Fictions of Culture

Fictions of Culture

Essays in Honor of Walter H. Sokel

Edited by
Steven Taubeneck

PETER LANG
New York · San Francisco · Bern
Frankfurt am Main · Paris · London

Library of Congress Cataloging-in-Publication Data

Fictions of culture : essays in honor of Walter H. Sokel /
edited by Steven Taubeneck.
  p. cm.
  Includes papers presented at a conference held in
April, 1988 at the University of Virginia.
  Includes bibliographical references.
  1. Arts, Modern—Congresses.   2. Aesthetics,
Modern—Congresses.   I. Taubeneck, Steven A.
II. Sokel, Walter Herbert, 1917-
NX449.5.F53   1991   700—dc20   91-19689
ISBN 0-8204-1714-9   CIP

Die Deutsche Bibliothek-CIP-Einheitsaufnahme

Taubeneck, Steven:
Fictions of culture : essays in honor of Walter H. Sokel /
Steven Taubeneck.—New York; Berlin; Bern; Frankfurt/M;
Paris; Wien: Lang, 1991
  ISBN 0-8204-1714-9

The paper in this book meets the guidelines for permanence and
durability of the Committee on Production Guidelines for Book
Longevity of the Council on Library Resources.

© Peter Lang Publishing, Inc., New York 1991

Printed in the United States of America.

700
F448

Table of Contents

Table of Contents

Walter H. Sokel

Introduction:
Walter H. Sokel and the Shift to Culture

This volume has two related aims. The first is to honor Walter H. Sokel, one of the leading scholars and teachers in the study of German languages and literatures and a well-known figure in American academics in general. As a teacher at Columbia, Stanford, and the University of Virginia, Walter Sokel has specialized in Expressionism, Kafka, and German intellectual history, and his teaching and writings have made many important contributions to these various fields.[1] This volume is meant to recognize his exemplary work. As an indication of the considerable impact of his teaching and writing, the collection includes several essays by his former students.

Walter Sokel's teaching and writing have helped to shape the practices of literary studies for over thirty years. His work has also contributed to the massive shift that is taking place in literary study, involving a thorough reconsideration of its most basic practices.[2] On one hand, the concept of "literature" has lost its honorific centrality, whereas on the other hand, the concept of "text" has been broadened enormously to include all social forms. This broadening of "text" has shifted attention towards the relations between literature and other kinds of artifacts, and brought literary study into closer contact with many other disciplines, such as anthropology, art, history, philosophy, political science, and sociology. In the process, the discipline itself seems to be changing its emphasis from literary to cultural studies. The second aim of the volume is to outline the emerging shape of cultural studies, and to suggest that Walter Sokel's work, especially in the field of intellectual history, has played a decisive role in that transition. The two aims of this volume together are meant to illustrate the process of transformation occurring within literary study as one generation leads to the next. With this the book takes a position in the vertiginous debate concerning the purpose of education today.

The majority of the essays arose on the occasion of a conference for Walter Sokel held in April, 1988, at the University of Virginia in Charlottesville, Virginia. Over two bright and warm spring days, several scholars from around the United States and Europe gathered in Charlottesville to present their papers in response to Walter Sokel's work. These essays pay tribute to his work by adding to the discussion of topics he addressed. At the conference itself, Professor Sokel compared the gathering to the ancient model of Plato's *Symposium*. The wide range of topics discussed in the volume demonstrates that this gathering involved a rich feast indeed.

Soon after the conference, numerous other scholars asked to contribute to the volume. Although this second wave of contributions has delayed the publication of the volume somewhat, it has enhanced the richness of the gathering. Walter Sokel has himself contributed an essay that offers an illuminating reading of his own reception of Austrian literature during the period of Nazi domination.

These expressions of and responses to a distinguished academic career generate a map of the interdisciplinary techniques and topics of cultural studies. Several of the essays, for example, develop the perspectives of critical theory. Ernst Behler sketches an intellectual history of cultural studies in general, extending from the eighteenth century to the contemporary situation. For Behler, one tradition follows from Herder, the Schlegel brothers, and the organic conception of art in Romantic aesthetics. From the same period a conflicting tradition arises that extends to Nietzsche. The paper describes both traditions in order to sharpen the debate over the past and future of cultural studies.

Further discussions of theory include the recent work of E. D. Hirsch, Jr., and Alan Bloom. In his paper Hirsch returns to the important distinction between meaning and significance to distinguish between naive and reflective intentionalists. For Hirsch, an intentionalist approach should continually limit and refine its claims, thus avoiding the wholesale acceptance of an overly simplistic view. My paper then discusses the work of Alan Bloom in the context of recent critiques of postmodernism. An important problem both Bloom and Hirsch raise is the articulation of cultural studies with practical educational reform.

Several of the papers apply an interdisciplinary, multigeneric, or broadly comparative perspective to literary and cultural history. One group interprets eighteenth and nineteenth century European culture in general and the tradition of German classicism in particular. Liliane Weissberg considers the interaction of philosophy and literature for Fichte and broaches the problem of reading. Bernhard Greiner applies a multigeneric approach to Goethe's novel *Wilhelm Meister* in order to uncover its sense of the theater and relations between stage and audience. The paper by Richard Gray interprets Schiller's early theater in terms of its sociosemiotic backgrounds and connotations. Peter Burgard illuminates Goethe's essays using the techniques and vocabulary of Derridean theory. And Karl Guthke's paper on "Last Words" employs an interdisciplinary, multigeneric, and comparative perspective to the rhetoric of "last words" since the eighteenth century. In sum, these papers deal with a number of important issues from the eighteenth to the twentieth century through a combinatory approach to culture. From the study of rhetoric and semiotics to drama, intellectual history, and politics, an assemblage of approaches and issues emerges as an underpinning for a program of cultural studies.

A second group of papers highlights cultural developments in the late nineteenth and early twentieth centuries. The subject of Vienna is broached by Judith Ryan in her study of the intellectual relations between "Viennese psychology and American pragmatism." Michael Morton argues that Hugo von Hofmannsthal, Fritz Mauthner, and Ludwig Wittgenstein were engaged in the "vindication of language" during the time. Benjamin Bennett discusses the "intransitive parody" in Hofmannsthal's style in the wider context of German prose at the turn of the century. From an explicitly feminist perspective, Sylvia Schmitz-Burgard criticizes

Freud's theory in relation to the recent gender discussions in the work of Laplanche.

Two essays deal with the work of Franz Kafka. The first, by Hans-Gerd Koch, looks very closely at the actual manuscript pages of Kafka's diaries. Koch's approach yields a more precise view of Kafka's composition practices. Michael Jennings locates Kafka's writing in the space between modernism and postmodernism. Jennings shows a crucial shift in Benjamin's reading of Kafka that would enable a somewhat clearer view of Kafka's conflicted position. This elaboration of his study of Benjamin enables Jennings to add an important piece to the difficult puzzle of Kafka's status in intellectual and cultural history.

Five papers deal with more recent cultural patterns. James Rolleston gives a powerful reading of Herbert Marcuse's work, and explains the controversies that have arisen in the reception of Marcuse's social critique. Karen Achberger relates the work of Ingeborg Bachmann to the music of Hans Werner Henze. Anton Kaes explores the ambivalence of contemporary German filmmakers in regards to their history. Ultimately, John Rodden raises an issue from the sociology of literature of reputation as a determining force in the fluctuations of power and popularity in literary history.

Taken together, the essays in this collection form a combinatory response to the work of Walter Sokel and the question of cultural studies. The response includes critical theory and the comparative, interdisciplinary study of cultural artifacts from the eighteenth to the twentieth century. These essays spring from the recognition of Professor Sokel's contributions to the "human sciences," and suggest ways of producing interdisciplinary, multi-perspectival cultural studies in the future. As we move into the twenty-first century and universities continue to face serious questions about their function in education, the project of cultural studies outlined here offers a useful path to follow.[3]

Notes

1 Among his many writings are two important books: *The Writer in Extremis. Expressionism in Twentieth-Century German Literature* (Stanford: Stanford University Press, 1959), and *Franz Kafka. Tragik und Ironie. Zur Struktur seiner Kunst* (Munich: Albert Langen Georg Mueller Verlag, 1964). Also see *Probleme der Moderne. Studien zur deutschen Literatur von Nietzsche bis Brecht. Festschrift für Walter Sokel*, eds. Benjamin Bennett, Anton Kaes, William J. Lillyman (Tübingen: Max Niemeyer Verlag, 1983) for a discussion of the many topics addressed by his work.

2 For a discussion of this shift in the discipline of German Studies in particular, see "*Germanistik* as German Studies. Interdisciplinary Theories and Methods," in *The German Quarterly*, 62, 2 (Spring 1989), and *German Studies in the USA: A Critique of "Germanistik"?* (Tempe: Arizona State University, 1989). On the effects of these changes in terms of literary study in general, see *The Future of Literary Theory*, ed. Ralph Cohen (New York: Routledge, Chapman and Hall, Inc., 1989).

3 I am grateful to Anton Kaes for suggesting the title, and to Mary Esteve and Gretchen Wiesehan for help with the editing. The aim of the editing was to keep each essay internally consistent.

PART I

ROMANTICISM AND ITS CONSEQUENCES

The Romantic Origins
of Cultural History
in a Nietzschean Perspective

Ernst Behler
University of Washington

However fascinating Nietzsche appears (in himself) on issues such as cultural history and historical interpretation, he immediately gains in scope and importance if he is seen in contrast to that tradition of hermeneutics, the humanities, human sciences, and cultural studies to which he directed his thought in these matters: the classical, romantic, and idealistic tradition of Germany, that of Humboldt, Schleiermacher, and Hegel. The present contribution attempts to confront the one tradition of cultural history and hermeneutics in Germany with the other, the classical-romantic tradition with that of Nietzsche, the cultural philosophy of unity, coherence, and continuity with that of division, discontinuity, and disruption. The range of authors in the field of the interpretative or humanistic disciplines to be discussed will differ slightly from the established canon of critics in this domain. Instead of Schleiermacher, Boeckh, and Dilthey, considered the pioneers of modern hermeneutics, the discussion will turn to Winckelmann, Herder, the Schlegel brothers, and Hegel. This will retrograde the historical period and focus more closely on the origins of the romantic theory. The purpose of the shift is to show that this tradition of cultural history found its counterpart not only with Nietzsche, but already among some of these early writers themselves, most noticeably in Herder, Friedrich Schlegel, and, in a certain way, even in Hegel, all of whom did not fully fit the scheme of organic unity, unbroken continuity and coherence usually associated with the romantic model of cultural history. Although formulated in a discourse that has become alien to us today, these modes of writing cultural history directly relate to us and our contemporary concerns, if not through their limited and antiquated content then as models of thought and interpretation.

1. There are good reasons for starting the theory of cultural history in Germany with Winckelmann, although there is always something arbitrary about such beginnings. One central issue of this discipline, however, can be found in the initial remarks of Winckelmann's *History of the Art of Antiquity* about the general purpose of his work.[1] Winckelmann stated in this instance that he did not intend to give a "mere narration of the sequence of time and the changes that took place in it," but understood "the word history in the broader sense it has in the Greek language," meaning a systematic, a structured, an organized account (*Geschichte*, 7). By distinguishing in the course of his presentation between different styles of artistic expression and by assigning these styles to different schools and stages in the development of Greek art, Winckelmann also furnished major conceptual tools for the task of cultural historiography in the sense of delineating a coherent structure, a progressively unfolding unity of the world he was depicting. This is indeed the most characteristic feature of Winckelmann's writing on Greek art, the presentation of a developmental or genetic unity. In his appreciation of individual works of art, Winckelmann had an astonishing ability to understand particular features of classical art from larger historical contexts as, for instance, reliefs on Roman sarcophages as scenes from Greek mythology. Conversely, however, he was at a loss when it came to an understanding of Roman images which did not derive from or apparently had no connection with Greek traditions.[2]

Winckelmann also insisted on the absolute origin and nonderivative character of the Greek world integrating whichever foreign element came to it with its own substance and giving it a new form (*Gedanken*, 7).[3] These thoughts are of course closely related to Winckelmann's cultural mission in Germany which can be described as establishing an intimate relationship between Germany and classical Greece. Winckelmann considered this possible because of a particular way of imitating the ancients. Their creations do not show us only the most beautiful nature, he argued, but also "certain ideal beauties" embedded in our reason and visible to the spiritual eye (*Gedanken*, 9). It is from this perspective, according to Winckelmann, that Michelangelo and Raphael have viewed the works of the ancients and that the imitation or rather incorporation of the Greeks should proceed again in Winckelmann's own time (*Gedanken*, 15). Indeed, this direct and unmediated relationship to classical Greece became the peculiar mark of German humanism during the romantic period and distinguished it from Renaissance humanism as well as from French Neoclassicism, both characterized by their strong orientation according to the Roman and Latin forms of classicism.[4]

Although Herder distinguished himself from Winckelmann's absolute veneration of the Greeks by a much broader cultural receptivity, his thoughts about cultural history start out directly from the author of the *Art of Antiquity*. The first entries in his *Fragments on Modern German Literature* take issue with Winckelmann's ideas about the interrelationship of history and system and introduce his own long sequence of thought on this topic. Herder too wants to maintain "the broad Greek meaning of history" in the sense of a systematic account (*Herder* II, 294)[5] and considers Winckelmann's history of Greek art the "most magnificent monument" of this kind, an "ideal of history." His only reservation, however, was that this work was perhaps "more system than a history might possibly be" (*Herder* II, 123-124), i.e., more organized, structured, and selected than the reality of life. In another instance, Herder thought that Winckelmann had been more intent on deducing from the ancients a "historical metaphysics of the beautiful" than a true history (*Herder* III, 10). His special effort in this domain can be characterized as maintaining a better balance, but also a more dynamic and antagonistic tension between the two poles of history and theory (system) (*Herder* IV, 202-204).

Herder was also critical of Winckelmann's axiom that art was original with the Greeks (*Herder* II, 123-124) and considered the exclusion of the Egyptians simply as a "prejudice of that system" (*Herder* II, 128).[6] His own ideal of a history of human reason, of a *histoire de l'esprit humain*, was based on the entirety of the human race and meant to show how "the spirit of literature after different peregrinations and transformations had assumed its present stature" (*Herder* I, 293). Yet this inachievable task soon had to be reduced for Herder to those nations who had exerted "a real influence" upon us (*Herder* I, 293). Among them, the Greeks certainly occupied a prime position. The history of their poetry and wisdom can very well instruct us about the nature of these arts and disciplines according to Herder, provided only that "before we imitate them, we first have to know them" (*Herder* I, 286). Herder's call for special investigations into this relationship produced a number of writings of that time which under titles such as "On the Study of the Greeks," "On the Study of the Greeks in Relationship to the Moderns," or "On the Study of Greek Poetry" thematized the particular relationship supposedly existing between the Greek and the German mind and discussed the appropriate way of imitating the Greeks. Herder also called for an improved philology of Greek literature (*Herder* I, 286-287) and for better and more extended translations of Greek works (*Herder* I, 289). In this context, Herder demanded a "Winckelmann of Greek poetry," that is, a critic who would unveil the nature of Greek literature just as Winckelmann had revealed the secret of Greek art to the artists of his time. Herder added that because of the abundance of Greek art objects in Rome, a Winckelmann of Greek art could only originate in that city, whereas a Winckelmann of Greek poetry could just as well appear in Germany (*Herder* I, 289).

We are here at the beginning of Friedrich Schlegel's critical career. His early writings on Greek literature emerge directly from these premises. They also bring the previous debate about the theoretical principles of cultural history to a synthesis and, without going into the details of Schlegel's history of Greek literature itself, deserve some attention in this regard. Winckelmann's holistic approach is obvious in Schlegel's genetic view of Greek literature as performing a complete cycle from epic poetry, as a mirror of nature, to lyric poetry, as an expression of the poetic ego, and to drama, as the unity of nature and the self, as an interrelationship of action and chorus.[7] Schlegel's use of categories such as style, school, and age, which he considerably improved under the guidance of the Hellenist Friedrich August Wolf, helped elaborate the view of the Greek world as a great and diachronic unity. The synchronic aspect of a structured totality in the world of the Greeks is obvious in Schlegel's concept of Greek culture or *Bildung* as a whole, according to which it is "impossible to understand perfectly and correctly one particular part of it in fragmentation," e.g., literature and poetry independent of rhetoric, philosophy, mythology, history, social reality, and political life (*KFSA* I, 206). All this reflects Winckelmann, whom Schlegel called "the systematic Winckelmann who read all the ancients as if they were one single author, who saw everything as a whole" (*KFSA* II, 188, No. 149). In another instance he characterized Winckelmann's manner of writing cultural history as a movement "from a whole to the whole." Casimir Ulrich Boehlendorff, Hölderlin's friend, wrote after reading Schlegel's history of Greek literature to Johann Friedrich Herbart that Schlegel's presentation was founded on an "inner living coherence, on a wonderfully great *whole* in becoming" and that Schlegel and his brother had abolished "mere formal criticism" through their device that "all criticism had to proceed from a *philosophy of art*."[8]

Schlegel's history of Greek literature also follows Herder's request for a balanced relationship between history and system or, in Schlegel's terms, between history and theory. In his letters to his brother (*KFSA* XXIII, 188), to Novalis (*KFSA* XXIII, 204), and in numerous instances of his work itself (*KFSA* I, 276, 283, 307, 317, 318), Schlegel insists that his research and writing is by no means merely a historical narrative undertaking but attempts to help found the theory of art and poetry through its history and that theory and history are inseparable in the critical, cultural, historical endeavor. This does not only apply to his writings on the Greeks but includes his criticism in general. One could even summarize the new level of cultural criticism brought about by the Schlegel brothers by this dictum which occurs throughout their writings: "The theory of art is its own history."[9]

With this formulation, the project of cultural history and historical investigation in the human sciences seemed to have found a position of irrefutable soundness and undeniable certainty of itself: unlimited investigation of historical material was accompanied by rigorous theoretical scrutiny of this material, just as its philosophical comprehension was prevented from emptiness and void abstraction through the supply of ever-new material. Both drives of the investigating mind, the one toward the material of knowledge and the other toward a comprehending form, supported each other in a movement toward ever higher levels of understanding and integrating knowledge. Such neat solutions and smooth reconciliations, however, appeared too perfect to the romantic mind not to provoke suspicion and be met with irony.

Whereas the intellectual work of the Schlegel brothers in the domain of the human sciences can very well be considered as a synthesis of history and theory and as never abandoning one side of the polarity, the dictum of "The theory of art is its own history" is often expressed with a grain of salt and carries along with it a self-critical note of amusement. Long before the interrelationship of history and philosophy had become a serious issue and an essential task in Hegel's philosophy, Friedrich Schlegel talked about such a project in the ironical mood of an impossible balancing act which eventually would yield to theory, to philosophy, to the system and be consumed, annihilated by this inclination. Just as critics in classical antiquity had called poetry "painting in words and painting a silent poetry," he mused in the *Athenäum* that one could say that "history would be a becoming philosophy, and philosophy a perfected history" (*KFSA* II, 221). He also coined the term "historical system" and used it for a type of investigation which is systematic throughout, i.e., general and completed, as well as downright historical, i.e., oriented toward everything individual. As is obvious, "historical system" was for Schlegel a metaphor for an absolute task, something equally desirable as impossible, and therefore to be viewed in an ironic mood.[10]

2. However, the phrase "The theory of art is its own history" still best expresses what can be described as the romantic turn or the turning point brought about by romanticism in the theory of cultural history and hermeneutics. August Wilhelm Schlegel's Berlin lectures *On Literature and Art* of 1802-04 offer the most elaborate presentation of this critical synthesis and the most precarious balancing or mediation of the two elusive principles. At first glance, history, especially in its "raw aspect," appears to be completely opposed to theory. History, in this sense, is "a mere aggregation of events, without connection, sense, and meaning as a whole showing no other common features than having occurred in the same place (in a city, in a country, etc.) and presenting no other order than sequence of time." From here, however, we have to move on to the realization, as Schlegel puts it, "that the real is truly necessary only that its necessity is often not directly and sometimes not completely recognized" (AWSV I, 11).[11] Of course, the historical view will never accomplish an insight into "absolute necessity" because it can never provide first causes, which instead get lost in the darkness of time and of which there can be no historical knowledge. One therefore should speak about history in a more careful manner as a discipline having its position in the intermediary field of a "transition between the real and the necessary" (*AWSV* I, 12). The question remains, however, what the ordering principle of history actually is.

Schlegel assumed that every "noble human being" is inspired by the desire to approximate something unattainable and that the same type of striving can be attributed to the entire human species (*AWSV* I, 12). All human history thereby turns into a history of culture, of *Bildung* of the human race and into a realization of that which is purpose as such, i.e., the morally good, the true, and the beautiful. The main tasks of history are political history, which produces the states of the league of nations, upon which the moral existence of the social human being relies; the history of science and philosophy; and the history of art (*AWSV* I, 13). In this sense, then, history can be called for Schlegel the "science of the becoming real of all that which is practically necessary," (*AWSV* I, 14) of what should be. To put this in less dense fashion:

> Theory proves what should happen, starting in this demand from the most general and highest postulates, while turning more and more to the particular without ever arriving at the individual. History, on the other hand, is driven from one individual appearance to the other having the most general and highest always invisibly present: their full appearance could only be realized in the whole which history can never completely establish. (*AWSV* I, 14)

As far as the relationships of theory and history in the realm of art are concerned, it appears to be clear to Schlegel on the basis of these considerations that, first of all, history cannot do without theory (*AWSV* I, 14):

> Only through reference to the idea of art can we assign each individual phenomenon of art its true position, and to do this is the business of theory. Whoever has this idea of art in some clarity, already possesses theory, even if he has not yet enunciated it otherwise. (*AWSV* I, 15)

Theory, on the other hand, cannot endure without history. Its very origin already presupposes the fact of art which has shaped itself "among different ages and different nations." Although first clinging to the most general, art theory soon adds "ever more precise distinctions" and finally arrives at "even national and local conditions" (*AWSV* I, 15).

This notion of history appears to be inseparably linked with the assumption of autonomous human individuals, groups of people, and entire nations who sovereignly create their history and collaborate in an effort which although founded in individual actions, transcends the merely individual and has collective results. Such a notion of history also assumes an overriding teleological orientation of all historical phenomena toward a higher and more comprehensive goal, a striving toward something absolute and unconditional, a process of formation of *Bildung* toward a state of completion of which all previous historical expressions are only anticipations. Schlegel was aware of the problems arising from these assumptions and attempted to cope with them from his position of an interaction of history and theory. As far as the remoteness of human activities and works of art from the highest goal of all historical striving is concerned, he would consider the observation of such a discrepancy the actual intent of all critical, theoretical statements about historical phenomena, as is obvious in assessments according to which one work, nation, or age is more poetic than the other (*AWSV* I, 16). This assessment, however, has to be complemented by the other, the historical one, according to which each work of art is to be contemplated from its own position and does not have to attain an absolutely highest point in order to be perfect as long as it is "a highest in its kind, in its sphere, in its world" (*AWSV* I, 17).

As far as the overriding teleology in the movement of history is concerned, its progression toward an absolute goal, its infinite perfectibility, Schlegel maintains that we should not operate with the "idea of an infinite progress" in every small and detailed portion of history because this is "a mere idea" leaving everything undetermined. We can even doubt whether during that period of history of which we can only have knowledge, that is, Western history, the history of the Occident, "a significant preponderance of progresses over regresses is recognizable" (*AWSV* I, 13). He refers to Hemsterhuis, who described "the increase and decrease in culture very meaningfully as an elliptic circular motion in which the human race during one age is in the perihelion and then again in the aphelion." Schlegel concludes: "It cannot be determined whether humanity during these revolutions really comes closer to its center" (*AWSV* I, 13).

In a more fundamental reflection upon our ascribing of meaning and goal-oriented movement to history, Schlegel admits that this is more the perspective of the philosopher (theory) who assumes human morality and freedom of the will, whereas the historian sees the human being more as a natural entity which is under the influence of elementary and sideric powers (*AWSV* III, 87). From this point of view, the historical revolutions of the human race "show a great analogy to physical revolutions and are perhaps connected with certain astronomical periods, with changes in magnetic power, climatic temperatures, etc." Schlegel knows of course that there is something ridiculous in the belief of certain chroniclers according to which comets and extraordinary meteors announce terrible and devastating events. Yet he admits with regard to such opinions that "at least the principle appears to be correct, although its application is wrong" (*AWSV* III, 88). He obviously wants to move away from an exclusively human-centered view of history and to detach himself from the idealistic interpretation of history in terms of human freedom dominant in his time by recognizing more elementary levels of historical events in which the human individual is simply inscribed and merely a partial expression. In another instance, he maintains that in both human and natural history there are creative and destructive forces and that the human being as a corporeal and spiritual being participates in both (*AWSV* III, 94).

August Wilhelm Schlegel's Berlin lectures seem to elaborate, in methodological and hermeneutic terms, that scientific model according to which the humanistic disciplines continued their formation during the nineteenth century and far beyond. If one concentrates on the basic principles of these disciplines in the realms of language, culture, art, and poetry, i.e., their particular mode of understanding, their movement in comprehension from "a whole to the whole," and their being embedded within an encompassing process of *Bildung*, of culture, of formation of the human race in the greatest possible manner of diversification, we could say that this romantic model is still operative in contemporary theories of the human sciences. We know of course that with August Wilhelm Schlegel's lectures, we are only at the beginning of this formative process which became enormously more diversified through the flowering of the historical disciplines in the nineteenth century. Yet the advantage of Schlegel's early position of a mediation of history and theory appears to be that it had not yet become subject to enforced dialectics and superimposed teleologies as they arose with Hegel, but instead provided an open-ended course for the development of the human race.

Hegel's model of historical knowledge comes indeed very close to this romantic notion of an interdependence of history and theory and aims at a similar intellectual comprehension of the interactive and contradictory interrelationship of the historical and the philosophical realms. Knowledge in these matters, for Hegel, is not centered in a beyond or a transcendence to finite beings but in the mutual and innerworldly interpenetration of the finite and the infinite, the accidental and the necessary, the historical and the philosophical, moving back and forth between the two realms in the process of comprehension (*Hegel* V, 156).[12] One could very well designate this interactive relationship as the "unity of the finite and the infinite" if this concept were not accompanied by the idea of a static fulfillment which is of course inappropriate for this entirely fluid and mobile relationship and thereby produces an "awkward expression" for Hegel (*Hegel* V, 156). The interactive determination of the finite and the infinite is rather to be thought of as a relationship which is both the unity and the negation of the two, in which none of the two can be comprehended without the other and in which "both determine each other in a mutual nega-tion" (*Hegel* V, 157-158). If they were only thought of as joined by an "and," Hegel says, the infinite would be made finite. In this manner of thinking, that is, in truly dialectical thought, we accom-plish a "doubled unity of the infinite and the finite," i.e., doubled through unity and negation.

These reflections of Hegel's *Science of Logic* culminate in the concept of the "concrete universal," the individual historical entity with a universal significance. This is perhaps the most concise expression for Hegel's model of knowledge and, although much more sophisticated and demanding in its philosophical content, at first glance in line with the romantic mediation of history and the-ory in the realm of the cultural sciences. The main difference, however, arises with the teleology of the historical process. For A. W. Schlegel, the goal of this movement had been something unattainable, the realization of something which is purpose as such, i.e., the good, the true, and the beautiful. Such principles were much too vague and abstract for Hegel, who aimed at concrete realizations of the infinite in finite terms. He summarized the assumption of an unattainable goal to be approximated only in endless efforts in pejorative terms as the position of an "infinite progress," of a "poor" or a "bad" infinity and concentrated all his polemical efforts in the realm of historical thought against this thinking of history in terms of progression, infinity, and unattainability. Hegel's critique of the infinite progress is mainly directed against Kant and Fichte but by implication also includes the romantic conception of an infinite progression or an infinite perfectibility, in general, every form or mode of action which declares its goal as unattainable and forces us to move on from one limit to the next, and this in infinity. For Hegel, this leads to a devaluation of finite being, of finite reality, which is declared as merely transitory. Infinite approximation seems to establish a link between the finite and the infinite, but in reality finite being in this line of thought is considered to be separate, independent, and persistent in relation to the infinite. An abyss, an insurmountable chasm is erected between the two with the infinite in an eternal "beyond" and the finite in a constant "here" (*Hegel* VIII, 201-202). This seems to be indeed the main difference between Hegel's and the romantic model of knowledge in the historical and interpretative sciences. Whereas the romantics assumed an infinite progression and open-ended development for cultural history, that which Hegel calls the "absolute method" does not permit such infinite continuation and proceeds from determination to determination, whereby these determinations become "ever richer and more concrete" (*Hegel* VI, 569). Hegel's "dialectical procedure" claims not only not to leave anything behind, "but to carry every acquisition along with it and to enrich and consolidate itself in itself" (*Hegel* VI, 569).[13]

It depends very much on our reading of the relevant texts, however, whether the difference between Hegel's dialectical mode of knowledge and the romantic mode of thinking in terms of an infinite progress are as opposed as Hegel gives us to understand. For there is also a way of understanding Hegel's "absolute method" as a screw without an end or, as Hegel put it himself, as a "circle of circles" which, returning to its origin, immediately forms the beginning of a new chain (*Hegel* VI, 571-572). Conversely, the infinite process, as it is assumed by Kant, Fichte, and the romantics, does not have to be understood as an endless repetition of the finite in unrelated steps, as Hegel presents it, but assumes the feature of a meaningful course through *a priori* structures of the human mind of an epistemological, moral, and aesthetic order which guide our orientation in the world and precede it. This process is thought of, for instance, in terms of an education of the human race, of a progressive formation (*Bildung, Ausbildung*) of all human faculties, or a harmonious deployment of the entire human nature in a free society. All this implies a goal-oriented movement of self-fulfillment. If the attainment of the goal is seen to take place only in infinite approximations, the goal still remains the principle of history, if not in the sense of an historical arrival, then as a structural or metaphysical determination of every type of human action.

Without going into all formative stages of a long and diversified development, we can say that this romantic-idealistic model of a progressive coherence and integration of all human activities in history formed the umbrella concept for the formation of cultural history and its manifold disciplines. When Dilthey attempted to establish the principles of the human sciences (*Geisteswissenschaften*) toward the end of the nineteenth century, he seemed to reemphasize the integration of history with theory. Gadamer sees the historicism implied in this approach as held together by the philosophical principle of a formation toward humanity. To think historically, he claims, means to grant each epoch its own right of existence, even its own perfection, whereas the idea of an unending process implies that the idea in history will always find imperfect representation.[14]

The intellectual model of cultural history established by the romantics and taken up in modern developments of hermeneutics can best be described by terms such as progressive coherence, gradual integration, genetic wholeness, enlarging of context, or expanding continuity. This view of history is determined by meaning and meaningfulness throughout, even if meaning is obscured in the past, does not fully occur in the present, and will not attain self-presence in the future. But the idea of a total congruity or a complete interrelationship of all historical phenomena is always operative in spite of the silent pages of history, its sunken civilizations, lost treasures, and forgotten periods.

3. There is yet another form of romanticism, which forms a contrast to this holistic view of history, although this type of romanticism has not yet found sufficient attention nor affirmed itself through a major form of reception. This is the romanticism of the fragment, of fragmentation, of a lack of coherence and congruity, of radical unpredictability, "incomprehensibility," and also of disbelief with regard to a retrospective foundation of truth. If the first model of a continuously progressive coherence can be characterized as a constant "enlarging of context," this model can best be described as one of a "discontinuous restructuring."[15] I am referring to the romantic theory of the early Friedrich Schlegel, his thoughts on fragmentary writing, the figurative, indirect communication of irony, his hermeneutics of incomprehensibility, but especially, in the present context, to his critical attitude toward a coherent and entirely comprehensible historical system.

Schlegel took his starting point from Winckelmann and Herder when he began to write his history of Greek literature. Winckelmann had provided him with the view of a comprehensive, genetic type of unity in historical development, and Herder had made him aware of the individuality and irreplaceable uniqueness of each historical phenomenon. Yet as far as the entire course of Western history was concerned, Schlegel was still in search of a guiding principle, and none of the contemporary philosophies could satisfy him. Winckelmann was too one-sidedly oriented toward the Greeks; Herder sacrificed the coherence of history for the sake of individual nations and epochs; Kant transposed everything into the future and made teleology the only valid point of view; and Fichte relied too much on human freedom and virtually neglected the forces of nature. Schlegel's own condition for a unified view of history can be defined as never subordinating this unity to an absolute in the past (classicism, golden age) or in the future (final goal, utopia), or as he put it, never paying "respect to the lofty prototype behind ourselves or to the higher goal in front of ourselves." He proceeded from the assumption "that it is not our destiny to live like *beggars* from the alms of the previous world, nor to work like *serfs* in forced servitude for the posterior world." He said: "As each individual does not exist for the species, but as a purpose in itself, no age can lose through conditional diminution its inalienable right of isonomy [equality]" (*KFSA* I, 640). On this basis, Schlegel believed that "each human being without exception could attain his individual destiny, that indeed each activity, as limited as it might appear, satisfied a moral infinitum, and granted the enjoyment of eternity" (*KFSA* I, 640).

In this frame of mind, Schlegel became acquainted with Condorcet's text *Sketch of a Historical Picture of the Progress of the Human Mind*. Condorcet, in contrast to German idealism, did not deduce the process of history from a progressive education of the human race nor from a gradual formation and integration of all human faculties, but from more basic data. The starting point for his calculation was the human ability, in contrast to the animal, to form from simple sense impressions complex ideas, and to compose moral laws from the feelings of pleasure and displeasure. Condorcet followed the influential philosophy of Condillac, which in turn was founded on Locke's empiricism. We could also describe Condorcet's theory of an infinite perfectibility as the formation of an advancing system of signs which proceeds from ever new combinations among the original sense impressions to the formation of language and writing, to a mathematical language, and finally, to a system of entirely artificial and perfected signs. The decisive turning point in this conception of history is consequently not the rise of Christianity or the transition from a national to a universal conception, but the invention of alphabetical writing. In a positivistic manner and in the style of a "mathématique sociale," Condorcet attempted to prove from the impact of each event upon the following, the unlimited perfectibility of man as a natural law of his development. Whereas in the idealistic model of history the human mind is governed from the beginning by *a priori* structures of an epistemological, moral, and aesthetic order which guide our orientation in the world and precede it, Condorcet's historical model starts out from an amorphous sensuality which accomplishes the formation of logical, epistemological, and moral concepts of its own accord and moves on from there to ever more complex combinations in the invention of signs.[16]

Traces of Condorcet are frequent in Schlegel's writings. He could certainly also find notions about the infinity of the historical process in Kant and Fichte. Yet the concept of infinite perfectibility in its mathematical configuration, precluding any state of accomplished perfection, is rarely used in German texts of the time and substituted by others like movement toward perfection (*Vervollkommnung*) which round off the process and give it a meaningful end. The particular feature of German Enlightenment on the whole can be seen in the notion of an education of the human race, of a progressive formation (*Bildung, Ausbildung*) of all human faculties, or a harmonious deployment of the human personality. In his writings about the history of literature, Schlegel employs the notion of an infinite perfectibility in the context of Greek literature, characterized as a "relative maximum," i.e., the highest accomplishment during that period (*KFSA* I, 288), and for determining the special feature of modern, post-classical literature which he condensed into the category of "the interesting." Since there is no possible way for us to figure out the "highest interesting" or the highest modern, Schlegel argues, these phenomena are the best illustration for the infinite perfectibility of aesthetics (*KFSA* I, 214). In another instance he says about the character of modern art: "Nothing appears to be as evident as the theory of perfectibility. The pure sentence of reason about the necessary infinite perfection of humanity is without any difficulty" (*KFSA* I, 263).

In similar fashion, Schlegel's speculations about the "highest ugliness" evolve from this theory. The "highest ugliness" was just as impossible for him as the "highest beauty," and the argument was the same for both phenomena: "An absolute maximum of negation, or perfected nothingness, can just as little exist in any representation as an absolute maximum of position; and the highest level of ugliness still comprises something beautiful" (*KFSA* I, 313). In another argument, Schlegel derives infinite perfectibility in aesthetics from the semiotic character of works of art, their combination of artificial signs. In this regard, it would already be daring according to Schlegel to posit a limit of perfection for music and painting. Poetry, however, because of its instrument of language, an entirely arbitrary and artificial system of signs, is by its nature infinitely perfectible and corruptible (*KFSA* I, 294). What attracted Schlegel in Condorcet's notion of infinite perfectibility was the lack of any determining and preconceived structure such as human nature or transcendental subjectivity. Of special interest is the following fragment:

> Analysis of *absolute infinity*, of the progresses which still remain for us. Not only the material is infinite, but also the form, each concept, every proof, every sentence is *infinitely perfectible*. Also mathematics is not excluded from this, cannot be excluded from this. Extremely important is the perfectibility of mathematics for philosophy, the theory of science, and logic. (*KFSA* XVIII, 506, 518)

With its emphasis on the absolute infinity for the steps of progress which still remain for us, this fragment seems to indicate a type of historical movement free from any preconceived goal. Schlegel by no means simply took over Condorcet's theory of infinite perfectibility, but only operated with it for a short period of time. He found in it the prototype of a historical movement free from any preconceived teleology, and when he formulated his own theory of history in the medium of romantic poetry, there was no recollection of the French model. Yet the thought of a decentered movement, irreducible to a final and foreseeable goal, had remained the same. Schlegel wrote in Fragment 116 of the *Athenäum*:

> Other kinds of poetry are finished and are now capable of being fully analyzed. The romantic kind of poetry is still in the state of becoming; that, in fact, is its true essence: that it should forever be becoming and never be perfected. It can be exhausted by no theory and only a divinatory criticism would dare try to characterize its ideal. (*KFSA* II, 183)

This infinite becoming, irreducible to a knowable principle in the beginning or in the end, seems to formulate Schlegel's notion of history most concisely, although there are many other expressions for this phenomenon in his writings. One way of describing our position in history is Schlegel's frequent use of formulas such as "as long as" or "not yet." In this sense, he justifies fragmentary writing "as long as" we have not yet established the completed system of knowledge; or he demands irony "as long as in oral or written dialogues we philosophize not yet fully in systematic fashion" (*KFSA* II, 152). In a similar argumentation, philosophy is in need of "genial inspirations" and "products of wit" because it is not yet entirely systematic. This will change, Schlegel assures us, once we move on to a safe methodology. Yet, as we realize, his words "as long as" and "not yet" are meant ironically. They do not designate a transitoriness to be overcome by accomplished knowledge, not a deficiency, but the actual state of our knowledge, its permanent form. Schlegel said: "One can only become a philosopher, not be one. As soon as one believes one is a philosopher, one stops becoming one" (*KFSA* II, 173). Yet Schlegel's position can also hardly be characterized as sheer skepticism, since he not only maintains the validity of limited, circumscribed structures of knowledge, but also considers systematic totality and coherence as a necessary, however unattainable, goal of knowledge. He said: "It is equally fatal for the mind to have a system, and to have none. One will simply have to decide to combine the two" (*KFSA* II, 173).

4. With these thoughts, hardly recognized in their consequence at the time of their origin, Schlegel seems to have anticipated essential aspects in the critique of the idealistic position in cultural history as it was conducted in unrelenting fashion by Nietzsche toward the end of the nineteenth century. There is no direct relationship between Schlegel and Nietzsche, and their discourses are separated by a century. Yet Nietzsche can make us aware of the self-critical, deconstructive elements in Schlegel's dealings with the principles of cultural history because his target is the same as that of Schlegel, namely, the genetic and teleological continuity of a type of knowledge which claims to comprehend a totality. Since the beginning of his writing, Nietzsche attempted to understand that as injurious, "a defect and deficiency," which in his time was considered with pride, namely, "the cultivation of history," historical consciousness (*KSA* I, 246).[17] Like Schlegel, Nietzsche was by

no means anti-historical but deeply convinced of the necessity of historical knowledge. Yet he was opposed to the "holistic," goal-oriented, teleological construction of history and saw the value of history and historical study rather as an exercise in discontinuity, in transposing oneself into ever new and changing historical horizons and perspectives. The modern representatives of hermeneutics consequently criticized Nietzsche's notion of history. Dilthey said about the early essay *On the Advantages and Disadvantages of History for Life* that it was Nietzsche's "refusal of or his farewell to history,"[18] whereas Gadamer saw in Nietzsche's perspectivism and his attempt to transcend customary points of view an alienated historical consciousness which had not established the appropriate relationship to its own presence.[19]

It seems, however, that these criticisms miss an essential point in Nietzsche's view of historical understanding which is critically concerned with the topics of unity, coherence, integration, and continuity and relates directly, if only as its counterpart, to the romantic and idealistic tradition in cultural history. This can be noticed in some of Nietzsche's earliest writings which more noticeably than his later texts refer to the romantic relationship of his thought. The essay of 1873 *On Truth and Lie in an Extramoral Sense* is a good example for this tendency. It begins in poetic fashion with a narration:

> In some remote corner of the universe, glittering in innumerable solar systems, there was once upon a time a star upon which clever animals invented *knowledge*. This was the haughtiest and most mendacious minute of 'world history,' yet only a minute. After a few last gasps of nature, the star froze and the clever animals had to die. (*KSA* I, 875-876)

In his text of the preceding year, *On the Pathos of Truth*, Nietzsche puts this fable into the mouth of a heartless demon who does not think highly of what we call with proud metaphors "world history" and "truth" and "fame" and who adds to his account of the death of these clever animals:

> It was about time. For although they prided themselves with a lot of knowledge, they eventually found out that they had gotten it all wrong. They died

and cursed truth while dying. This was the kind of those desperate animals who had invented knowledge. (*KSA* I, 760)

The relationship of these essays to historical knowledge and historical understanding is obvious from the beginning in the references to world history, world historical moment, and world historical knowledge which is confronted with a complete arbitrariness of events transcending any possibility of human comprehension. We can see this relationship also in the fabulistic framing of the essays which present, like historians or philosophers of history, what cannot be known by way of a story, a narrative, a récit. Yet the focus of the early texts is not so much the question of truth and lie in historical accounts and constructions of cultural history but the impact of language, of our metaphorical manner of talking about things upon thought, philosophy, and science. The theme of history, however, is taken up by Nietzsche one year later in the second of his *Untimely Meditations*, the essay *On the Advantages and Disadvantages of History for Life*.

Although the critique of the holistic view of cultural history is by no means the only concern of this text, it forms an important part of it under the title of "monumental history." In one of the first sections Nietzsche asks of what use the "monumentalistic conception of the past is to a person of the present" and finds it in the assumption that the great moments form a chain, a ridge of humanity, in which one also participates (*KSA* I, 259). Such a person, Nietzsche says,

learns from it that the greatness that once existed was in any event once *possible* again; he goes his way with more cheerful steps, for the doubt which assailed him in weaker moments, whether he was not desiring perhaps the impossible, has now been banished. (*KSA* I, 260)

Whereas this concept of monumental history and world-historical vision represents a desirability, Nietzsche also depicted the reverse effect such views of historical wholeness and integrality must have on the spectator. "I believe," he says,

there has been no dangerous vacillation or crisis of German culture this century that has not been rendered more dangerous by the enormous and still
continuing influence of this philosophy, the Hegelian. The belief that one is a
latecomer of that age is, in any case, paralyzing and depressing; but it must
appear dreadful and devastating when such a belief one day by a bold diver-
sion raises this latecomer to godhood as the true meaning and goal of all previous events, when his miserable condition is equated with a completion of
world-history. Such a point of view has accustomed the Germans to talk of a
'world-process' and to justify their own age as the necessary result of this
world-process; such a point of view has set history, insofar as history is 'the
concept that realizes itself,' 'the dialectics of the spirit of the people' and the
'world-tribunal,' in place of the other spiritual powers, art and religion, as the
sole sovereign power. (*KSA* I, 308)

The most concise example in Nietzsche's text for the opposite
treatment of human history, outside of any preconceived structure
and finality, is perhaps his dealing with the phenomenon of punishment in the Second Part of *On the Genealogy of Morals* (*KSA* V,
313-318). The origin and purpose, beginning and goal, of a phenomenon like punishment, Nietzsche argues in this text, ought to
be kept separate from each other, although in our historical conception they are usually confounded. One naively seeks some purpose in punishment, for example, revenge or deterrence and
guilelessly places this purpose at the beginning, considering the
ensuing history as a progressive unfolding of this purpose. This is
for Nietzsche the cardinal fault of historiography in general,
including of course cultural history. He says: "The cause of the
origin of a thing and its eventual utility, its actual employment and
place in a system of purposes, lie worlds apart," and continues:
"Whatever exists, having somehow come into being, is again and
again reinterpreted to new ends, taken over, transformed, and redi-
rected by some power superior to it" (*KSA* V, 313). I pass here
over Nietzsche's claim that in all such redirections and reinterpre-
tations "*a will to power* is operating" and that "purposes and utili-
ties are only *signs* that a will to power has become master of something less powerful and imposed upon it the character of a function." This would already be another, namely, Nietzsche's own
mode of interpretation which diverts from the more basic discovery
that

the entire history of a 'thing,' an organ, a custom can in this way be a continuous sign-chain of ever new interpretations and adaptations whose causes do
not even have to be related with one another, but on the contrary, in some
cases succeed and alternate with one another in a purely chance fashion.

Looked at from this point of view of "genealogy," the concept of
punishment "possesses in fact not one meaning but a whole synthesis of 'meanings,'" which finally crystallize into a certain "unity that
is hard to disentangle, hard to analyze and, as must be emphasized
especially, totally *undefinable*." "All concepts," Nietzsche maintains, "in which an entire process is semiotically concentrated elude
definition; only that which has no history is definable" (*KSA* V,
317).

5. Nietzsche attempted similar analyses with regard to cruelty,
envy, love, or conscience and said: "All kinds of individual passions
have to be thought through different ages, peoples and great and
small individuals . . . So far, all that has given color to existence still
lacks a history" (*KSA* III, 379). With regard to "revenge" he
thought:

The word "revenge" is said so quickly, it almost seems as if it could not contain more than one root concept and feeling. And so people are still trying to
find this root — just as our economists still have not become tired of smelling
such a unity in the word "value" and of looking for the original root concept
of value. As if all words were not pockets into which now this and now that
has been put, and now many things at once. (*KSA* II, 564)

Whereas Schlegel's critique of the idealistic conception of cultural history appeared to be directed against the preconceived goal
of this movement and its teleological character, Nietzsche seems to
strengthen this argument by emphasizing the chance character of
historical movement — a chance sequence also comprising that
philosophical consciousness which claims to be above chance. In
order to highlight this critique of idealistic thought, one is inclined
to refer to Derrida who injects the notion of play into this
critique — a notion of great importance to both Schlegel and
Nietzsche. Concentrating on the concept of historical knowledge
and understanding in its Hegelian version, Derrida said:

The necessity of *logical* continuity is the decision or interpretative milieu of all Hegelian interpretations. In interpreting negativity as labor, in betting for discourse, meaning, history, etc., Hegel has bet against play, against chance. He has blinded himself to the possibility of his own bet, to the fact that the conscientious suspension of play . . . was itself a phase of play; and to the fact that play *includes* the work of meaning or the meaning of work, and includes them not in terms of *knowledge*, but in terms of *inscription*: meaning is a *function* of play, is inscribed in a certain place in the configuration of a meaningless play.[20]

Yet we should remain aware of the fact that the critique launched against the romantic-idealistic notion of cultural history by Schlegel, Nietzsche, and Derrida is by no means only an opposition to or a negation of this thought but remains inseparably bound to it. To use the terminology employed in the initial parts of this paper, we could say that the deconstructive critique constitutes the part of theory, the theoretical, philosophical counterpart to history, which is of course inseparable from our dealing with history.

Notes

1 Johann Joachim Winckelmann, *Geschichte der Kunst des Altertums*, ed. Wilhelm Senff (Weimar: Böhlau, 1964). References to this text with the designation "*Geschichte*."

2 Nikolaus Himmelmann, "Winckelmanns Hermeneutik," in *Akademie der Wissenschaften und der Literatur, Abhandlungen der Geistes – und Sozialwissenschaftlichen Klasse*, Jahrgang 1971, Nr. 12, Mainz.

3 Johann Joachim Winckelmann, *Gedanken über die Nachahmung der griechischen Werke in der Malerei und Bildhauerkunst, Deutsche Literaturdenkmale*, Vol. 20 (Heilbronn: Henninger, 1885). References to this text with the designation "*Gedanken*."

4 See on this my essay "The Force of Classical Greece in the Formation of the Romantic Age in Germany," in *The Paths From Ancient Greece*, ed. Carol Thomas (Leyden: Brill, 1988), 98-120.

5 Johann Gottfried Herder, *Sämtliche Werke*, ed. Bernhard Suphan (Berlin: Weidemann, 1878). References to this edition with the designation "*Herder*."

6 This was a prejudice apparently widely shared in Germany of that time. See Martin Bernal, "Black Athena denied: the tyranny of Germany over Greece and the rejection of the Afroasiatic roots of Europe: 1780-1980," *Comparative Criticism* 8 (1987), 3-69. Bernal takes issue with what he calls the construction of an "Aryan Model" of ancient Greece.

7 See on this Schlegel's early, however, unfinished work with the title *History of the Poetry of the Greeks and the Romans* (1798): *KFSA* I, 395-568: Friedrich Schlegel, *Kritische Ausgabe in 35 Bänden*, ed. Ernst Behler with the collaboration of Jean-Jacques Anstett and Hans Eichner and other specialists (Paderborn-München: Schöningh, 1958–). References to this edition with the designation "*KFSA*."

8 Karl Freye, *Casimir Ulrich Boehlendorff, der Freund Herbarts und Hölderlins* (Langensalza, 1913), 90.

9 See on this my essay "'The Theory of Art is its Own History': Herder and the Schlegel Brothers," in *Herder Today. An Interdisciplinary Colloquium.* Stan-

ford University, November, 1987, ed. Kurt Müller-Vollmer (Berlin: de Gruyter, 1990), 246-67.

10 See on this the essay cited in the preceding footnote.

11 *August Wilhelm Schlegels Vorlesungen.* Kritische Ausgabe von Ernst Behler in Zusammenarbeit mit Frank Jolles. 6 vols. (Paderborn-München: Schöningh, 1988-). References to this edition with the designation *"AWSV."*

12 Georg Wilhelm Friedrich Hegel, *Werke in 20 Bänden.* Suhrkamp-Taschenbuch-Wissenschaft (Franfurt: Suhrkamp, 1986). References to this edition with the designation *"Hegel."*

13 See on this my essay "Zum Verhältnis von Hegel und Friedrich Schlegel in der Theorie der Unendlichkeit," *Kodikas/Code. Ars semiotica* 11 (1988), 127-147.

14 Hans-Georg Gadamer, *Wahrheit und Methode.* Grundzüge einer philosophischen Hermeneutik. Fourth Edition (Tübingen: Mohr (Siebeck), 1975), 7, 118, 189, 190.

15 I am employing these terms from the philosophical debate between Gadamer and Derrida on text and interpretation: *Text und Interpretation.* Deutsch-französische Debatte mit Beiträgen von J. Derrida, Ph. Forget, M. Frank, H.-G. Gadamer, J. Greisch und F. Laruelle, ed. Philippe Forget (München: Fink, 1984), 57.

16 Condorcet, *Esquisse d'un tableau historique des progrès de l'esprit humain.* Texte revu et présenté par O. H. Prior. Nouvelle édition présentée par Yvon Belaval (Paris: Vriss, 1970).

17 Friedrich Nietzsche, *Kritische Studienausgabe in 15 Bänden*, ed. Giorgio Colli and Mazzino Montinari (Berlin: de Gruyter, 1980). References to this edition with the designation *"KSA."* The translation of the essay *On the Advantages and Disadvantages of History for Life* is quoted from Friedrich Nietzsche, *Untimely Meditations*, trans. R. J. Hollingdale. With an Introduction by J. P. Stern (Cambridge: Cambridge University Press, 1983).

18 Wilhelm Dilthey, *Die Jugendgeschichte Hegels und andere Abhandlungen zur Geschichte des deutschen Idealismus*, ed. Hermann Nohl, in Wilhelm Dilthey, *Gesammelte Schriften*, Vol. 4 (Göttingen: Vandenhoeck and Ruprecht, 1959), 528-529.

19 H.-G. Gadamer, *Wahrheit und Methode.*

20 Jacques Derrida, *L'écriture et la différence* (Paris: Seuil, 1967).

Puppet Show and Emulation of Hamlet: Wilhelm Meister's (Re)mission of the *Theatralische Sendung*

Bernhard Greiner
University of Freiburg
(Translated by Cora Schenberg)

I

Wilhelm Meisters theatralische Sendung depicts an attempt to realize a modern subject's establishment of itself in terms of the world of aesthetics, and to tell this subject's story in the form of a theater novel.

"Theatralische Sendung" therefore means having been sent to the theater to complete the search for the self; conversely, it is a mission (*Sendung*) on the part of the theater as the realm where one's identity is realized. With this double meaning, the novel divides contemporary "theatromania,"[1] which expected the theater to fulfill the predominant wish to find one's identity and establish oneself as an individual, since bourgeois reality did not promise this fulfillment.[2] But the novel comes to an abrupt end just at the moment when Wilhelm's theater-dream appears to fulfill itself.

Ten years later, the *Lehrjahre* appear to abandon the theater as the realm where individual as well as social identity is realized. The theater becomes a "false tendency"[3] and Wilhelm the actor is later marked in Jarno's judgment as a dilettante (see L 551).[4] The "tower society," not the theater, becomes Wilhelm's final authority of legitimization. However, this understanding of the "remission" of the *Theatralische Sendung* is an inexact one. My thesis is that the art forms of play and theater referred to in the *Theatralische*

Sendung would have interrupted Wilhelm's progression, allowing him to attain the social identity represented by the tower society from the subjective-aesthetic ego foundation gained through the theater. Thus, the journey from theater to tower society was already foreseen in the *Theatralische Sendung.*

The interruption which would necessarily have followed in the story of Wilhelm's life is avoided in the *Lehrjahre.* In this, the meaning of the revision is revealed. This is possible because Goethe has his hero arrive at a new concept of the theater, which may now be recognized. For the ensuing self-discovery in this theater already contains transcendence of the realm of the theater into other spheres of realization of identity. This also explains the surprising phenomenon that the understanding of the theater and play at which Wilhelm ultimately arrives—the concept of a "symbolic theater"—is in keeping with what Goethe practiced as head of the Weimarer Hoftheater. And yet it is this same understanding which makes Goethe extend his character beyond the theater. In the task at which Goethe arrives for the theatrical mission, the theater concept finally outlined by the *Lehrjahre* both recognizes and transcends the *Theatralische Sendung.* Key areas of modern ego foundation are integrated into the new theater concept.[5]

II

With which forms of acting and theater does Wilhelm come into contact in the *Theatralische Sendung*, and where do their limitations lie? In the beginning there is the puppet theater—more precisely, the marionette theater.[6] The puppets themselves, independent of what each represents, are nothing but lifeless objects, scraps of material and paper carelessly thrown into boxes (see ThS 12). The materiality of the puppets, their individual reality, has symbolic value only; the puppet theater is solely a theater of signification, which knows no tension between the player and the signified play. If Wilhelm prefers occupying himself with the materials of the puppet theater, with its costumes and props, he is already living in the plays, since the puppets themselves are nothing and have only symbolic value. We can thus understand the "parapraxis"[7] Wilhelm and his friends make after going from the puppet theater to amateur acting. They still prefer to occupy themselves with the props, and only at the moment when the play is to be presented do they realize that they have no script. Occupied with costumes and sets, they were living totally in the world of the signified play. The bridge from the actor to the signified play—which should have been the script—had been drawn up.

The inverse of a theater of signification alone is a theater with no signification, or one for which the signified is only secondary. Rather than building up a signified world, the latter type of theater merely presents the actor's body, performing its skills. This is the first professional "theater" which Wilhelm encounters on his trip: a company of "tightrope walkers, acrobats and jugglers" ("Seiltänzer, Springer, Gaukler" [ThS 107]). These artists' performances, their "signs," carry no primary meaning; i.e., they do not refer to anything other or absent. Rather, they merely present themselves, bodies performing their stunts in the here-and-now, with their agility and skill, their seeming transcendence of natural laws. From this troop of tightrope walkers and pole vaulters comes Mignon. She makes it clear what this kind of theater represents— elaborate physical technique (the egg-dance),[8] and how this technique is acquired: through the trainer's physical force.

These physical skills are developed and handed down (as shown in the report on Serlo's training as an actor; see L 268 f.) through force imposed on the body. The *Theatralische Sendung* portrays Serlo as a genius of mimicry (ThS 294); the *Lehrjahre* trace this genius back to his perfected bodily control. Like the puppet, the body, which perfected technique has rendered all-flexible, lets no relations of tension arise between actor and played meaning.

The above-mentioned forms of acting are limited in that they only accent one pole of "theatrical doubling."[9] Theater exists in the simultaneous presence of performers and audience, both of which are at once producer and product, both part of reality and a representation of reality. The actor who comes on stage indicates that he is doubled. He is a person who comes on stage, and is yet something other than himself. That which is signified is also doubled: if the role calls for it, the actor may for example perform a real death, without dying in reality.

In both versions of the novel, the puppet theater accents only the pole of the signified world. The actor's reality disappears into this world. The same is true of artificial physical technique, insofar as its goal is mimicry and quick-change artistry. Taken in itself, the theater of artificial physical technique points toward the opposite possibility, that of accentuating only the pole of the actor. Using its technique, the respective body "quotes" a paradigm (pole vaulter, strongman, tightrope walker) in the present, and through his body and his reality, endows it with a new being.[10] This concept of the theater is not limited to the "lower world" of the circus or acrobatics, i.e., the world of the fair or market. On his journey, Wilhelm becomes acquainted with it as a demanding theater concept, even the leading form of theater. It is theater in which each actor represents a specific character type which is "written on his body": the leading man, the heroine, the lover, the pedant, etc.

In such a theater, the actors are set into character types; each plays his respective character type: himself. The connection between the "character type" and the actor is therefore not "natural," but coincidental. It is fixed and inscribed according to the demands of the situation. The Count illustrates this principle when he presents the pedant as a great actor. The transference of this character type brings about a definite physical and spiritual attitude in the actor, which he does not relinquish when he leaves the theater. It is therefore now a "character trait," and no longer an act. It is shown that as a consequence of the theater of type-casting, the actor's "own" character type affects him beyond the boundaries of the theater, and that he continues to play the role outside the theater. However, in the 18th century, the theater of "type-casting" complied with a social need.

Gottsched's theater reforms and the influence of Lessing's critiques of the theater point toward a process in which the theater —

in contrast to the courtly tradition—established itself as a bourgeois institution, a forum within the "bourgeois public sphere."[11] It appears as the place where a person of the middle class can experience himself as a "whole person," a person able to operate using all his capabilities. In this manner the theater becomes the aim of a longing for another, more intensive life than bourgeois reality could ever make possible. Wilhelm's pilgrimage to the theater bears witness to the "theatromania" which developed out of this longing—as does *Anton Reiser* in a more tragic turn. However, in order to accomplish and experience this functioning as a "whole person," both scenery and acting must be made as lifelike as possible. In this way, the theater's social function in the 18th century, to become a forum within the bourgeois public sphere, leads to the kind of theater of illusion already promoted by Diderot in France.[12] In Germany, where the bourgeoisie was much more excluded from the socio-political process, this was transposed more rigorously into practice in the theater. The theater of illusion demands the best possible mimesis of an individual's behavior and relinquishes contact with the audience. The principle of the theater of illusion is to obliterate the boundaries between art and reality. It is in just this instance where theater of illusion corresponds to theater of "type-casting." By continuing to play his "character type" in his own life, the actor has similarly abolished the boundary between art and reality.

The theater of illusion, whose effect has lasted from the 18th century into the present, and which Goethe, as head of the Weimarer Hoftheater, opposed, stands at the crossroads of two developments. It came about when social demand for theater as a forum within the bourgeois public sphere confronted the tradition of a theater of "type-casting." It was a time when the bourgeois lifestyle insisted on a bourgeois, rather than a courtly theater, and also when bourgeois, rather than plebeian actors—with their character types—urged themselves onto real life. Wilhelm portrays this kind of inscription of character type—in his case, the tragic hero. He reads Shakespeare and finds things previously unclear in his life now fulfilled and developed (see ThS 239). Fascinated by this newly revealed world, he completely forfeits himself to the character of the Shakespearean hero. He passes himself off as Hamlet in real life as well, imitating his dress and treating others as a prince would treat them (see ThS 244 f.). In the end, he dissolves into the character: "He was even willing to take on the burden of deep melancholy, and the role entwined itself with his lonely life so much that finally he and Hamlet began to become one."[13]

Finally, in the figure of Hamlet, Wilhelm summarizes his sporadic, undetermined journey to the theater. The description of the character becomes a self-interpretation: "Here not the hero, but the play, has a plan."[14]

The view given by the *Theatralische Sendung* is the concept of the theater of illusion, in which the demand for theater as a setting for the bourgeois public sphere is united with the tradition of theater of type-casting: Wilhelm, who has already become Hamlet in the reality of his life, and who expresses himself and his time through Hamlet, will enter Serlo's theater and play Hamlet. The boundary between theater and reality will be abolished.

The *Lehrjahre* delineate the two theater concepts more sharply by progressively building up a distance from both. The theater of type-casting is explicitly called by name; the Count's partiality to the pedant and the harpist can be explained by the view that these actors continued to play their role even in "normal life" (see L 208). On the other hand, Wilhelm's letter to Werner, which also first appears in the *Lehrjahre*, is well-known. In this letter, it is not the theater of type-casting, but rather the theater as the realm of a more intensely-lived life, of the middle-class citizen's experience of himself as a whole person, which is celebrated, along with the establishment of a bourgeois public sphere: "I have an irresistible inclination to that harmonious development of my nature which was denied me by my birth . . . you understand that I can only find it in the theatre, that only there can I behave and develop as I wish."[15]

This praise to the theater is echoed not only in the "Flee, youth, flee!" ("Flieh! Jüngling, flieh!" L 328) following the performance of *Hamlet*. It is only now, during his work on the *Hamlet* production, that Wilhelm learns to see the dissolution of boundaries between character and actor, between stage and reality which follow from imagining a more intensely-lived life as a whole person in the theater, as a false tendency. He comes up with this surprising insight: "with all my study of the play, my wish to play Hamlet led me entirely astray. The more I work into the role, the more I realize that my appearance has not the slightest resemblance to the Hamlet Shakespeare imagined."[16] Wilhelm now knows himself different from Hamlet, but still expresses himself here as Hamlet; he therefore has Hamlet in himself. He is still Hamlet, although he knows Hamlet as completely other. In this process, Wilhelm recognizes and develops both poles of theatrical doubling—whereby a principally different theater concept is attained.

III

While the previous theater concepts cancelled one pole of theatrical doubling, Wilhelm learns in the *Lehrjahre* to recognize this principle: that he is at once actor and character, and that neither of these may be allowed to disappear into the other. With the *Hamlet* production, which is not brought to performance until the *Lehrjahre*, Goethe gives us the outline for a new theater concept, a "symbolic theater." This is the pivotal issue of the novel, the starting point for the shifted emphasis in theater concepts made in the revision, and which will confront Wilhelm in the *Lehrjahre* as well. At the same time, new fields of identity discovery outlined by the novel come together in this issue.

A substantially new category is the intimacy of the nuclear family and its drive-dynamics as the setting for ego formation.[17] In the *Lehrjahre* it is no longer a neutral narrator, but rather Wilhelm himself who re-tells the story of the puppet theater to his mother. Now it is she (rather than his grandmother on his father's side) who gave Wilhelm the puppet theater, and not because Wilhelm was already fascinated by it—only after he received the gift did this fascination begin—but because she herself loved the theater (see L 11 f.). Hence, from the beginning, the puppet theater is raised into a "higher context," thrown into a constellation of displaced desire. The mother projects her desire for the theater onto the gift of the puppet theater, awakening in the boy a wish for the theater, which is synonymous with desiring the mother's desire which she had projected onto the theater. In the intimate relationship between mother and son, the puppet theater is libidinously charged, and stands in opposition to a denying third person, the father, who scoffs at it. Accordingly, the narrator is able to make the following comment on Wilhelm's love: "his passion for the stage joined with his first love for a female creature."[18]

This may definitely not be said to refer to his love of Mariane. Mariane falls asleep over Wilhelm's account of the puppet theater, because it shows her that she is only a surrogate in his love of the theater. From the beginning, Wilhelm's journey to the theater and through the various theaters is a production directed by his mother, while his progression beyond the theater is shown to be directed by the fatherly authorities of the tower society.

The puppet theater, in whose memory mother and son joyfully indulge themselves, is not the wish fulfillment itself. It is the expression of a love, which is—still, but not to be for long—possible, under the domination of a denying third person. The novel thus introduces Wilhelm into the "symbolic order:"[19] as a transformation of a denied wish. The essence of the theater is therefore related to another central category of ego formation. The theater in its constitutive doubling of the actor's being and the signification constructed by the "played" world—its doubling of body and required expression—repeats the process undergone in the history of the formation of every ego. This is the process—under the domination of a denying authority—of transformation from an orderless desiring body to the symbolic order of signs, which sets down the first limits and thereby creates the first instance of form: ego formation as transformation from body into symbol, from nature into culture. Introduced in such an instinctual-dynamic fashion, the theater in the forms in which Wilhelm encounters it always contains a moment of lack, as long as it cannot organize its *Aufhebung* (sublation) within a higher frame of reference. This is first accomplished in the recognition of theatrical doubling and the related symbolic theater.

The revision of the *Lehrjahre* culminates in the *Hamlet* production. Wilhelm now learns — despite all his identification with the hero — to differentiate himself, as an actor, from the character being played. Ultimately, he is even able to imagine his hero as the physiognomical opposite of himself ("blond and fat," L 306).

However, it is not only the hero who gains insight into theatrical doubling; rather, it takes an additional function in the novel itself: the author makes definite use of it. To begin with Wilhelm: he becomes a dramatic adviser only after gaining awareness of theatrical doubling. When it is no longer possible for him as an actor to put himself in the place of the protagonist or to become one with the character being played, a bridge must be built from the here-and-now of the actors and spectators, to the reality of the play and the hero. Wilhelm finds this bridge when he distinguishes between the "great inner relations between people and events"[20] which are actually dramatic, and the external circumstances of the plot, which are more novelesque (L 296). It is the distancing from Shakespeare as too novelesque which will later be reinforced by Goethe (in the essay "Shakespeare und kein Ende," 1815). Here, the differentiation serves in a historical-hermeneutic argument. For the English, who were used to circumstances concerning ships, sea journeys, changes of location, pirates' voyages etc., the novelesque external circumstances would not be confusing. However, the German reader of the 18th century, who had a different constellation of experiences, would have to be permitted "to toss out the distracting elements and substitute for them a single motif."[21] In this way Wilhelm introduces the dramatic "revision" of plays ("Dramatische Bearbeitung," L 302);[22] he becomes the first *Dramaturg* (dramatic adviser).

Fascinated by the character he is playing, Wilhelm lets himself be pulled into the illusion of the piece; as *Dramaturg*, he is both representative of the author ("I am convinced that Shakespeare would have done it this way himself"[23]) and advocate of the audience (by entering their historical-hermeneutic situation). In this way he is producer and product, under illusion and not under illusion, portrayed character and spectator, as long as he does not dissolve one position in favor of the other.

The author makes use of theatrical doubling in another way. He orchestrates, on the levels of the play being performed and the reality of the actors, dramas which are in a certain respect similar, but in another, exact opposites. Wilhelm plays the leading role in the bourgeois theater of a large city, wooed by the theater director and as the *spiritus rector* of the entire production. In doing so he fulfills the dream of the theater awakened by his mother, which stands for the mother's and son's symbiotic desires. He realizes this dream as an actor, but in the portrayed world he gives life to a figure and a drama, a life which presents the oedipal constellation as a tragic one. Here, symbiotic wishes remain unfulfilled, and Hamlet is crushed by the power of a denying third person. As an actor in the theater, the realm of representation, Wilhelm acts out the very symbiotic wishes which he reiterates in his performance as impossible to act out. Goethe defines the symbol as just such a paradox: "[the symbol] is the thing, without being the thing, and yet the thing; a picture formed in the mental mirror, and yet identical with the object."[24]

In its paradoxical content, the theater performance re-stages the oedipal constellation of the entrance into the symbolic order. In this process, the field of tension between displaced fulfillment and renewed negation of the aroused wish remains, pointing toward continual repetition of this constellation. Thus, in his theater acting, Wilhelm stands under the spell of the first enactment of his mother's desire. However, when he repeats the oedipal constellation as Hamlet, something new happens at this level of acting, which removes him from the spell of his mother's enactment of desire. In dealing with the play as an actor and *Dramaturg*, Wilhelm has not only gained distance from the character; rather, during the performance, the oedipal constellation is decidedly changed for the actor. A spirit appears, in whom the actor Wilhelm (and not only Hamlet, the character being played) believes he recognizes his own father. This father no longer dismisses the theater, but rather "plays along." His puzzling appearance contributes decidedly to the success of the play, by leading Wilhelm to an especially rousing performance.

Through a surrogate, the actor fulfills for himself what is denied in the played world. The *Hamlet* performance becomes the pivotal point of the novel. The performance looks back, once again re-enacting the mother's desire until its fulfillment through a surrogate. For after the play, Wilhelm finds a substitute for his mother in his bed: Philine, who plays the queen in the play-within-the-play in *Hamlet*. This queen alludes to Hamlet's mother, the very woman whose love Hamlet is denied. At the same time, the play looks ahead, since it breaks the spell of a "development" in the sign of the mother. With help from a father-surrogate, Wilhelm gains distance from the theater which was, until now, the location of the mother's desire, which had been transformed, maintained and constantly rekindled.

In this manner, the narrator makes use of the same theatrical doubling which he has his hero learn. Through backward and forward development, he makes the *Hamlet* play into a comprehensive system of references. This single performance contains the whole of the novel, with its theory of education as well as its theory of the theater. The scene is therefore raised to the level of the symbol according to Goethe's definition: the particular is expressed "without thinking of or referring to the general. Whoever grasps the particular receives at the same time the general without being aware of it immediately."[25]

It is only in the *Hamlet* scene that Wilhelm's journey becomes a progression in which his defining characteristics are developed. The novel gives only a limited view of its theory of education in the much-quoted letter to Werner. This is because the concept of education formulated there, which lays the foundation for Wilhelm's entrance into the theater, is retracted in the progression of the plot. The theater scenes develop another theory of education. There, the parameters of education are not the development of skills and talents, nor the tension between the individual and society. Rather, judging by the puppet theater scene, they seem to be an awakening of desires into which early symbiotic yearning is transformed. Education is therefore an enactment, a progression over a long period of time, the continual re-enactment of implanted desires. In the *Hamlet* production, in which both protagonist and author decisively make use of theatrical doubling, this rut of re-enactment is escaped and, for the first time, a stable ego is formed. The *Hamlet* production portrays this detachment by bringing together two processes, which psychoanalysis terms "work of mourning" and "triangulation."

On the subject of "work of mourning:"[26] as Hamlet, Wilhelm re-enacts the oedipal drama, but now knows to distinguish himself as an actor from Hamlet. Thus he once again goes through the constellation to which he is bound, because symbiotic desires are transformed in it, but he repeats the constellation with the knowledge that he, as an actor, is other (than the hero). This is how detachment from the theater of the mother comes about. The detachment is assisted (this is the "triangulation" aspect[27]) by the appearance, in the performance, of a father-surrogate who leads Wilhelm toward success and cancels the signified constellation. Once again, a theater comes to Wilhelm's aid, but this time it is one which detaches him from the theater of continual re-enactment of his mother's desire. Quite fittingly, in the act of handing over the letter of apprenticeship, it is finally revealed as a theater of "letting go" (as traditionally marks the end of an apprenticeship period), and at the same time, of Wilhelm's being proclaimed a father (whereby Wilhelm becomes what he is).

The masculine-defined "theater" of initiation into the tower society is the inverse response to the previous initiation into the maternal spell of the puppet theater. The society of fatherly surrogates, who take helpful action by self-sacrifice, rather than negative and destructive behavior, breaks the spell of the previous image (the personal myth) of the suffering King's son who loves the King's mother. As a new authority of legitimation, it assigns social functions. At the same time it transforms the personal myth of bloody passion (the Amazon as a return of the Tankred-Chlorinde constellation referred to earlier in the puppet show; see ThS 18) into the domestic structure of marriage by bringing Natalie, the "beautiful Amazon" to the hero (L 605 ff.).[28] While the break from theater is portrayed as socialization of personal myths, legitimation authorities for symbolic fields of new ego formation are also outlined.

The *Hamlet* performance contains not only the novel's theory of education, but also a new theory of the theater. It is a theater which develops theatrical doubling, rather than dissolving it into one of the poles. This theater is "symbolic" in two senses. From the point of view of drive psychology, it is established as a re-enactment of the entrance into the symbolic order, i.e., as a repetition of the constellation which, destined for the theater, awakened the desire for it. The *Hamlet* production therefore presents a story which has achieved its end (entelechy). However, this theater also enacts the letting go of itself, the giving up of itself which is necessary in order for its full potential, for ego formation, to be achieved. Therefore, retraction of itself as reference to something beyond itself is an integral part of the symbolic theater outlined by Goethe; this theater is simultaneously regressive and progressive. What has to be achieved in this extensive content of theatrical doubling is the process of symbolization. Accordingly, it is no surprise that Goethe's own theater work, reflected upon in his writings, has its vanishing point in this symbolization.

Goethe's theater work distinguishes itself from the theater of illusion which was prevalent during his time. It emphasizes the distinction between actor and played world, between the illusion of the performance and the audience. Hence, Goethe praised Roman comedy, in which "the concept of imitation, the awareness of art, remained alive, and the clever play brought forth only a kind of self-conscious illusion."[29]

Creation of illusion is limited in favor of a will to stylization, which reminds us of the doubling of actor and character, performance and audience, according to this maxim: "only the stage and the hall, the actors and the audience together make up a whole,"[30] from which this claim, among others, is derived: "for the actor must always divide himself between two things, namely between the object with which he speaks and his listeners."[31]

However, theatrical doubling is always subject to the law of reference, as recorded in these remarks:

Strictly speaking, nothing is theatrical except what is also visually symbolic: an important plot that points to one even more important.[32]

Goethe devotes the *Lehrjahre* to just this symbolic reference.[33] It is agreed in the *Lehrjahre* that the theater cannot become an end in itself, that it must always point beyond itself, continuously enhance itself. However, since theatrical doubling was outlined in *Wilhelm Meister*, the theatrical as the symbolic has been put to the following mission: not to neglect the charm revealed by theatrical doubling, that special charm, grace and charisma of the theater, captured by Goethe in this maxim: "actors steal hearts without giving theirs in return; they deceive, however, with grace."[34]

Notes

1   See also: Eckehard Catholy, "Die geschichtlichen Voraussetzungen des Illusionstheaters in Deutschland," in *Festschrift für Klaus Ziegler*, ed. E. Catholy and W. Hellmann (Tübingen: Niemeyer, 1968); Rolf Selbmann, *Theater im Roman.   Studien zum Strukturwandel des deutschen Bildungsromans* (Munich: Fink, 1981).   See in particular Chapter II: "Theatromanie im Roman."   Selbmann reminds us of the origin of the concept of "theatromania," first referred to by Catholy: a document written by a pastor Anton Reiser in 1681, in strong opposition to the theater.   It is to this document which Moritz probably refers: *Theatromanie, oder Die Werke der Finsterniß in den öffentlichen Schauspielen, von den alten Kirchenlehrern und etlichen heidnischen Skribenten verdammt* (Theatromanie, or The Works of Darkness in Public Plays, damned by the old church teachers and some pagan scribes).

2   This idea is concisely developed in Wilhelm's well-known letter to Werner, in which he declares himself in favor of a theater career (*Lehrjahre*, Book 5, Ch. 3).   The opposition of theater and bourgeois reality can be so decisively formulated here because it dissolves as the plot develops.

3   *Tag- und Jahreshefte*, "To 1786" (X, 432).

4   Unless otherwise specified, quotations from Goethe in this text will be taken from the Hamburger Ausgabe (Roman numeral: volume number; Arabic numeral: page number).   To facilitate identification of quotations from the *Lehrjahre* and the *Theatralische Sendung*, quotations from the *Lehrjahre* will be designated by an 'L' (instead of VII); quotations from the *Theatralische Sendung* will be identified under 'ThS' (quotations from the *Sendung* will be from *Wilhelm Meisters theatralische Sendung*, dtv complete edition, Vol. 14, which is identical to the Artemis edition, Munich, 1962).

5   For greater detail see also Gerhard Neumann, "Der Wanderer und der Verschollene.   Zum Problem der Identität in Goethes 'Wilhelm Meister' und in Kafkas 'Amerika' -Roman," in *Paths and Labyrinths.   Nine Papers from a Kafka Symposium*, ed. J. P. Stern and J. J. White (London: Publications of the Institute of Germanic Studies, 1985).

6   Cf. ThS 12, 15 et al.

7   The concept is derived from Sigmund Freud, "Zur Psychopathologie des All-
tagslebens," in Freud, *Gesammelte Werke*, Vol. IV, ed. Anna Freud (London:
Imago Publishing [Fischer], 1940).

8   Cf. ThS, Book 4, Ch. 3; L Book 2, Ch. 8.

9   The term "theatrical doubling" is used according to Manfred Wekwerth,
*Theater und Wissenschaft. Überlegungen für das Theater von heute und
morgen* (Munich: Hanser, 1974).

10 The difference between the puppet theater of signification alone and the
theater of artificial physical technique is disregarded if Mignon is interpreted
only through extrapolation of one section of the text (ThS 162, L 115 f.) in
terms of the concept of marionettes: Hellmut Ammerlahn, "Wilhelm
Meisters Mignon—ein offenbares Rätsel," in *DVJS* 42, 1968.

11 This concept is used according to Jürgen Habermas, *Strukturwandel der
Öffentlichkeit* (Neuwied, Berlin: Luchterhand, 1962).

12 For greater detail see also E. Catholy, n. 1.

13 "Auch die Last der tiefen Schwermut war er geneigt auf sich zu nehmen, und
die Übung der Rolle verschlang sich dergestalt in sein einsames Leben, daß
endlich er und Hamlet eine Person zu werden anfingen" (ThS 269).
[Translations by the editor.]

14 "Hier hat der Held keinen Plan, aber das Stück hat einen" (ThS 283 f.).

15 "Ich habe nun einmal gerade zu jener harmonischen Ausbildung meiner
Natur, die mir meine Geburt versagt, eine unwidersprechliche Neigung . . .
du siehst wohl, daß das alles für mich nur auf dem Theater zu finden ist, und
daß ich mich in diesem einzigen Elemente nach Wunsch rühren und
ausbilden kann" (L 291 f.).

16 "eigentlich hat mein Wunsch, den Hamlet zu spielen, mich bei allem Studium
des Stücks aufs äußerste irregeführt. Je mehr ich mich in die Rolle studiere,
desto mehr sehe ich, daß in meiner ganzen Gestalt kein Zug der
Physiognomie ist, wie Shakespeare seinen Hamlet aufstellt" (L 306).

17 This complex in Wilhelm Meister is thoroughly examined in Friedrich A.
Kittler, "Über die Sozialisation Wilhelm Meisters," in G. Kaiser und F. A.
Kittler, *Dichtung als Sozialisationsspiel* (Göttingen: Vandenhoeck &
Ruprecht, 1978).

18 "seine Leidenschaft zur Bühne verband sich mit der ersten Liebe zu einem
weiblichen Geschöpfe" (L 14).

19 The term "symbolic order" is used in the sense of Jacques Lacan, "Funktion
und Feld des Sprechens und der Sprache in der Psychoanalyse," in Lacan,
Schriften I, ed. and trans. N. Haas (Olten: Walter, 1973). Julia Kristeva fol-

lows Lacan, insofar as the "entrance into the symbolic order" occupies a central position in her theory of literature. See J. Kristeva, *Die Revolution der poetischen Sprache* (Frankfurt: Suhrkamp, 1978).

20 "großen innern Verhältnissen der Personen und Begebenheiten" (L 295).

21 "die zerstreuenden Motive alle auf einmal wegzuwerfen und ihnen ein einziges zu substituieren" (L 296).

22 On the theory of "dramatic revision" ("Dramatische Bearbeitung") based on hermeneutics and intertextuality (proceeding from earlier evidence of dramatic revision in Shakespeare's *Hamlet* itself), see also Bernhard Greiner, "'Explosion einer Erinnerung in einer abgestorbenen dramatischen Struktur:' Heiner Müller's 'Shakespeare Factory,'" in *Deutsche Shakespeare Gesellschaft West, Jahrbuch,* 1989.

23 "ich bin überzeugt, daß Shakespeare es selbst so würde gemacht haben" (L 295).

24 "Es [das Symbol] ist die Sache, ohne die Sache zu sein, und doch die Sache; ein im geistigen Spiegel zusammengezogenes Bild, und doch mit dem Gegenstand identisch" ("Philostrats Gemälde," Weimarer Ausgabe, Section I, 49.1., p. 142).

25 "ohne ans Allgemeine zu denken oder darauf hinzuweisen. Wer nur dieses Besondere lebendig faßt, erhält zugleich das Allgemeine mit, ohne es gewahr zu werden, oder erst spät" (XII, 471).

26 This concept is used in the sense of Alexander and Margarete Mitscherlich, *Die Unfähigkeit zu trauern* (Munich: Piper, 1977).

27 On the concept of triangulation, see Michael Rotmann, "Über die Bedeutung des Vaters in der 'Wiederannäherungs-Phase,'" in *Psyche* 32, No. 12, 1978.

28 For the point of reference for both "personal myths," see Hans-Jürgen Schings, "Wilhelm Meisters schöne Amazone," in *Jahrbuch der deutschen Schillergesellschaft* 29, 1985. For a selection of more recent interpretations of *Wilhelm Meister,* see Ilse Graham, "An Eye for the World: Stages of Realisation in *Wilhelm Meister,*" in I. Graham, *Goethe. Portrait of the Artist* (Berlin, New York: de Gruyter, 1977); Per Ohrgaard, *Die Genesung des Narcissus. Eine Studie zu Goethe: Wilhelm Meisters Lehrjahre* (Copenhagen: Univ. Inst. for germansk filologi, 1978); David Roberts, *The Indirections of Desire: Hamlet in Goethe's 'Wilhelm Meister'* (Heidelberg: Winter, 1980); Hannelore Schlaffer, *Wilhelm Meister. Das Ende der Kunst und die Wiederkehr des Mythos* (Stuttgart: Metzler, 1980); Ivar Sagmo, *Bildungsroman und Geschichtsphilosophie. Eine Studie zu Goethes Roman 'Wilhelm Meisters Lehrjahre'* (Bonn: Bouvier, 1982); Winfried Barner,

"Geheime Lenkung: Zur Turmgesellschaft in Goethes *Wilhelm Meister*," in *Goethe's Narrative Fiction. The Irvine Goethe Symposium*, ed. W. J. Lillyman (Berlin, New York: de Gruyter, 1983); Jochen Hörisch, *Gott, Geld und Glück. Zur Logik der Liebe in den Bildungsromanen Goethes, Kellers und Thomas Manns* (Frankfurt: Suhrkamp, 1983); Wulf Köpke, "Wilhelm Meisters theatralische Sendung," in *Goethes Erzählwerk. Interpretationen*, ed. P. M. Lützeler (Stuttgart: Reclam, 1985); Monika Fiek, "Destruktive Imagination. Die Tragödie der Dichterexistenz in *Wilhelm Meisters Lehrjahren*," in *Jahrbuch der deutschen Schillergesellschaft* 29, 1985. On the Hamlet motif in *Wilhelm Meister*, see David Roberts, "Wilhelm Meister and Hamlet. The Inner Structure of Book III of *Wilhelm Meisters Lehrjahre*," in *Publications of the English Goethe Society*, N. S. 45, 1974/75; Mark Evan Bonds, "Die Funktion des 'Hamlet'—Motivs in *Wilhelm Meisters Lehrjahre*," in *Goethe Jahrbuch* 96, 1979; Kurt Ermann, *Goethes Shakespeare-Bild* (Tübingen: Niemeyer, 1983).

29 "der Begriff der Nachahmung, der Gedanke an Kunst immer lebhaft blieb und durch das geschickte Spiel nur eine Art von selbstbewußter Illusion hervorgebracht wurde," "Frauenrollen auf dem römischen Theater durch Männer gespielt," *Schriften zur Literatur*, Erster Teil (Munich: Deutscher Taschenbuchverlag, 1962), Vol. 31, p. 8.

30 "die Bühne und der Saal, die Schauspieler und die Zuschauer machen erst ein Ganzes" (82, XII, 260).

31 "Denn der Schauspieler muß sich immer zwischen zwei Gegenständen teilen: nämlich zwischen dem Gegenstande, mit dem er spricht, und zwischen seinen Zuhörern" (Par. 40), ("Regeln für Schauspieler," in *Schriften zur Literatur*, Erster Teil. See n. 20, p. 45).

32 "Genau aber genommen, so ist nichts theatralisch, als was für die Augen zugleich symbolisch ist: eine wichtige Handlung, die auf eine noch wichtigere deutet" (XII, 296). Analogously, Eckermann notes the following on July 26, 1826: "Ich fragte, wie ein Stück beschaffen sein müsse, um theatralisch zu sein. 'Es muß symbolisch sein,' antwortete Goethe. 'Das heißt: jede Handlung muß an sich bedeutend sein und auf eine noch wichtigere hinzielen,'" J. P. Eckermann, *Gespräche mit Goethe*, ed. H. H. Houben (Wiesbaden: F. A. Brockhaus, 1949), p. 137.

33 Conversation with Chancellor von Müller, Jan. 22, 1821 (quoted in L 613), and conversation with Eckermann on Dec. 25, 1825 (quoted in L 614).

34 "Schauspieler gewinnen die Herzen und geben die ihrigen nicht hin; sie hintergehen aber mit Anmut" (MuR 933, XII, 497).

Epistemic Conflict, Hermeneutical Disjunction, and the Subl(im)ation of Revolt: A Sociosemiotic Investigation of Schiller's *Die Räuber*

Richard Gray
University of Washington

"Deiner heiligen Zeichen, o Wahrheit, hat der Betrug sich /Angemaßt ... "
— Schiller, "Der Spaziergang"

I
"Revolution" as Conflict of Semiologies

In his "archaeology of the human sciences" entitled *The Order of Things*, Michael Foucault has plotted three epochs in the history of Western culture, distinguishing them on the basis of their characteristic epistemological paradigms (epistemes) and their essential semiologies.[1] Deliberating on the evolution of the institution of literature in the 18th and 19th centuries, Foucault suggests that literature's autonomous status in the bourgeois age derives from its preservation of a superannuated semiology discordant with that which dominates bourgeois thought in general (*OT*, 43-44). Modern literature "achieved autonomous existence, and separated itself from all other language with a deep scission, only by forming a sort of 'counter-discourse,' and by finding its way back from the representative or signifying function of language [characteristic of Western thought since the Classical age] to this raw being that had been forgotten since the sixteenth century" (*OT*, 43-44). Three aspects of this theory hold out promise for investigations into the evolution of the institution of autonomous bourgeois literature in Germany in the final decades of the eighteenth century: the first is Foucault's insistence on the *semiological* dimension as that realm in which autonomous literature attains its self-constitution; the second is the implied *historicizing* thesis that suggests that autonomization occurs when literature "finds its way back," i.e., historically returns to a semiotic mode antecedent to the "paradigm shift" to Classical (i.e., "Enlightenment") thought; the third, finally, is Foucault's assertion that in the counter-discourse of modern literature, language escapes the merely *representational* function to which it is reduced in Classical thought.

As Manfred Frank has recently maintained, the inherent weakness of Foucault's historical "archaeology" rests in its veritable anti-historical obsession with genealogical "formations" of history to the total exclusion of the processes or mutations which might account for the transformation from one paradigm to the other.[2] What Foucault's analyses purposely ignore, as his metaphor of archaeological "strata" indicates, are the breach-points, the ruptures that mark the transformation from one episteme to another. Foucault's historical archaeology thus needs to be supplemented by a theory which attempts to define the space of discontinuity between epistemic paradigms as the locus of revolution.

In his contribution to the *Yale French Studies* volume on "Literature and Revolution," Jacques Ehrmann theorizes a structural conception of revolution which locates it at the fault line between two antagonistic conceptual systems. "Revolution is situated at the juncture of two histories, appearing as the moment when the relationships between politics and history become disjointed for lack of a suitable language to articulate these relationships, and also for lack of a language (that is, a symbolic conceptual system) fit to articulate reality."[3] Ehrmann's reflections are basically consistent with Foucault's conception of historical "strata," but they point to a more dynamic configuration that is better rendered with the metaphor of the fault between two continental plates, a metaphor which stresses the factors of tension, resistance, and conflict at work at the juncture of two "histories." Such a conception of revolution, it seems to me, can fruitfully be applied to the incipient bourgeois era in Germany and especially to the writers of the *Sturm und Drang*.[4]   A further aspect of Ehrmann's reflections seems especially relevant to a reinterpretation of the "revolutionary" features of the *Sturm und Drang*: this is his notion of the revolutionary period as one characterized fundamentally by a struggle for *articulation* that evolves out of the conflict of competing and inimical discourses. Viewed from such a standpoint, the near-obsessive reflections on language proffered by this generation, including their concern with issues of semiotics and the process of signification, as well as the characteristic verbal "flailing about" of their dramatic characters, take on added significance. The literature of the *Sturm und Drang* can be productively understood, as I hope to show on the example of Schiller's inaugural drama *Die Räuber* (1781), as a product of this discursive conflict which manifests itself as the struggle between two competing semiologies.[5]

II
Semiotic Re-Turn and Schiller's Sentimental Redemption of the Naive

If, as John Frow claims, the "sentimental redemption of the naive" represents the prototypical strategy of modernist literature, then Schiller—like the *Stürmer und Dränger* in general—is the modernist par excellence, and not merely because he has authored the terminology that makes this definition possible.[6] Indeed, Schiller's entire literary-aesthetic project, from the rebellious early plays to the *Ästhetische Erziehung* and *Über naive und sentimentalische Dichtung*, can be characterized as a critical rejection of the devolving contemporary world in favor of a nostalgic return to the lost origin of an authentic, unalienated, and immediate existence. As late as 1803, in the essay "Über den Gebrauch des Chors in der Tragödie," Schiller could formulate the task of the modern tragic poet as the retro-transformation of the "moderne gemeine Welt in die alte poetische . . . " (II, 819-20). His attack on the contemporary age continues in these characteristic and telling terms:

> Der Palast der Könige ist jetzt geschlossen, die Gerichte haben sich von den Toren der Städte in das Innere der Häuser zurückgezogen, die Schrift hat das lebendige Wort verdrängt, das Volk selbst, die sinnlich lebendige Masse, ist, wo sie nicht als rohe Gewalt wirkt, zum Staat, folglich zu einem Begriff geworden . . . (II, 820)

The poet's mandate is to reverse these circumstances, to restore the "immediacy" that has otherwise disappeared from the practical interaction between individuals and the life world, to undo the processes of abstraction, internalization, and privatization which have transformed the interactive community of the "Volk" into the monadic, modular "subjects" of the modern State.

Schiller's various aesthetic theories are "revolutionary" in the sense of that word as employed by Jean Baudrillard, who defines revolution as "planned reversal."[7] Schiller conceived his aesthetic theories as guidelines for a return to genuine human worth. This aesthetic redemption of humanity is characterized by the paradox that the ultimate renunciation of dissimulation can only be accomplished by exploiting dissimulation in the form of aesthetic semblance. "Die Menschheit hat ihre Würde verloren," Schiller writes in a celebrated passage from the ninth aesthetic letter, "aber die Kunst hat sie gerettet und aufbewahrt *in bedeutenden Steinen*; die Wahrheit lebt in der Täuschung fort, und aus dem Nachbilde wird das Urbild wiederhergestellt werden" (V, 594; emphasis added). The crisis of modernity, if we take Schiller at his word, is the crisis of the human counterfeit: humanity has lost its original value, has become a counterfeit of itself; but in art there exists the last true copy of human dignity, from which the original can and will be restored. Implied in Schiller's metaphor of "signifying stones" is a conception of the aesthetic as a hieroglyphic tablet, i.e., as a durable if yet illegible text which preserves an enigmatic mode of signification in which "truth" hibernates, so to speak, waiting to be decoded and to announce with the reappearance of its authentic "meaning" the return of an unalienated (i.e., im-mediate) humanity. The "signifying stones" of art preserve an alternate semiotic whose code has been lost to the modern world. This semiotic undercurrent runs throughout much of Schiller's thought on an almost subliminal level; turning out the semiological lining in some of his aesthetic-theoretical statements exposes precisely the degree to which Schiller, like many of his contemporaries, conceived the struggle between the "ancients and the moderns" as a fundamental conflict of semiologies.

Reflections from the "Theosophie des Julius," part of the "Philosophische Briefe" Schiller composed in conjunction with Christian Gottfried Körner—i.e., a work whose conception, like that of *Die Räuber*, goes back to Schiller's final years at the academy in Stuttgart—suggest that even at this early date Schiller discerned two different epistemological-conceptual systems whose distinctness was attributable to their reliance on variant *semiotic* relations. Early in his theosophical deliberations Julius formulates a conception of the symmetry between the physical, objective world and the internal realm of the human soul, a conception which reads like an extension of Johann Caspar Lavater's physiognomical semiotic, allowing it to encompass all of nature as the signifying material which gives expression to the human soul.

> Jeder Zustand der menschlichen Seele hat irgendeine Parabel in der physischen Schöpfung, wodurch er bezeichnet wird, und nicht allein Künstler und Dichter, auch selbst die abstraktesten Denker haben aus diesem reichen Magazin geschöpft. Lebhafte Tätigkeit nennen wir Feuer, die Zeit ist ein Strom, der reißend von hinnen rollt, die Ewigkeit ist ein Zirkel, ein Geheimnis hüllt sich in Mitternacht, und die Wahrheit wohnt in der Sonne. Ja, ich fange an zu glauben, daß sogar das künftige Schicksal des menschlichen Geistes im dunkeln Orakel der körperlichen Schöpfung vorhergekündigt liegt. (V, 345)

The external, organic world takes on the role of a secondary phenomenon: it exists as the perceptible metaphorical vehicle which lays bare the imperceptible tenor of the human soul; it is the external signature of the internal world of the human spirit, and what binds these two spheres together is a tertium comparationis revealed by the power of analogy. For Michel Foucault it is precisely this principle of similitude, the analogical understanding of the visible as "signs" for the invisible, which defines the semiotic of the Renaissance episteme.

> [T]he face of the world is covered with blazons, with characters, with ciphers and obscure words—with 'hieroglyphics' . . . And the space inhabited by immediate resemblances becomes like a vast open book; it bristles with written signs; every page is seen to be filled with strange figures that intervene and in some places repeat themselves. All that remains is to decipher them . . . The sign of affinity, and what renders it visible, is quite simply analogy. (*OT*, 27)

While he apparently subscribes to just such a quasi-oracular relationship between the visible world as sign and the human spirit as its signified, Schiller's Julius simultaneously formulates a specifically modern and contrary conception of a semiotic relation grounded in conventionality rather than in resemblance.

> Unser ganzes Wissen läuft endlich, wie alle Weltweisen übereinkommen, auf eine konventionelle Täuschung hinaus, mit welcher jedoch die strengste Wahrheit bestehen kann. Unsre reinsten Begriffe sind keineswegs *Bilder* der Dinge, sondern bloß ihre notwendig bestimmte und koexistierende *Zeichen*. Weder Gott, noch die menschliche Seele, noch die Welt sind das wirklich, was wir davon halten . . . Aber die Kraft der Seele ist eigentümlich, notwendig und immer sich selbst gleich: das Willkürliche der Materialien, woran sie sich äußert, ändert nichts an den ewigen Gesetzen, wornach sie sich äußert, solang dieses Willkürliche mit sich selbst nicht in Widerspruch steht, solang das Zeichen dem Bezeichneten durchaus getreu bleibt . . . Wahrheit ist also keine Eigenschaft der Idiome, sondern der Schlüsse; nicht die Ähnlichkeit des Zeichens mit dem Bezeichneten, des Begriffs mit dem Gegenstand, sondern die Übereinstimmung dieses Begriffs mit den Gesetzen der Denkkraft. (V, 355-56)

Here Schiller/Julius explicitly subscribes to a theory of conventionality and arbitrariness as a way of explaining the linkage between expressive signs and their referents. Moreover, he admits that this conventionality is a *deception* which, nonetheless, is capable of sustaining the most rigorous truths. Abstract signs, in this view, are incommensurable with the intellectual or physical objects to which they refer; signs are not re-presentations, similitudes of the objects they signify, but are symbolic proxies whose representational function is vouchsafed by "eternal laws" which are themselves *extrinsic to* the relation of signification. "God," "soul," and "world"—

indeed, all "referents"—acquire the virtual unattainability of the Kantian thing-in-itself; the principle of adequation as the condition of possibility of veritable signification is replaced by a structure of relationality, the coincidence of "concept" with the "laws of cogitation" or with the "necessary" self-identity of the power of the "soul." Schiller thus articulates a paradigmatically modern—if yet rudimentary—conception of a formal or structural model of truth in which verity is guaranteed by the conformity of expression with certain eternal (logical or rational) *laws*. Nothing could contrast more starkly with the substantivist, iconic semiotic grounded in similitude propagated earlier in the same essay; and the rather confounding side-by-side of these two semiologies is symptomatic for Schiller's intellectual-historical position on the fault line between two antagonistic epistemic structures.

The proximity of Schiller's conventional semiotic grounded in formal-structural relations to modern semiological thought is brought out further by the examples he himself provides to elucidate his conception. He cites, interestingly enough, the ability of mathematics to calculate, on the basis simply of signs on paper, the future appearance of a comet, as well as the daring of the explorer Columbus, who traverses uncharted seas in the conviction that the laws of logic guarantee that reality will conform to his conceptual map of the world. This "structural," logical, and conventional semiotic, then, not restricted to mere reiteration of the known, allows for productive, projective calculation on the basis of unchanging and infallible rules. What Schiller outlines, in fact, accords perfectly with the symbolically mediated semiotic of the Classical age as characterized by Foucault.

> In the Classical age, to make use of signs is not . . . to attempt to rediscover beneath them the primitive text of a discourse sustained, and retained, forever; it is an attempt to discover the arbitrary language that will authorize the deployment of nature within its space, the final terms of its analysis and the laws of its composition. It is no longer the task of knowledge to dig out the ancient Word from the unknown places where it may be hidden, its job now is to fabricate a language, and to fabricate it well—so that, as an instrument of analysis and combination, it will really be the language of calculation. (*OT*, 62-63)

The coexistence of the modern symbolic semiotic of arbitrariness and calculation with the superseded iconic, "re-iterative" semiotic in Schiller's early thought points to a fundamental equivocation that he shares with many of his contemporary bourgeois intellectuals. The nostalgia for an iconic semiotic in which the adequacy of signifier to signified is immediately guaranteed by resemblance is the persistent symptom of a skepticism and deep-seated uneasiness about the modern, bourgeois semiotic by these thinkers who themselves are representatives of the bourgeoisie. If they were among the first bourgeois intellectuals to gain insight into what has come to be called the dialectic of Enlightenment,[8] then this critical awareness was grounded in fundamental perceptions about the *semiotics* of bourgeois exchange and the potential repercussions of this structural-conventional system of value when transported to the realms of human interaction and moral conduct in the life world.

In the treatise *Über naive und sentimentalische Dichtung* Schiller addresses once more this semiological problematic; in this instance, however, he does so in order to valorize the iconic semiotic which he identifies with the genius endemic to the naive mode of cognition. Contrasting naive thought and expression with the logic and grammar of bookish erudition [*Schulverstand*], Schiller's reflections culminate in a juxtaposition of the semiotic relations that govern these conceptual systems.

> Wenn dort [im Falle des Schulverstands] das Zeichen dem Bezeichneten ewig heterogen und fremd bleibt, so springt hier [in der naiven Denkart] wie durch innere Notwendigkeit die Sprache aus dem Gedanken hervor und ist so sehr eins mit demselben, daß selbst unter der körperlichen Hülle der Geist wie entblößet erscheint. Eine solche Art des Ausdrucks, wo das Zeichen ganz in dem Bezeichneten verschwindet, und wo die Sprache den Gedanken, den sie ausdrückt, noch gleichsam nackend läßt, *da ihn die andre nie darstellen kann, ohne ihn zugleich zu verhüllen*, ist es, was man in der Schreibart vorzugsweise genialisch und geistreich nennt. (V, 706; emphasis added)

Naive cognition is characterized by a remainderless conjunction between signifier and signified: the signifier, language, is produced by the signified, thought, not vice versa. Moreover, the process by which the signifier is produced derives from *internal necessity.* Semiosis here, in other words, consists in a relation of self-determination, self-identity, and immediacy whereby the signified "organically" gives birth to its expressive signifier. Schiller's language in this passage makes amply clear that the noncommittal juxtaposition in the "Theosophie des Julius" of a substantive iconic semiotic and a formal-structural semiotic of manipulative control has been resolved with the result that the former finds its rightful place in the counter-discourse of "naive" art. The rules of logic, held up by Schiller/Julius in the earlier work as the basis of correspondence between thought and world, are condemned in the later treatise as the cross on which words and concepts are crucified: " . . . der Schulverstand, immer vor Irrtum bange, [schlägt] seine Worte wie seine Begriffe an das Kreuz der Grammatik und Logik . . . " (V, 706). But more important yet is Schiller's projected dichotomy between transparency and concealment which distinguishes naive semiosis from that of bookish erudition. The former is characterized by auto-nomy expressed in the pure transparency of the signifier—it "disappears" into the signified, leaves it "naked" and immediately perceptible. The latter, which Schiller associates with "representation," attains expression only by simultaneously *concealing* what it aims to portray: representation by heteronomous, arbitrary, or conventional signs is thus inextricably caught up in a dialectic of disclosure and simultaneous enshroudment in which expression automatically and necessarily is accompanied by occultation. This moment of concealment not only clouds the desired transparency of truth, it opens up an ungovernable, unpoliceable blind spot which prevents the validity of a specific representation from being tested or guaranteed.

Schiller's early drama *Die Räuber* examines questions about the compatibility or incompatibility of the iconic and the structural, or symbolic, semiotic. The play poses, in essence, questions about the viability of an iconic semiotic in a world increasingly dominated by calculation, arbitrariness, exchange, and economically legitimated deceit. While Schiller himself sought to underwrite an iconic semiotic, preserving it at least in the aesthetic and ethical spheres, he was well aware of the perils to which it is subject and which threaten to undermine its efficacy. His own aesthetic practice in this "dramatic novel" which fuses dramatic immediacy and the mediative reflection of the written-read text aims at a corrective to the arbitrariness of abstract, manipulable, and manipulating signs.

III

Semiotic Conflict and Hermeneutical Disjunction in *Die Räuber*

> "The written word and things no longer resemble one another. And
> between them, Don Quixote wanders off on his own."
> — Foucault, *The Order of Things*

In the preface to the first edition of *Die Räuber* Schiller characterizes Karl Moor as a "strange Don Quixote" whose ideals and "enthusiastic dreams of greatness and effectiveness" are smashed by prevalent conditions in the "unideal world" of the time (I, 486). I propose to take this assertion literally and construe Schiller's protagonist as a direct descendent of the naive, idealizing fool, Don Quixote, who, taking the superseded books of chivalrous romance at their word, set out on an absurd campaign in which the banal reality of the life world was confronted with the ideality of the written word. Schiller's allusion clearly suggests that the problematics of *reading* and the adjudication of written text with really existing social, cultural, and political conditions—"bürgerlich[e] Verhältnisse," as he refers to them in his preface (I, 486)—are central to this drama.

In his ground-breaking essay on the function of letters in Schiller's early plays, Oskar Seidlin situated the conflict between the brothers Franz and Karl in *Die Räuber* in the linguistic realm, describing it as the struggle between two distinct conceptions and uses of language.[9] Written texts, specifically letters, are associated throughout the drama with Franz, who, as Seidlin points out, exploits the distance between the writer of such messages and their readers, setting himself (and others) up as "intermediaries and middlemen" (131) who manipulate and falsify the original messages. Franz capitalizes, in other words, on the moment of "concealment" Schiller diagnosed in the representational dialectic of modern semiosis: as self-established "mediator" between Old Moor and Karl, father and son, Franz, the veritable incarnation of the abstract, heteronomous sign, controls and distorts their relationship.[10]

Schiller made no secret of the fact that his Franz was intended to represent the negative potentials inherent in the "enlightened" and "modern" tendencies of the age. In the "Selbstbesprechung" of the play Schiller identifies the reasoning underpinning Franz's "Lastersystem" as "das Resultat eines aufgeklärten Denkens und liberalen Studiums" (II, 627). His persistent objections to Dalberg's transposition, in the stage version, of the action of the drama into the historic past is founded on his sense that in such a setting his characters, whom he describes as "zu aufgeklärt, zu modern angelegt,"[11] would inevitably appear anachronistic. Schiller realizes, in short, that to dramatize his play in any other time but the historical present would be as absurd as retro-contextualizing Cervantes *Don Quixote* in the era of chivalry: the entire structure of the dramatic conflict, which is predicated precisely on the opposition between modern reality and the "naive" ideals of the past, would thereby collapse.

Seidlin's desire to project Karl as a tragic hero, rather than to conceive him as a comic figure in the tradition of *Don Quixote*, prevents his insights into the linguistic nature of the struggle between the brothers from bearing real fruit.[12] Seidlin accuses Karl, thereby implicitly integrating him in the tradition of the tragic hero, of committing an act of "hubris" with his "decision[!] . . . to fuse sign and meaning into immediate and self-evident communication" (134). Such a critique sides with the corruption of Franz and fails to perceive the marginalization of Karl's naive semiotic as a threat. If Schiller criticizes his protagonist, it is certainly not because he relies on a naive semiotic, the same semiotic Schiller himself later defended and explicitly associated with poetic genius; rather, it is the *insufficiency* of this semiotic principle in the context of a world given over to the manipulative power of the semiotic of mediacy and arbitrariness to which Schiller calls our attention. As a result of this crucial misreading, Seidlin goes on to interpret Karl's ultimate reconciliation with the law of the land, whose hypocrisy he has otherwise attacked, as a renunciation of "his heroically sinful insistence on directness" and his "acceptance of the communicative sign" (134-35). Karl's resignation thus becomes re-signation in a more specific sense: he is "re-signed," i.e., re-oriented and re-integrated into the bourgeois order of mediative signs. But such a "re-signing" interpretation has the effect of completely stripping the revolutionary impetus away from this work, making out of a utopian project of "planned reversal" a drama of conciliation with and capitulation to the principles represented by Franz and the rest of the counterfeiters in this "tintenklecksendes Säkulum (I, 502)." Karl's submission, in other words, would signify the surrender of the ideal of naivité, the enemy of dissimulation, to the paramount power of dissimulation. Such a conclusion is not only out of keeping with the parameters of Schiller's play, but also inconsistent with the entire aesthetic-pedagogical project he pursued in different ways over the course of his life. Instead, I propose that we comprehend Karl's actions at the conclusion of the play in the context of recognitions he makes about the *practical* ineffectiveness of a naive semiotic when confronted with the "treacherous signs" deployed by the likes of Franz and Spiegelberg.

Karl Moor's position with regard to written texts is from the outset a paradoxical one. His famous first words, "Mir ekelt vor diesem tintenklecksenden Säkulum, wenn ich in meinem Plutarch lese von großen Menschen" (I, 502), establish a number of fundamental points about his character and his assessment of the contemporary life world. His position vis-à-vis the present historical conditions is one of outspoken inimicality, grounded in his assertion of the degeneracy of this age in contrast to a past ideal. Most important in the context of the arguments pursued here is that the measure Karl employs to gauge this discrepancy between past ideal and present reality is the contrast between their modes of textuality. He does not play off writing against speech as do, for example, Rousseau and Herder,[13] and even Schiller himself in other instances; rather he juxtaposes one *kind* of writing, Plutarch's *Lives*, to the type of texts proliferating during his own time.[14] This nuance is of crucial importance, especially given Schiller's self-conscious defense of his own reliance on the textual medium for the composition of this very drama. The valorization of Plutarch's *Lives* as an "authentic" form of textuality over against the degenerate writing which proliferates in the modern era probably derives from Rousseau's remark in the *Confessions* that Plutarch cured him of his dependence on popular novels,[15] and it thus points to the incipient bifurcation within the bourgeois literary institution of two distinct literary endeavors, "serious" literature, on the one hand, and the "popularized" literary commodity, on the other. This phenomenon, as Christa Bürger has argued, is a side-effect that accompanies the subjection of literature to the bourgeois marketplace.[16] The distinction Karl draws between the "ink smears" of modern textuality and the genuine writing of Plutarch's *Lives* is thus essentially one between disingenuous textual commodities, whose authors are incapable of immediate identification with the conjunctures they relate—"ein schwindsüchtiger Professor . . . liest ein Kollegium über die *Kraft*" (I, 502-03)—and genuine textualizations whose authority is guaranteed by an immediacy and identity with their subject matter grounded either in direct personal experience or, in historical investigations such as Plutarch's, in a projective hermeneutical empathy that conjoins authorial character with the subject matter related. The fundamental paradox of Karl's character, however, is grounded in the disjunction between this theoretical insight into the functioning of disingenuous textual commodities and his *practical* inability to recognize such texts and interpret them appropriately.

Karl shares this interpretive gullibility, as we shall see, with Old Moor and Amalia. But to condemn the interpretive incompetence of these figures as improbable and artificial, as critics have tended to do,[17] is to pass over the very conflict that Schiller seeks to examine. It is precisely the inadequacy of a naive, iconic semiotic when confronted with the manipulative and deceitful practices made possible by the inter-mediative semiotic of modernity mastered by such beguilers as Franz and Spiegelberg that Schiller's drama throws into relief. Franz's dissimulations catapult the play's naive protagonists into a pervasive state of hermeneutical confusion precisely *because* their idealizing mode of cognition does not permit them to interpret messages as other than perfect similitudes of authorial essence. Figures like Karl, Amalia, Old Moor, and even Kosinsky are successfully marginalized in the "tintenklecksendes Säkulum" because their semiotic expectations and resulting hermeneutical practices are out of touch with dominant tendencies. However, Schiller's drama not only presents a protest against such marginalization, it initiates a kind of problem-solving search for a means to remedy this situation as well; it seeks a solution, in other words, that will permit figures like Karl to preserve their "naive" ideals as an outpost in which the counter-discourse of iconic semiosis can be preserved and protected from the encroachments of semiotic inter-mediacy and its all too effective calculative manipulations.

Franz, as representative of this inauthentic inter-mediacy, functions primarily as an alienator of meanings who extends and exploits the distance between authorial expression and its codification in written signs,[18] on the one hand—interference in the symptomatic functioning of language—and between scriptive symbols and their interpretations, on the other—disruption of the appellative linguistic function. He interferes, in other words, both in the productive and receptive dimensions of semiotic-communicative transfer, and in this sense he embodies those socially grounded mechanisms of "systematic distortion" which, according to Jürgen Habermas, disrupt and displace any naive and immediate hermeneutical interchange.[19] Despite his awareness that such systematic distortion is typical of communicative exchanges in the modern world, Karl proves himself to be a hermeneutically naive reader, and it is this interpretive maladroitness, not simply Franz's willful corruptions, that structures the misunderstandings which drive the dramatic plot. Karl's reading of the letter from home in the second scene of the play exemplifies the hermeneutical disjunction between him and his brother, the "author" of the note. This scene reveals Karl's interpretive naivité with regard to written expression, his own inability to recognize in Franz's letter a paradigmatic example of the hypocritical and mendacious textuality he has just vehemently attacked. Karl's initial words of response upon seeing the letter, "Meines Bruders Hand!" (I, 508), encapsulate the irony of his interpretive gullibility: while correctly recognizing Franz's "hand" as the author of the written symbols, he fails to perceive Franz's "hand," his devious authorship, in the substance of the message itself.[20] What Franz communicates as his father's "eigene Worte" are in fact Franz's, as we as readers know based on the discrepancy between this message and the actual statements of the father presented in the previous scene. Dramatic irony thus places us in a position superior to that of Karl and discloses to us his fatal misinterpretation. Karl falsely concludes on the basis of this letter "in his brother's hand" that Old Moor has rejected his repentant plea for forgiveness; and he goes on to accuse his elder of lovelessness and hypocrisy. Karl's inability to understand Franz's misrepresentation of the father's attitude is predicated on a fundamental principle of the naive hermeneutic with which he operates: the supposed transparency of the mediative sign. Thus, because Karl assumes that Franz is playing the role of a simple, transparent, noncorrupting communicative intermediary between him and his father, he fails to apprehend that this mediation brings with it intentional obfuscations and distortions. For Karl, true to Schiller's conception of a naive semiotic, mediative "signs" should be purely transparent transmitters of authorial expression; hence it is Karl's gullible reliance on this idealized semiotic of immediacy, his failure to penetrate the moment of occultation in the dialectic of representation, which allows Franz's distortions to pass unnoticed.

Karl's misreading, although understandable (given the parameters of his thinking), elicits a series of ironic effects. For one, it prevents him from following up on his resolution to abandon his misguided intrigues in Leipzig and return "home" to an "authentic" existence. His diagnosis of this deviant behavior as the product of a disjunction between speech and genuine sentiment is consistent with his indictment of the modern age in general, whose representative he obviously understands himself to have become: "mein Herz hörte nicht, was meine Zunge prahlte" (I, 506), Karl asserts in self-condemnation when Spiegelberg reminds him of their roguish exploits. But his resolve to unify the sentiments of his heart with the expressions of his tongue is dissolved after reading Franz's letter. Only at this point of total disillusionment does Karl succumb to Spiegelberg's suggestion that they form a robber band. The most bitter irony, perhaps, is that with this move Karl fulfills Franz's earlier prophecy that his brother will become the leader of a band of highwaymen (cf. I, 496). Indeed, what makes Franz's deceitful mediations so pernicious is that they ultimately proliferate those principles of self-alienation around which his conceptual system is structured. Not only does he succeed in changing the image that the father has of Karl, and that which Karl has of his father, making each believe that the other has succumbed to the hypocrisy so rampant at this time; he actually maneuvers Karl into a position, through the treacherous manipulation of mediated signs, of carrying on an existence that is out of keeping with his own desires and his essential character. In his monologue of protest against his father, Karl unwittingly evokes the transmogrifying power of Franz's calculating semiotic: " . . . wenn Blutliebe zur Verräterin, wenn Vaterliebe zur Megäre wird, o so fange Feuer, männliche Gelassenheit, verwilde zum Tiger, sanftmütiges Lamm . . . " (I, 514). Convinced that his father's love has somehow been perverted, he takes this conviction as legitimation for his own conversion from "gentle lamb" to "furious tiger." Thus ultimately one must ascribe to Franz's calculating, "enlightened" semiotic veritable alchemical powers: reality conforms to the manipulative might of his words, his arbitrary signs take control over and master their signifieds.

Amalia too suffers calamitous defeats when confronted with Franz's (textual) deceptions. In a scene which closely parallels in its substance and images the depiction of Karl's misinterpretation of the letter from home, Amalia likewise falls victim to one of Franz's textual hoaxes (cf. 529-33). Trying to convince Amalia that Karl has died in battle, Franz produces the conventional bloody

sword as final evidence. Franz adds to this convention a characteristic twist, however: he forges a text, written putatively by Karl
with his own blood, in which the dying hero bequeaths Amalia to
his brother. Amalia is duped by this rather obvious ruse into
believing she recognizes Karl's "hand" as the author of the bloody
text: "Heiliger Gott!," she exclaims, "es ist seine Hand, — Er hat
mich nie geliebt!" (I, 532). Amalia's error is more severe than is
Karl's in the parallel scene, for while he at least correctly recognized Franz's signature in the written symbols, she fails here even
to recognize Franz's rather blatant forgery. Her mistake is
excused, of course, by the fact that Franz has miraculously produced some overwhelmingly convincing evidence, not least of
which is the portrait of Amalia Karl carried with him.

While it is easy to cite the improbability of this scene as testimony to Schiller's literary immaturity or attribute it to carelessness,
it seems more instructive from a critical-interpretive standpoint to
analyze the possible text-strategic impulses that might have moti-
vated such improbability. We must assume either that Schiller's
reasons for implementing such far-fetched devices outweigh the
logical deficiencies, or that improbability itself is a strategic device
which serves to call attention to specific motivic complexes in the
play. The latter, indeed, seems to be the case in this instance. It is
no coincidence, first of all, that Franz supplies a portrait to support
his assertions, since throughout the play portraits function as symbols which represent the guarantee of resemblance that underwrites the iconic semiotic employed by the naive protagonists.
Secondly, as Seidlin recognized, the portrait is associated throughout the drama with Karl, as an emblem of his insistence on immediate communication, whereas the epistle and its manipulable mediacy is connected with Franz.[21] The portrait, which in Seidlin's
words "is what it represents" and thus "appears as the seal and
voucher of genuineness" (134), is skillfully exploited by Franz in
this scene: it "vouches," so to speak, for the genuineness of the
counterfeit Karl that he seeks to bring into circulation.

Throughout Schiller's play hand and portrait are the vouchers of
intrinsic genuineness; in the scene in which Amalia is deceived by

Franz, this deception is predicated on his ability to counterfeit *both*. His success, improbable as it may seem, thereby underscores two complexes we have already examined: on the one hand it testifies again to the overwhelming, near-alchemical powers of Franz's cunning, his ability to produce practically at will convincing if yet counterfeit signs; on the other hand it stresses Amalia's reliance on the semiotic of similitude and underscores the insufficiency of this conceptual pattern as a hermeneutical strategy given the distortive capacity of Franz's semiotic counterfeits. Once duped into believing the forged text was authored by Karl, Amalia, replicating Karl's spurious condemnation of his father, moves directly to a misguided indictment of Karl: "Er hat mich nie geliebt." Following the principles of an iconic semiotic which identifies expression with authorial character, she associates the infamy of the message with the character of its putative author.

The problematic of naive misreading is augmented by a further dimension as this scene develops. Convinced finally that Karl has died, Old Moor asks Amalia to read him the Biblical story of Jacob and Joseph. At the point in her narration where the jealous sons produce Joseph's bloody garment as evidence of his death, Franz suddenly leaves the room, only too aware that the deceit perpetrated in the Biblical tale is the perfect "similitude" of his own deception (cf. I, 534). But the guileless interpreters fail here to draw the analogy between the Biblical parable and the reality of their own circumstance: Old Moor and Amalia take the parable merely as confirmation of Karl's death, instead of understanding it as a key which unlocks the prison of Franz's hoax. Shortfall of interpretation, predicated on an innocence that prevents penetration of the simple face-values of textualizations, is the common denominator of all these examples of misreading.[22] This single failing leads to divergent results, however, depending upon whether the interpretive object is an example of genuine textuality such as the Bible, or a disingenuous, inter-mediary textual commodity such as Franz's forgeries. In the latter case their misprision causes the naive interpreters to take fiction for fact; in the former case they fail to recognize the analogical factuality of fiction, i.e., to comprehend the profound relevance of the authentic, non-commodified Biblical text as a similitude of their actual situation. This suggests that in an age dominated by "Falschmünzer der Wahrheit" (I, 553), it has become impossible adequately to distinguish genuine from counterfeit texts. Schiller does not repeatedly expose the interpretive incompetence of these naive readers in order merely to condemn their gullibility; he is concerned, rather, with the hermeneutical confusion into which good-willed and guileless individuals are thrown in a period marked by the conflict of competing semiologies and their respective textualities. The incipient bourgeois age, to keep within the economic and numismatic metaphors Schiller exploits throughout the drama (I, 500; 501; 511; 539; 553; 616), is characterized by the dissemination of counterfeit textual currencies, worthless symbolic inscriptions (texts) that make pretense to authoritative value; the naive readers in Schiller's play take these counterfeits, on the one hand, to be empirical verities, and, on the other hand, they are no longer capable of recognizing in genuine textual currency, in Scripture, the similitude of their actual circumstances. Schiller's own play, the dramatic novel *Die Räuber*, is addressed as a caveat to just such naive readers and as a lesson in the segregation of the authentic, "serious," literary text, of which he intends his own to be an example,[23] from the cheap dissimulating counterfeits, the literary commodities, that he sets out to expose.

IV
Semiotics, Economics, and the "verkehrte Welt"

"Da das Geld als der existierende und sich betätigende Begriff des Wertes alle Dinge verwechselt, vertauscht, so ist es die allgemeine *Verwechslung* und *Vertauschung* aller Dinge, also die verkehrte Welt, die Verwechslung und Vertauschung aller natürlichen und menschlichen Qualitäten."
— Karl Marx, *Ökonomisch-philosophische Manuskripte aus dem Jahre 1844*

According to Jean Baudrillard, throughout the history of Western society fundamental mutations in the law of value are paralleled by mutations in the order of representation.[24] For the "classical" period from the Renaissance to the industrial revolution, grounded in the natural law of value, counterfeit is the dominant representational scheme (83). An obsession with the counterfeit, of course, is by its very nature nostalgic to the extent that its aim is the rediscovery of the lost original, of the unique and individual (cf. 96). Schiller's dramatic novel *Die Räuber* tells the story of the victory of the counterfeit over the original as the ascendancy of exchange semiotics over the naive principles of iconic similitude. However, it does not therefore cease to register its protest against the scheme of the counterfeit, but it does, on the other hand, argue for a fundamental change of strategies in the struggle against the modern episteme. We have witnessed how Schiller lays bare the relative incompetence and inefficacy of the iconic semiotic when confronted with a world of disseminating counterfeits; the only alternative left to the guilelessly beguiled, it would appear, is to play the part of counterfeits themselves: only by counterfeiting counterfeits, as it were, can they survive in the world of exchange and simultaneously struggle against its determining principles. Just as the naive can only be restored through the medium of the sentimental, and original truth recreated from the counterfeit semblance of art, the iconic semiotic, paradoxically, can only be reconstituted if one is able to work within the semiotic of the dissimulative counterfeit to ensure the survival of similitude. In this project of strategic adaptation, "aesthetics," high art, makes a double move: on the one hand, it sets out to establish itself as a semiotic Other in the world of bourgeois exchange, serving as a reminder of the longed-for guarantee of iconic similitude; on the other hand, it seeks to function simultaneously as a pedagogical instrument which models and thereby discloses hermeneutical strategies appropriate to an unmasking of the counterfeit. Insofar as it teaches one how to reveal the intrinsic essence concealed behind the extrinsic guise, art becomes a tool of ideological critique. Conceived in terms of literature's semiological otherness vis-à-vis the bourgeois semiotic of conventionality and exchange, aesthetic autonomy is by no means incompatible with pedagogical function; on the contrary, semiotic autonomy is the condition of possibility for literature's re-volutionary effectiveness.[25]

The brothers Franz and Karl Moor represent what Theodor Adorno and Max Horkheimer portray as the only two possible responses left to human subjects when confronted with the "Urprinzip" of the bourgeois world structured on calculative exchange as the motor behind the profit motive: "Man hatte die Wahl, zu betrügen oder unterzugehen."[26] Franz opts for deceit and its financial rewards; Karl chooses, at least initially, to "go under," in the specific sense of "going underground": he establishes himself as the leader of a counter-society of "robbers" whose acts of theft become for him a protest against "legitimated deceit" as the fundamental economic and moral principle of the bourgeois world. In order to determine whether the ultimate moral-political thrust of Schiller's drama is integrative, as Seidlin suggests, or retains yet the design of re-volution, we must examine whether Karl's "going under" at the play's conclusion is an act of total capitulation or itself a strategy of dissimulation which merely drives his re-volt deeper underground. But in order to arrive at this point we must establish the *economic* nature of the conflict of epistemes as manifest in the text.

For the young Karl Marx, money, which he dubbed a "*verkehrende* Macht,"[27] came to represent the transformative, value-perverting power of bourgeois exchange. One year after the composition of Marx's economic-philosophic manuscripts Moses Hess drew a similar conclusion about the devaluation of human worth that follows necessarily from the inversion of being and appearance characteristic of the economic-semiotic principle of mediative exchange:

> Was nicht *vertauscht*, was nicht *verkauft* werden kann, hat auch keinen Werth. Sofern die Menschen nicht mehr verkauft werden *können*, sind sie auch *keinen Pfennig* mehr werth—wohl aber sofern sie sich selbst *verkaufen* oder 'verdingen.'[28]

In this essay, significantly enough, Hess ultimately equates writing and money, condemning them both as "tödtende *Verkehr*smittel!"

(346; emphasis added) which are responsible for the "*verkehrte Welt.*" The pun on the word "Verkehr," denoting at once "commerce," "intercourse," and "inversion," runs like a leitmotif throughout Hess's writings on the problematics of money,[29] and it is around the semantics of this word that his attack on mediacy as the root of all evil in the bourgeois episteme crystallizes. His vision of a utopian future includes a world without "dead letters" that choke off spirit or "dead money" that strangles life (346): "kein fremdes Wesen, kein drittes *Mittelding* wird sich mehr zwischen uns eindringen, um uns äußerlich und scheinbar zu 'vermitteln', während es uns innerlich und wirklich trennt und entzweit" (347). Schiller shares with Hess, as the previously cited passage from *Über naive und sentimentalische Dichtung* indicates, this utopian vision of a world that would return to the naive and immediate semiotic of iconicity, where the need for mediation would disappear and transparent signifiers would expose their signifieds in their naked verity.

Franz Moor incarnates this calculating semiotic which functions on the basis of exchange and deceptive mediacy. To the extent that exploitation of these principles permits him to become a magical transformer who shapes reality by manipulating mere signs, he embodies the limitless transmogrifying capacity which Marx ascribed to money as an abstract medium of exchange.

> [Das Geld] verwandelt die Treue in Untreue, die Liebe in Haß, den Haß in Liebe, die Tugend in Laster, das Laster in Tugend, den Knecht in den Herrn, den Herrn in den Knecht, den Blödsinn in Verstand, den Verstand in Blödsinn. (*Werke*, Ergänzungsband I, 566)

Later in the same treatise, Marx derogatorily describes logic as the money of the mind, the abstract system of exchange that makes speculative, exploitative thought possible: "Die *Logik* — das *Geld* des Geistes, der spekulative, der *Gedankenwert* des Menschen und der Natur . . . , das *abstrakte* Denken" (571-72), suggesting by association that logic as well is a great transformer which manipulates and alters reality by abstracting from its concrete and immediate givenness.

This abstractive exchange-value function of Franz's entire mode of cognition is brought out especially well in the scene that portrays his response to the falsely proclaimed death of his father:

> *Tot*! schreien sie, *tot*! *Itzt* bin ich *Herr*. Im ganzen Schlosse zetert es, *tot*!—wie aber, *schläft* er vielleicht nur?—freilich, ach freilich! das ist nun freilich ein Schlaf, wo es ewig niemals "Guten Morgen" heißt—Schlaf und Tod sind nur Zwillinge. Wir wollen einmal die Namen wechseln! Wackerer, willkommener Schlaf! Wir wollen dich Tod heißen! (*Er drückt ihm die Augen zu*). (I, 535)

Franz's initial words divulge that behind his linguistic manipulations there lies a fundamental purpose of exchange: the long-awaited death of the father will finally allow him to transfer the sign "master" from the referent "father" to the referent ":Franz." Upon discovering that the father is merely unconscious, however, he exploits the metaphorical proximity of the signifieds "sleep" and "death" to exchange their signifiers and thereby alter reference, allowing him to pass off his father's "sleep" as "death." He employs the manipulative exchange of "equi-valent" signs, in other words, to produce equi-vocations that permit him to intervene in and alter the reality these signs signify. Franz thus is the paradigmatic representative of the "verkehrte Welt," of the inversion of the semiotic relation between signifier and signified. Instead of the signifier evolving necessarily and immediately out of its signified, as Schiller envisioned for the ideal(ized) semiotic of naive thought, here the signifier controls and masters its signified, enforcing upon reality the manipulations it has effected in the abstract, mediative realm of pure signs.

Franz is not the sole representative of this transformative "money of the mind" in Schiller's play; his role is replicated in the figure of Moritz Spiegelberg, and it is no coincidence that these two characters consistently turn to metaphors of money, credit, and exchange when deliberating on their own aims and strategies. In the extended monologue which concludes the first scene of the play, Franz carries on a diatribe against nature and its "holy" bonds, an excursus which serves as the philosophical legitimation of his devious plot to gain mastery in his father's house, even if it means transgressing all natural laws of blood and kinship. This "might makes right" speech of self-justification turns on a rhetoric which blatantly exploits economic metaphors.

> Das Recht wohnet beim Überwältiger, und die Schranken unserer Kraft sind unsere Gesetze. Wohl gibt es gewisse gemeinschaftliche Pakta, die man geschlossen hat, die Pulse des Weltzirkels zu treiben. Ehrlicher Name! — Wahrhaftig, eine reichhaltige Münze, mit der sich meisterlich schachern läßt, wers versteht, sie gut auszugeben. Gewissen, — o ja freilich! ein tüchtiger Lumpenmann, Sperlinge von Kirschbäumen wegzuschröcken! — auch das ein gut geschriebener Wechselbrief, mit dem auch der Bankerottierer zur Not noch hinauslangt. (I, 500-01)

Franz's identification of the limits of law with the limits of self-empowerment and overpowerment succinctly characterizes his conscienceless drive for mastery. Franz overwrites the laws of nature in the name of "cultivated" laws of abstraction and exchange: the central image in his monologue is that of the "well-written promissory note" — the "*Wechsel*brief," whereby "Wechsel" denotes both exchange and change, alteration — and this image joins into a single symbol the issues of corrupt writing and of deceptive economic practices, both grounded in false "signs" that make "promises" inconsistent with the reality they signify.

In what Pierre Bourdieu refers to as the pre-capitalist "good-faith economy," the trader "practises no exchanges involving money and all his relations are based on total confidence; unlike the shady dealer, he has recourse to none of the guarantees (witnesses, written documents, etc.) with which commercial transactions are surrounded."[30] Franz represents the "shady dealer" interested solely in "commercial transactions," and he mercilessly exploits those "naive" figures who do not operate with similar structures. The result of his practices, as he himself foresees, is the demise of those "gemeinschaftliche Pakta, die man geschlossen hat, die Pulse des Weltzirkels zu treiben." The principles of abstract, symbolic exchange, in short, destroy the immediate "confidences" and obligations which vouchsafe economic interaction in the good-faith economy, just as the principles of semiotic exchange which Franz so masterfully deploys disrupt communicative interaction and hermeneutical understanding. Suspension of the confidence in an interpersonal obligation grounded in "name" and "conscience" thus parallels in the economic sphere the suspension of the guarantee of similitude in the semiotic realm.

Baudrillard stresses this coincidence of the institution of the modern, arbitrary sign with the demise of interpersonal obligation.

> The arbitrary sign begins when, instead of linking two persons in an unbreakable reciprocity, the signifier starts referring back to the disenchanted universe of the signified, common denominator of the real world toward which no one has any obligation. End of the *obliged* sign, reign of the emancipated sign . . . The modern sign dreams of the signs of the past and would well appreciate finding again, in its reference to the real, an *obligation*: but what it finds again is only a *reason*: this referential reason, this real, this "natural" off which it is going to live. (*Simulations*, 84-86)

Baudrillard describes here not only the shift to a semiotic of arbitrariness, but also its repercussions in the dimension of human interaction on diverse levels. Accompanying the emergence of the arbitrary sign comes a shift from emphasis on the *symptomatic function* of language and economics, the stressing of their roles as immediate and transparent bonds that link *individuals* in a relationship of mutuality and trust, to concentration on their *representational function* as symbolic mediators between abstract thought and objects in the world. The paradigm shift from the "Renaissance" to the Enlightenment semiotic, in other words, bespeaks a displacement of the semiotic relation from the sphere of interpersonal interaction in the life world, from communicative action, to employ Habermas's terminology,[31] to instrumental reason, i.e., to concerns about the *deployment* of objects in the (life) world. No longer a system of "Wertung," of evaluation, semiotics/economics becomes a structure for "*Ver*wertung," for (d)evaluation and exploitation. Franz's intrusive mediations between Old Moor and Karl, we should recall, are aimed at the destruction of the natural bond of *Blutliebe*, a word which he uses with scorn (I, 501). His intervention into this natural bond succeeds in transfiguring it, at least in the mind of Karl, who legitimates his own transformation from a loving son to a murderous robber by pointing to the degeneration of just such natural laws.

Only in the context of a society caught up in the process of instituting breach of promise as its *modus vivendi*, a society bent on reifying living things and commodifying natural objects, does Karl's perverse, even pathological obsession with the oath of brotherhood that binds him to the robber band make any sense whatsoever: the "price" of release from this oath is the death of his beloved Amalia, and the necessity of this "payment" ultimately signals for Karl the failure of this counter-project, its insufficiency over against the principles of abstract exchange. The scene in which the robbers, surrounded and heavily outnumbered, reject the temptation to buy their own freedom at the price of turning their leader Karl over to the authorities (II, iii) elucidates how Karl attempts to reestablish in this "brotherhood" the blood-bond he has lost with his real brother and his father, instituting a counter-society structured around the principles of reciprocity and obligation. Two arguments that tie in closely to the thematics and motifs examined thus far figure centrally in the robbers' decision to fight for their lives and that of their ringleader. They are offered the choice between the *verbal oath* that unites them as a group, and the *written contract* offered them by the priest as an assurance of amnesty.

> *Pater* Sorgt ihr etwa, daß dies eine Falle sei, euch lebendig zu fangen? — Leset selbst, hier ist der Generalpardon unterschrieben. (*Er gibt Schwiezern ein Papier*) Könnt ihr noch zweifeln? (I, 554)

Given the pattern established throughout the play that written texts are the index of deceit and that signatures, easily forged and not necessarily given in good faith, have lost all power of obligation, we, and the robbers as well, have every reason to assume that, despite the priest's assertion to the contrary, he is indeed leading them into a trap. Karl, at any rate, responds by admonishing his comrades that they would have to break their oath to him and each other in order to accept this written offer, and he points out that by thus making themselves into traitors they establish a basis that legitimates breach of the promise made to them.

> *Moor* Seht doch, seht doch!   Was könnt ihr mehr verlangen? — Unterschrieben mit eigener Hand — es ist Gnade über alle Grenzen — oder fürchtet ihr wohl, sie werden ihr Wort brechen, weil ihr einmal gehört habt, daß man Verrätern nicht Wort hält? (554)

Here, as in his speeches throughout this scene, we witness how Karl, no longer a naive Don Quixote who takes language at its face value, has become a master of irony.   Finally we no longer are dealing with a naive fool who is duped by "signatures" and texts; on the contrary, here Karl shows himself to be a master of arbitrary signs, exploiting them to perpetrate a classical instance of ironic double-speak.   The priest, unable to decipher the ironic undertones in Karl's words as he ostensibly encourages his comrades to accept the pardon offered them, responds with understandable shock and disbelief.   When Karl's challenge culminates in the provocative rhetorical question "Wer ist der erste, der seinen Hauptmann in der Not verläßt?" (555), the robbers jump to his support and send the priest away with the message that "keinen einzigen *Verräter*" (555; emphasis added) can be found in Moor's entourage.   For Karl this is the decisive point in the entire action of the play, and he responds to the faithfulness of his comrades with the emphatic statement "Itzt sind wir frei — Kameraden!" (555), implying that only now that their oath of brotherhood has been put to and survived this crucial test are they truly "comrades" and "free" men — free, we suppose, from the institutionalized structures of deceit rampant in the "first" world of bourgeois exchange.   The challenge presented to the outlaws' *verbal* oath by the *written* pardon offered by the "Pater" — the designation itself suggests the association of this false "father" with the ostensibly "false" father, Old Moor, against whom Karl's rebellion is directed — becomes for Karl the fundamental test case of their true fidelity and the genuineness of their interpersonal obligation.   The robbers' victory over vastly superior military forces underscores the superiority of this bond of obligation over the bond that unites the mercenary soldiers they fight against.

The "improbability" of this victory represents another case in point where logical deficiencies in the motivational structure of the drama can be attributed to Schiller's desire to underwrite the specific thematic complexes we have been pursuing here. Thus, just as the robbers are distinguished from the institutionalized powers by the dichotomy between verbal oath and written promise, they are also differentiated on the basis of their personal motivations. Although they are outnumbered twenty to one, Schweizer remains unperturbed, reminding his "comrades" that the opposition soldiers have none but monetary interests: "Brüder, Brüder! so hats keine Not. Sie [the mercenaries] setzen ihr Leben an zehen Kreuzer, fechten wir nicht für Hals und Freiheit?" (548). It is the outlaws, in other words, who, as true "brothers," are fighting for genuine and immediate values, for life and liberty, as well as for the bonds of interpersonal obligation, while the mercenary soldiers fight only for *symbols* of value, for abstract (monetary) signs of worth. Interpersonal obligation is demonstrated to be superior to the monetary, symbolic dependencies which structure human relationships in society at large. In the "brotherhood" of the robber band, thus, Karl seeks to reconstitute the immediate blood-bond of nature, the bond between brother and brother and father and son that Franz's mediacy has successfully undermined.[32] That such relationships of reciprocity and mutual obligation are wholly marginalized, choked off into a counter-societal underworld, renders a devastating commentary on the perverse structures that govern human inter(ex)change in the dominant society.

Karl's and Spiegelberg's competing conceptions of the outlaw band and its societal function represent a displacement of the conflict of semiologies manifest in the antagonism of the two blood brothers. In a drama that consistently presents the triumph of the mediative semiotic of exchange over the naive semiotic of iconic similitude and interpersonal obligation, it comes as no surprise that, despite Karl's ability to waylay the threat to the oath of solidarity presented by the written pardon, Spiegelberg's principles

ultimately reign supreme. When Karl knuckles under to the juridi-
cal authority of the state and to the laws of a "prostituting" economic exchange, he signals his own apparent co-optation by the
ruling logic of abstract value. Upon turning himself in for the
monetary price placed on his head—irrespective of the extenuating
factors which motivate this move—he implicitly abandons the
axiom of *intrinsic* value that he has otherwise upheld throughout
and embraces the convention of *extrinsically determined* abstract
worth. We recall here Moses Hess's assertion that in the bourgeois
world whatever cannot be exchanged or sold has no value, and that
even human beings only attain worth "sofern sie sich selbst
verkaufen oder 'verdingen'."[33]   Abandoning the integrity he has
struggled to uphold, Karl subjects himself to the reifying mediation
of symbolic equivalences. If his own being is already rent by the
breach between essential character and societal (inter)action at the
moment he becomes the robbers' ringleader, it is yet not until this
point of literal "sell-out" that he accepts and accedes to this situation.

Karl's ultimate capitulation to the structures of mediated
exchange seems to be corroborated by the rhetoric that informs the
language in the closing scene of the play, which is dominated by
allusions to commodity-exchange economics. The oath of brotherhood, as the murder of Amalia makes clear, has metamorphized
into an economic contract: with her sacrifice Karl repays the
"debt" he incurred when the robbers saved him from capture at the
hands of the mercenaries, i.e., her life is given in exchange for the
rescue of Karl's.

Moor . . . Ihr [the robbers] opfertet mir ein Leben auf, ein Leben, das schon
nicht mehr euer war . . . —ich habe euch einen Engel geschlachtet . . .

Grimm Du hast deine Schuld mit Wucher bezahlt . . .

Moor Sagst du das? Nicht wahr, das Leben einer Heiligen um das Leben der
Schelmen, es ist ungleicher Tausch? . . . Die Narben, die böhmischen
Wälder! Ja, ja! dies mußte freilich bezahlt werden. (616)

Karl's words here are charged with bitterness and irony. At this
moment he appropriates the economic metaphors characteristic of

Franz and Spiegelberg, thereby signaling the failure of his campaign to establish a counter-society structured according to the principles of trust, reciprocity, and interpersonal obligation. The principle of abstraction that underwrites bourgeois exchange-value economics becomes operative on the level of human interchange as one "life" is exchanged for another. But Karl's capitulation does not necessarily imply surrender to and acceptance of the principles of mediated exchange, as most critics, like Seidlin, have tended to read the play's conclusion[34]—an interpretation almost certainly grafted onto Schiller's original text by analogy to the later, revised version.[35]   Instead, it merely indicates that his *overt* rebellion against these principles has miscarried. There is evidence to suggest that with this capitulation Karl accedes to the real ascendancy of the principle of mediative exchange, without however embracing this principle as his own. Read as an *ironic* appropriation, Karl's ostensible compliance would indicate that his revolt has now gone deeper underground than it had in the failed resistance manifest in the robber band. He recognizes, in other words, the futility of *overt* insurrection and turns instead to the subtler forms of *covert* revolt: his exploitation of the metaphors of economic-semiotic exchange hence betoken an exploitation of the game-rules of bourgeois society that turns these rules against the principal players themselves. Earlier in the drama, Amalia opted for a similar stratagem when confronted with Franz's open hostility: only by appropriating the strategy of dissimulation was she able to avoid being overpowered by Franz (cf. III, i; esp. p. 558). Karl likewise "buys in" to the principles of exchange only as a last-ditch effort to rescue his resistant rebellion. From this moment on, when the ascendancy of the bourgeois status quo is recognized and accepted, overt rebellion is appropriate only to fools like Don Quixote, and the revolutionary project of planned reversal to the epistemic status of the naive semiotic of similitude becomes a sentimental redemption of the naive, a covert, underground resistance operation which outwardly accepts mediative exchange in order to carry on its struggle under the dissimulative disguise of "re-signed" collusion.

"Quae medicamenta non sanant, ferrum sanat, quae ferrum non sanat, ignis sanat," Schiller reminds us in his epigraph from Hippocrates (I, 491). It is important to note that Schiller deletes the concluding line of the original Hippocratean aphorism when he appropriates it for his *Räuber*. This line reads: "quae vero ignis non sanat, insanabilia reputari oportet."[36] This deletion suggests, if the epigraph can be taken as a "similitude" for Karl Moor's and Schiller's originary social-critical operation, that such resigned conclusions have no place in this project and must consequently be "effaced": when faced with the failure of specific cures, one must regroup and turn to the implementation of new methods and strategies. This suggests that when Karl Moor is confronted by the principles of bourgeois society and must either "deceive" or "go under," as Horkheimer and Adorno expressed it, he ultimately chooses *both*. If in the underground of the outlaw existence his rebellion proved unsuccessful, then this is true because he sought to adhere to naive principles of similitude, of identity between character and action, which were doomed to failure given the really existing socioeconomic conditions. Only when he consciously appropriates deceit as a weapon against deceit, paradoxically, can Karl's potential for rebellion be salvaged. This suggests that insurrection must go yet farther "under," be absorbed into the very being of the rebellious subject itself, which now, unable to preserve the iconic principle of resemblance between the internal self and the external expressive signs of the self, must sublate/sublimate its rebellion as a fracture which runs through the rebellious subject. Indeed, in the final analysis, even Karl's position as ringleader of the highwaymen is possible only by means of implementing such a strategic disjunction: outwardly a robber and murderer, he never ceases inwardly and in his *private* actions to be a benefactor to the oppressed and downtrodden. Karl ultimately gives in to this oppression only insofar as he transmogrifies it into repression, *internalizing* his re-volt, turning what for robber Moor had been a *public* campaign into a *private and secret* crusade that lies outside the confines of bourgeois "self-expression."

This interpretation is borne out by the Hamletesque monologue Karl delivers in the final scene of the fourth act, in which he deliberates on and then rejects the possibility of suicide.

> Nein! Nein! Ein Mann muß nicht straucheln—sei, wie du willt, namenloses *Jenseits*—bleibt mir nur dieses mein *selbst* getreu—Sei wie du willt, wenn ich nur mich *selbst* mit hinübernehme.—Außendinge sind nur der Anstrich des Manns—*Ich* bin mein Himmel und meine Hölle. (591)

The generalizing, objectified statement which Karl distills from his self-reflections, "Außendinge sind nur der Anstrich des Manns," is clearly inconsistent with the principle of iconicity as the guarantor of human truth and integrity which he has defended and represented up to this point. This insight must be viewed as the culmination of a painful process of education: throughout the course of the drama Karl is effectively "weaned" from his dependence on naive principles of immediacy. He does not abandon, however, an insistence on the integrity of the self; indeed, his monologue is marked by an insistence on selfhood which is independent of the external varnish of the "individual." To be sure, the bourgeois individual proves itself to be a "dividual," an entity divided between external expression and a now wholly *internalized* (self-)being. Self-identity has become something which is wholly private and insular, existing solely in the internal realm of the soul and independent of the external signs and actions carried out by the *empirical* self. That is, self-identity is no longer configured as the similitude between the external and the internal, but becomes *a property inhering in the internal itself.*

In Karl's ultimate turn to and acceptance of the principle of self-division, we witness the birth of the classically divided bourgeois rebel, split between public personality and private sentiment, action and concealed desire, openness and secrecy, self-assertion and self-repression. Fidelity to the private, internal "self," irrespective of the external actions and expressions of the public person, become the measure of human self-worth. Outmaneuvered by the semiotics of arbitrariness, the principle of iconicity and wholeness, which had vouched for the moral integrity of the naive individual, retreats into the sphere of internal self-identity. Hypocrisy is institutionalized and legitimated as the necessary behavioral paradigm in a world governed by the axioms of symbolic abstraction and exchange-value economics.   Nevertheless — and this is the crucial point — the reversion of the potential revolutionary to the inner-worldly asceticism of the bourgeois subject remains marked by the dialectic between rebellion and its concealment: revolutionary public ambitions are repressed and relegated to the realm of the private, i.e., they become "heimlich" in both senses of that word as analyzed by Freud.[37]   Paradoxically, only by being drawn within is Karl's revolutionary potential able to survive, and with this interiorization Karl, as rebellious bourgeois subject, subjects *himself* to the dialectic of representation as constituted in the bourgeois episteme, to self-(re)presentation and self-occultation.   It is this paradox of revolution and its repression that marks the constitution of the German bourgeois intelligentsia in this period, and which allegates to future bourgeois revolutionary projects the strategy of the sentimental redemption of the naive, the covert recapturing of a moral highground that has proven itself practically indefensible in the context of the modern episteme.   Reinhart Koselleck has demonstrated the degree to which "secrecy" evolves as a necessary consequence out of the conflict between "enlightened" burgher and the absolutistic state in eighteenth-century Germany.[38]   The burgher develops a "private" and "secret" sphere in which bourgeois morality both takes refuge from the corrupting influence of the politico-economic realm, and defines the locus from which it will launch its own revolt against this corruption: "Das Geheimnis war . . . die Grenzscheide zwischen Moral und Politik: es schützt und umgrenzt den sozialen Raum, in dem sich die Moral verwirklichen sollte."[39] Karl Moor paradigmatically embodies, at least in the initial version of Schiller's play, this circumscription of a private, internal realm in which "integrity" is insulated and protected from the "corruption" of the sociopolitical, economic world beyond the "self"; but as his case demonstrates, this interiorization is a by-product of the bourgeois's encounter not so much with the constraints of the feudal-absolutistic state, as with his own alter ego, his own Franz/Spiegelberg as the embodiment of abstract value, corrupt intermediacy, and exchange. Sentimental redemption of the naive defines the recovery project by which the socioeconomic life world will eventually be salvaged and re-turned to the semiotic-economic integrity of similitude; but prerequisite for this long-range re-volution is the retreat of iconicity into the "privatized" and "secret" core of the bourgeois subject, as well as into the "privatized" and "secret" revolutionary kernel of bourgeois art. Karl Moor, in this sense exemplary for the German bourgeois artist of the period, implements a strategy defined by outward collusion with the enemy in an attempt to circumscribe and thus preserve a realm of private and secret revolt. Covert rebellion is not simply the path of least resistance, as one might be tempted to surmise, rather it is the *only available viable path* of resistance. Only by himself embracing deceit — *Täuschung* and *Schein* — as well as exchange and the symbolic mediacy of money — *Tausch* and *Scheine* — can Karl preserve *within the subject itself* a *potentially* explosive kernel of resistance. This sublimation of rebellion marks the bourgeois intellectual as an *aesthetic* construct, divided between semblance and essence, bourgeois "formality" and repressed rebellious drives. Given this, it is not surprising that aesthetics would appear to Schiller and his contemporary bourgeois intellectuals as the paradigmatic battleground from which the campaign for the sentimental redemption of the naive, the rescue mission intent on delivering the bourgeois subject from the condition of self-alienation, would have to be launched. It is in the field of aesthetics, i.e., by means of "aesthetic education," that the rift that divides the (self-)rebellious bourgeois subject, a rift that signals internalization of the revolutionary conflict of semiologies, must eventually be mended.

In his early essay "Über den affirmativen Charakter der Kultur," Herbert Marcuse expounded a theory which ties the evolution of the institution of autonomous art and the advent of idealist aesthetics to the repressive disciplining of the bourgeois subject. "In der affirmativen Kultur ist die Entsagung mit der äußeren Verkümmerung des Individuums verbunden, mit seiner Disz+plinierung zum Sich-Fügen in eine schlechte Ordnung."[40] What Marcuse suggests in this essay, and what our interpretation of *Die Räuber* confirms, is that the emergence of the (self-)divided bourgeois subject and of the institution of aesthetic autonomy are co-temporal. Both are characterized by the dialectical interplay between collusion with and rebellion against the epistemic-economic principles of the bourgeois age. From the point onward at which Karl Moor, the epitome of the intellectual bourgeois rebel, represses his utopian aims and submits his empirical existence to the exchange-value economy, rebellion submerges below the "beautiful semblance" of the reified, commodified burgher.[41] In a central passage from *Über naive und sentimentalische Dichtung,* Schiller characterized the "sentimental" poet as one caught in his very constitution between the world as liminal, limiting phenomenon, and the infinity of the ideal.

> Der sentimentalische Dichter hat es daher immer mit zwei streitenden Vorstellungen und Empfindungen, mit der Wirklichkeit als Grenze und mit seiner Idee als dem Unendlichen zu tun, und das gemischte Gefühl, das er erregt, wird immer von dieser doppelten Quelle zeugen. (V, 720-21)

In *Die Räuber* we witness Karl's transmogrification from an "integral," unified, "naive" character who has difficulty comprehending that he is out of step with reality, into a sentimental, (self-) divided character who, after butting his head against the limits of socioeconomic, epistemic reality, interiorizes this disaccord as an internal struggle between public concession to the real and "secret"/"private" assertion of the ideal.

Notes

1 Michel Foucault, *The Order of Things: An Archaeology of the Human Sciences* (New York: Random House [Vintage], 1970), esp. pp. 17-76; henceforth *OT*.

2 Manfred Frank, *Was ist Neostrukturalismus?* (Frankfurt: Suhrkamp, 1983), pp. 146-48.

3 Jacques Ehrmann, "On Articulation: The Language of History and the Terror of Language," *Yale French Studies*, 39 (1967), p. 13.

4 Cf. Jochen Schulte-Sasse, "Einleitung: Kritisch-rationale und literarische Öffentlichkeit," *Aufklärung und literarische Öffentlichkeit*, ed. Christa Bürger, et al. (Frankfurt: Suhrkamp, 1980), pp. 27-28: "Gerade in der Umbruchszeit des achtzehnten Jahrhunderts, in der sich die zweckrationale Vernunft immer rascher durchsetzt, konnte Literatur die Aufgabe übernehmen, an zurückgedrängte Formen kollektiver Vergesellschaftung zu erinnern und ihre Erinnerung ins Bild zu setzen. Die Sozialgeschichtsschreibung *dieser* Funktion bürgerlicher Literatur hat nicht einmal in Ansätzen begonnen." The project undertaken here is conceived as just such a sociohistorical examination of this "re-volutionary" function of bourgeois literature.

   The essays in the volume *Aufklärung und literarische Öffentlichkeit* treat specifically the demise of the Enlightenment project of literary education and its connections with the development of the bourgeois episteme; see especially Christa Bürger, "Literarischer Markt und Öffentlichkeit am Ausgang des achtzehnten Jahrhunderts in Deutschland," pp. 162-212; Onno Frels, "Die Entstehung einer bürgerlichen Unterhaltungskultur und das Problem der Vermittlung von Literatur und Öffentlichkeit," pp. 213-37; and Jochen Schulte-Sasse, "Das Konzept bürgerlich-literarischer Öffentlichkeit und die historischen Gründe seines Zerfalls," pp. 83-115. See also Christa Bürger's introduction to the volume *Zur Dichotomisierung von hoher und niederer Literatur* (Frankfurt: Suhrkamp, 1982), pp. 9-39; esp. pp. 18-20.

5 Jochen Schulte-Sasse has pointed to the semiotic undercurrent which marks the revolutionary projects of literature in this period, "Das Konzept bürgerlich-literarischer Öffentlichkeit und die historischen Gründe seines Zerfalls," pp. 90-91; David Wellbery's groundbreaking investigation into Lessing's semiotics also provides much background into the general evolution of semi-

otic thinking at this time, *Lessing's* Laokoon: *Semiotics and Aesthetics in the Age of Reason* (Cambridge: Cambridge University Press, 1984), esp. pp. 1-98.

6 John Frow, *Marxism and Literary History* (Cambridge, Ma: Harvard University Press, 1986), p. 117. In *Über naive und sentimentalische Dichtung* Schiller defines the sentimental poet as the seeker after lost nature; cf. *Sämtliche Werke*, ed. Gerhard Fricke and Herbert G. Göpfert, 2nd ed., 5 vols. (Munich: Hanser, 1960), V, 712; all references to Schiller's works follow this edition and are cited parenthetically in the text by volume and page number.

7 Jean Baudrillard, *Simulations* (New York: Semiotext(e), 1983), p. 112.

8 This assertion has been made by Andreas Huyssen, *Drama des Sturm und Drang: Kommentar zu einer Epoche* (Munich: Winkler, 1980), pp. 48 and 75; Manfred Wacker has objected to this contention, viewing it as a projection of Horkheimer and Adorno's insights back onto the generation of the *Sturm und Drang*; see his "Einleitung" to the volume *Sturm und Drang*, Wege der Forschung, Bd. 559 (Darmstadt: Wissenschaftliche Buchgesellschaft, 1985), p. 12.

9 Oskar Seidlin, "Schiller's 'Treacherous Signs': The Function of Letters in His Early Plays," in *Schiller 1759/1959: Commemorative American Essays*, ed. John R. Frey (Urbana: University of Illinois Press, 1959), pp. 129-46.

10 Such disruptive inter-mediacy, according to J. G. A. Pocock, is the very definition of corruption: "Every theory of corruption, without exception, is a theory of how intermediaries substitute their own good and profit for that of their supposed principals." See Pocock, "The Mobility of Property and the Rise of Eighteenth-Century Sociology," *Virtue, Commerce, and History: Essays on Political Thought and History, Chiefly in the Eighteenth Century* (Cambridge: Cambridge University Press, 1985), p. 122.

11 *Schillers Briefe*, ed. Fritz Jonas, 7 vols. (Stuttgart: Deutsche Verlags-Anstalt, 1893-96), I, 45-46.

12 This criticism is valid *mutatis mutandis* for Bruce Kieffer's interpretation as well, since he follows Seidlin in most essential points; see his chapter "The Tragedy of Ideal Language," in *The Storm and Stress Language: Linguistic Catastrophe in the Early Works of Goethe, Lenz, Klinger, and Schiller* (University Park: University of Pennsylvania Press, 1986), pp. 111-38.

13 See the section entitled "On Writing" in Rousseau's *Essay on the Origin of Language,* in *The First and Second Discourses and the Essay on the Origin of Language*, trans. and ed. Victor Gourcvitch (New York: Harper and Row, 1986), pp. 249-54. Jacques Derrida, of course, develops his theory of "grammatology" on the basis of an interpretation of Rousseau's denigration

of writing, *Of Grammatology*, trans. Gayatri Spivak (Baltimore: Johns Hopkins University Press, 1976), esp. pp. 164-268. See also Herder, *Abhandlung über den Ursprung der Sprache,* in *Sturm und Drang: Kritische Schriften,* ed. Erich Loewenthal, 3rd ed. (Heidelberg: Lambert Schneider, 1972), pp. 407-10.

14 Bruce Kieffer, in his otherwise stimulating expansion on Seidlin's investigation of this drama, is stumped by the paradox that Karl's complaint about the bookishness of the age derives from the reading of a book; *The Storm and Stress of Language*, p. 125. The inability to provide an answer to this paradox points up the limitations of the solution Seidlin and Kieffer offer.

15 See Jean-Jacques Rousseau, *The Confessions*, trans. J. M. Cohen (Harmondsworth: Penguin, 1954), p. 20: "Plutarch . . . was my especial favourite, and the pleasure I took in reading and re-reading him did something to cure me of my passion for novels."

16 Christa Bürger, "Literarischer Markt und Öffentlichkeit am Ausgang des achtzehnten Jahrhunderts in Deutschland," pp. 165-69; see also her "Einleitung: Die Dichotomie von hoher und niederer Literatur. Eine Problemskizze," *Zur Dichotomisierung von hoher und niederer Literatur*, pp. 9-31, esp. pp. 17-19.

17 Jürgen E. Schlunk also argues against this critical tendency, "Vertrauen als Ursache und Überwindung tragischer Verstrickung in Schillers *Räubern*: Zum Verständnis Karl Moors," *Jahrbuch der deutschen Schillergesellschaft*, 27 (1983), pp. 185-201, esp. p. 186. Schlunk maintains that trust is the central quality of Karl's character, and that his gullibility is just the negative aspect of this positive trait which Schiller wishes to underscore.

18 Cf. Seidlin, p. 131.

19 See Jürgen Habermas, "Der Universalitätsanspruch der Hermeneutik," *Kultur und Kritik* (Frankfurt: Suhrkamp, 1973), p. 277.

20 Even Schweizer, after all, perceives upon reading the letter that its author is "[e]in zuckersüßes Brüdergen" and a "Kanaille" (I, 509).

21 Seidlin, p. 134.

22 The gullibility and childishness of which Schiller himself accuses the father in his review of the play (I, 633) seems to me to be applicable to Karl and Amalia as well, at least in terms of their interpretive shortcomings.

23 Schiller's own employment of Biblical allusions and motifs, one might hypothesize, reflects a desire to underwrite the authenticity of his own text by associating it with Biblical verity.

24 Jean Baudrillard, *Simulations*, p. 83.

25 Aesthetic autonomy has thus often been too narrowly construed as a reaction against the pedagogical, moralizing impulse of the literature of the enlightenment; see, for example, Rolf-Peter Janz, *Autonomie und soziale Funktion der Kunst: Studien zur Ästhetik von Schiller und Novalis* (Stuttgart: Metzler, 1973), pp. 1-2; on autonomy as a response to bourgeois economics and the principles of commodification see Berthold Hinz, "Zur Dialektik des bürgerlichen Autonomie-Begriffs," in *Autonomie der Kunst: Zur Genese und Kritik einer bürgerlichen Kategorie* (Frankfurt: Suhrkamp, 1972), pp. 173-98, esp. pp. 188-91; see also the other essays in this volume as well as Harry Olechnowitz, "Autonomie der Kunst: Studien zur Begriffsbestimmung einer ästhetischen Kategorie," Diss. Berlin 1981, pp. 92-98; Bernd Jürgen Warneken, "Autonomie und Indienstnahme: Zu ihrer Beziehung in der Literatur der bürgerlichen Gesellschaft," in *Rhetorik, Ästhetik, Ideologie: Aspekte einer kritischen Kulturwissenschaft* (Stuttgart: Metzler, 1973), pp. 79-115. Marcuse and Adorno, of course, are the theoreticians of an aesthetic autonomy which preserves socially redemptive elements otherwise eliminated in the bourgeois world. However, neither deals with the specific *semiotic* autonomy of literary discourse.

26 Horkheimer and Adorno, *Dialektik der Aufklärung: Philosophische Fragmente*, Fischer Taschenbuch, 6144 (Frankfurt: Fischer, 1969), p. 57.

27 Karl Marx, *Ökonomisch-philosophische Manuskripte aus dem Jahre 1844*, in *Karl Marx — Friedrich Engels: Werke*, Ergänzungsband, Teil I (Berlin: Dietz, 1968), p. 566.

28 Moses Hess, "Über das Geldwesen," *Philosophische und sozialistische Schriften 1837-1850*, eds. Auguste Cornu and Wolfgang Mönke (Berlin: Akademie Verlag, 1961), p. 336.

29 See, for example, his "Rede über Kommunismus," *Philosophische und sozialistische Schriften 1837-1850*, p. 354.

30 Pierre Bourdieu, *Outline of a Theory of Practice*, trans. R. Nice (Cambridge: Cambridge University Press, 1977), p. 173.

31 Jürgen Habermas developed this notion in *Erkenntnis und Interesse* (1968; rpt. Frankfurt: Suhrkamp, 1981), esp. pp. 72-76; 176-78; see also his *Theorie des kommunikativen Handelns*, 2 vols. (Frankfurt: Suhrkamp, 1981).

32 Peter Michelsen, *Der Bruch mit der Vater-Welt: Studien zu Schillers* Räubern, Euphorion Beihefte, Heft 16 (Heidelberg: Winter, 1979), pp. 86-89, views Karl's revolt as an attempt to reestablish paternal authority; this thesis seems questionable, given Karl's earlier rejection of the father and the implicit rejection of the father a second time in the scene with the "Pater." It seems to me

much more likely that Karl is attempting to reconstruct the blood-bonds of obligation that he feels have been disrupted.

33   Moses Hess, "Über das Geldwesen," p. 336.

34   Cf., for example, Otto Best, "Gerechtigkeit für Spiegelberg," *Jahrbuch der deutschen Schillergesellschaft*, 22 (1978), p. 301; H. C. Finsen, "Bürgerliches Bewußtsein zwischen Heroismus und Legalität am Ende des achtzehnten Jahrhunderts: Eine literatursoziologische Skizze," *GRM*, 59 (1978), pp. 23 and 31; and Hans-Jürgen Schings, "Schillers *Räuber*: Ein Experiment des Universalhasses," in *Friedrich Schiller: Kunst, Humanität und Politik in der späten Aufklärung*, ed. Wolfgang Wittkowski (Tübingen: Niemeyer, 1982), p. 21. In all these instances Karl's capitulation is interpreted as acceptance of the principles of the world against which he has hitherto struggled.

35   In the "Trauerspiel" rendition of *Die Räuber*, i.e., the version Schiller rewrote specifically for the stage production, Karl advises the robbers in the concluding scenes "Dienet dem König, der für die Rechte der Menschheit streitet" (I, 934); Kosinsky and Schweizer he admonishes "werdet gute Bürger" (ibid.), and he even concludes about himself "Und auch ich bin ein guter Bürger" (ibid.). Far from simply making explicit implications contained in the original version, these revisions eradicate entirely the revolutionary thrust of the drama, and as such they mark Schiller's own repression of his rebellious design—unless, of course, we understand the word "Bürger" here ironically to imply and include the self-division which Karl displays in the original text of the drama.

36   Quoted from the Ciceronian translation, cited by Buchmann, *Geflügelte Worte*, 26th ed. (Berlin: Haude und Spenersche Buchhandlung, 1920), p. 352.

37   Sigmund Freud, "Das Unheimliche" (1919), *Freud-Studienausgabe*, ed. Alexander Mitscherlich et al. (Frankfurt: Fischer, 1970), IV, pp. 241-74; see esp. p. 248.

38   Reinhart Koselleck, *Kritik und Krise: Eine Studie zur Pathogenese der bürgerlichen Welt* (1959; rpt. Frankfurt: Suhrkamp, 1973), pp. 49-76.

39   Koselleck, p. 60.

40   Herbert Marcuse, "Über den affirmativen Charakter der Kultur," *Kultur und Gesellschaft I*, edition suhrkamp, 101 (Frankfurt: Suhrkamp, 1965), p. 100.

41   Fritz Wolfgang Haug analyzes the process of aesthetification, the creation of semblance, as the fundamental principle of bourgeois society, culminating in the production of the pure "Bedeutungsding," the commodity whose only "significance" resides in its own signifying, a pure "semblance" detached from any use; see his *Kritik der Warenästhetik* (Frankfurt: Suhrkamp, 1971), esp.

pp. 17, 127, and 173. Karl Moor represents the turning of this process of aesthetification against the bourgeois subject itself; the detachment of semblance
from use-value and essence, the process in which the commodity is constituted, likewise constitutes the (self-)alienation of the bourgeois subject.
Haug's thesis is expanded on and generalized in Baudrillard's notion of
"simulation" and the "hyperreal," the always already reproduced sign which
contains no "reference"; see *Simulations*, p. 146.

Goethe's Transgressions

Peter J. Burgard
Harvard University

Let me begin by digressing. By at least appearing to digress from the main focus of my essay—from the law of the text and from Goethe's playful subversion of that law within the dialogic fabric of his essays.

One of the essays I will address is the longest of those written for the *Propyläen: Der Sammler und die Seinigen.*[1] It is a collection of eight letters written to the editors of a journal by an art collector and by various members of his circle. The essay classifies the types of bias in artistic creation and reception and ends with a diagram that both outlines the relationships of those biases and demonstrates how their combination results in "true" art, which is described with the word "style." There are two general categories of bias—the overly object-oriented and the extremely subjective. On the side of the former we find the "Nachahmer," who would reproduce the object with no trace of her*his interpretive consciousness, the "Charakterist," who devotes her*his energy only to the idea or meaning of the object, and the "Kleinkünstler," who is so fascinated with the object that s*he attempts to make its depiction ever more exact in detail. On the side of those who lose sight of the object in their striving for artistic individuality are the "Phantomist," whose art is seen as nebulous and incoherent in its concentration on the expression of the subject's imagination, the "Undulist," who likes all that is soft and pleasant and disregards the meaning of the object, and the "Skizzist," the producer of a symbolic art that always remains only an outline and thus speaks to the mind, not to the senses.

Der Sammler begins on an anti-systematic note. The collector refuses to give a consistent theory of art and criticizes a young friend for having become a systematic philosopher. This opposition to systems disappears, however, in the course of the text: first the collector himself presents a rudimentary classification of the artistic types and then the essay ends with the system of relationships I have just described, which the young friend prepares at the collector's request. However, closer examination of the text shows the attitude toward systematic thought to be oppositional after all. The system is ironized both in its presentation—by the collector's niece Julie and by the young philosopher—and within the conceptual structure of the system itself. But the text's most forceful subversion of the system it presents lies in its proposed syntheses. We hear, for example, that the art of the "Kleinkünstler" and that of the "Skizzist" combine to produce "Vollendung," whereas both biases had represented the very impossibility of completion. More significant is the use of the concept "Stil." There is nothing in the philosopher's treatise or in the essay as a whole that can provide us insight into the meaning of the term. The word itself has occurred only once before this point, in passing and without discussion or definition (XIII, 296), and suddenly we find it at the geometric center of the system. The effect of using such an undefined term is to undermine the supposed closure of the system; we are forced to search for definitions elsewhere, either by extrapolation or by looking to other Goethean texts, such as "Einfache Nachahmung der Natur, Manier, Stil," but this search proves just as futile.[2] In *Der Sammler*, Goethe plays with our desire for systematic understanding and its inherent closure; his text makes the obvious gesture of presenting a system, but ultimately undermines that system by breaking it open at the center, by failing to define the central category.

This subversion is a form of a deconstruction, in that a discrepancy between explicit and implicit levels of signification is produced; and it is produced by a "double-edged word, which serves as a hinge that both articulates and breaks open the explicit statement being made."[3] "Stil," it seems to me, is just such a word. The deconstructive force of the term lies not only in its apparent explicit articulation of the system's goal and its actual inability to do so, but also in its position at the *center* of the system. In "Structure, Sign and Play in the Discourse of the Human Sciences" Derrida discusses systems as structures that depend on a center to limit the play that would otherwise threaten their certitude and coherence: "The concept of centered structure is in fact the concept of a play based on a fundamental ground, a play constituted on the basis of a fundamental immobility and a reassuring certitude, which itself is beyond the reach of play."[4] The effect of decentering, of the absence of the center *qua* center, is the loss of that certitude. In *Der Sammler* the subversion of systematic discourse operates by means of such a decentering. The non-definition and incomprehensibility of the central term "Stil" in both the system and the essay as a whole decenters that system by rendering its center effectively absent. Or, to be more specific, the center is absent in its function as a systematic element; it remains 'present,' of course, insofar as it fulfills an apparently indispensable communicative function in the discussion of art.[5]

What has all of this to do with "Goethe's Transgressions"? I have summarized my reading of *Der Sammler* because I think the subversion of systematic discourse that occurs there, as well as in most of Goethe's essays, shows in the most general sense his law-breaking tendency, the breaking of the law that the system, as such, represents. In what follows I will focus on another, but related, aspect of Goethe's transgression: the breaking of the law of the monologic and thus teleologically oriented text, the text that, by virtue of its monologism, implicitly makes claims to absoluteness, to truth, or at least to the achievability and formulability of truth. Using *Der Sammler* and another *Propyläen* essay, "Über Wahrheit und Wahrscheinlichkeit der Kunstwerke," as examples, I will attempt to show how Goethe's essays break that monologic textual law and in so doing enact the dialogic.

In the middle of the first letter of *Der Sammler* we discover the reason for the correspondence that comprises the essay. The collector writes:

Sie haben für die Schrift, die Sie herauszugeben gedenken, durch diese Probestücke [die beigefügten Manuskripte] meine Hoffnungen und meine stille Teilnahme verstärkt, und gern will ich auch auf irgendeine Weise, deren ich mich fähig fühle, zu Ihren Absichten mit beitragen. Theorie ist nie meine Sache gewesen, was Sie von meinen Erfahrungen brauchen können, steht von Herzen zu Diensten. Und um hiervon einen Beweis zu geben, fange ich sogleich an, Ihren Wunsch zu erfüllen. Ich werde Ihnen nach und nach die Geschichte meiner Sammlung aufzeichnen . . . . (XIII, 260)

With these words the collector formulates the law of the text—the avoidance of theory and the concentration on an historical account and perspective. However, he has barely finished writing that law before he begins to break it. While he promised to start "sogleich" with the history of his collection, he goes off on a tangent the moment he begins, and the remainder of the first letter contains nothing of that history; at the end of the letter he then reprimands himself for this deviation from his course—"Ich schließe diesen Brief, ohne meinen Vorsatz erfüllt zu haben. Ich schwätzte anstatt zu erzählen" (XIII, 262). Furthermore, the history of the collection, which was to constitute the correspondence "nach und nach," is completed within the second and third letters; the remaining five letters address different and more general questions about art and its appreciation.

The collector's deviation in the first letter, what he calls prattle, is an excursus into just what he had promised not to discuss: theory. Theory—theoretical meditations on the reception of art—fills most of the second half of the letter. The paragraph immediately following his formulation of the law of the text introduces a theory of the effects of both personal and cultural history on the appreciation and accumulation of works of art:

Freilich kommt es viel auf den Charakter, auf die Neigung eines Liebhabers an, wohin die Liebe zum Gebildeten, wohin der Sammlungsgeist, zwei Neigungen, die sich oft im Menschen finden, ihre Richtung nehmen sollen, und ebensoviel, möchte ich behaupten, hängt der Liebhaber von der Zeit ab, in die er kommt, von den Umständen, unter denen er sich befindet, von gleichzeitigen Künstlern und Kunsthändlern, von den Ländern, die er zuerst besucht, von den Nationen, mit denen er in irgendeinem Verhältnis steht. (XIII, 261)

Then, after he has quickly run through the history of his collection in the second and third letters, the collector allows theoretical considerations to govern the rest of the correspondence: his classification of the types of art lovers, his debate with a visitor to the collection who is called the "Charakterist," and the further refinement of the classification that culminates in the philosopher's system. Even in the midst of his historical narration, the collector again and again falls into theoretical reflections; for example, when describing his father's love of portrait-painting, he theorizes about the advantages and disadvantages of this genre as well as about its relationship to art-collecting (XIII, 264). No matter that the collector criticizes himself at the end of the first letter for a lapse into theory and later ironizes his classifications by referring to them as "wunderlich" (XIII, 284-5); what he has produced *is* still theory. *Der Sammler* thus transgresses the law it has formulated for itself.

The text does not then descend immediately into lawlessness. 'Theory' itself, especially as it appears here in the form of classification and system, carries with it the quality of law. Because of this particular result of the collector's infraction, the transgression of the initial law of the text leads paradoxically to the establishment of a new law, the law of a system of aesthetics. This unstated but implied law rules the remainder of the text, but, as I suggested at the beginning, only on the explicit level. Examination of the subtext, of the implicit signification, of the discursive strategies of *Der Sammler*, enables us to gain access to the transgression of that new law, to the subversion of the essay's apparently systematic discourse.

We might describe that subversion of the system as an undermining of the authority of a unified, totalized, 'centralized,' closed text. However, that undermining can also be seen to have begun at a much earlier point in the text and to have facilitated or at least reflected the transgression of the law of the text all along. I would locate this feature of the text in the growing attenuation of the authority of the collector's *voice*, an attenuation that begins already in the second letter. The deconstruction of the system in *Der Sammler* implies non-closure and, in that this implication occurs at the end of the essay, in its culmination, the text breaches its own closure; it then calls attention to this open-endedness in Julie's assertion that the debate will continue where she leaves off. The text thus forces our attention to its own process, its own strategies. Once discourse has lost its center, its teleological orientation, all that is left *is* that process. The undermining of the authoritative voice of the collector occurs in what I consider the most important aspect of the essay's process or discursive strategy—in its dialogism.

Collecting Voices

The collector himself makes the first move toward undermining the univocality of the text, toward opening 'his' text to a dialogue of voices. He does this, however, at a point where he does not yet seem quite ready to relinquish his authority. Near the end of the second letter he discusses the obsession that overcame his brother-in-law after the death of his sister, and is then overcome by his own melancholy ruminations—to the point where he feels he can no longer continue to write. Because he is unwilling to end the letter on a sad note, he asks Julie to close the letter: "Und doch soll dieser Brief mit einem so traurigen Schlusse nicht in Ihre Hand kommen, ich gebe meiner Julie die Feder, um Ihnen zu sagen—" (XIII, 269). The ellipsis at the end of this remark indicates that he expects Julie to write exactly as he would have liked to have been able to write, to be an extension of his voice. But she does not meet these expectations. She begins her postscript with an explanation of why it is impossible for her to do as her uncle wishes:

> Mein Oheim gibt mir die Feder, um Ihnen mit einer artigen Wendung zu sagen wie sehr er Ihnen ergeben sei. Er bleibt noch immer der Gewohnheit jener guten alten Zeit getreu, wo man es für Pflicht hielt am Ende eines Briefes von einem Freund mit einer zierlichen Verbeugung zu scheiden. Uns andern ist das nun schon nicht gelehrt worden; ein solcher Knicks scheint uns nicht natürlich, nicht herzlich genug. (XIII, 270)

In other words, Julie is very much aware that she has a voice and she plans on using this opportunity to exercise it.

Julie herself then brings up the notion of authority in connection with the voice of her uncle *and* reflects on her inability, her unwillingness to abide by that authority. She speaks of the "task" he has set for her, but then corrects herself and chooses the more accurate word, "command": "Wie machen wir's nun um den Auftrag, den Befehl meines Onkels, wie es einer gehorsamen Nichte geziemt, zu erfüllen?" (XIII, 270). She asks the rhetorical question, "Will mir denn gar keine artige Wendung einfallen" (XIII, 270), and then indicates that such a closing remark, which would complete her task, is not sufficient. She justifies her deviation from the uncle's command by pointing out that he did not see fit to show her all of his letter, indeed that he *forbade* her (again, the language of law, of authority) to read the last page. This lack of trust in her, this unpleasant 'legislation,' gives her license not to feel bound to finish the letter as her uncle would have, license to say what she wants, and this is precisely what she does.

The emergence of her voice takes the form of a challenge to her uncle's opinions about the young philosopher friend:

> Genug er hat mir erlaubt den Anfang seines Briefes zu lesen, und da finde ich, daß er unsern guten Philosophen bei Ihnen anschwärzen will. Es ist nicht artig noch billig vom Oheim einen jungen Mann, der ihn und Sie wahrhaft liebt und verehrt, darum so strenge zu tadeln, weil er so ernsthaft auf einem Wege verharrt, auf dem er sich nun einmal zu bilden glaubt. (XIII, 270)

Julie even goes so far as to criticize the collector for being "einseitig" and for not being willing, "jedem sein Recht widerfahren [zu] lassen" (XIII, 270).

It is not only *vis-à-vis* her uncle that Julie attempts to define her own voice, but also *vis-à-vis* the correspondents, the editors of the *Propyläen*. Since she apparently knows that they do not think highly of the kind of art that interests her, she senses ridicule in the engravings they have sent her as a gift. In order to defend herself, she employs the rhetorical device of feigned self-ridicule: "Was kann die arme Julie dafür, daß etwas Seltsames, Geistreiches sie aufreizt, daß sie gern etwas Wunderbares vorgestellt sieht und daß diese durcheinander ziehenden und beweglichen Träume, auf dem Papier fixiert, ihr Unterhaltung geben!" (XIII, 271). This first introduction of another voice into the text, while it was intended to be nothing more than a continuation of the collector's voice, already succeeds to a great extent in challenging the authority of that first voice.

Julie does not then forbid her uncle to read her postscript and thus does not, as he had done, make a claim to authority. He begins the next letter with an attempt to re-establish his authority: "Julie hat in ihrer letzten Nachschrift dem Philosophen das Wort geredet, leider stimmt der Oheim noch nicht mit ein" (XIII, 272). He evidently feels challenged, for he does not leave his difference of opinion at this simple statement, but rather presents a long argument about why he thinks she is wrong. This insistence on his own authority diminishes, however, in the course of his letter. The last part of his historical narration deals mainly with his education and development as an art-collector. More specifically, it deals with the important role "Widerspruch" played in that education and with the significant effects of having viewed the collections of *others*. It is as a result of *this* discussion, I would suggest, that by the end of the letter he is prepared to give up his authority altogether, to abandon the further expression of his ideas, *to stop writing*: "Für diesmal und für immer genug von mir selbst. Möge sich mein ganzer Egoism innerhalb meiner Sammlung befriedigen!" (XIII, 277). He does not carry out this plan. The editors draw him back into the dialogue by sending him essays from their journal, and he finds it impossible to ignore them, especially since they recall for him the productive discussions he and his correspondents have had in the past.

In the fifth letter, the last time we hear directly from the collector, he takes a further step toward un-privileging his own voice and attributing equal validity to the voices of others. The characterist visits him in order to see the collection; the extreme divergence in their views on art leads to an intense, sometimes heated argument. The collector at first conveys this argument in his letter by reporting what his opponent said. However, this reportage gives way to a direct transcription of their debate in the form of a dramatic dialogue. By choosing this form of writing, the collector shows his willingness to allow others equal rights of expression, no matter how 'threatening' the other's position may be to his own. He no longer finds it necessary, as he had after letting Julie write for him the first time, to subordinate the discourse of others. He has developed a dialogic attitude.

The next two letters are written by the philosopher and by Julie, respectively. They serve to dialogize the essay further by both reproducing debate in the form of dramatic dialogue and, more generally, by varying the writing voices of the text. Any sense of superior authority in the collector's voice has disappeared by now; that voice returns, but only as one among others in a debate or in reports of what was said.

Julie writes the final letter. But we would also be justified in saying that she does *not* write it. Her remarks after describing the first of the artistic biases, imitation, explain this paradox:

> (Notabene! Daß Sie ja nicht irre werden und, weil Sie meine Hand sehen, glauben, daß das alles aus meinem Köpfchen komme. Ich wollte erst unterstreichen was ich buchstäblich aus den Papieren nehme die ich vor mir liegen habe; doch dann wäre zu viel unterstrichen worden. Sie werden am besten sehen wo ich nur referiere, ja Sie finden die eignen Worte Ihres letzten Briefes wieder.) (XIII, 312)

For the most part, we *are* able to tell where she is simply reporting, since she often indicates whose idea it is that we are currently reading. But not always. And without "underlining" or quotation marks or some other cue to the presence of another voice, we cannot be certain whether the philosopher, the collector, Julie or Karoline, the collector's other niece, is responsible for the words on the page. This is especially the case with Karoline, whose voice we never read, even though we are told that she takes part in the discussions. Thus Julie's voice, given her warning and the fact that she is conveying the results of what we know was a communal effort, loses the aspect of authority, the fiercely independent quality it seemed to have when we first read it. What emerges, then, is a dialogue of voices in which the very idea of one's 'own,' independent voice is compromised. Moreover, this dialogue of voices is a dialogue that involves the reader. Julie remarks that her readers, the editors, will find in her letter the words of their own letter. But we have not had access to that letter, or to any of their responses, and are unable to recognize their voice in the text. With the introduction of this extreme indeterminacy, the sense, the possibility, of any single authoritative voice is lost. The text thus not only reproduces dialogue and reflects on the value of dialogue; it *becomes* dialogue.

Der Sammler und die Seinigen provides a particularly potent example of how dialogically saturated Goethe's essays are.[6] Besides the dialogism I have just described, *Der Sammler* is dialogic in a number of other ways as well. The classifications and categorizations that lead to the final system themselves arise out of dialogue. And the essay as a whole represents several different dialogues. Most obviously, it is a dialogue between the collector, Julie and the philosopher on the one hand and the editors of the *Propyläen* on the other. However, it is also a dialogue between that first group and *us* as readers. The editors' letters are never reproduced; we are therefore implicitly forced into the position of the respondents and must try to supply the missing part of the dialogue by gleaning from the letters we read what the editors might have written. *We* thus 'write,' however inexactly, the missing letters.[7] Furthermore, the letters we read imply another, broader dialogue between the collector and his circle and the literary public sphere, in that these letters are to be published in the editors' journal. Indeed, they *are* then published, and herein lies one of the text's great self-reflective moments. In that the editors' journal is the *Propyläen* —that is, *Goethe's* journal—and in that the letters are actually published there (as we read them), the essay constitutes a highly ironic public dialogue *between Goethe and himself.*

Goethe's essay not only directly represents various dialogues and implies others. It also openly discusses dialogue and its advantages. At one point the collector comments on the significance of dialogue in a way that points beyond the specific help he elsewhere says it affords in intellectual endeavors. Just after expressing his intention to stop writing and find another way to subsume his "Egoism," he signs off with the following proclamation: "Mitteilung und Empfänglichkeit sei übrigens das Losungswort"

(XIII, 277). He conflates "communication" and "receptivity" into one concept by using the singular verb and equating the two terms with one "Wort"; the result is a definition of dialogue. The emphasis on bi-directionality is crucial, for "Mitteilung" by itself, without "Empfänglichkeit," would be a uni-directional, univocal communication equivalent to monologue. In the early stages of the essay, this is the state in which we find the young philosopher—insistent on his new-found philosophical passion, unreceptive to the collector's ideas on art, and thus unable to be a part of the dialogue. Only by 'opening up,' by becoming receptive to the ideas of others (and thus implicitly relinquishing the notion of autonomous ideas) does he then join in what is for him, for the collector, for Julie, for the editors and for us an 'edifying' dialogue. But there is more to the collector's remark than this. By designating dialogue as "das Losungswort"—the password—he simultaneously alludes to dialogue's power to carry us over thresholds and cross boundaries, boundaries, I would say, between types of discourse and between subjects.

The Law of the Text, or: Playing with Plato

In another of his *Propyläen* essays, Goethe brings together more explicitly the dialogic and the circumvention, even subversion, of law. "Über Wahrheit und Wahrscheinlichkeit der Kunstwerke" in its outward form is the most obviously dialogic of Goethe's essays. Not only does it carry the subtitle, "Ein Gespräch," but whenever Goethe referred to the essay, he used this designation.[8]

But "Wahrheit und Wahrscheinlichkeit" is not just any kind of dialogue. Its fictional situation and its rhetorical strategy reveal its quality as a specific type of dialogue steeped in tradition. The situation is an argument between a spectator and the representative of an artist who has offended the spectator by painting a background scene for a theater that portrays an audience watching the performance on stage. The representative is placed in what seems an intellectually superior position to that of the spectator, and the course of their discussion consists in his gradually leading the spectator out of his aesthetic naiveté into 'enlightened' awareness. For example, he asks the spectator, whose complaint arose out of a conviction that everything he sees in the theater should appear "true and real": "Was werden Sie sagen, wenn ich Ihnen einwende, daß Ihnen alle theatralische Darstellungen keineswegs wahr scheinen, daß sie vielmehr nur einen Schein des Wahren haben?" (XIII, 176). The spectator at first objects to this word-game, but eventually accepts the point. Having gained this much, the representative is then able to carry his argument further and argue his opponent into relinquishing even his diminished ground:

> Wenn aber die guten Leute da droben singend sich begegnen und bekomplimentieren, Billets absingen, die sie erhalten, ihre Liebe, ihren Haß, alle ihre Leidenschaften singend darlegen, sich singend herumschlagen, und singend verscheiden, können Sie sagen, daß die ganze Vorstellung, oder auch nur ein Teil derselben, wahr scheine? ja ich darf sagen auch nur einen Schein des Wahren habe? (XIII, 176-7)

This purposeful questioning is augmented by a more powerful, if less appealing, rhetorical strategy—the use of examples analogous to the opponent's position, but designated to shock the opponent out of his position by making it impossible for him to continue insisting on it without appearing foolish. Thus the representative uses two examples—that of the sparrow that mistook the cherries in a painting for real cherries and that of the monkey who ate all of the insects out of a naturalist's engravings—in order to show that only the most uncultured of art-lovers would want a work of art to be a fully accurate representation of the real world. Finally, the spectator himself comments on the dialogic strategy being employed against him; at a moment of confusion, the representative asks, "Wollen Sie mir erlauben auf dem Punkt, wo wir stehen, einige Fragen zu tun?," to which the spectator replies, "Es ist Ihre Pflicht, da Sie mich in diese Verwirrung hineingefragt haben, mich auch wieder herauszufragen" (XIII, 177). Given this rhetorical structure I would suggest, then, that what "Wahrheit und Wahrscheinlichkeit" presents us with is a *Platonic* dialogue.[9]

Goethe introduces the issue of law into his text with his designation of the artist's representative. He does not call him a "representative" and does not, for example, have the director or the artist himself defend the painting. Rather, it is "Der Anwalt des Künstlers" who takes on the task of defending the stage set; and in the use of the word "advocate" there is a strong suggestion of "lawyer" and "law." It should strike us as odd that Goethe would have an advocate, not an artist or critic, debating on the relationship between art and nature. This oddity is explained, however, by the fact that it is in the general sense a *legal* problem that is at issue in the essay. And the legal problem under consideration is the problem of law *in general*, insofar as questions of *truth* and *probability* are at issue. Moreover, these issues are related to the Platonic tradition in thought evoked by the essay's form, as well as to the problem of system and systematic discourse. In "Pragmatism, Relativism, and Irrationalism" Richard Rorty relates the Platonic search for truth to the problem of method, which he describes in terms that point toward the problem of legislation: the insistence on method "is the myth that rationality consists in being constrained by rule."[10] The issue of truth ties that of law into questions of the system, both in a very specific sense—that of the functioning of a *legal system*, which depends on the discovery of 'the truth'—and in a general sense, in that all systematic discourse has truth as its implied goal.

Already in the connections among law, truth, system and Platonic tradition, we should become suspicious of Goethe's composition of an apparently Platonic dialogue. When we examine how the essay treats the law (truth), we discover that in this dialogue truth, the notion of truth, is not served, but rather subverted. This subversion receives special emphasis in the text's basic irony. It is the artist's representative who performs the subversive act. That is, the lawyer breaks the law—the law of truth and by extension the law of the text. In discussing the rhetorical strategy of this essay, I already outlined the way in which the advocate educates the spectator *away* from the belief that works of art must "appear to be true" by first substituting for that notion the idea that they only have an "appearance of the true" and then showing how this as well is not the case. The only sense of truth in art that the advocate allows to survive is the possibility of an "inner" truth, "eine innere Wahrheit, die aus der Konsequenz eines Kunstwerks entspringt" (XIII, 178). After the spectator has agreed with him, we discover his reason for positing such an inner truth: "Sollte nun nicht daraus folgen, daß das Kunstwahre und das Naturwahre völlig verschieden sei, und daß der Künstler keineswegs streben sollte, noch dürfe, daß sein Werk eigentlich als ein Naturwerk erscheine?" (XIII, 178). By eliminating the possibility of correspondence between a work of art and a work of nature, the advocate has succeeded in subverting what Rorty refers to as the Platonic myth of "truth as accuracy of representation" (164). In other words, he uses truth in order to move away from the notion of truth.

Near the end of the text the advocate discusses why it was possible for the spectator to perceive a "vollkommenes Kunstwerk" as a work of nature, and by so doing addresses the *reception* of art:

> Weil es mit Ihrer bessern Natur übereinstimmt, weil es übernatürlich, aber nicht außernatürlich ist. Ein vollkommenes Kunstwerk ist ein Werk des menschlichen Geistes, und in diesem Sinne auch ein Werk der Natur. Aber indem die zerstreuten Gegenstände in eins gefaßt, und selbst die gemeinsten in ihrer Bedeutung und Würde aufgenommen werden, so ist es über die Natur. Es will durch einen Geist, der harmonisch entsprungen und gebildet ist, aufgefaßt sein, und dieser findet das Vortreffliche, das in sich Vollendete, auch seiner Natur gemäß. (XIII, 180-1)

The recipient of art reinscribes the work within the harmony of her*his own mind, which at the same time perceives *itself* as nature, and is thus able to identify nature and art (the connection between nature in general and a person's nature is made here in the language of the text as well—in the rhythmic interchange of the general "die Natur" and the possessively modified "Natur"). The only 'inner truth' of the artwork resides, then, in the artwork as it is re-created in the mind of the educated recipient. As a result, we can no longer speak of the inner truth of the work of art *itself*. And the truth of the work for one recipient will differ from its truth for another. The advocate thus makes the point that truth is possible, but only in the individual's complete isolation. This in turn eliminates the possibility of truth in *re-presentation* as well as, paradoxically, in active *reception*, which the advocate himself describes as a process of repeated viewing ("es wiederholt anschauen" [XIII, 181]).[11] The only truth possible in reception would then be the result of a single viewing and of a refusal to see the work again, and would thus imply a denial of the continued existence of the work. Repeated re-viewing would mean entering into a 'dialogue' with the work of art, a dialogue that would open up a play of constantly changing meanings and temporary 'truths'—temporary because they will always be relativized by the difference incurred through repetition.[12] Any concern with *the* truth of the work of art becomes superfluous.[13]

Goethe employs the form of the Platonic dialogue in order to ironize it and its attendant philosophical tradition. Rorty describes that tradition as follows:

> According to th[e] Platonic myth [that rationality consists in being constrained by rule] . . . . One simply arrives at true beliefs by obeying mechanical procedures. Traditional, Platonic, epistemologically-centered philosophy is the search for such procedures. It is the search for a way in which one can avoid the need for conversation and deliberation and simply tick off the way things are. (164)

My summary of the treatment of systematic discourse in *Der Sammler* should explain why Goethe would challenge that tradition. However, the question remains: why would Goethe attack, on the implicit level of this dialogic essay's discourse, the Platonic dialogue itself?

We can attempt to answer that question by turning to Goethe's own explicit discussion of that kind of dialogue in an essay of 1796 (two years prior to "Wahrheit und Wahrscheinlichkeit"), entitled "Plato als Mitgenosse einer christlichen Offenbarung." In the critique of a new translation of Plato, particularly of the elevation of "Ion" to the status of a canonical text, we find as well a critique of the Platonic dialogue. In reference to "Ion" we read: "Überhaupt fällt in diesem Gespräch, wie in andern Platonischen, die unglaubliche Dummheit einiger Personen auf, damit nur Sokrates von seiner Seite recht weise sein könne" (XIV, 693). Earlier

Goethe had mentioned Plato's polemical tendency (691), and here we see that what such a tendency leads to is one-sidedness in his dialogues, and thus not to dialogues at all, but rather to texts that tend toward monologism. The essay emphasizes the unfairness of this tendency by discussing "die alberne Frage" of the "wise" Socrates (XIV, 693). This criticism then leads to consideration of the detrimental effect of that monologism in its failure to address sufficiently the questions it raises; Goethe suggests that a discussion between more equally privileged and able dialogic partners would have produced something more than the discussion we find in "Ion." Goethe thus supplies some details for Rorty's argument that Platonic philosophy looks for a way to "avoid the need for conversation." In terms of my current discussion, that criticism of monologism is especially significant, since the question "Ion" raises but fails to address is at the heart of "Wahrheit und Wahrschein-lichkeit"—the problem of truth in art and truth in nature: "Diese Fiktionen, diese Hieroglyphen [e.g., alte Gemmen . . . worauf die Pferde ohne Geschirr dennoch den Wagen ziehen sollten], deren jede Kunst bedarf, werden so übel von allen denen verstanden, welche alles Wahre natürlich haben wollen und dadurch die Kunst aus ihrer Sphäre reißen" (XIV, 693).

Again, "Über Wahrheit und Wahrscheinlichkeit der Kunst-werke" leads the spectator, and the reader, away from the notion of truth. Moreover, it does not replace that lost notion with some other *telos*, but remains open-ended, stopping as almost all of Goethe's essays do with an intimation of or invitation to continuing dialogue.[14] The essay does not portray the more experienced advocate's partner in dialogue as "unbelievably stupid." The advocate takes advantage of nearly every opportunity to diminish any impression of his great "wisdom": he emphasizes that anyone can achieve a higher level of aesthetic judgment and that the specta-tor's misconceptions are understandable—the points he makes important ones that deserve and require consideration. The essay is an anti-Platonic Platonic dialogue, dialogic rather than polemi-cally monologic, law-breaking rather than law-making.

In *Der Sammler und die Seinigen* and "Über Wahrheit und Wahrscheinlichkeit der Kunstwerke" Goethe's dialogic strategies not only *accompany* the transgression of laws, but also *perform* that transgression. And I would like to suggest that the transgression of the law of the monologic text is at the same time a transgression of the law represented by the notion of an autonomous subject. The subversion of the authoritative voice that we witness in the dialogism of Goethe's essays is perhaps another way of talking about the deconstruction of the autonomous subject, since it is in dialogue that the boundaries of and between not only texts but also subjects are crossed.[15] Texts like *Der Sammler* and "Wahrheit und Wahrscheinlichkeit" enact the inevitability of dialogue and hence illustrate the hypocrisy of system, which in its attendant claim to truth would deny that inevitability. Recognizing the inevitability of dialogue implies recognizing the impossibility of a single authoritative voice, of an autonomous, self-identical subject, of a unitary language.[16] The constant postponement of final decisions that dialogue engenders, its open-endedness through deferral, undermines the illusion of presence.[17] Perhaps it is dialogue's disclosure of the subject as *différance*, for that is what I am talking about here, that Hölderlin also means when he writes the words, "Seit ein Gespräch wir sind."[18]

But Hölderlin's words are not my last. Goethe's novel *Unterhaltungen deutscher Ausgewanderten* ends with a digression, with the enigmatic fairy tale, and I would like to end with a digression on that digression. In "Das Märchen" the snake, with her newly acquired glow, enters the cavern in order to satisfy her curiosity and finally see what she had hitherto only been able to feel in this dark, secret place. Just as she peers at the golden king, he begins speaking to her and directs a series of questions at her: "Wo kommst du her? — Aus den Klüften, versetzte die Schlange, in denen das Gold wohnt. — Was ist herrlicher als Gold? fragte der König. — Das Licht, antwortete die Schlange. — Was ist erquicklicher als Licht? fragte jener. — Das Gespräch, antwortete diese" (IX, 374-5). As with so many statements and descriptions in this tale, this strange comparison between light and dialogue is never explained, but simply abandoned. Within the context of the narration we can perhaps explain the references of the two terms in isolation from one another. "Light" might refer to the light of the old man's lamp that has the capacity to turn stone into gold, wood into silver, and dead animals into gems; but we might also understand it as a reference to the snake's glow, or to the "Irrlichter." "Dialogue," especially since it is the snake who brings it up, is related to the apparent theme of the tale—the sacrifice of the autonomous individual for the sake of the collective (the snake's "Entsagung"). If one accepts this interpretation and reads "light" as a reference to the lamp, then we could say that dialogue, which changes things in society for the better, is seen to be of greater value than light, which changes things, but only material things. Or, if we concentrate on the progression of phenomena the golden king elicits with his questions, and attempt to explain why one surpasses the other, we could say that the progression is one of increasing enhancement of that which precedes: in other words, light is that *by which* gold is "herrlich" and conversation is that *by which* knowledge (i.e., light understood in the Enlightenment sense of *Erkenntnis*) is "erquicklich." But in order to explain more exactly why it is specifically *dialogue vis-à-vis light* that is so important, I would suggest a reading that moves further beyond the bounds of the text. "Dialogue" need not be read as an expansion or enhancement of "light," in the sense of a progression, but, given the comparative construction, can also be seen in juxtaposition to "light." In keeping with the evocation of the 'ages' of mankind in the tale (the golden, silver and bronze kings), we could then read "light" as referring not only to "Licht der Erkenntnis," but specifically to the *age* of the Enlightenment, the age of Wolff, Baumgarten and Gottsched, the age of *monologic, systematic discourse*. "Dialogue" could then be seen to refer to the ages that followed the Enlightenment, not as enhancements, but as radical questionings of their predecessor—that is, to the *Sturm und Drang*[19] and *Klassik*, to the questioning of Enlightenment discourse that occurs in the writings of Lessing, Herder and Goethe.

Notes

1 Johann Wolfgang [von] Goethe, *Gedenkausgabe der Werke, Briefe und Gespräche*, ed. Ernst Beutler, 27 vols. (Zürich: Artemis, 1949ff.), XIII, 259-319. All quotations from Goethe's works will be documented in the text with volume and page numbers from this edition.

2 I carry out this search for Goethe's understanding of the concept, "style," in my book, *Goethe and the Essay* (University Park, PA: Penn State Press, forthcoming). The present essay is a slightly modified version of an argument carried out in greater detail in Part Two of that study.

3 Barbara Johnson, "Introduction," in Jacques Derrida, *Dissemination*, ed. Barbara Johnson (Chicago: University of Chicago Press, 1981), pp. xiv-xv.

4 Jacques Derrida, "Structure, Sign and Play in the Discourse of the Human Sciences," in his *Writing and Difference*, trans. Alan Bass (Chicago: University of Chicago Press, 1978), p. 279.

5 This discussion of the treatment of system in *Der Sammler* originally appeared in my "Unlikely Affinities: Warhol and Goethe," *MOSAIC: A Journal for the Interdisciplinary Study of Literature* 21, 1 (Winter 1988), 37-47. In both cases it is the summary of an argument carried out in Part One of *Goethe and the Essay*, op. cit.

6 Mathijs Jolles (*Goethes Kunstanschauung* [Bern: Francke, 1957]) bases his entire study on a reading of *Der Sammler* and discusses at length the significance of dialogue in the essay. He makes the general statement that "Das Gespräch ist der Inhalt und die Form des 'Sammlers'" (p. 54), but concentrates only on the more obvious manifestations of dialogue—that of the correspondence with the editors and that between the members of the collector's circle. And while he discusses the essay's unsystematic quality and attempts to show that its dialogic character interferes with any theoretical intentions, he undermines this argument by positing dialogue itself as a kind of system when he calls it "eine höhere Gesetzlichkeit" (p. 53) and claims that it, even more than a systematic treatise, leads to closure (p. 47).

7 In *Werther*, Goethe had practiced a similar textual strategy. We find essentially the same situation in the novel: we have only one side of the correspondence and must thus 'supply' the other side. For a discussion of this aspect of

the text and of its implications for the novel as a whole, see: Benjamin Bennett, "Werther and Montaigne: The Romantic Renaissance," *Goethe Yearbook*, 3 (1986), 1-20, especially 12-13.

8 For example, in the "Anzeige der Propyläen" we read, "diese Frage [Wahrheit und Wahrscheinlichkeit der Kunstwerke] [ist] in einem heitern Gespräch ausgeführt" (XIII, 195), and in a letter to Schiller of 24 May 1798 he writes: "Zugleich erhalten Sie das Gespräch, von dem ich neulich sagte" (XX, 586).

9 Joachim Wohlleben (*Goethe als Journalist und Essayist* [Frankfurt: Lang, 1981]) also asserts that "Wahrheit und Wahrscheinlichkeit" is a Platonic dialogue (p. 95), but does not bring the actual process and strategies of Goethe's dialogue into a comparison with the philosophical implications of the form of the Platonic dialogue.

10 Richard Rorty, "Pragmatism, Relativism, Irrationalism," in his *Consequences of Pragmatism (Essays: 1972-1980)* (Minneapolis: University of Minnesota Press, 1982), p. 164.

11 Goethe's *Propyläen* essays are generally held to represent his most thorough development of the idea of the autonomous work of art. One of the more important consequences of my reading of "Wahrheit und Wahrscheinlichkeit" is the disclosure of Goethe's *questioning* of that idea. In that it restricts the truth of the work of art to an "inner truth" and then makes that 'truth' dependent on reception—on that which is allegedly 'outside' the work, on us—the essay constitutes a subversion of that notion of autonomy.

12 There is a parallel here to Roland Barthes' discussion of the "writerly" and the "readerly" in *S/Z* (trans. Richard Miller [New York: Hill and Wang, 1974]). In re-reading (i.e., the writerly), Barthes says, we maintain the plurality and non-closure of the text, the subversion of any supposed final signified, and a play of differences—"that play which is the return of the different" (p. 16). Barthes' goal in positing the writerly as his value is "to make the reader no longer a consumer, but a producer of the text" (p. 4). The reader who acts as a consumer is the "readerly" reader; s*he does not re-read and thus reduces the text to a commodity:

Rereading, an operation contrary to the commercial and ideological habits of our society, which would have us 'throw away' the story once it has been consumed ('devoured'), so that we can then move on to another story, buy another book . . . rereading is here suggested at the outset, for it alone saves the text from repetition (those who fail to reread are obliged to read the same story everywhere). (pp. 15-6)

That Goethe, in "Wahrheit und Wahrscheinlichkeit," had in mind what Barthes calls the writerly, is not only implied. The view of the recipient of art as at the same time its producer is made explicit in the essay, where their conflation forms the final argument *against* the possibility of the truth of a work of art. Here Goethe brings together the notions of 're-reading' and of the proper reception of art as a 'reading' in which the recipient must *become* the producer in order to appreciate the 'text' (the work of art): "der wahre Liebhaber . . . fühlt, *daß er sich zum Künstler erheben müsse*, um das Werk zu genießen, er fühlt, daß er sich aus seinem zerstreuten Leben sammeln, mit dem Kunstwerk wohnen, *es wiederholt anschauen* . . . müsse" (XIII, 181; my emphasis). Preceding this definition of the ideal recipient is a description of the usual manner of reception that, in its use of the metaphor of consumerism, further demonstrates the remarkably extensive affinity between Goethe's and Barthes' views on reception: "der gemeine Liebhaber . . . behandelt ein Kunstwerk wie einen Gegenstand, den er auf dem Markte antrifft" (XIII, 181).

13 Given my reading of "Wahrheit und Wahrscheinlichkeit" we could then attempt to justify to the spectator the painted audience behind the stage. (The essay itself never returns to the question.) First of all, we could say that the painting reminds us, the audience, that we are watching a play, a *Kunstwerk*, and thus not a representation of the real world. Beyond this, it reminds us that we are not the only recipients of the performance, that there are other interpretations that might call ours into question, and that the fact of these other interpretations prevents us from determining the absolute "inner truth" of the work of art.

14 In the case of "Wahrheit und Wahrscheinlichkeit" a continuation was actually planned. In the letter to Schiller of 24 May 1798 we read: "ich bin neugierig, . . . ob Sie die angekündigte Fortsetzung wünschen und fordern" (XX, 586).

15 In his discussion of dialogue in *Der Sammler*, Jolles makes what seems to be a similar point about the dis-integration of the autonomous subject in dialogue. However, he then attempts to rehabilitate that subject by claiming that the "Unterordnung des Ich" (a phrase that itself maintains the subject as part of a hierarchy) occurs only for the sake of eliminating "willkürliche Verabsolutierung"; in the place of that individual subject he posits a more general subjectivity that results from dialogue's combination of elements—what he calls "eine höhere Würde" (p. 53). The image of a unity, a totality, remains in his insistence on the prerequisite for dialogue of a "gemeinsame Mitte," a center (p. 53).

16 Bakhtin's understanding of dialogue in "Discourse in the Novel" (M. M. Bakhtin, *The Dialogic Imagination: Four Essays*, ed. Michael Holquist, trans. M. H. and Caryl Emerson [Austin, Texas: University of Texas Press, 1981], pp. 259-422) would also seem to call into question the possibility of a unitary language (Holquist alludes to this in his introduction, p. xxi). However, Bakhtin mitigates his own subversion of the notion of a unitary language by reinstating such language as a quality of poetic genres other than the novel.

For a discussion and critique of Bakhtin's restriction of dialogue to the novel and his concomitant reduction of poetic/lyric language to the monologic, see: Renate Lachmann, "Dialogizität und poetische Sprache," in *Dialogizität*, ed. R. Lachmann, Vol. 1 of *Theorie und Geschichte der Literatur und der schönen Künste, Reihe A: Hermeneutik, Semiotik, Rhetorik* 1 (München: Fink, 1982), pp. 51-62. Lachmann also discusses Kristeva's subtly modifying interpretation of Bakhtin and how her notions of intertextuality and "paragrammes" subvert Bakhtin's reduction of poetic language and demonstrate the dialogic quality of language beyond generic boundaries.

17   In discussing Goethe's famous description of his "ideelle Unterhaltung" in *Dichtung und Wahrheit* (X, 630-1), Jolles claims that the dialogue leads not to a problematization of the self's 'presence,' but rather to a "zeitlose Gegenwart" (p. 61). In other words, while he seemed to be saying that dialogue undermines the 'absoluteness' of the self (the "Verabsolutierung" of the subject mentioned in note 15), he ends up positing dialogue as a means of *achieving* the subject's absoluteness—its complete presence.

18   Friedrich Hölderlin, *Sämtliche Werke und Briefe*, ed. Günter Mieth, 2 vols. (München: Hanser, 1970), I, 368.

19   I include Storm and Stress here mainly because of Goethe's own views. In *Dichtung und Wahrheit* he describes the movement, first, as having arisen out of contradiction to the age that preceded it (X, 285) and, second, as having come about through dialogue (X, 567-8). Even though the writers of the time openly criticized Enlightenment thought and writing, seeing the movement in strict opposition to the Enlightenment remains problematic, since in at least one aspect the movement can be seen as a radicalization of Enlightenment systematics—in its glorification of the "Genie," the hypertrophied manifestation of the autonomous subject.

A Philosopher's Style:
Reading Fichte's "Geist und Buchstab"

Liliane Weissberg
University of Pennsylvania

How is one to read?

This question was answered early on in the history of Western letters, with a remark by Paul in the New Testament (2 Cor 3:6; Rom 2:29; Rom 7:6). The text Paul refers to, the Mosaic ten commandments, is an undoubtedly fixed one, carved in stone. To be able to read this text and understand it as the foundation-stone of a new culture, Paul presupposes and demands an act of separation: the spirit differs from the letter. This act of division, of posing the difference between the physically present script and the unseen, is a lesson that itself has turned into the form of a commandment, the letter of law. The question "how is one to read?" henceforth no longer doubts the existence of this separation, but asks for the rules of its performance.

Early readers, following Paul's example, outline already different models for this production of meaning. Origin, for example, parallels the distinction between a literal and an allegorical reading with that of the body and the soul. The law of the letter, gaining its physical substance, is contrasted with the *spiritus vivificans* in Augustine's works. *Signum* and *res* rather than body and soul or spirit finally form the difference here that provides the basis of his hermeneutics. According to Augustine, the literal reading forms the "rule," the reading of the spirit (*sensus spiritualis*) the exception.[1]

Martin Luther draws upon these models. The distinction between spirit and letter takes on a central importance for him. According to Luther, the spirit is hidden in the letter, and this process of veiling determines the task of the theologian himself. He has to perform the act of division as an unfolding of the spirit from the letter, not only to reach the religious word, but to reveal the true one. While the opposition between the spirit and letter instigates the theologian's quest, the true word, the word of God, is at the same time able to undo this opposition. The recognition of the true word, and therefore the knowledge of the difference between spirit and the letter, distinguishes the theologian and the proper reader from the enthusiast or *Schwärmer*, and makes him "true" as well: "Item in Scripturis Sanctis optimum est Spiritum a litera discernere, hoc enim facit vero theologum."[2]

Luther foregrounds the discussion of spirit and the letter as a language theory that is inseparable from a concept of religion. Christianity is a religion for the reader. But his interpretation of "how is one to read?" as the question of "how is one to be a Christian or a theologian?" draws itself upon a framework of discussion that will be clearly articulated again in the period generally defined as that of German Idealism.[3]

Let us consider Johann Gottlieb Fichte. If Luther was concerned with the definition and task of the true theologian, Fichte offers for the academic year 1794-1795 his "Vorlesungen über die Bestimmung des Gelehrten." Fichte, a candidate of theology, had become well-known because of his *Versuch einer Kritik aller Offenbarung*, a book published anonymously two years earlier, and first thought of as Kant's long awaited critique of religion. Fichte had come to Jena in 1794, and his new appointment at the university was greeted with enthusiasm. Goethe in nearby Weimar speaks positively of the "boldness" and "audacity" of this choice,[4] and Schiller, a professor of history at Jena since 1789, knew Fichte's *Kritik* and was looking forward to his lectures.[5] Students crowded the auditorium.

Fichte gave two lecture series in this first year. One was based on his *Wissenschaftslehre*; the other, the already mentioned "Vorlesungen über die Bestimmung des Gelehrten," was intended as a more popular propaedeuticum. Robert Adamson describes these lectures as studies of the "effects of philosophical culture in general upon character and life."[6] The notion of philosophical "culture" as well as that of the "effect" of such a culture is problematized in Fichte's discussion, however. After an initial "Examination of Rousseau's Remarks on the Contribution of the Arts and Sciences to the Welfare of Mankind,"[7] Fichte turns his thoughts from the task of the scholar to that of his own philosophical propaedeuticum:

> A scholar should, among other information, also have a certain knowledge of philosophy. This is the point which we have reached now, and at which we have some prejudices that hinder a thorough study of philosophy; I wanted to indicate the means in general, with which one could acquire a complete knowledge [vollständige Kenntniß] of this science.[8]

To show "of what the *spirit*, in contrast to the *attachment to the letter itself [den Buchstaben überhaupt]*, consists, and what its business is especially in philosophy,"[9] becomes henceforth the task of Fichte's lectures, and turns the question of a theological reading into that of a proper philosophy. Spirit, the spirit in philosophy, is determined here in opposition to the letter, and with an image that had to evoke for his Jena students the figure of Luther himself. It may be ironic therefore, that Fichte does not mention Luther in his lectures, nor refer to theology as such, while his lectures' formal presentation on Sundays provoked the accusation of an "intended step against the public national church services."[10] Soon afterwards, Fichte will be charged with "atheism."[11]

Fichte, the orator, the writer on the revolution, stages himself as the knight of the new philosophy. The notions of "task," "definition," and "vocation" meet in Fichte's term *Bestimmung*, as he attempts to describe a scholar capable of pursuing philosophy. In three further lectures of this series, Fichte concentrates on a description of this philosophy within the dichotomy of "Ueber Geist und Buchstab," placing himself in the role of the scholar whose philosophy is now at stake.

These three lectures seem of special importance to Fichte. Shortly after their presentation, Fichte revises them in 1795, and again in 1798, into epistolary form.[12] In the lectures, Fichte enacts a dialogue with a skeptic to outline his ideas and save philosophy from its enemies. The revised letters "Ueber Geist und Buchstab" address instead a reader, thematizing the issue of reading while putting their own text forth as one to be read. To be able to deal with the spirit and the letter in philosophy (333), Fichte's propaedeutic is in need of a propaedeutic: "Before I can clarify for you [deutlich machen] what I understand as spirit in philosophy, we have to agree upon what it is that we call spirit in general [müssen wir uns darüber vereinigen, was wir überhaupt Geist nennen]" (334). This agreement on what can be called "spirit," and "spirit" *überhaupt*, can only be achieved by studying the question of reading. It is as if in the act of reading itself spirit can arise more clearly; or rather, the issue of spirit can come forth in the discussion of reading in a most pointed way: *deutlich. Deutlich machen*, making clear, and pointing at that which is already there and can offer itself to clear view, so that the agreement is not just made, but made clear, is the philosopher-correspondent's task.

Fichte approaches his scientific project with a scientific propaedeuticum, staging the difficulty of beginning with this, or any, systematic philosophy, but also the difficulty of separating the issue of finding the spirit in philosophy from the spirit's general definition. Does not the example of reading itself lead us precisely to the question, as Adamson describes it vaguely, of "philosophical culture" as well?

Fichte seems to concentrate on the effects of reading, and the question "how is one to read?" changes into the investigation of the conditions of the text's production, the genesis of the work as "human product" (336). To discover these conditions, Fichte studies the properties of the text itself that make successful reading possible. Paradoxically, however, these properties are only open to description if tested by the reader. The reading's effect, the text's effect on the reader, is a successful or unsuccessful engagement with the book. This effect becomes evidence itself; the letter read establishes thereby what kind of letter is at stake.

Fichte tells two anecdotes. The first one refers to the reader's own past experience:

You probably remember the complaints that you have made when reading a certain book which was praised highly by some people. You could not read yourself into it [Sie konnten sich in desselbe nicht hinein lesen]. You had it placed before you, and your eyes were fastened on it; but, as often as you reflected upon yourself, you found yourself far away from the book; every one of your attacks on its content, on that content's course, slid off [gleitete ab], and as often as you believed you had grasped the unyielding [spröden] spirit, it slipped out of your hands [entschlüpfte er Ihnen unter den Händen]. It was necessary for you to remind yourself, again and again, that you wanted to study this book, that you had to study it; and it took the often repeated thought [Vorstellung] of its usefulness, and its educational impact [Belehrung], that you have expected from it, to stand the continued resistance; until you were finally persuaded by other reasons that you could leave it as well unread, and that even the spoliation [Ausbeute] could only be a small one, and not worth the effort. (334)

Fichte calls upon the reader's memory twice. While the anecdote itself is remembered, memory reappears as an issue in this described reading event. To be able to continue with his reading, the reader has to recall his own intention of doing so.

The book in question, while of excellent reputation, seems to split curiously into an inside and an outside. Reading encounters the physicality of the object in more ways than one. It seems possible to fix the eyes on the surface image, but impossible to attack the content, and study the progress of the argument. The metaphors of warfare are often used in Fichte's lectures to stress the violence implicit in his rescuing efforts for the subject of philosophy; they are matched in the present description with the image of the impenetrable mirror. It is indeed reflection, or rather, the reader's reflection upon himself, that issues forth the slippery movement, the attack's gliding away. The answer to the question of what the spirit could be *über-haupt*, is frustrated by the disappearance of its subject, moving in the opposite direction: *unter den Händen*. The attack on the content is paralleled by the attempt to grasp the text's spirit. Eyes and hands are used in vain, they can neither penetrate a surface, nor hold on to what seems to be unstable and moving away.

The process of reflection and the movement of grasping are attacks that deal with different subjects. Reflection is here described as self-reflexive; the grasp, on the other hand, tries to hold on to the spirit of the book. This interrelatedness of self and other, the reader and his text, becomes more complicated in the continuation of this chronicle of defeat. The reader has to remind himself of his intention of reading to suffer the text's resistance. Intention and resistance cooperate to perform a split in the reader. He is both the tactical warrior, and his own voyeur who tells him of his task and of his duty, which is, as we learn, that of putting the book and its lesson to use.

Reading here seems necessary because the book is said to promise a didactic message. The peculiar educational effort of reading results, however, in a split of the book's integrity; while its text becomes a deceptive mirror and inconquerably deep, the reader attempts to reflect himself in the text and to reflect upon himself in regard to the text. He tries to read and has to think about his action. This characterizes finally the reading process's movement of attack followed by resistance as a series of initiations and interruptions: "again and again."

Fichte is reluctant to blame this disruptive movement on the reader. The reader is innocent, tempted by the book and its reputation, and thwarted by its text despite all efforts. Mirroring himself in the text, not even narcissistic pleasure seems possible. The "union" which Fichte intended to achieve as the agreement on the definition of "spirit" — "müssen wir uns vereinigen, was wir überhaupt Geist nennen" — is one that cannot come to pass by this seduction. To contrast this failure of reading with another, successful attempt, Fichte introduces the notion of *Stimmung*, a musical tuning, used to describe an atmosphere or a state of mind. It is another book, another text that can produce a mood in the reader which cannot be described otherwise than as a tuning by the text. An agreement between book and reader, as this specific attunement of spirits, may be closer in the second example:

> The mood in which you found yourself while reading other, not less thorough writings, encouraged you to form a more favorable opinion of yourself. You felt attracted to, and captivated by them; there was no need to remind you of your resolution to study the book, and the advantage, that you had hoped to

gain from the study of it. In a reading, which alone had filled your mind [Geist] entirely, you did not have to look for a purpose [Zweck] outside of it, and only this cost you, to tear yourself away from it, when some other business called you away. Perhaps you were often in a similar situation as a certain French woman. In the hour in which the court ball opened, she was reading the new *Héloise*. It was announced to her that the carriage was ready, but it was still too early to make the trip to court. Two hours later, when she was reminded again, there was still time enough; and two hours later still, she thought it was too late. She read the whole night through and, for this time, sacrificed the ball. (334-335)

With his example of the French woman, Fichte refers to an anecdote recounted by the author of the *Nouvelle Héloise* in his *Confessions*.[13] Rousseau gives this woman the pseudonym of "la princesse de Talmont" (547), because he does not know her name; the story itself had been told to him as a comment to the reception of his works. For him, it produces a flattery beyond words: "I was reassured by an event that in itself alone has flattered me more than all the compliments that one has given me for my work" (547). Rousseau expresses his desire to meet this woman, to assure himself of the truth of this story, and of an evidence for his own theory of reading: "I always thought that one could not take such a vivid interest in the *Héloise* without having that sixth sense, that moral sense which so few hearts seem to have, and without which nobody would be able to perceive mine" (547). For Rousseau, reading properly, with that "vivid interest," is an act unthinkable without the sentiments of the morals that are placed in the heart. His theory of this proper reading includes the answer to the question of why precisely women seem to like his work. They believe in the truth of Rousseau's story, but also that this story is his very own, that he himself is no other than the "hero of this novel" (457).

These questions of truth—that of Rousseau's theory of reception and of women, or the women's theory of the status of Rousseau's book—are answered in Fichte's text with his concept of *Stimmung*. Placed within contrasting examples of reading, the metaphors of surface and depth, the notions of reading and memory, are highlighted and put in different positions. Instead of a spoliation which has to be relinquished, the desirable reading may offer gain, a gain great enough to sacrifice other amusements or the business of the outside world.

The inside and outside no longer seem characterized by the surface and depth of the book, but by the contrast of book and world. The reader, on the other hand, needs another, different person to remind her of her reading; but to recall the duties of the outside world rather than the usefulness of the present text.   Time, stretching itself in the first example as a repetitive series of interruptions, seems now to contract in reading, to defy the measurement of a time "outside."

Paradoxically, the usefulness of duty and business coincides with the amusement of the ball. Memory comes here from the outside and reminds the reader of the world beyond the book. It takes the form of the servant calling upon the mistress, and not the master calling upon his delinquent double whose reading has gone astray. The reminders interrupt a reading that opposes memory itself, as forgetting. Fichte draws his conclusion:

> This is the way of books, this is the way of other products of art as well as nature. One leaves us cold and without interest, or even repels us; the other draws us closer, invites us to dwell in its contemplation, and to forget ourselves in it. (335)

Successful reading offers the reflection of the self as a reflection of the book, independent of its genre. Fichte makes this explicit, not only by these examples: there are many people, he indicates, who would prefer to reason with Voltaire or polemicize with Lessing, than read Gellert's epistolary novel.

Fichte's examples of reading clearly go beyond statements of readability. In his further explication of the anecdote, the reputation of the first book was easily revised; not only by Fichte's reader who had problems reading it, but also by others who changed their minds about the book's value. The second example, however, offers an engagement between reader and text that forms a moment of intimacy beyond common worries of time and place. There is no need to be concerned about the reputation of the text: reading it is almost literally a timeless process in which the reading situation itself speaks for and as the book's content. But what is it in this book that would call for such a bond and bonding between the reader and the text, independent of the question of the reader's guilt or the book's genre?

Another question of "genre" may be of importance here. The intimate relationship between reader and text receives a model already indicated by Rousseau. In his *Confessions*, it is the female reader who enjoys the text while thinking of the author as its hero. In Fichte, the examples are gendered as well. If the first reader is rebuked by a text that only seemingly offers education, the French woman, taking the association of the seductress as well as the role of the reader, proceeds to find this bond previously described as a special mood or tuning, *Stimmung*, and later as the forgetting of the self.

This forgetting of the self corresponds to the calling to life of the text. In taking the examples of reading as a study of the conditions of the production of a work of art, Fichte can phrase his question as follows: "How does a human product receive that enlivening power, and whence does the spirited [geistvolle] artist take the secret to breathe it into his product?" (336) In describing the difference between the two books as either the lack or presence of an enlivening force that may be called spirit, Fichte turns the *Vereinigung* as the agreement on the term's definition to the agreement or *Stimmung* produced in reading. At the same time, the anonymous author becomes an artist who owns this spirit, and can convey it with his text. Neither Rousseau's nor Gellert's styles, nor the books' genres, nor their praised contents are focused upon. As with Rousseau, there is an author behind the text who enters into the reading relationship. But Fichte goes further than Rousseau's brief notes. A consideration of the lecture transcript can help to trace another story behind Fichte's examples of reading. The discussion in the first lecture does not quite correspond to that of the first letter of Fichte's later version. In the earlier version, Fichte discusses the artist and his creation of sculpture; he touches this issue only briefly in the third letter of the later version of his text.[14] As a true artist, Fichte names Pygmalion. He differs from the artisan who would simply like to imitate the artist's art, and would only take art's measure. The breath of life, described as the enlivening force in the essay, differs from the artisan's account of measures and is, quite literally, no business of this sort. Instead of taking measure, Pygmalion has his love for Galatea, a power that turns the marble sculpture into a living being with whom, again, a union could be achieved.[15]

Who is the artist and what is the sculpture in the example of reading? And how is his example of sexual attraction translated into the gendered desire for the text? The enlivened text had effected the withdrawal of the French woman from the world, and fixed her, seemingly motionless, to her place. At the same time, it seems unclear whether it is the text which is the author's artistic product, or the reader whose reaction and transformation Fichte made us witness. Fichte proceeds with his argument, however, by turning to the second example first:

> So much is clear, that work of the first kind would inspire, animate, strengthen our sense for its object; that such a work would not only give us the object of our spiritual occupation, but, at the same time, the talent to occupy ourselves with it. It would not only present us with the gift, but also with the hand to grasp it. It would create the drama and the audience at the same time, and, as the living force in the universe, communicate with the same breath motion and organization to the dead substance, and spiritual life to the organized one: because, on the other hand, a product of the latter class arrests and hinders especially that sense, which one would need to one's enjoyment, and tires and kills because of the continued resistance; so that the mechanism of the spirit, run down in every minute, has to be reconstructed again, because of a new pressure of the mainspring in it, namely the absolute self-reliant action [Selbstthätigkeit], only to be interrupted again in the next moment. (336)

The life and death of the reader's inner organism are at stake, a mechanism that is kept alive by insisting not on the author's power, but on the reader's *Selbstthätigkeit*. The proper effect of reading is not just to receive a message or a didactic lesson, but to turn, as reader, into an author. Here, then, Fichte's *Bestimmung* of the reader answers his *Bestimmung* of the scholar and philosopher. To turn the difference author/reader into the agreement of author/author is a true union — *Vereinigung* — carried by *Stimmung*, and made possible by the imagination:

> In the first case our reason thinks, or our imagination composes on its own, and together with the artist, and just as he wants it, and we do not give it any orders; the appropriate terms, or the intended characters form themselves and produce an order before our spiritual eye, and we do not believe we had even touched them with our hands. (336)

Eye and hand reappear in this description. The eye is, however, replaced by the inner eye, and hands are no longer necessary. The enlivening force of the product, the spirit itself, forms its own order; spiritual becomes, moreover, the attribute of the inner or invisible eye.

Thinking and composing poetically, *denken* and *dichten*, draw close together here as does reason and imagination, *Verstand* and *Einbildungskraft*. The imaginary position before one's spiritual eye marks the order common to both in reading. It may only be necessary to indicate here that the structure of this dramatic *Vorstellung*, here discussed in regard to artistic production, is central in Fichte's various versions of the *Wissenschaftslehre* as well, in which he attempts to capture the establishment, *Setzung*, of the Self, *Ich*, via that of the Other, *Nicht-Ich*. The close relationship between "Geist und Buchstab" and the project of the *Wissenschaftslehre* insists on the concerns of aesthetics as central ones for philosophy. Fichte's sketch of reading dramatizes, moreover, this constitution of the self: it forgets itself and is reminded of its existence; it hopes for a reading as an imaginary union that poses the self while questioning the boundaries of its identity. Not the effect of the text, but the exchange of effect, *Wechselwirkung*, between the author and the reader, establishes the author as artist and the reader as artist and blurs the boundaries of their places as the subject and the object.

This is the issue, and between them is the issue of philosophy. Fichte clarifies it in his *Sonnenklarer Bericht*, written shortly after "Geist und Buchstab."[16] Author and reader enter into a dialogue here; this time not to decide upon a common definition of spirit, but on the difference between the self and the reality outside of it. "Are you thinking of your reading, observing, listening, or speaking of the object, while engaged in this act itself?" the author asks. "Not at all," the reader answers.

> In this case, I do not think at all about myself; I forget myself entirely in the book, in the object, in the conversation. Therefore, one may well say: *I am included therein [Ich sey drin begriffen]*; also: I am *immersed* in it.

The author answers:

> And this only, to remember it in passing, — only more so, if your consciousness of the object was more intense, fuller, and more animated. That half-consciousness, that dreamlike and diverted consciousness, that inattentiveness and thoughtlessness, that has become a character trace of our age, and the most powerful hindrance to a thorough philosophy, is just this state in which one does not *throw* oneself completely *into* the object, bury and forget oneself in it; but wavers, and quivers between it and oneself. (337-338)

The intimate union, exemplified in the French woman's reading of the *Héloise*, is a subject's inclusion and forgetting in the text that marks the desired relationship of the philosopher to his subject. Only in this way, we have to learn, the true spirit in philosophy may appear for us to agree upon.[17]

Fichte, the scholar and philosopher, sees it as his task to tell about philosophy, to write down version after version of his scientific system, the *Wissenschaftslehre*, ceasing finally to prepare them for publication, depending on oral performance and his own voice only, a temporary solution, but one that seeks a distance from the printed page. He works on new abstractions while despairing over that proper word that would be able to formulate it correctly, do away with the separation of the subject and its object that prevents the spirit's rise.[18] To be able to let the spirit come forth, Fichte has to proceed while going back to that original situation, the original leap (*Ursprung*) that marks the state of philosophy:

> Originally, *the* philosophy does not have any letters, but it is pure spirit, and there was the task of capturing this spirit and putting it forth [aufzustellen]. How would people have decided to philosophize, if for instance philosophy would have been cut off precisely from all proper knowledge [Erkenntniß]?[19]

This "original" state of philosophy devises therefore the need of the propaedeuticum, of moving back to some earlier, more fundamental question that already presupposes philosophizing itself. Fichte's letters "Ueber Geist und Buchstab" were doomed not just to be a propaedeuticum, but the propaedeuticum of a propaedeuticum, preparing a philosophy that cannot be formulated, or perhaps not be formulated yet, while presupposing its existence in its introduction.

Philosophizing, while waiting for philosophy to articulate itself, Fichte rewrites the theological tradition of the spirit and the letter as one in which the spirit in philosophy would undo the letter, so that philosophy could become that "pure spirit" itself. This spirit, as the secularized word of God, guides Fichte's words, escapes his articulation, and points forward in and as a movement of initiation and interruption that marks a failed reading but also describes the fate of the Romantic project itself. This may elucidate the full irony of Fichte's Sunday lectures. It also comments on the significance of a rhetorical endeavor about which Fichte may have despaired, but which has become of so much interest for literary critics today.

Notes

The present paper is part of a larger project, *"Geistersprache*: Philosophical and Literary Discourse in the Late Eighteenth Century." I would like to thank the American Council of Learned Societies for its support.

1 For a concise history of the early tradition of the opposition of "spirit" and "letter," see G. Ebeling, "Geist und Buchstabe," in *Die Religion in Geschichte und Gegenwart*, I-VI, eds. Kurt Galling, Hans von Campenhausen, Erich Dinkler, Gerhard Gloege and Knud E. Logstrup (Tübingen: J. C. B. Mohr, 1957-65), 1290-1296.

2 Martin Luther, *Werke. Kritische Gesamtausgabe*, I-XXXXXVIII (Weimar: Böhlau, 1883-1948), XXXXXV I 1, 4, 25-26; quoted after Werner Führer, *Das Wort Gottes in Luthers Theologie* (Göttingen: Vandenhoek & Ruprecht, 1984), 24. For a general outline of Luther's philosophy of language, see Peter Meinhold, *Luthers Sprachphilosophie* (Berlin: Lutherisches Verlagshaus, 1958).

3 See, for example, Rudolf Malter, *Das reformatorische Denken und die Philosophie: Luthers Entwurf einer transzendental-praktischen Metaphysik* (Bonn: Bouvier Herbert Grundmann, 1980), 202, 365-366 n. 3 and 4.

4 Quoted from the "Tag- und Jahreshefte" by Elisabeth Winkelmann, "Schiller und Fichte," *Zeitschrift für Geschichte der Erziehung und des Unterrichts* 24 (1934): 177-248, esp. 186.

5 See Winkelmann, 189.

6 Robert Adamson, *Fichte* (1903, rpt. Freeport, N.Y.: Books of Libraries Press, 1969), 45. The catalogue for the fall term 1794/95 lists three lectures: 1. philosophiam theoreticam specialem; 2. philosphiam practicam specialem; 3. the continuation of de officiis eruditorum; see Johann Gottlieb Fichte, *Gesamtausgabe der bayrischen Akademie der Wissenschaften*, I-IV, eds. Reinhard Lauth et al. (Stuttgart: Fromman, 1962–), III, 2, 347n.

7 "Prüfung der Rousseauschen Behauptungen über den Einfluß der Künste und Wissenschaften auf das Wohl der Menschheit." This lecture is published as number five in the *GA* I, 3, 59-68. Only five lectures of this series are known and published; see Reinhard Lauth, "Einleitung," in Johann Gottlieb

Fichte, *Von den Pflichten der Gelehrten: Jenaer Vorlesungen 1794/95* (Hamburg: Felix Meiner, 1971), VII-LXVI; esp. XIX, XXVI-XXVIII. The translations of Fichte's texts are mine.

8 Johann Gottlieb Fichte [Fichte über den Hauptgedankengang, der von den ersten fünf Vorlesungen zu den folgenden noch vorhandenen leitete], *Von den Pflichten der Gelehrten*, 55. See also the beginning of the first lecture "Ueber den Unterschied des Geistes, u. des Buchstabens in der Philosophie," *GA* II, 8, 315.

9 Fichte, "Schlußwort der Vorlesung über die Bestimmung des Gelehrten," *Von den Pflichten der Gelehrten*, 89. This "Schlußwort" differs from the "Schlußwort der Vorlesungen," *GA* II, 3, 345-353.

10 Official statement of the Jena Konsistorium (November 16, 1794) and Weimar Oberkonsistorium (November 18, 1794); quoted in Lauth, XX. Fichte quotes Luther in his other writings, of course; see for example his *Beitrag zur Berichtigung der Urteile des Publikums über die französische Revolution*, published in the previous year, which names Jesus, Luther, and Kant as the holy patrons of freedom. Fichte, *Sämmtliche Werke*, I-VIII, ed. Immanuel Hermann Fichte (Berlin: Veit und Comp., 1845-1846), IV, 104.

11 See the account of this charge, and the publication of the material related to the charge, in *GA* I, 6. Duke Karl August von Sachsen-Weimar encouraged Fichte's resignation from his position in Jena in 1799.

12 For a history of the revisions of Fichte's essay, see Günter Schulz, "Die erste Fassung von Fichtes Abhandlung 'Über Geist und Buchstab in der Philosophie,'" *Goethe. Neue Folge des Jahrbuchs der Goethe-Gesellschaft* 17 (1955): 114-141. "Ueber Geist und Buchstab" was first published in the *Philosophisches Journal einer Gesellschaft deutscher Gelehrten* IX (1798) which appeared in 1800. I am quoting Fichte's essay from the *GA* I, 6, 333-361. Page references appear in the text after the quotations.

13 Jean-Jacques Rousseau, *Les Confessions. Oeuvres complètes*, I-IV (Paris: Gallimard, 1959-1969), I, 547-548. The translation of Rousseau's text is mine.

14 Compare *GA* II, 3, 321, and *GA* I, 6, 359-360.

15 With his reference to Pygmalion, Fichte remains, of course, within the context of Rousseau's works that include a brief theatrical scene of Pygmalion and Galathée.

16 Fichte, "Sonnenklarer Bericht über das Wesen der neuesten Philosophie" (Berlin: Realschulbuchhandlung, 1801). The text is quoted here from *SW* I, 2, 323-420. Page references appear after the quotations in the text.

17 Fichte's concept of reading seems to prefigure the fate of his own essay "Ueber Geist und Buchstab." In 1795, he submitted it in its first version to Friedrich Schiller's journal *Die Horen.* Schiller rejected the essay, and the correspondence between Schiller and Fichte following this rejection is very much a reflection on proper or improper reading (and philosophical writing). See *GA* III, 2, 227-368. Schiller's "Über die ästhetische Erziehung des Menschen" seems to have influenced Fichte's terminology as well as his concept of the human being, as described in "Geist und Buchstab." Schiller's essay on aesthetic education was published in the *Horen* in 1795.

18 My reading parallels here John Sallis's reading of Fichte's *Wissenschaftslehre* in *Spacings — of Reason and Imagination in Texts of Kant, Fichte, Hegel* (Chicago: University of Chicago Press, 1987), 23-66.

19 Letter to Friedrich Schiller, June 27, 1795. *GA* III, 2, 336.

PART II

THE DIMENSIONS OF MODERNITY

Intransitive Parody
and the Trap of Reading
in Turn-of-the-Century German Prose

Benjamin Bennett
University of Virginia

1

One of the most striking stylistic features of "Bahnwärter Thiel" is the shift in tense, from the conventional narrative past to the present, and then back again, at the point where Tobias is struck by the train.

> Thiel keuchte; er mußte sich festhalten, um nicht umzusinken wie ein gefällter Stier. Wahrhaftig, man winkt ihm — "Nein!"
> Ein Aufschrei zerreißt die Luft . . .

And then, after two pages of nothing but present tense:

> Thiel begleitet den Zug [the procession carrying Tobias] bis an die Grenze seines Reviers . . . Er meint sich zu erwecken; denn es wird ein Traum sein, wie der gestern, sagt er sich. — Vergebens. — Mehr taumelnd als laufend erreichte er sein Häuschen. Drinnen fiel er auf die Erde, das Gesicht voran. (pp. 58, 60)

Evidently this change of tense operates as a signal to the reader. But what kind of signal, and a signal for what?

I dismiss out of hand the idea that the present tense creates a more intense or immediate relation between the reader and a supposed "experience" of the narrated world, the idea that the present tense reflects back at us a sudden increase in our emotional involvement with the fiction. Present-tense narration is not, of itself, any more immediate or intense or vivid than past-tense narration, especially where it operates as a clear *signal* to the reader, which asks the reader to stop and reflect upon his situation. In fact, I propose to question the whole idea of intensity or immediacy in reading, the whole idea of a *linear* reading of fictional narrative, the idea of a kind of sympathy or resonance between "Erzählzeit" and "erzählte Zeit," mediated by the supposed cumulative linearity of our intellectual consumption of the text. I question the whole idea that reading, for the reader, is a discriminable and in some ways distinctly privileged type of *experience*, the idea that reading is a doubling and a complication of experience, indeed a multiplication—thus at once both a subversion and an expansion—of the reader's very ego. I thus question the whole idea of reading that is presupposed in the theoretical meditations of Henry James and Percy Lubbock, in Georges Poulet, in the systematics of, say, Lämmert and Genette, and especially in Wolfgang Iser, who asserts that reading is a kind of radically self-transformative "learning" on the reader's part. I maintain, moreover, that this questioning is not merely theoretical, but is an integral component of all three of the texts I will talk about: "Bahnwärter Thiel," the "Reitergeschichte" and "Der Tod in Venedig." These texts *themselves* undermine the "phenomenological approach" to them.

But how are we to make sense of the shift in tenses we began with? If we read very carefully, we will perhaps associate that shift with the exercise of self-control on Thiel's part. The present tense enters at just the moment when Thiel must get hold of himself ("sich festhalten") in order not to collapse under the shock of what he has just seen; the past tense is reëstablished at just the moment when he again loses control, stumbles blindly into his shack and collapses on the floor. This suggestion can be developed easily enough. The present tense, we might continue, signals the momentary possibility of *contact* between Thiel and the reader. Thiel is otherwise held up for our inspection as a markedly narrow character, by contrast with the broad and distanced character we put on as readers. But now, in his exercise of self-control, Thiel achieves a kind of reader's distance from his own fate, which he now actually confronts for the first time. For a few moments, his mental situation becomes analogous to ours, as readers, and the possibility of contact, of something like identification, arises, which is reflected in the present tense. Thiel, so to speak, for a short time pulls himself up out of the restrictive narrative past, and into our own immediate present, by becoming a kind of reader with respect to himself.

I think this idea has some merit, but it must be modified by the recognition that that present-tense passage also contains a very clear and very uncomfortable *image* of the process of reading. The train approaches, and Tobias is struck. The train stops, and the passengers, "die todbleichen, erschreckten Gesichter der Reisenden," stare out of their windows for a few moments into another world, a narrow, tragic world with which they have nothing in common, and which they misunderstand completely—"'Das arme, arme Weib,' heißt es in den Coupés, 'die arme, arme Mutter.'" Then they throw money, which ostensibly expresses sympathy but actually asserts distance. And then the train leaves. It is as if, for a moment, our reading of the story had become visible inside the fiction; for the rôle of the suddenly visible train passengers, I contend, is the rôle of the reader. *We* are cast as those passengers. What, after all, do we actually do when we read? The progress of our lives in a larger world (a world mapped by "Zugverbindungen") is interrupted, arrested, by a narrated event that catches our attention, an event that we observe from the comfort of our "Coupés," as if through windows. We perhaps even manage to feel a few real emotions, which we then take as evidence of contact with that narrated world. But then the story is over, "Die Zeit ist kostbar," and we move on.

This picture of the process of reading is clearly an *attack* on the reader—who is attacked *for* being a reader, not for anything more specific—and as such, it goes together with numerous passages in the story that parody the style of a sensational popular press. (Filling in of background, summaries of what "people" thought and said, ostentatiously "human" touches, concerning Thiel and the neighborhood children for example, etc.) After the faces in the train windows are described, we read of Thiel: "Was geht's ihn an?

Er hat sich nie um den Inhalt dieser Polterkasten gekümmert."
"Der Inhalt dieser Polterkasten," "the contents of these noisy
boxes": that means us, the readers. The idea of reading as a
broadening of our experience, as a multiplication of our ego, as the
achievement of contact with a world that is otherwise strictly external to our own: this idea of reading is *suggested* in the long present-
tense passage, but is also *unmasked* as a mere pose. The passage
thus becomes a parody of itself, a parody without an object, what I
will later call an "intransitive parody." And a similar parodistic
move is present in the text's powerful poetic descriptions of natural
scenes, descriptions that obviously engage, in us, conventional aesthetic sensibilities from which the characters in the fiction, however, especially Thiel, are specifically (and brusquely) dissociated.
(Thiel walks through the compellingly described forest "ohne
aufzublicken"; and when he finally does look up, his only response
is to think, "Ein furchtbares Wetter" [pp. 44-5].) Thiel dissociates
himself from us in every possible way; he even refuses to entrust his
child's smashed body to the train that represents us.

Reading "Bahnwärter Thiel," therefore, is not a process of liberation or self-multiplication, but has become a trap for us. In the
very process of recognizing how mistaken the passengers are in
their view of the story's situation — "die arme, arme Mutter" — we
are compelled by analogy to question the validity of our view of
that situation, the genuineness of our contact with it, as well — or
rather, we are compelled to recognize that the very concept of
"validity" or "contact" has no real meaning in this context to begin
with. The assumption that reading fiction is somehow an expansion of our personal horizons here leads us into a trap, leads to an
absurdity, leads to the recognition that reading is in truth only a
narrowing of our horizons, like the popular press, that reading is
not a form of contact with the external, but merely a delusive exercise of our own aesthetic preconceptions, a staring out through
windows that are in truth nothing but mirrors. And there is no way
for us to avoid this trap. For by the time we recognize what this
text shows us — indeed, *in order* to recognize it — we have *already*

adopted the conventional reading posture that is unmasked in the image of the train passengers, "der Inhalt dieser Polterkasten."

This approach to "Bahnwärter Thiel," however, creates a number of problems. The question arises: why do we read the novella in the first place? what do we get from it? Is the text's whole function here merely to destroy itself as an object of reading? And this question is related to the question of the *linearity* of the process of reading, which I began by doubting. Does the idea of a "trap" of reading, which must be first prepared and then sprung, not imply at least the analogy of a linear temporal process? If reading, as I have suggested, "is" something other than a cumulative linear process in time, then how can the operation of a "trap" in the text have any significance, indeed any effective existence, whatever? I will return to this question shortly from another angle.

2

There is also a problem in my use, and what I contend is Hauptmann's use, of a *visual* metaphor for reading. The train passengers become mirror images of the reader by looking (and imagining they see) into Thiel's existence and experience. The trouble is that in order for this mirroring (another visual metaphor) to become effective, it appears necessary that *the reader* "see" into the fictional world after all, that we not only "see" the train and its passengers, but also see *through* them, apprehend them not only as image, but also as experience, as an experience that resonates significantly with our own immediate experience as readers. Or to look at the same problem more generally, if the trap of reading, for us, takes the form of a sudden recognition of *inadequacy* in our relation to the fictional world, then precisely this recognition endows that world with an experiential *integrity* (our apprehension is inadequate with respect to *what?*) that might, after all, eventually admit an adequate relation on our part—indeed does already admit the adequacy of our sense of exclusion. Or if we insist that the trap of reading enforces, in us, not merely a recognition of inadequacy, but a radical criticism of the very idea of adequacy, we have still only succeeded in occupying the untenable position of limitless hermeneutic relativism.

But are we speaking here of an inconsistency in the present argument, or of a complication in the trap of reading itself? The point, it seems to me, is that in responding to the trap, we find that we inevitably *continue* to expose ourselves to it. The discrediting of the visual metaphor for reading, again, is accomplished only by way of yet another visual metaphor; any "recognition" afforded us by the springing of the trap thus turns out to be only another form of the delusion that had lured us into the trap to begin with. The trap, that is, is never actually sprung—never sprung once and for all, so that we can say we now *know* what the trap has to teach us—but rather is always only still about to be sprung. The springing of the trap is thus deferred interminably into the future—and in fact interminably into the past as well, if we reflect that the trap is inevitable (thus in effect already sprung) as soon as we begin to read the text, or indeed as soon as we read any comparable text, or indeed as soon as we become the kind of creature who *might* read such a text.

Therefore, while the trap of reading, at least in "Bahnwärter Thiel," does occupy a definite place—as it were, a visible place—in the text, it also lacks entirely the quality of an *event* that might assume the relation "before" or "after" to other events; it cannot occupy a particular point in any experienced temporal continuum whatever. (And precisely the analogy between places in the text and events in the actual experience of the reader, it seems to me, is crucial in any form of the Iserian "phenomenological approach.") In the very process of happening to us as we read, the trap of reading thus explodes not only certain superficial preconceptions about reading, but also the very idea of an event in experience. It thus in the end explodes the possibility of its own operation as a trap, and so (by this paradox) directs our attention toward a mechanics of entrapment in reading that is located on a level incommensurately different from the one defined by the question of adequacy in the communication of experience, a level of inquiry on which the question of what reading "is" is itself called into ques-

tion. In any case, we must *beware* of entanglement in misleading
metaphors, but we cannot *avoid* such entanglement.
    Let us conclude by looking at one further trap-like structure in
"Bahnwärter Thiel," a structure that engages precisely the idea of
the visual metaphor as applied to reading. When Thiel arrives at
his post, after having discovered Lene in the act of abusing Tobias,
we read:

> Die Strecke schnitt rechts und links gradlinig in den unabsehbaren grünen
> Forst hinein; zu ihren beiden Seiten stauten die Nadelmassen gleichsam
> zurück, zwischen sich eine Gasse frei lassend, die der rötlichbraune, kiesbe-
> streute Bahndamm ausfüllte.   Die schwarzen, parallellaufenden Geleise
> darauf glichen in ihrer Gesamtheit einer ungeheuren eisernen Netzmasche,
> deren schmale Strähne sich im äußersten Süden und Norden in einem
> Punkte des Horizontes zusammenzogen. (pp. 48-9)

Since the two tracks, in each direction, do appear to converge at a
point, the idea of an iron mesh—two strands of iron joined at both
ends but separated in the middle—is logically plausible. But this
idea is presented in the form of a visual image, which it *cannot be
literally*, since no actual observer could ever see simultaneously
both the north and the south points of convergence. The iron
mesh is unquestionably there, and we unquestionably do in a sense
see it, as readers, even while recognizing, at the same time, that it
cannot be seen. Thus *we* are trapped—caught in a "mesh" of our
own—in a situation that makes both perfect sense and perfect
nonsense, and so calls into question the very idea of making sense
(or experiencing by the senses) in our reading.
    Or perhaps the adherent of a phenomenological approach would
respond: "Even if we are thus trapped for a moment, the truth
must soon dawn upon us: that our seeing of the unseeable is not
really a trap after all, but a token of our transcendence, as readers,
of the limited empirical ego, the token of a kind of temporary
quasi-divinity that reading affords us. God, after all, does see the
whole of the iron mesh." And it is as if the text itself were deliberately making a mockery of *this* possibility when, later, Tobias spies
a squirrel and asks, "Vater, ist das der liebe Gott?" (p. 57). For the
squirrel, with eyes on the sides of its head, perhaps *can* see both

north and south at the same time. This is what happens, in "Bahnwärter Thiel," to the idea of reading as a quasi-divine transcendence of our particular ego and condition; at every possible point, the text reduces it to the absurd. Nor is this relation between the reader and the squirrel as utterly far-fetched as it might seem at first glance. Given our aesthetic enjoyment of nature in a world where the real humans (the story's characters) are enmeshed in a blind struggle to subsist, what *are* we really, as readers, if not a species of idyllically imagined woodland creature?

3

Hofmannsthal's "Reitergeschichte" provides, at the very least, a marked stylistic contrast to "Bahnwärter Thiel." But in fact there are strong points of similarity between the two texts. The combination of deferred sexual desire and indirect discourse, for example, in Thiel's encounter with Lene after he finds her beating Tobias, is matched almost exactly in Anton Lerch's encounter with Vuic. And I maintain that the assault upon the idea of reading as an expansion of our experiential horizons is also present in the "Reitergeschichte," perhaps on a level more deeply submerged than in Hauptmann, but in a form no less profound and radical.

The central character of the "Reitergeschichte," Anton Lerch, is not the focus of attention at the beginning of the story. Not until after the ride through Milan, not until after he sees a familiar female face in the window of the yellow house, does he become the center of our quasi-experience as readers. Not, in other words, until after *he himself becomes a kind of reader*, dreaming himself into a realistically founded but increasingly fantastic "Zivilatmosphäre," just as we, in reading, might be considered to be dreaming our way into a realistically founded but increasingly fantasmal "kavalleristische Atmosphäre." The symmetry here is exact. Given the central thematic opposition, in the story, between the military and the civilian, it must occur to us that our reading of fiction, here and now, is a civilian act, characterized by freedom and leisure. And if reading were in truth a relaxation of the limits of our ego, a transcending of its boundaries, then in this particular case, we should expect that transcending to operate in the direction of the military. Not, of course, in the sense that our civilian experience would be *replaced* by a military experience; the whole point of reading (supposedly) is that the multiple components of our experience continue to exist side by side, each affording us a perspective upon, an enjoyment of, a learning from, the other.

And this transcending of the boundary between military and civilian seems to be exactly the structure of Anton Lerch's experience:

> der Wachtmeister [lebte sich] immer mehr in das Zimmer mit den Mahago-nimöbeln und den Basilikumtöpfen hinein und zugleich in eine Zivilatmo-sphäre, durch welche doch das Kriegsmäßige durchschimmerte, eine Atmo-sphäre von Behaglichkeit und angenehmer Gewalttätigkeit ohne Dienstver-hältnis, eine Existenz in Hausschuhen, den Korb des Säbels durch die linke Tasche des Schlafrockes durchgesteckt. (p. 42)

But does this mean that our reading has now become a true libera-tion for us? I contend, on the contrary, that it has become a trap. Our reading, which at first appears to extend the range of our experience, now suddenly brings us back face to face (in Anton Lerch) with nothing but a mirror image of *ourselves as readers*, an image that shares with the actual image in a mirror even the quality of symmetrical reversal. Anton Lerch's "reading" moves in the opposite direction from ours, toward the civilian, and so is, as it were, an unreading of our reading of the story, places us in the position of both the subject and the object of reading, involves us therefore in a reading that now has no object whatever beyond the narrow, self-indulgent self that is doing the reading.

Nor should it surprise us unduly that the act of reading is thus mirrored here, for the story as a whole is made of mirror-like repe-titions. The ride through Milan is repeated in the ride through the dirty village, Vuic is repeated in the woman who later crosses in front of Lerch's horse, the muzzle of the enemy officer's pistol is repeated in Baron Rofrano's pistol; the stout man who becomes the focus of Lerch's dreaming is actually seen in a mirror; and the climax of the story is Lerch's meeting himself (a self-meeting we also enact, as readers) at the bridge. The story is made of nothing but mirrors, mirrors that reflect in the end nothing but the process of mirroring, and so show back to us, over and over, the exclusively self-referred futility of the process of reading. "Handpferde auslassen!" is the command that brings the story to its close. And we too are given that command, in our recognition that we bring away no "Beute," no gain, no learning, no self-development or self-renewal, from the process of reading.

The operation of the trap of reading, the inevitable recognition of *futility* that belongs to the process of reading, is represented with minute exactness in the structure of the "Reitergeschichte." The long and wonderful sentence that describes the squadron's ride through Milan is an irresistibly readable piece of prose, a kind of invitation to the dance of reading.

> Unter dem Geläute der Mittagsglocken, der Generalmarsch von den vier Trompeten hinaufgeschmettert in den stählern funkelnden Himmel, an tausend Fenstern hinklirrend und zurückgeblitzt auf achtundsiebzig Kürasse, achtundsiebzig aufgestemmte nackte Klingen; Straße rechts, Straße links, wie ein aufgewühlter Ameishaufen sich füllend mit staunenden Gesichtern; fluchende und erbleichende Gestalten hinter Haustoren verschwindend, verschlafene Fenster aufgerissen von den entblößten Armen schöner Unbekannter; vorbei an Santo Babila, an San Fedele, an San Carlo, am weltberühmten marmornen Dom, an San Satiro, San Giorgio, San Lorenzo, San Eustorgio; deren uralte Erztore alle sich auftuend und unter Kerzenschein und Weihrauchqualm silberne Heilige und brokatgekleidete strahlenäugige Frauen hervorwinkend; aus tausend Dachkammern, dunklen Torbogen, niedrigen Butiken Schüsse zu gewärtigen, und immer wieder nur halbwüchsige Mädchen und Buben, die weißen Zähne und dunklen Haare zeigend; vom trabenden Pferde herab funkelnden Auges auf alles dies hervorblickend aus einer Larve von blutbesprengtem Staub; zur Porta Venezia hinein, zur Porta Ticinese wieder hinaus: so ritt die schöne Schwadron durch Mailand. (pp. 40-41)

What attracts us here is not merely the flow and rhythm of the language, but especially the multiplication of perspective it offers us. In reading, we are invited to occupy the position of both spectators and participants in a scene composed—by a corresponding paradox—of watchful actors (the riders) and visible spectators (the populace). For a moment (it appears) the walls of the ego are breached, the opposition of subject and object disappears, and we lead a philosophically liberated existence as it were *in* the language. Or at least this is the way we customarily account for what we imagine happens to us in reading a passage of this sort.

The very next sentence, however, marks the point at which the story begins to focus on Anton Lerch. The multiplication of perspective in reading, namely, turns out to be not a dissolution and renewal of the ego, but merely an instance of that taking of the subject as object, that self-detaching process of reflection, by which the ego constitutes and perpetuates itself in the first place. The ego is no longer joyously dismembered in the language, but rather—since that dismemberment, and that joy, are in truth only an exercise in solitary self-reflection—it is again concentrated (as in truth it always had been) into a *person*, a person who, as the fictional Anton Lerch, had actually ridden through Milan, had actually been a vessel of that miraculous watchful visibility, and a person who now, in that he becomes more and more a kind of reader in reverse, leads our consciousness in a circle that confronts us more and more clearly with our own true condition as particular, limited, unexploded, civilian persons. Reading, in other words, in the form of the ride through Milan, is itself the process that produces the *need* for reading, that sense of inescapable finitude which prompts us to seek the extraordinary, the adventurous, "das Andere" (as Hofmannsthal puts it elsewhere), the dissolution and renewal of the ego. And it is at this point, accordingly—after having been developed as a reader in reverse—that Anton Lerch notices the little village which then turns out to be a horribly parodistic *rereading* of the ride through Milan, indeed a revelation of what that ride had in truth been to begin with, the revelation that reading in truth is never anything but a rereading, the reading of a parody, of an intransitive parody, of a text that never does anything but imitate confusedly the text we had wanted it to be, that nonexistent "original" text—like Anton Lerch's dream of a "feindlicher General mit geringer Bedeckung"—at which our actual reading never arrives. And then, finally, the trap of reading is sprung, when at the end of the village, at the end of this reading, at the end of every reading, like Anton Lerch, I encounter myself—not even myself *as a reader*, which is still a generalization, a multiplication of myself—but simply, absolutely, myself, the utterly finite, undeveloped, unimproved, ungeneralized, *mortal* thing that I, inescapably, am. The ego-dismemberment of reading turns out to have been mere confusion, the joy of reading a mere concealment of my actual undeniable condition.   And that confusion and concealment, being a movement of *repression*, in the end inevitably focusses upon, and reveals, precisely the inadmissible reality it had existed for the purpose of negating.

4

The "Reitergeschichte," like "Bahnwärter Thiel," is thus an *unreadable* text. And again the question arises: what are we doing when we do read it after all? Namely, if we cannot adequately read these texts, in the sense of "reading" that is established in the tradition from, say, James to Iser, then does it not follow that our reading must here take a more active or productive form, the form of something closer to *writing*? These texts, I claim, in that they trap and in effect destroy their "reader," refuse to be anything *but* "writable" or "writerly" texts, characterized by what Roland Barthes calls the "scriptible." Barthes says: "le texte scriptible, c'est *nous en train d'écrire*." The text is not a thing produced *by* us, but *is* "us, in the process of writing."

   This formulation, and my claim, require elucidation. We must be careful, above all, about how we imagine *what* is "written" or produced by us in the process of reading. For neither in hermeneutic theory, say in Gadamer, nor in reader-response theory, and certainly not in Iser, is it ever assumed that reading is *not* a productive activity. In fact, an important goal of hermeneutic theory is to understand the historical operation of precisely the productive component of reading, while an important goal of reader-response theory is to understand the productivity of the individual reader. The key is the question of *what* we imagine to be the product of reading as an activity. From a hermeneutic point of view, that product is ordinarily the meaning, or the very identity, of the text considered as an utterance, whereas from a reader-response point of view it is the text's fictional content, which, in being productively constituted, is now contiguous with the reader's own experience, with his very self. And I think I have shown that with reference to the two texts we have looked at so far, the same question can be answered in neither of these ways. If the trap of reading operates as I have suggested, in "Bahnwärter Thiel" and the "Reitergeschichte," then it follows that the product of reading can be *nothing but* the reader's own strictly particular self. Not the historically engaged self posited by hermeneutics, not the self-developing and self-renewing self posited by reader-response theory, but rather the self in the sense that "nothing but" might be said of it, the self stripped of every attribute, every relation, stripped of everything that might be fictionalized and presented to it as an object of readerly contemplation. Anton Lerch's encounter with himself, in other words, his encounter with a thing that is *nothing but* Anton Lerch, is exactly what is enacted by us, in reading. The text, as Barthes suggests, stands in no particular experiential or revelatory relation to us, but in some sense simply *is* us.

This concept of the self, if it is a "concept" at all, is definable only by a kind of negation. Any statement (however defensible) of the form, "the self is this or that," merely names a quality, "this or that," that must be *subtracted* in order to arrive at the self I am talking about. As soon as we introduce, say, the general notion of identity as opposed to alterity, or the idea of some specific communal or interpersonal function, or of a supposed principle or structure in the process of consciousness, we have missed the point. Or if we try to visualize the self by way of our sense or image of our own selves, then the process of visualization inevitably insinuates itself into the object, and we find ourselves thinking about that self-developing readerly self which is precisely not what we mean.

And yet, the minimal, utterly particular self, which Anton Lerch encounters at the bridge, is also undeniably a part of our knowledge of life. It is that happening of the self which Goethe, for example, calls not DAIMON but ANANKE. (I say a "happening" of the self, not an "experience," for terminological reasons that are fairly clear already, and will become clearer as we go on.) It is the repeated, and repeatedly sudden and shocking knowledge of our finitude and mortality; it is the repeated, and repeatedly inescapable recognition that I am nothing but my utterly particular self, within limits so perfectly narrow and rigid as to be strictly untouchable by the inevitably generalizing operation of concepts.

But in what sense can we assert that this "happening" or "knowledge" of the self is *not* an "experience" that arises from our reading, *not* a deepening of our experience in general, *not* a "learning" of the sort Iser envisages? Or if what we are talking about is a perfectly primitive knowledge, prior to all actual experience, then how can this knowledge be regarded as a "product" of reading? My contention is that the two texts we have looked at do trap us into enacting, as readers, a perfectly primitive form of knowledge, but that this is a knowledge, or a happening, which we *come to* only by way of the more complicated structures of "experience," and especially of reading. Experience, as a process, is itself already a constant self-expansion, self-multiplication, self-renewal; and the expansion or multiplication or renewal *of* our experience, which the tradition of romance associates with the process of reading, is thus *practically identical with experience itself in the general sense.* (Lubbock develops this relation with unparalleled clarity and economy.) But if, in Hauptmann and Hofmannsthal, the imagined experiential self-complication of *reading* is suddenly collapsed, then the practical identity of reading with experience as such—even if this is merely an imagined identity, belonging to a specific literary and critical tradition—must bring about a more general collapse that leaves us with nothing but that happening or knowledge I have spoken of.

Like Anton Lerch, we undergo experience, and experience our experience, and experience the experiencing of our experience, in a process that inevitably makes readers of us, until (in a kind of trap) that process finally becomes wholly self-conscious, parodies itself, makes a subtractable object of itself, and leaves us confronted with its absolute opposite, that mere, that horrifyingly *mere* thing which now appears across the sudden bridge to ourselves. Or we might think of Goethe's "Urworte. Orphisch," to which I have already alluded, and which begins by unfolding the basic components of experience, DAIMON and TYCHE, in Schiller's terms "Person" and "Zustand," the indomitable Self and the intractable Other. The initially confusing and interesting interaction of these components, which is experience, eventually assumes a directed shape of its own, a focus, which Goethe identifies as EROS. And once experience as such has thus concentrated itself in itself, it also thereby becomes subtractable from *my* self, which now appears as the *mere* self, utterly subject to ANANKE.

Of course this notion of the mere self is not yet at all satisfactorily defined, and must be regarded as heuristic. But I contend nonetheless that the account it suggests of an adequate reading of "Bahnwärter Thiel" or the "Reitergeschichte" is already substantially better than any account in terms of a supposed experiential resonance between reader and fiction. The reading of these stories is not an "experience" at all, not a fictionalizable shape, but mere life, nothing but life. In reader-response theory, reading is seen as life to the second power, life squared, life multiplied by itself, developed, given an extra dimension. In the two stories we are concerned with, by contrast, reading is the square root of life, life stripped of everything it can be stripped of, left as nothing but the shock of particularity, finitude, mortality. We might make a certain ethical sense of this situation by saying that in reading, we are offered the opportunity to realize the shock of finitude, the sheer particularity of ourselves, which we can never *receive* from any narrated fiction, as a positive writerly achievement, an active decision on our part—in that the "act" of reading must now truly *be* an act, since it is denied the possibility of being a mere response to the text. Thus we perhaps find ourselves in the vicinity of eighteenth-century German aesthetics—of Schiller's idea, for example, that our "Zustand" must be transformed into our "Tat"—as well as in the vicinity, say, of Nietzsche and the idea of "amor fati."

Reading is life. Or I might as well have said, reading is death. Or reading is the transforming of death into an achievement, a decision. But there is still a difficulty in our readings. In "Bahnwärter Thiel" the reader is left more or less to himself, except for the moments at which he sees himself in train windows or finds himself mockingly mirrored in a sciouromorphic God. In the "Reitergeschichte," however, in Anton Lerch's meeting himself, we receive something like a *direct representation* of what ultimately happens to us as readers. And how can the story now *continue*? Why does Anton Lerch die precisely as he does? Why does he not at least die quickly, in the skirmish? Before attempting to deal with this matter, let us turn to one more text. Reading, I have said, is death. And more specifically, reading is "Der Tod in Venedig."

5

The idea of "intransitive parody" is obviously applicable to "Der Tod in Venedig." As soon as we read Chapter 2, it becomes clear that the style in which the story is written is a parody of Aschenbach's own "classical" style. But on the other hand, we know that the texts this style parodies *do not exist*, and we have a perfect case of parody without an object. Moreover, the idea of intransitive parody and the idea of the trap of reading are indissolubly related to one another. For if reading is nothing but life, in the radical sense in which I have made that statement, then it follows that the integrity of the literary text, its very identity as a "work," must somehow be nullified in the process of reading. If it is possible to regard the text as a cohesive communicative entity, if the text conveys any specific content whatever, then this content is superadded to the act of reading, and reading is no longer strictly nothing but life.

Reading as I envisage it, therefore, requires that the text contain nothing that is originally its own. The text must be (or—somehow —become) nothing but intertext, in the strict sense of the idea of the "intertextual," as, for example, Kristeva develops it—which creates a problem. For in Kristeva's argument, and from a semiotic perspective in general, it is simply *true* that every text, in its entirety, is intertextually constituted, that at a sufficiently deep level of analysis there is never anything but intertext, just as there is nothing prior to difference in the universe of signs. Here, however, we are not concerned with truth in this sense, but with the process of reading. And how shall the ultimate intertextual nature of a specific text (its specificity is already a problem!) be conveyed to the text's *reader*? If it is conveyed at all, then how shall it avoid taking the form of a content or meaning that gives a particular identity to the text being read? If a text focusses upon its own intertextuality, then precisely *by* focussing, it presents itself to its reader as something more than merely intertextual. It *presents itself* thus, whatever the truth of the matter may be.

Obviously parody can be considered a response to this difficulty, for parody is always at least a gesture in the direction of the intertextual. But if the text is supposed to be realized, in its reading, as nothing but life, this gesture is not enough. For the object of parody, the text that is parodied, *is* inevitably presented as *a* text, a "work," a communicative endeavor with a specific identity, however much the present parodistic text may distance itself; and the idea of an "original" text is thus still present. What is required, therefore, is intransitive parody, parody without an object, a text that is clearly parodistic, but whose object is either non-existent or else necessarily itself a parody. Hence the parodistic technique of "Bahnwärter Thiel," in which the nature descriptions, and the passages that show marked subtleties in the use of verb tense and mood, are parodies of the non-existent texts which *they themselves* would have been if our reading of them had not turned out to be a trap; hence also the parodies of a popular press whose identifying qualities (especially its typical pandering to its reader) turn out not to be *its* qualities at all, but also inexorably characterize our own relation to the text before us. And hence, in the "Reitergeschichte," the complex parodistic relation between the ride through Milan and Anton Lerch's ride through the dirty village. The latter passage is clearly a parody of the former, in that the situation of the earlier "experiencing" reader is now shown forth in the figure of Anton Lerch. The effect of the parody, therefore, is precisely to strip the original text, the ride through Milan, of its identity as a text, to unmask that text as itself necessarily a parody of whatever non-existent text is responded to in what we had fondly imagined as our reading of it—whereupon both passages, both rides, assume the character of intransitive parody, parody referring to no original whatever.

But the parodistic operation of "Der Tod in Venedig" is even more economical. For the main text of the novella, the text we read, in that it parodies certain non-existent texts that we read about, is also *paralleled* with those non-existent texts, which means that the question of its own existence is raised, the question of the existence of "Der Tod in Venedig." In what sense is that text actually *there* for us, more immediately *there* than, say, Aschenbach's Friedrich novel? Where exactly is that absolute readerly present in which we are "actually" reading "Der Tod in Venedig"—that immediate present which must be there in order for us to distinguish adequately between works that we can and works that we cannot "actually" read? Do we not find ourselves in the same dilemma as Hans Castorp with the second-hand on his watch? Is that readerly present not always already past? Does our reading not always reduce itself to a rereading, a remembering of reading, a parody of reading? Do we really have, of Thomas Mann's work, anything *different in kind* from what we have of Aschenbach's works by hearing about them? The parodistic move thus doubles back and reinforces its own questioning of the text's substantiality, gestures with redoubled insistence in the direction of the text's quality as intertext. I of course do not mean that the strategy of intransitive parody actually *establishes* for the reader the character of the text as nothing but intertext. Such a claim would be nonsense, contradicted by the very idea of establishment. The texts I am talking about do not somehow magically overcome the logical constraints that follow from the very ideas of text and intertext. My point, rather, is that the structure of these texts opens the possibility of an entirely radical revision of our sense of what reading is, a revision in which—assuming it has been accomplished—we can discern, or deduce, the effect of the text's ultimate intertextual nature.

6

In Hauptmann and Hofmannsthal, then, intransitive parody is naturally associated with the use of reading as a trap for the reader; and I maintain that the same association operates in "Der Tod in Venedig." Let us begin by organizing chronologically the story of Aschenbach's career as it is described in Chapter 2. Of his youth we read:

> Aschenbach war problematisch, war unbedingt gewesen wie nur irgendein Jüngling. Er hatte dem Geiste gefrönt, mit der Erkenntnis Raubbau getrieben, Saatfrucht vermahlen, Geheimnisse preisgegeben, das Talent verdächtigt, die Kunst verraten ... (p. 454)

Irony and cynicism had characterized him; he had *been* a writer, but only in order to subject that profession, that activity, to a radical and destructive questioning. And the work with which he had rescued himself from this futile self-questioning had been his novel on Frederick the Great. But it is clear that this work had really been a *self*-portrait on Aschenbach's part, and more specifically, a portrait of himself *in the process* of creating the novel. The novel is about "Durchhalten," and "Durchhalten," sheer arbitrary perseverance in the face of his own self-questioning, is how Aschenbach had produced it. This means, however, that Aschenbach's "Sympathie mit dem Abgrund," his radical questioning of the validity of all norms and values, is not in truth overcome after all; for the novel acknowledges that *only its own genesis* is available to it as a valid object. Moreover, that novel is still a giving away of secrets ("Geheimnisse preisgeben") on Aschenbach's part; he achieves the conquest of his suffering artist's condition only by depicting that conquest, which in turn involves displaying the original suffering itself, thus *revealing* precisely the basis of radical doubt on which his achievement is built. Aschenbach has not yet climbed free of the abyss.

Hence his next major work, "der figurenreiche, so vielerlei Menschenschicksal im Schatten einer Idee versammelnde Romanteppich, 'Maja' mit Namen." Clearly the "idea" that unites the characters here is still basically the content of the Frederick novel, what the narrator later calls "Heroismus der Schwäche," except that it is now presented not in the form of an ultimately humiliating confession, but as something closer to a philosophical theory of personality. ("Maja" of course suggests both Nietzsche and Schopenhauer.) Aschenbach here generalizes from his own experience, the experience of *becoming* the person he creates in the very process of creating. All personality, he now suggests, is constituted in this manner, by "Selbstgestaltung" in the face of a gaping void of truth that is concealed from us only by the veil of "maya," the effort of a constantly self-creating fiction. Thus, again, he attempts to suppress, or *re*press, the experience of radical self-doubt on which his own existence is founded, by presenting it as the human condition in general, not as a personal confession.

But again he fails, and the manner in which he fails is very interesting.

> Damit ein bedeutendes Geistesprodukt auf der Stelle eine breite und tiefe Wirkung zu üben vermöge, muß eine geheime Verwandtschaft, ja Übereinstimmung zwischen dem persönlichen Schicksal seines Urhebers und dem allgemeinen des mitlebenden Geschlechtes bestehen. Die Menschen wissen nicht warum sie einem Kunstwerke Ruhm bereiten. Weit entfernt von Kennerschaft, glauben sie hundert Vorzüge daran zu entdecken, um so viel Teilnahme zu rechtfertigen; aber der eigentliche Grund ihres Beifalls ist ein Unwägbares, ist Sympathie. ["Sympathie," that dangerous word.] Aschenbach hatte es einmal an wenig sichtbarer Stelle unmittelbar ausgesprochen, daß beinahe alles Große, was dastehe, als ein Trotzdem dastehe, trotz Kummer und Qual, Armut, Verlassenheit, Körperschwäche, Laster, Leidenschaft und tausend Hemmnissen zustande gekommen sei. Aber das war mehr als eine Bemerkung, es war eine Erfahrung, war geradezu die Formel seines Lebens und Ruhmes, der Schlüssel zu seinem Werk; und was Wunder also, wenn es auch der sittliche Charakter, die äußere Gebärde seiner eigentümlichsten Figuren war? (pp. 452-3)

There is a non sequitur here. The narrator begins by suggesting that he will *explain* Aschenbach's popularity, the "sympathy" readers feel with his work; but then he backs off and simply describes the content of that work. Only after an interval is the question of sympathy again taken up, when we hear: "betrachtete man all dies Schicksal und wieviel Gleichartiges noch [all this 'heroism of weakness,' all the figures, the 'vielerlei Menschenschicksal' of the 'Maja' novel], so konnte man zweifeln, ob es überhaupt einen anderen Heroismus gäbe als denjenigen der Schwäche." And then—finally—we hear that this type of heroism is "zeitgemäß," characteristic of the age, that Aschenbach is "der Dichter all derer, die am Rande der Erschöpfung arbeiten ... all dieser Moralisten der Leistung" who are "die Helden des Zeitalters." The non sequitur, however, suggests the question of whether Aschenbach's readers recognize in his work a personal situation they *already* experience, or whether, rather, that situation is one they create for themselves and put on *in response to their reading.* "Betrachtete man all dies Schicksal ... *so konnte man zweifeln*, ob es einen anderen Heroismus gäbe." After all, Aschenbach's own theory of personality implies that personality types do not exist as prior givens, but are the product of an ever renewed fictional creation.

It is not clear, in other words, that Aschenbach has not himself *propagated* that idea of the age on which "sympathy" for his work is based. It is possible that Aschenbach, in attempting to conquer the experience of suffering and radical self-doubt, has not only confessed that experience, but has now made it available, *as an experience,* to the general public, to the ignorant crowd, that he has thus cheapened and trivialized and prostituted his own self-conquest; and it is this possibility that is embodied in the main character of his next major work, the novella "Ein Elender," in the character of that "Halbschurke, der sich ein Schicksal erschleicht, indem er sein Weib, aus Ohnmacht, aus Lasterhaftigkeit, aus ethischer Velleität, in die Arme eines Unbärtigen treibt und aus Tiefe Nichtswürdigkeiten begehen zu dürfen glaubt." Ethical velleity, or ambiguity, is exactly Aschenbach's situation. In the very process of presenting himself and his characters as a model of ethical resolve, he also offers his readers an experience of the abyss, of radical doubt, that necessarily undermines such resolve. Therefore, in the story "Ein Elender," he attacks not only his own fictional personage, but also *the whole practice of fiction,* of "art," which inevitably produces that ethical ambiguity. He now creates a fictional personage only in order to destroy him; and as far as we can tell, he never creates another work of fiction. His next major work, the essay "Geist und Kunst," proclaims his triumph over himself simply *by* being an essay, by no longer displaying the questionable and shameful conditions of its own genesis in the form of a narrated fiction. Aschenbach, so to speak, has written himself out of his own work, and into a kind of monumental existence.

But even in thus writing himself out of his work, Aschenbach is of course still *writing himself.* The movement of repression, by its nature, is inevitably also a movement of confession. And the text of the actual novella, "Der Tod in Venedig," is nothing but the fictional, confessional subtext of Aschenbach's own later essayistic texts; it is the text Aschenbach writes (hence the stylistic parody) precisely by refusing to write it. The day when the story opens, significantly, is a day on which Aschenbach's creative energy troubles him by refusing to *stop* operating at the usual time. Aschenbach is now writing in spite of himself; the repressed truth from which he had separated himself, the fiction he no longer permits himself, now begins to *write itself* as what appears to him in the form of an external world—a world filled with images of uncreated chaos (the jungle, the sea), images of a precarious artistic mastery of that chaos (Venice, Tadzio), and above all, as if the novel "Maja" were writing itself again, multiple images of Aschenbach himself, in the man with red hair, the ticket-seller on the boat to Venice, the old man made up as a young man, the illegal gondolier, the guitarist, the hairdresser—incessant images of Aschenbach himself, even in inanimate things, like Tadzio's vulnerable sand castle, or the abandoned camera in the last scene. Like Anton Lerch, Aschenbach comes face to face with himself; and as in the case of Anton Lerch, this encounter means death, a death with which Aschenbach eventually acknowledges his own complicity. Aschenbach's fate can in this sense be read straight out of Schopenhauer. Individual existence is in truth nothing but the self-creating struggle for individuality in the face of nothingness; and such existence, as soon as it is wrapped in the illusion of its own established identity, is thus also helplessly exposed to its true nature as struggle (as it were, it encounters itself), which inevitably destroys it.

It is true that Aschenbach's encounter with himself is radically different from Anton Lerch's. Aschenbach, who lives uninterruptedly in the shadow of the knowledge that personal existence is never anything but an act of self-fictionalizing, encounters himself (appropriately) in fictionalized images, whereas Anton Lerch's meeting himself is a representation of that primitive, unfictionalized self-knowledge which is the true product of reading. And of these two self-encounters, Anton Lerch's is still the more problematic, being a representation of the strictly unrepresentable. Clearly there is a profound relation between the two texts in their manner of operation, but we have not yet worked out that relation in satisfactory detail.

7

Aschenbach strives to write himself into existence, which means that he must write himself out of his writing, and his existence collapses under this contradiction. This, in a nutshell, is the action of "Der Tod in Venedig." But where, with respect to this structure, is the reader located?

In the first place, it follows both from the idea of reading suggested by Aschenbach's relation to his public, and from the idealist philosophical background of Aschenbach's self-fashioning, that reading is not basically different, as an activity, from writing. For if, in truth, there is no such thing as the individual, the personality, in the form of a simple given, if the person in truth exists only in the process of its own self-articulation, then it follows that just as the author writes himself into existence, so the reader, in reading, reads himself or herself into existence. But this does not mean that we read our way *into the story*, that we "identify" with some character in it, any more than Aschenbach identifies with any of the characters he writes of. On the contrary, Aschenbach's aim is always to move a step *beyond* the still questionable, still endangered character he is writing about, which is why the revelatory or confessional quality of narrative fiction always subverts its own aim for him. And the process of reading, correspondingly, is always a leaving behind of the text, a using of the text, on our part, for self-articulation, self-development, self-establishment. (We recall Barthes' idea of "readerly" reading as consumption.) Hence the parallel that is drawn, by parody, between "Der Tod in Venedig" itself and the works of Aschenbach that are described in it. Even now, even *in* reading—this parallel suggests—we have already left the text behind, relegated it to a distance from which it is no more immediately *there* for us than those non-existent works which we also in a sense know quite well. And distance is also enforced by the narrator's repeated distancing of himself from Aschenbach; identification is out of the question.

We are invited to read, and to recognize that reading for us, like writing for Aschenbach, is an instance of that necessary process of self-fashioning on which our existence depends. But we are invited to understand, in addition, that even now we also exist beyond our reading, like Aschenbach beyond his fiction, in a more achieved form of existence from which we can look at our reading and grasp and judge it. And then the "lisible" takes its revenge; the trap of reading is sprung. At the moment when Aschenbach eats the strawberries that will kill him, we read:

> Er saß dort, der Meister, der würdig gewordene Künstler, der Autor des "Elenden," der in so vorbildlich reiner Form dem Zigeunertum und der trüben Tiefe abgesagt, dem Abgrunde die Sympathie gekündigt und das Verworfene verworfen hatte, der Hochgestiegene, der, Überwinder seines Wissens und aller Ironie entwachsen, in die Verbindlichkeiten des Massenzutrauens sich gewöhnt hatte, er, dessen Ruhm amtlich, dessen Name geadelt war und an dessen Stil die Knaben sich zu bilden angehalten wurden,—er saß dort, seine Lider waren geschlossen, nur zuweilen glitt, rasch sich wieder verbergend, ein spöttischer und betretener Blick seitlich darunter hervor, und seine schlaffen Lippen, kosmetisch aufgehöht, bildeten einzelne Worte aus von dem, was sein halb schlummerndes Hirn an seltsamer Traumlogik hervorbrachte. (p. 521)

The narrator points out contemptuously that Aschenbach, the contemptuous author of "Ein Elender," has now become the object of his own contempt, that his rejection of fiction has exposed him more completely than ever to the danger and the degeneracy that fiction represents. But the narrator, in this passage, is himself doing exactly what Aschenbach had done. He is narrating himself into existence; he is detaching himself, raising himself above, the inevitable ethical and existential velleity associated with fiction; and in doing so, he is exposing himself to the conditions of his existence in exactly the same way Aschenbach had. But once I understand the replication of this process from the level of Aschenbach, the character, who is a writer, up to the level of the narrator, who is positioned somewhere between the conditions of writer and reader, I cannot fail to acknowledge the further replication by which the same reasoning applies to myself. In the very process of looking down at the narrator (with a detachment not far from contempt) and recognizing the manner in which he has exposed himself to a fate exactly like Aschenbach's, I find myself making exactly that gesture *by which* both he and Aschenbach had exposed themselves. There is no escape. Like Aschenbach's gondolier, the reader is perhaps, for the moment, more in control of his or her situation than either the narrator or the character, but he or she is still in the same boat. Precisely the clarity of my vision, the clarity of my abstract grasp of the relation between "Geist und Kunst," between achieved self-possession and its unstable, unsavory precondition, precisely that clarity *is* the move that entraps me. My reading is no longer comfortably "readerly," no longer left behind after all, but now suddenly catches up with me in the form of nothing but life, nothing but the immediate exposure to mortality of *my* particular self, a self that protrudes (and so is exposed) entirely beyond the otherwise perhaps comforting limits of a fictional rôle.

It must be understood that the result of this trap is not a form of "identification" between the reader and Aschenbach—any more than we might speak of "identification" with the glimpsed railway passengers in Hauptmann. For the trap, in order to operate, requires precisely our assertion of *difference* from Aschenbach. And indeed our *continued* assertion of difference: for if, at the end, we acknowledge our similarity with Aschenbach and pretend to learn from it, if we pretend to *accept* our "sympathy with the abyss," then we are not like Aschenbach after all, but have merely joined up with the "respektvoll erschütterte Welt" that reads of his death in the papers. What we have in common with Aschenbach is nothing but a fundamental contradiction of existence: we read ourselves into existence by pretending to read ourselves out of our reading, which eventually destroys us. And this contradiction is not an object of experience, to be grasped and learned from. If it were, then the story would be called simply "Der Tod," referring to death as an experience we all share. The actual title, "Der Tod in Venedig," denies us this form of participation, excludes us, leaves us alone with a contradiction that is nothing but our entirely primitive self-encounter, our own mortality.

The connection between the reader and Aschenbach is definitely there, but is always occult and problematic. We think, for instance, of the abandoned camera on the beach. The story's allusions to Oedipus—the Apollo and Dionysus chapters, which suggest tragedy in general; the hero of intellect, infected with guilt, who finds himself in a plague-stricken city—associate that three-legged camera, by way of the Sphinx's riddle, with the figure of an old man, Aschenbach, who has become nothing but eye, nothing but the vessel of a delicious vision that is now "scheinbar herrenlos," now governed by no formative moral will. But that camera is also obviously, as it were, a pinhole in the text, which betrays the presence of the reader, the presence of a detached "aesthetic" seeing that turns out, in truth, to be not a seeing, not an experiencing, at all, but the mere *gesture* of seeing, carried out by an apparatus that is in truth nothing but a helpless, particular, abandoned material object at the brink of oblivion. The problematics of the visual metaphor is here the same as in Hauptmann. The nullity of our supposed experiencing as readers, the nullity of our seeing, is conveyed only by being shown us in an image.

8

But in this reading of "Der Tod in Venedig": who is Tadzio? Tadzio could be omitted from the story—replaced by some completely different type of figure or narrative—with no damage to the work's structure as I have presented it.

Tadzio is clearly the *content* of "Der Tod in Venedig"—just as he is the content of the fictional bridge by which Aschenbach arrives at his death. But the idea of content has become problematic. In order to do what it does to the reader's sense of reading, we have seen, the story must be *devoid* of any substantial content, must be intransitive parody, nothing but intertext. The story cannot, however, by definition, *present itself* as nothing but intertext; its "presenting itself" already contradicts this possibility. "Der Tod in Venedig" must therefore have a content after all—otherwise it would simply not be there—but a content that manages to become transparent with respect to its own irrelevance, its own insubstantiality, its own strictly arbitrary or accidental quality as a kind of generalized happening of what Barthes calls "la voix du lecteur." And the constitution of the story's content, in this manner, is itself strikingly fictionalized in Aschenbach's deliberate constitution of Tadzio as the object of desire, in his avoidance of the opportunity to regularize and conventionalize his relation to the boy.

Moreover, the idea of Tadzio as the content of a contentless text is reflected exactly in the page and a half of prose that Aschenbach writes on the beach while looking at Tadzio. That text, like the other writings of Aschenbach we hear about, is a parody of (or, indifferently, is parodied by) "Der Tod in Venedig" itself, and in fact combines the idea of parody with the mechanism of *reversal* that we have also discussed. "Der Tod in Venedig," again, *is* the fictional text that Aschenbach represses in writing his own later non-fictional texts, which means that the relation between visible and invisible texts, for the reader, is exactly the reverse of what it is within the fictional world. And similarly: whereas the *ostensible* content of Aschenbach's page and a half is "ein gewisses großes und brennendes Problem der Kultur und des Geschmackes" (p. 492) — about which he had been invited to write, which gives it a strong intertextual flavor — while the *true* content is the figure of Tadzio, exactly the reverse is the case in the whole novella. The ostensible content, the needful identifying veil spread over the truth of limitless intertextuality, is now Tadzio, while the true content is indeed a burning cultural problem, the problem of reading. Nor is it insignificant that Aschenbach's failure to make Tadzio's acquaintance in a relatively harmless manner immediately follows his writing of that page and a half. It is as if we, having understood the novella, were attempting to convince ourselves that the problem of reading (the novella's submerged or repressed content) has now been dealt with, rendered harmless by our understanding. But the parallel with Aschenbach reminds us that we do not even really *want* such an "Ernüchterung" (p. 494), that we ourselves still insist on the problem — just as Aschenbach insists on the object of desire — that we still constitute the problem for ourselves *by* reading, that it is thus a problem we are *alone* with, our own perfectly primitive self-encounter.

Similar considerations emerge from the discussion of "Bahnwärter Thiel" above. Given our basic sense of the work's literary genre, plus various parodistic gestures in style, the ostensible content, Thiel's life and its crisis, as it were peels away to reveal a second layer: the relation, the gulf, between a coarse popular press and the relatively finer literary sensibility and human sympathy that we bring to the material such a press merely exploits. And when it then turns out that our relation to the text is *not* really distinguishable from that of the reader of the popular press, the work's true content is revealed, accordingly, as nothing but the journalistic sensation at the end, the murder. But this still cannot be the text's content *for us*. Just as our inveterate readerly self-multiplication inevitably excludes us from Thiel's dogged self-narrowing, so also precisely the process that makes newspaper readers of us tells us, by *being* a literary and critical process, that we are not newspaper readers after all, so that even the text's sensational content is not really available to us. Thiel's story, like Tadzio's, is thus the content of an empty text, of a maximally intransitive parody.

This brings us, finally, to the question of the end of the "Reitergeschichte." Anton Lerch's meeting himself across the bridge, I have argued, represents the reader's true situation, the happening of a primitive self-knowledge; but *as* a representation, we must now continue, that image *relegates the actual happening to the past*. Like the trap of reading in Hauptmann, the happening of primitive self-knowledge in Hofmannsthal is not locatable at any particular point in real or in fictional time; it is deferred interminably into the future and recollected interminably into the past. The moment of representation (in the story) is thus itself already a movement *beyond* that unlocatable and in a sense non-existent moment of truth (for the reader), which means that the continuation of the story beyond the moment of representation is absolutely necessary—if never demonstrably sufficient—precisely to *validate* the representation. The story moves beyond Anton Lerch's self-encounter just as we have moved beyond what that event represents.

Or more generally, not only must we *come* by way of experience *to* the knowledge that reading produces, but we must also *come away* from it by way of experience. Hence the *inevitability* of representation (which is such a coming away) in the "Reitergeschichte," problematic as that representation may be. Hence also the inevitability of Barthes' complicated formulation: for the writable text is not, strictly speaking, the utterly particular "us" (or me) of primitive self-knowledge, but rather always finds us in the process of writing ourselves *away* from such knowledge, "nous en train d'écrire." And Goethe's ANANKE stanza, similarly, *must* be followed by something like an ELPIS stanza. The happening of the strictly mortal self cannot itself effectively happen except in being superseded by the *experience* of mortality, by our turning our backs on it, our holding fast to something learned or, as it were, *rescued* from it. Otherwise it must simply lose the character of knowledge; for we do actually die only by becoming a person and exposing ourselves in experience.

And Anton Lerch's captured horse clearly represents, or indeed allegorizes, what we inevitably (if contradictorily) rescue from our reading. His fate, from the moment at the bridge onward, is a perfect circle. He confronts the thing that is nothing but Anton Lerch, the happening of nothing but life, which, in the skirmish, inevitably receives content, substance, the quality of possessible experience, which possession in turn, is his actual exposure to death and so at once repeats and validates the original happening. And this circle, in turn is itself repeated in the process of reading. Our reading of the story gradually unmasks itself as nothing but life, which idea then necessarily assumes the quality of a *content* belonging to the story, a captured prize we bring away with us, a victory like Anton Lerch's in the skirmish, an achieved fictional *experience*; and this possession in turn exposes us precisely to our mortality, to that death we had already known directly in the moment of nothing but life. Like Anton Lerch, we *cannot* let go of our prize—we cannot stop knowing what the story means—even though we know (for this knowledge *is* the prize) that that possession means literally our death.

There are of course complications here. We pass beyond the blind self-indulgence of readerly "experience," at the end of the story, only by finding ourselves mirrored yet again in the fiction. Thus the end of the story parodies the story as a whole and so relocates *my* primitive self-encounter in a non-time before my even beginning to read. Moreover, the allegorical circle of Anton Lerch's fate at the end, like the self-encounter which initiates it, is itself a representation that relegates its object to the past and so initiates, for us, a still larger circle by which we eventually return and validate it. But we do not need to work out these complications in detail. That they exist, and can be multiplied indefinitely, is already implied by the story's radical operation upon the idea and the experience of reading.

9

I have argued that the stories treated above all unmask the insufficiency of a particular idea of reading, which means, paradoxically,
that the *persistence* of that insufficient idea of reading is required in
order for those stories to operate. Where, then, does that idea of
reading come from—the idea of reading as a joyful and instructive
self-multiplication of the self-multiplication that is already
experience—and how is its persistence justified? Clearly we are
dealing here with a *tradition*, in fiction itself and in the study of fiction, which I call the tradition of romance; and clearly the Iserian
"phenomenological approach" to reading, far from being an adequate objective description of literary practice, is itself a relatively
unreflected manifestation of that tradition. But exactly what
stance is assumed, vis-à-vis the tradition or within it, by the three
stories we have looked at?

It could be argued, I suppose, that these texts employ the
romance tradition, and our presumed entanglement in it, as a kind
of *lever*, in order to make available to us—or indeed, to impose on
us—that utterly solitary happening of our own mortality which is
posited in existentialist thought. But an argument of this sort, it
seems to me, would require that we assume a radical historical
break in the tradition, a leap of self-reflection by which we are suddenly enabled to lay hands on the tradition as a whole and make
use of it as a mere lever, a tool. And in what sense, then, does the
tradition persist after all?

I think it is more reasonable to say that from the perspective of a
certain segment of turn-of-the-century German prose, the *whole*
tradition of romance, which culminates in a Jamesian idea of reading, is recognized as a movement of repression, and indeed an
inevitable movement, a repression that *must* in some form persist,
since the repressed content—what reading in truth *is*, what I have
gestured at in the phrase, "primitive happening of the self"—is
strictly inadmissible and incommunicable. Intransitive parody, after
all—if it is related to the idea of the intertextual in the manner I

have suggested—must ultimately characterize all fictional texts. And the trap of reading is nothing but a particular form of that covert revelatory gesture, that moving toward the brink of a full but impossible consciousness, which is by definition characteristic of repression. Our three texts, therefore, not only accept the persistence of the tradition they unmask, but actively develop that tradition, and show that comparable gestures of self-unmasking must be present in the tradition at every stage.

An important question remains. To what shall we attribute the particular form of self-reflection that romance tradition carries out in turn-of-the-century German prose? To the rise of literary modernism in general, and especially to symbolist theory and sensibility? Or to a specifically German situation, perhaps to the unique nineteenth-century development of the "Novelle" as a genre, as far back as the Romantics and Kleist and Goethe? But this question does not belong to the present argument.

Note

I presented an earlier version of this argument at The Johns Hopkins University in 1987. I trust that the participants in the discussion that followed—including especially Liliane Weissberg, Lieselotte Kurth, Rainer Nägele, Richard Macksey, Werner Hamacher, and two students whose names I am ashamed to have forgotten—will recognize their own important contributions to the present version, for which I am deeply grateful. Page references are to:

Gerhart Hauptmann, *Sämtliche Werke*, Centenar-Ausgabe, ed. H.-E. Hass, 11 vols. (Frankfurt/Main, 1962), vol. 6.

Hugo von Hofmannsthal, *Sämtliche Werke*, veranstaltet vom Freien Deutschen Hochstift, 37 planned vols. (Frankfurt/Main, 1975 -), vol. 28.

Thomas Mann, *Gesammelte Werke in dreizehn Bänden*, 2nd ed. (Frankfurt/Main, 1974), vol. 8.

Viennese Psychology and American Pragmatism

Judith Ryan
Harvard University

William James's turning towards pragmatism in the second half of the 1890s, which culminated in the publication of his Lowell lectures under the title *Pragmatism* in 1907, is generally held to be a quintessentially American phenomenon. It is also usually presented as a response to his particular biographical situation: his need to break away from the towering influence of Josiah Royce.[1] I would argue, however, that its cause was more profoundly embedded in the kind of questions James was investigating and that its origins can be traced to Viennese, as much as to American sources.

To make this argument effectively, I will need to say a little more about James's thought and its development. Most commentators draw a dividing line between the completion of *The Principles of Psychology* (1890) and what is thought of as his subsequent return to philosophy. At the same time, most studies of James also recognize that pragmatism was latent in James's earlier thought, linking it implicitly or explicitly with his decision of 1870 to accept the notion of free will even though it might well be an illusion: "My first act of free will shall be to believe in free will."[2] In making this choice, James not only saved himself from the depths of a severe depression, he also illustrated *avant la lettre* his later precept that ideas are true if they can be shown to be useful in the conduct of everyday life.[3]

The depression to which this early pragmatic decision was the resolution had begun in 1867, when James, concerned about his health, departed for Germany to improve his command of the language and study physiology in German laboratories. This move both precipitated the crisis and provided him with a basis for resolving it.

German itself was one of the problems, and he wrote an amusing letter to his mother describing its effects upon him. Having reached the point where he could readily skim through any book "writ in a style at all adapted to the requirements of the human, as distinguished from the German, mind,"[4] he still found himself frustrated by more scholarly prose: "The profounder and more philosophical German requires, however, that you should bring all the resources of your nature, of every kind, to focus, and hurl them again and again on the sentence, till at last you feel something give way, as it were, and the Idea begins to unravel itself" (L, 92). This method cannot have failed to make James acutely aware of the functioning of his own mind. Underlying his amusing recipe for unravelling difficult German is a contrast between two different ways of looking at language: the word-by-word approach, on the one hand, and the whole sentence approach, on the other. Only the whole sentence approach actually worked. His experience is, of course, not an unusual one for learners of German as a foreign language. But his description of it gains an entirely new dimension if we map it onto some of the contemporary debates of which his exposure to life in Germany was making him aware. In a letter of the month before, just two weeks after his arrival in Germany, he gives a number of examples, taken from the newspaper, of the strange German mode of expression—but though he introduces them as "elephantine ways of saying things" (L, 88), they are not that at all. They are in fact early clues to the quite specific perturbation into which he was thrown by his sudden immersion in a foreign cultural context. The Emperor of Austria is said to have given a speech that was "more *atomistisch* than *dynamisch*"; a historian of German literature is said to have failed to illuminate the *Lebensgrund* of his subject; and another is said to have developed it "without entirely losing sight of what was *menschlich*" (L, 88-89). James is not picking out random linguistic items here: on the contrary, he is pointing to a consistent source of puzzlement to which the "context gave no explanation" (L, 89). The source of his confusion is his relative ignorance of two important controversies then raging in the German-speaking world: the debate over atomistic, as opposed to holistic, views of thought and reality; and the debate whether the human factor should be included or excluded in positivistic science. Exactly what these controversies meant was not to become clear to him until somewhat later.

The split between two forms of thought, as yet only intuited by James, was reinforced by a split between theory and practice that made his trip to Germany deeply disappointing. Although able to attend lectures on physiology and do a great deal of reading, he was not permitted to work in the laboratory. Writing home to Henry Bowditch, he wishes the two could "take counsel together concerning the world and life": "how you would pour into my astonished ear all that is new and wonderful about pathology and microscopical research, all that is sound and neat about operative surgery, while I would recite the most thrilling chapters of Kolliker's 'Entwickelungsgeschichte' [sic] or Helmholtz's 'Innervationsfortpflanzungsgeschwindigkeitsbestimmungen'!" (L, 123) He imagines a fantastic partnership between the two of them in which Bowditch will have more experience, James more learning than anyone else in the world. James put a more practical plan into effect in the spring of 1868 when he moved from Berlin to Heidelberg to hear Helmholtz and Wundt and learn more about the connections between physiology and psychology (L, 118-119, 137). But this attempt to bridge the gap between the physical and the mental was interrupted by an event that any Germanist will immediately recognize as, under the circumstances, inevitably fatal: James began to read Kant (L, 138). "Whether right or wrong (and it is pretty clearly wrong in a great many details of its *Analytik* part, however the rest may be), there it stands like a great snag or mark to which everything metaphysical or psychological must be *referred* (L, 138). Now the terms have shifted. The focus is no longer the

gap between physiology and psychology, but that between metaphysics and psychology. For the next twelve or fifteen years, James
spent his time on the thin ridge between these two abysses:
whether he stepped to the left or to the right, he threatened to fall
into one or the other of them.

In the grip of a full-blown *Kantkrise*, but clutching an essay by
the Frenchman, Renouvier, whose views on free will were ultimately to provide the antidote, James returned home. This point
in the edition of his letters is appropriately marked by a sketch
from James's pencil of an elephant turning tail and lumbering off
(L, 139).[5] In the months that followed James "about touched bottom" before arriving at his first pragmatic decision simply to
believe in the freedom of the will (D, 1 February 1870). The
unstated corollary, of course, was to believe in reality even though
it may be a delusion. With phenomenalism and positivism thus no
longer pitted against each other, the immediate Kant crisis was
solved. James's early (if still unnamed) pragmatism was a kind of
"as if" philosophy. It enabled him, in the twenty years between the
free will decision and the completion of the *Principles of
Psychology*, to explore such topics as sense-perception without
having to worry whether the world of things was actually "out
there" or not. One simply acted as if it were. By the same token, a
number of other problems could be neatly side-stepped. In
Cambridge, the big debate was over the merits of monistic, as
opposed to dualistic, philosophies. Was the world all made up of
one single, consistent "stuff" or was it divided into inside and
outside, subjective and objective reality? Here was a different way
of turning the Kantian question. James answered it in the
Principles of Psychology by the "as if" method: "The dualism of
Object and Subject and their pre-established harmony are what the
psychologist as such must assume, whatever ulterior monistic
philosophy he may, as an individual who has the right also to be a
metaphysician, have in reserve."[6] To "do psychology" was
precisely to act as if the larger philosophical questions could be
provisionally bracketed off.

In the main, this technique works out very well for James in the *Principles* — indeed, had he not adopted it, it is doubtful whether he could have written the work at all. But one of the principal sources of some of James's key chapters was an Austrian philosopher who neither bracketed off the metaphysical issues nor adopted the pragmatistic stance. This was Franz Brentano, whose *Psychologie vom empirischen Standpunkte* (1874) represented precisely the kind of theory James took issue with in his early essay "On Some Omissions of Introspective Philosophy" (1884),[7] several passages of which he included in chapter IX of the *Principles*. This chapter, "The Stream of Thought," has since become a canonical text for literary studies as much as for psychology. In the new Harvard edition of James's works the editors comment that there are "some two thousand references" to the writings of other scholars in the *Principles* (P, 1300), but James is in fact rather canny in his references to Brentano. If we look at his own index to the *Principles*, we find that he lists only two of them, one a direct quotation and the other an account of some experimental results of Fechner's cited by Brentano. Several other references make no appearance. Two of these are quite significant, since they bear upon whole chapters of Brentano's book. The first of these is Brentano's Chapter Four on "The Unity of Consciousness" ("Die Einheit des Bewußtseins"), of which James remarks that it is "as good as anything with which I am acquainted" (P, 234). The other is his Chapter Seven, "Vorstellung und Urtheil zwei verschiedener Grundclassen," whose thesis James defines as the idea that "conception and belief (which he names *judgment*) are two different fundamental psychic phenomena" (P, 916). To be sure, James refers the reader in both instances to whole chapters and expresses his admiration of them without hesitation, but, in contrast to his presentation of Wundt, Helmholtz or Fechner, he does not cite specific details or quarrel with particular points.

An extraordinary thing appears to have happened here. Though not convinced by the rather extreme version of introspective philosophy developed by Brentano, James was evidently so struck by his idea of the "Unity of Consciousness" that he adopts it and gives it a new meaning entirely his own.

Franz Brentano was a key figure in late nineteenth-century psychology. Under his influence psychologists at the universities of Vienna, Graz and Prague came to regard the introspective method as the only proper method of their discipline. Even Sigmund Freud, different though his psychology is from those of the other *Brentano-Schüler*, relied on introspection rather than experimentation.

To look through James's markings in his copy of Brentano's *Psychologie vom empirischen Standpunkte*, now in Houghton Library, is to begin to trace the path that led from Vienna to Cambridge in the 1880s. In accordance with James's notes in the *Principles of Psychology*, the two chapters he singles out for special admiration bear the largest number of markings. One can observe him already searching for grist to his own mill. A central point in Brentano's thinking was the notion that "inner perception" ("innere Wahrnehmung") is true in itself. This was, in a sense, Brentano's answer to Kantianism: although we cannot testify to the reality of the object-world, we can testify to that of our inner perception, since this certainly is true for us. This statement is one of the first passages James marks.[8] But further on in Brentano, James also marks a passage that suggests a kind of proto-pragmatism in Brentano's thinking: "And when, from the phenomena of our perceptions, we posit a three-dimensional world as their cause, we assume something which is never directly present to experience, and yet this conclusion is perhaps not unjustified."[9] Sense-perception does not actually present us with a three-dimensional world "out there"—this is merely a conclusion we draw from the evidence of our senses. But it may not be wrong to draw this conclusion, since, as Brentano goes on to explain, it helps us orient ourselves in reality and even predict things that will happen by deducing them from generalizations based on the assumption of an objective reality (Brentano, 140). This argument is of course the backbone of Jamesian psychology and what he was ultimately to call pragmatism. In *The Principles of Psychology* James also makes clear that he thought he found something very much like his own "will to believe" in Brentano's thought. By translating Brentano's category "Urteil" as "belief" James conveniently pragmatized his Austrian predecessor. Similarly, he converts Brentano's definition of "psychological phenomena" as those phenomena in which the perceiving subjectivity contains an object[10] into his own idea that thought appears both "as part of personal consciousness" and as "dealing with objects independent of itself" (P, 220).

But by far the most remarkable change is that undergone by the notion of unity. Brentano's argument is directed at two opposing views that were very much the subject of debate in the latter nineteenth century: the Romantic notion of "levels of consciousness" and the Kantian notion that consciousness also entailed self-consciousness. Brentano's tenet of the unity of consciousness was intended to collapse both sets of dualisms. But although James refers to Brentano's "unity of consciousness," his real argument in this chapter is directed against Wundt. Despite the fact that James depends on Wundt for a good deal of the experimental evidence adduced in the sections on sense-perception in the *Principles*, he was a staunch opponent of Wundt's underlying philosophy throughout his life. This was the philosophy that thought was composed of "elements"—in fact, the very view of which James's reading of German newspapers in 1867 had given him a first inkling. "Atomistisch" and "dynamisch," the terms that had then seemed so mysterious in their application to a speech by the Austrian Emperor, were code words for two opposing views of reality: elementaristic and holistic. Was the world made up of innumerable particles randomly linked together, or was it a coherent unity? Invoking Brentano, James argued in the *Principles of Psychology* not that the world, but that thought was a unified whole rather than a composite of disparate parts. His famous image contrasts a line of coupled railway carriages with the flow of a river or stream. But he also had a better image up his sleeve: "The transition between the thought of one object and the thought of another is no more a break in the *thought* than a joint in a bamboo is a break in the wood. It is a part of the *consciousness* as much as the joint is a part of the *bamboo*" (P, 234).   In appropriating Brentano's holism in this way, James was also completely remolding him in his own image.

But there is one feature about this remolding that remains puzzling.   Despite James's insistence throughout the body of the chapter on the personal character of thought, he opens his discussion with the contention that it is really impersonal.   "If we could say in English 'it thinks,' as we say 'it rains' or 'it blows,' we should be stating the fact most simply and with the minimum of assumption.   As we cannot, we must say that *thought goes on*" (P, 220).   We Germanists have heard this before: "One should say 'it thinks,' just as one says 'it thunders.'"[11]   Its original author is Lichtenberg, but James did not have to go so far back for this idea.   He found it in Ernst Mach, who cites Lichtenberg's aphorism and develops it in his own way.   Though James has no note to Mach at this point in his argument, other references show that he had before him while he was writing the *Principles* the first edition of Mach's treatise on sense-perception, then titled *Beiträge zur Analyse der Empfindungen* (1886).[12]   The quotation from Lichtenberg is part of Mach's famous argument that "the self is unsalvageable."[13]   Mach's discussion is in many ways much closer to James's argument in "The Stream of Thought" than is Brentano's: he writes, for example, that the sense of continuity is only a means of pulling the contents of thought together: "this content, not the self, is what matters."[14]   But although Mach emphasizes the irreality of the self, he also recognizes that the concept has practical value in everyday life.   "*Cogito* is already an overstatement as soon as it is translated 'I think.'   To assume the self, to postulate it, is a practical necessity."[15]   The difference between Mach and James on this point is merely a tip of the balance—though to be sure, a significant one: Mach accepts our practical need to postulate a self but claims that it is not a real entity; James accepts the essential impersonality of thought but claims (following Brentano) that any introspective truth is a truth plain and simple, and since we think of ourselves as having a self, the notion of personal consciousness is in this sense true.

The most surprising feature of James's presentation of these ideas is the unbridged gap between his opening postulate of the impersonality of thought and his principal thesis that thought tends to be part of a personal consciousness. Mach, by contrast, is much more careful to mediate between abstract philosophy and everyday ideas. Perhaps James had Mach's articulation so vividly in mind that it simply didn't occur to him to spell out the connection. Oddly enough, he does not refer to Mach at this point; nonetheless, this opening page or so of "The Stream of Thought" is conspicuously absent from James's earlier article, and it is the only one of the additions to add a substantially new idea, as opposed to elaborations of the old. It is reasonable to assume, therefore, that Mach's 1886 treatise is the hidden link between James's 1884 essay and the 1890 *Principles of Psychology*.

In 1903, Mach sent James a copy of the fourth edition of his book, now called *Analyse der Empfindungen*. Although he was familiar with the first edition, James read this new version particularly attentively; the copy preserved in Houghton Library bears numerous underlinings and marginal markings, as well as a brief personal index pencilled into the back flyleaf. The first three items on James's list are "Pragmatic resumé," "Common Sense" and "Ich" (Self). A glance through the marginal markings reveals that James reread Mach with a special view to discovering his latent pragmatism. He marks, for example, a passage at the beginning of the book in which Mach explains that words like "body" ("Körper") and "Ich" are "only aids to preliminary orientation and for certain practical ends"[16] and places the annotation "prag." in the margin against a longer passage in which Mach maintains, not only that the concept of self can be useful for practical purposes, but also that any concept developed for a specific purpose has real value for this purpose (Mach, 25-26). Two other passages, in which Mach expresses his respect for the "naive realism" ("naiver Realismus") of the common man and emphasizes that he has not intended in any way to discredit this point of view, are marked with "Common Sense" and "prag" respectively (Mach, 30). James was clearly combing the *Analyse der Empfindungen* for pragmatistic leanings that might confirm his own belief in the value of everyday reasoning.

The reward came for James in 1907 after he had sent Mach a copy of his book *Pragmatism*. Mach himself now agreed that his thought had always been pragmatistic at bottom: "Although my training has been that of a natural scientist, my way of thinking is very close to pragmatism, though I have never used that name."[17] Mach's letter continues: "If this line of thought is successful, it could finally resolve the troublesome differences between philosophers and natural scientists."[18] In a postscript he regrets the fact that pragmatism is not better known in the German-speaking world and passes on a colleague's request for permission to translate the book into German.[19]

But James was not the only one to have discovered Mach's own implicit pragmatism. Hermann Bahr's essay of 1904, whose title consists of the key phrase in Mach's discussion of the self, "Das unrettbare Ich" (the unsalvageable self), brings out the pragmatism behind Mach's apparently negative idea: "What counts for me is not what is true, but what I need, and so the sun still rises, the earth is real, and I am I."[20] Bahr's response was in effect an elaboration of Mach's insistence in the preface to the fourth edition of the *Analyse der Empfindungen* that his views on the unsalvageable self were not intended to lead to despair.

Writing psychology and bracketing out philosophy was for the William James of the Eighties a way of insulating himself from this despair. If our inner perceptions can be treated as true, we don't have to worry about the possibly illusory status of external reality. But there were moments, such as when he appropriates Mach's contention that the *cogito* should be translated "es denkt (it thinks)," or adapts Brentano's complex conflation of subject and object—both of which run counter to our inner perception of things—when James allows the philosophical underpinnings to show through his psychological overlay. In the *Principles* these tears in the fabric appear as logical discrepancies; but his later pragmatism is a wonderful kind of invisible mending. Just as physics and psychology are "two universes of discourse—

depending on the direction of your business with it,"[21] so critical empiricism and common sense are in James's view simply two ways of looking at the same set of phenomena. That Ernst Mach ultimately accepted James's deconstruction of his attack on the concept of self is the proof of a very strange pudding: the Austrian ingredient in that very American recipe, pragmatism.

Notes

Reprinted with kind permission from *Raritan* VIII: 3 (Winter 1989), 45-54.

1 Bruce Kuklick, *The Rise of American Philosophy. Cambridge, Massachusetts, 1860-1930* (New Haven: Yale University Press, 1977), 264.

2 William James, *Diary*, 30 April, 1870. References in the text will be to "D."

3 First formulated in his 1898 Berkeley lecture "Philosophical Conceptions and Practical Results."

4 *The Letters of William James*, ed. Henry James (Boston: Atlantic Monthly Press, 1920), vol. I, 92. References in the text will be to "L."

5 Pencil sketch from a pocket notebook.

6 William James, *Principles of Psychology*, 1300. References in the text will be to "P."

7 William James, *Mind*, IX (1884), 1-26.

8 Franz Brentano, *Psychologie vom empirischen Standpunkte*, vol. I (Leipzig: Duncker und Humblot, 1874), 24-25.

9 "Auch wenn wir aus den Erscheinungen unserer Empfindungen auf eine räumlich ausgebreitete Welt als ihre Ursache schließen, nehmen wir etwas an, was nie als unmittelbare Erfahrungstatsache gefunden wurde, und doch ist dieser Schluß viellecht nicht unberechtigt" (Brentano, 140). [Translations by the editor.]

10 "Phänomene, welche intentional einen Gegenstand in sich enthalten" (Brentano, 116), also marked by James.

11 "Es denkt, sollte man sagen, so wie man sagt: es blitzt."

12 Ernst Mach, *Analyse der Empfindungen*, 4th ed. (Jena: Gustav Fischer, 1904), 20.

13 "das Ich ist unrettbar" (Mach, 19).

14 "Dieser Inhalt und nicht das *Ich* ist die Hauptsache" (Mach, 19).

15 "Zu sagen *cogito* ist schon zuviel, sobald man es durch *Ich denke* übersetzt. Das *Ich* anzunehmen, zu postulieren, ist praktisches Bedürfnis" (Mach, 23).

16 "nur Notbehelfe zur vorläufigen Orientierung und für bestimmte praktische Zwecke" (Mach, 10).

17 "Obwohl ich meiner Erziehung nach durchaus Naturforscher bin, stehe ich doch in meiner Denkweise dem Pragmatismus sehr nahe, ohne jemals den Namen gebraucht zu haben," letter of June 28, 1907 (Houghton box no. 543).

18 "Mit dem Durchschlagen dieser Richtung könnten endlich die unerquicklichen Differenzen zwischen Philosophen und Naturforschern eine Lösung finden," letter of June 28, 1907.

19 "Es wäre sehr schön, da man hier wohl wenig mit der Bedeutung des Pragmatismus vertraut ist." Letter of June 28, 1907.

20 "Für mich gilt, nicht, was wahr ist, sondern was ich brauche, und so geht die Sonne dennoch auf, die Erde ist wirklich, und Ich bin Ich." Hermann Bahr, *Zur Überwindung des Naturalismus. Theoretische Schriften 1887-1904*, ed. Gotthart Wunberg (Stuttgart: Kohlhammer, 1968), 192.

21 Marginal note in pencil in James's copy of Mach's *Analyse der Empfindungen*.

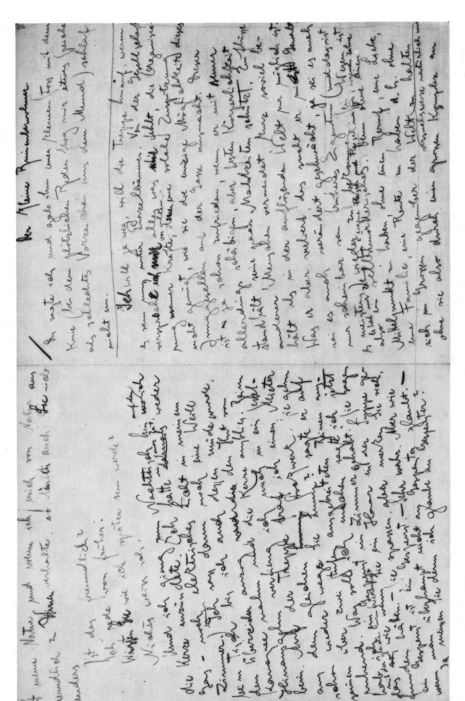

Pages from the second quarto notebook of Kafka's diaries.

The First Two Quarto Notebooks of Franz Kafka's Diaries: Thoughts on Their Genesis and Date of Origin

Hans-Gerd Koch
University of Wuppertal

Franz Kafka's diaries have been handed down to us in the form of twelve quarto notebooks. Of these, the first two notebooks, which Kafka used alternately up to September 1911, make up the theme of this essay. It is difficult to determine when Kafka started these diaries as none of the early entries are dated, and we do not have any other record made by Kafka as to when he started keeping a diary. Previous estimates of their date of origin range from the early part of 1909 to the beginning of 1910. However, it must be added that these attempts used the text of Max Brod's edition as a basis. Brod published the diary entries in their chronological order and with many omissions.

In addition, information on the actual nature of the texts, such as the fact that Kafka wrote both in ink and pencil in these diaries, has been ignored up to now, even though this information is of particular importance when attempting to date texts. It is particularly striking that the few entries in pencil that can be dated approximately were written on occasions when Kafka was away from Prague or, to be more precise, when he was not at home. Using those entries that can be accurately dated or reliably deduced as a framework, it is possible to create a logical sequence by ascribing all the passages in pencil to periods when Kafka was not at home.

To back up this hypothesis, an examination of all Kafka's existing correspondence of the time reveals that the bulk of postcards written to friends or relatives in the years 1909 to 1911 while on business trips or on brief stays away from Prague are written in pencil.

Only on rare occasions are these postcards written in indelible pencil, in black ink or in an ink different from the black one Kafka normally used in Prague. This last fact in particular is of great significance: an entry in the second notebook two sides long and written in pencil, which includes only one three-line passage in blue ink, must have been written on a journey to Berlin in 1910, according to my hypothesis. Consulting Kafka's postcards to Max Brod from Berlin to provide a comparison, we discover that the first one from December 4 is written in pencil, while the second two, both dated December 9, are written in the same blue ink as the three-line passage in the second notebook.

Of course, it is not possible to produce such convincing evidence in all cases, but it seems to me that this adequately supports the theory that the diary entries which are not written in the black ink Kafka normally used were not written at home. This theory, supported by parallels in content in Kafka's letters and postcards and in Max Brod's unpublished diaries of that time, lays the foundations for my thoughts on the origins of the two notebooks. Along with my thoughts on how to date the entries up to the end of 1910, I intend to show the changes that take place in his manner of recording notes in his diary. Furthermore, I intend to show how he gradually develops his own manner of keeping a diary over this period.

According to Kafka's letters and Max Brod's biography, the year 1909 was one of deep depressions and literary crises for Kafka. Max Brod describes how he managed to revitalize Kafka's creative zest on their excursion to Riva at the beginning of September 1909: he tells how the notes on *Die Aeroplane in Brescia* (Bi 315) were written as part of a contest between the two of them, and that the diaries are to a certain extent a continuation of these travel notes (Bi 93). But Brod's conception of writing as a "sporting competition" was probably formed a few weeks before this vacation.

Brod writes in his diary at Whitsun 1909: "Indescribably beautiful excursion with Kafka and Weltsch to Dobrichowitz, spent the night, Mnisek—slept outdoors. —7 or 8 hours on foot."[1] Brod's literary description of this journey appears under the title of

"Zirkus auf dem Lande" in the periodical *Die Schaubühne* on July 1, 1909. A letter written by Kafka to Brod a few days later shows, however, that he is not able to share Brod's enthusiasm: "'The silence of a large area—etc.' The friends in the story did not say that, I think; if one were to tear it apart, they did not say that."[2] I suspect that Brod's publication provided the catalyst for Kafka's more sober literary recollections of this excursion (or of one of the later ones). Why do I suspect this?

The friendship between Max Brod and Felix Weltsch was based largely on their interest in epistemological philosophy. They read together publications of the Prague philosophy professors Anton Marty and Christian von Ehrenfels and also visited their lectures. Ehrenfels, in particular, worked on epistemic problems which had emerged as a result of Einstein's theory of relativity. For example, Einstein's theory had had repercussions for the perception of objects while in a state of motion, something Einstein liked to demonstrate with the example of a locomotive. It seems reasonable to suppose that the first entry in Kafka's diary, "the viewers stiffen when the train goes by" ("Die Zuschauer erstarren, wenn der Zug vorbeifährt," T 9), records a comment made during the conversations between Brod and Weltsch on their mutual excursions. It was out of these excursions that the concrete plan of Brod and Weltsch's joint book *Anschauung und Begriff* emerged some six months later. This comment may even have been an illustration for Kafka, who, years later, still voiced his disinterest in the theory of relativity. He wrote to Felice Bauer after *Anschauung und Begriff* appeared in print (Leipzig, 1913): "I have to force myself to read and understand; if there is nothing one can lay one's hand on, my attention flies away too easily."[3] In connection with the above-mentioned outings in 1909 this would also explain Kafka's entry in the diary: "The forest was apparently still there. But my gaze had hardly moved ten paces away when I gave up, caught again by a dull conversation."[4] Brod notes one of Kafka's comments made on one of the summer outings of 1909, "about someone who talks uninterruptedly": "Conversation grows out of his mouth like a branch."[5] In its pictorial nature, this comment bears a great resemblance to the diary entry: "'Wenn er mich immer frägt.' The 'ä,' freed from the sentence, flew away like a ball in a field."[6]

Immediately following this entry we find the passages on the dream sequences about the dancer Eduardova (T 9), whose "Czardas" Kafka had seen the week before the Whitsun outing, on May 24, 1909. Later Kafka wrote to Felice Bauer saying he had dreamed about it for months (F 254), most certainly meaning the summer of 1909.

On the basis of these parallels, however speculative, I think it is fair to assume that the initial entries in the diary up to and including the unpublished "Aus dem Coupeefenster," which are in the same characteristic handwriting and the same color ink, were all written in the summer of 1909. In fact, it is highly probable that these entries can be dated even more precisely as having been written in the first half of July 1909. As letters to Brod show, the period following this was a time of deep depression for Kafka and a time in which he suffered under a heavy workload at the Workers' Accident Insurance Bureau. Both of these factors led to a creative crisis which obviously continued until December 1909, only interrupted by "Die Aeroplane in Brescia," written at Brod's insistence.

Towards the end of 1909, Kafka undertook a longish business trip to northwest Bohemia. It is probably here that the first passage of "Unglücklichsein" (E 22) was written in pencil, not in the first notebook which was started in the summer and contained autobiographical notes, but in a second notebook, obviously intended for literary notes. My dating of the text is based upon a comparison with cards written by Kafka to his sisters Ottla and Elli on the journey, in lead or indelible pencil. Moreover, the fact that November is mentioned in the first sentence of the text is a fairly reliable indication of the date of writing, taking other Kafka texts into consideration. Furthermore, this date also corresponds to the entry in this first notebook made after he returned from this journey around Christmas 1909 and which directly follows the entry from July: "Finally, after five months of my life in which I could not write anything with which I would have been satisfied, it occurred to me to talk to myself again."[7]

As far as we know, over this period he only wrote the article on the airplanes, written at Brod's insistence, and the fragment "Unglücklichsein." Apart from the reference to the five-month break in "talking to himself," this entry can be dated by the fact that Kafka mentions the Japanese jugglers who visited Prague November 17 to 30, 1909, i.e., before Kafka's business trip to northwest Bohemia. A further guide is the mention of Halley's comet: reports on its approach and about astronomers' observations first appeared in the press in December. Kafka's comment, "last Christmas, as I was so far gone that I could hardly collect myself, and as I really seemed to be on the last rung of my ladder,"[8] could quite easily refer to Christmas 1908, when his relationship with Hedwig Weiler obviously underwent a crisis. The affair ended with a very formal letter from Kafka dated January 7, 1909 with which he returned all his letters from her (Br 65). This date is further substantiated by the fact that it is also in keeping with Kafka's habit of taking a "critical look back" over the previous year, something he continues to do in the years following with a certain regularity, even though he claims on December 31, 1914 that it is not really in line with his character to do so (T 453). His entry, however, is above all to be seen as an attempt at avoiding a renewed writer's block after abandoning "Unglücklichsein." Comments such as "if I really asked myself, there was always something to beat out of me, out of this pile of straw I have been for the last five months"[9] are an indication of this. The remark, "such a question does not yet bring me to speak,"[10] hints that Kafka was indeed faced with a "question" from outside which finally prompted him to speak: on January 16, 1910, a review entitled "Ein Roman der Jugend" appears under Kafka's name in the Prague daily paper *Bohemia*.

Inspired by this success, which Brod also supported by quoting from "Hochzeitsvorbereitungen auf dem Lande" in his lecture on January 28, "Gibt es Grenzen des Darstellbaren in der Kunst?," and who described Kafka as an "underrated young Prague author" (PK 90), Kafka begins a second version of his novella "Beschreibung eines Kampfes," but not in either of the two notebooks under discussion here.   An indication that this must have been written at least at approximately the same time as the "Unglücklichsein" fragment in the second notebook is provided by the sentence "I held my mouth open a little while, so that the excitement would leave me through the mouth,"[11] which Kafka inserts unchanged in the second version of "Beschreibung eines Kampfes" (BeK 29).   Another clear indication is provided by the sentence "In February they say to him: come to the Laurenziberg":[12]   the first version does not mention the month February.   According to an entry in Max Brod's diary, Kafka read part of the new version of "Beschreibung eines Kampfes" to him on March 14, 1910.   However, it emerges in later entries that Kafka's despair gets worse and worse, and that he writes of plans to commit suicide.   This phase of Kafka's literary production of his novella is abandoned after the brief continuation of the "Gespräch mit dem Beter" (BeK 115).

Kafka starts making entries in the first notebook again from May 1910 onwards.   He records the "night of comets," which he mistakenly dates as "17./18. Mai" (T 14), instead of 18-19 May, as it should have been according to reports in the Prague daily newspapers.   Furthermore, he makes entries on May 29 and June 19.   Brod's diary of 1910 records a great many meetings with Kafka in the Moldau baths in Prague and a few outings into the surrounding area, some of which lasted several days.   A card from Kafka to Brod tells of a summer vacation taken in the latter half of August (Br 81).   The last passage of the "Unglücklichsein" fragment in the second notebook written in pencil was possibly written on one of these long outings, but it is more likely that it was written over this short summer vacation.   Without noticing, Kafka changes from the "Sie"- to the "Du"-form in this passage.   After just one side of text, this fragment is abandoned again after "I know nothing" ("Nichts weiß ich").   Kafka does not in fact correct his mistake until the early part of 1911 when he takes up the fragment again in ink in the blank space remaining on the page (see facsimile).

However, having failed to continue this literary text for the time being, Kafka obviously hits upon the idea of writing a largely autobiographical piece, which he executes in nearly the same handwriting in the first notebook soon after failing to pick up the thread of "Unglücklichsein"; possibly this was also written in this August vacation. There are two pieces of text, both about one side in length and written in pencil, beginning: "When I think about it . . ." ("Wenn ich es bedenke . . . " T 14). Kafka tries to continue these pieces when he returns to Prague. After these two sides written in pencil, the first notebook continues with four further attempts written in ink which start "I often think" ("Oft überlege ich") and "I think often" ("Ich überlege oft"). In all, these texts take up twelve pages of the notebook.

Among the autobiographical elements included here we find further confirmation of the approximate date we have just suggested: "if I were that small dweller in the ruins, burned by the sun."[13] It is easy to see this as an echo of the journey undertaken with Brod, Weltsch and Werfel on July 16-17 to the Sazawa valley, which according to a contemporary guidebook "is surrounded by wooded heights," with "countless towering castles and ruins." Brod mentions on several occasions the sunburn Werfel suffered on this journey (Bi 91).

These attempts grew further and further removed from their autobiographical beginnings, so that probably shortly before the trip to Paris in October 1910, Kafka planned to undertake a new attempt, or to make a fair copy in the second notebook, the one reserved for literary texts. On the facing page to the final temporary end of the "Unglücklichsein" fragment, Kafka notes the following title in ink: "Der kleine Ruinenbewohner" (T 695). However, he did not find the time to carry out his plan before the journey to Paris. Possibly intending to write out a fair copy on the journey, he takes the second notebook with him and the first one in which Kafka must have written the passage about "men in danger" ("Männer in Gefahr," i.e., the text beginning: "It is reported, and we are inclined to believe . . . "[14]) shortly before setting off on his journey. At this time, both notebooks closed with entries written in ink.

On October 8, 1910, Kafka travelled with Max and Otto Brod to Paris, where he made brief travel notes, partly in shorthand. These notes are recorded on the front and rear covers of both the first and second notebooks; they are written in lead and indelible pencil. The first notebook includes three further entries in pencil (unpublished) right after "Men in Danger." These entries are separated from "Men in Danger" and from one another by horizontal lines which extend right across the page. Previously Kafka used a short horizontal stroke in the middle of the page to separate the entries. These notes make up the last entry in the first notebook which falls in the period I wish to talk about here.

Kafka uses this new method of separating his texts in the second notebook too. Here he attempts to carry on with the second version of "Beschreibung eines Kampfes," which he started in the early part of the year and which he abandoned after "Gespräch mit dem Beter." He continues writing under the title "Der kleine Ruinenbewohner," not even crossing it out (see facsimile). This text written in pencil traces Kafka's attempt to find his way back into the text: fresh starts alternate with reflections of the author/ narrator on the text and references to motifs of the abandoned text, such as "This bachelor with his thin clothes, his art of praying" and "that time in front of the church."[15] The very first attempt begins with the words: "'You,' I said" ("'Du,' sagte ich" T 17). Here too, in the middle of the revised version of "Beschreibung eines Kampfes," he changes to the "Du"-form, just as he had done before in the short passage in pencil in "Unglücklichsein" on the facing page, broken off shortly before setting off on his journey. However, unlike in "Unglücklichsein," where Kafka later corrected the address form, this sudden change is not just preserved in the rough drafts in the notebook, but also in the later fair copy of the second version (BeK 119). That these entries in the second notebook are indeed an attempt at a continuation of the second version of Kafka's novella is further substantiated by an event recorded in Max Brod's diary of the summer of 1910. Brod writes on June 11:

Afternoon swimming. Rowed with Kafka and his cousin. —Premonitions of death. —At that moment the suicide, we see him pulled out onto the deck, trembling, staring, sweating guards, onlookers in boats and on the bridge.[16]

This experience finds its way into the fresh start on the novella in the second notebook with the image: "the poisonous world will flow into my mouth like water into a drowning man."[17] This experience is even more in evidence, however, in the final version we have of "Beschreibung eines Kampfes," which is preserved separately from the diaries. The first paragraph after the continuation closes with the sentence: "Like an idler on the quay, you stand there and I lie as though drowned."[18]

A clue as to the date of these fresh attempts, made, according to our theory, during the trip to Paris is supplied by the expression: "just as one suddenly notices a boil on one's body."[19] If one interprets this as an indication of Kafka's physical condition at the time of writing, it is quite reasonable to suspect that this was written towards the end of the journey: a worsening furunculosis forced Kafka to return alone to Prague on October 17, 1910.

In December 1910, Kafka confesses in a letter to Brod that he has not written much since the trip to Paris (Br 85). He does not write anything more in the second notebook until November 6 (T 24). The notes following this date, all written in pencil, form a sequence which ends before an entry written in ink on November 15 (T 26). These are mainly further attempts at continuing the second version of "Beschreibung eines Kampfes." Right after the first attempt, however, follows the description of the lecture on Musset and that on Hebbel. All three entries are dated by Kafka afterwards. The new beginning of the story was obviously dated to keep a record of the fresh start to the entries, while the descriptions of the lectures visited were probably merely dated for the sake of precision, although reviews in the Prague daily newspapers show that Kafka dated both events a day too late.

The purely literary nature of the second notebook is relinquished as Kafka dates his entries for the first time and also describes events at which he was actually present. Although it has not yet been shown that Kafka undertook a journey from November 7-14, 1910, I assume that the sequence of entries made at this time was recorded on a journey, possibly a business trip. This theory is supported not only by the fact that the notes made at this time are in pencil, but also by the fact that Brod's diary does not record a meeting with Kafka between November 6 — the date of the Hebbel lecture — and November 16.

Back in Prague after this presumed journey, after drawing a long horizontal line underneath the last attempt at finishing "Beschreibung eines Kampfes," Kafka notes in black ink: "15 November, 10 o'clock. I will not let myself get tired. I will plunge into my novella even if it kills me."[20] This is a confession that, despite all his efforts, he had not been successful in his attempt at continuing the second version of "Gespräch mit dem Beter." Kafka obviously realizes that, with the entries he made on this assumed journey, this notebook has taken on the nature of a diary. The second notebook 'officially' becomes a diary with the immediate and precise system of dating Kafka introduces and through the discussions with himself which he now holds. In line with this, further entries dated immediately follow on the next few pages: November 16 on the "Iphigenie" lecture, and November 27 on the Kellermann reading, both of course in black ink.

Between the 3rd and 9th of December Kafka travels to Berlin. Over this period he writes further fragments commencing with "'Du,' sagte ich" in pencil, including the three lines in blue ink, both of which I mentioned earlier. A comparison with the cards written in Berlin in pencil and blue ink shows that these notes were quite definitely made on this journey.

After a final line that runs right across the page underneath the last fragment beginning with " 'Du,' sagte ich" (unpublished), Kafka takes a critical look back in the second notebook on December 15, 1910, similar to the one he took in the first notebook the previous year. Despite all his attempts — it must have been many more than are actually included in the diary, as he admits later that he has crossed out "five times as much as I have ever written"[21] in this one year — he has not successfully managed to continue the second version of "Beschreibung eines Kampfes" that he broke off in March. He did not manage to "jump into" his novella after all. In order to overcome this situation, "now almost a year long,"[22] he opts for the same solution as the previous year: discussions with himself in his diary.   However, much more decidedly than the previous year, he notes on December 16: "I will never leave the diary again.   This is where I must hold myself steady, for only here can I do so."[23]

Kafka's return to his diary is to be taken literally, as he recalls the last three entries made in the first notebook before his look back over the year in December 1909. "Writers talk nonsense" ("Schriftsteller reden Gestank" T 11) probably refers to the sharp criticism of a novel by W. Fred (T 28); with regard to "Die Weißnä-herinnen in den Regengüssen" (T 11), Kafka now explains in detail his interest in "secondary characters," such as the above-mentioned seamstresses in "Die Jungfern vom Bischofsberg" (T 29). "Aus dem Coupeefenster" (unpublished) is probably—in connection with the above-mentioned space-time theories—taken up again in "when asked whether anything is ever still, Zeno answered, yes, the flying arrow is at rest."[24]   The next entry strengthens even further the impression that Kafka also leafed through the first and original diary notebook when he returned to the diary. "How much more would the Germans admire the French if the French were German"[25] is obviously a commentary on the last entry made in the first notebook at this time: the travel notes from Paris. After this Kafka notes: "Of course my writing is also greatly hindered by the fact that I have crossed out and discarded so much, in fact almost everything I have written this year."[26] By this, he most certainly means the fresh starts on "Oft überlege ich" in the first notebook, "Unglücklichsein," which was at this time fragmentary, and the fragments beginning " 'Du,' sagte ich" in the second notebook. He is, in fact, probably referring to many more notes apart from these two notebooks, notes which have not survived.

As if to record his return to the diary, Kafka stops using the long line drawn right across the page, which he had been using since his trip to Paris. After his Berlin notes, he returns once more to the short stroke which he used to divide diary entries in the first notebook. With his almost daily entries towards the end of 1910 (T 29) and with the next fragment beginning " 'Du,' sagte ich," written at the beginning of 1911 (T 36), Kafka begins to return to literary productivity once more and starts to develop his own style of diary. He retains this style of diary more or less unchanged until 1923. This mixed bag of autobiographical and literary notes was certainly strongly influenced by Kafka's reading of Hebbel's and Goethe's diaries in the decisive phase of November-December 1910. An attempt at showing these influences on Kafka would, of course, go beyond the bounds of this essay. Finally, we may conclude that Kafka's entries in the first notebook, originally reserved for "talking to himself," clearly began in the summer, possibly July, of 1909. The first entries in the second notebook were probably made at the end of November 1909; though he began this one as a literary notebook, Kafka used it from November 1910 as a diary like the first. In these two notebooks, which Kafka used interchangeably until September 1911, his style develops out of the combination of autobiographical observations and literary sketches. The fragments beginning " 'Du,' sagte ich" belong in the context of the development of Kafka's novella "Beschreibung eines Kampfes," for they document his search, using the notebooks, for a way to continue the second version of the novella.[27]

In my inquiry, I have disregarded the strict principles of our edition and have presented some thoughts which have developed through my own knowledge of the author and his work and for which I can provide no strict scientific evidence, because they belong to the forefield of research work for the critical edition of the *Tagebücher und Reisetagebücher*.[28] However, I do hope that I have succeeded in making clear the aims of this critical edition: namely, to show the genesis of the texts and to show the author's method of working. We want to provide a basis for further research work on interpretation, on motifs, on influences of a literary and philosophical nature; to provide a basis for attempts at placing Kafka's work in its cultural context. In short, we want to provide a basis for work as we have come to expect it from Walter Sokel and which we expect to receive from him for many years to come.

Notes

The abbreviations used in the text refer to the following editions:

BeK   Franz Kafka, *"Beschreibung eines Kampfes." Die zwei Fassungen*, eds. M. Brod and L. Dietz (Frankfurt, 1969).

Bi   Max Brod, *Franz Kafka. Eine Biographie* (Frankfurt, 1954).

Br   Franz Kafka, *Briefe 1902-1924*, ed. M. Brod (Frankfurt, 1958).

E   Franz Kafka, *Sämtliche Erzählungen*, ed. P. Raabe (Frankfurt, 1970).

F   Franz Kafka, *Briefe an Felice*, eds. E. Heller and J. Born (Frankfurt, 1967).

PK   Max Brod, *Der Prager Kreis* (Stuttgart, 1966).

T   Franz Kafka, *Tagebücher 1910-1923*, ed. M. Brod (Frankfurt, 1951).

1   "Unbeschreiblich schöner Ausflug mit Kafka und Weltsch nach Dobrichowitz, übernachtet, Mnisek—Schlaf im Freien. —7 oder 8 Stunden zu Fuß." [Translations of Brod and Kafka by the editor.]

2   "'Die Stille aus einer großen Gegend—u.s.w.' das haben die Freunde in der Geschichte nicht gesagt, glaube ich; wenn man sie zerreißt, haben sie das nicht gesagt" (Br 70).

3   "Ich muß mich zum Lesen und Verstehen zwingen; wo nicht etwas dasteht, auf das man die Hand auflegen kann, verfliegt meine Aufmerksamkeit zu leicht" (F 317).

4   "Der Wald war noch so ziemlich da. Kaum aber war mein Blick zehn Schritte weit, ließ ich ab, wieder eingefangen vom langweiligen Gespräch" (T 9).

5   "Das Gespräch kommt ihm wie ein Stock aus dem Mund."

6   "'Wenn er mich immer frägt.' Das ä, losgelöst vom Satz, flog dahin wie ein Ball auf der Wiese" (T 9).

7 "Endlich nach fünf Monaten meines Lebens, in denen ich nichts schreiben konnte, womit ich zufrieden gewesen wäre . . . komme ich auf den Einfall, wieder einmal mich anzusprechen" (T 11).

8 ". . . letzte Weihnachten . . . wo ich so weit war, daß ich mich nur noch gerade fassen konnte, und wo ich wirklich auf der letzten Stufe meiner Leiter schien" (T 12).

9 ". . . wenn ich mich wirklich fragte, hier war immer noch etwas aus mir herauszuschlagen, aus diesem Strohhaufen, der ich seit fünf Monaten bin" (T 12).

10 "eine solche Anfrage bringt mich noch nicht zum Reden" (T 12).

11 "Ein Weilchen lang hielt ich den Mund offen, damit mich die Aufregung durch den Mund verlasse" (E 23).

12 "Im Februar sagt man ihm: Du komm auf den Laurenziberg" (BeK 23).

13 ". . . wäre ich jener kleine Ruinenbewohner gewesen, abgebrannt von der Sonne" (T 14).

14 "Es wird berichtet, und wir sind aufgelegt es zu glauben . . . " (T 16).

15 "Dieser Junggeselle mit seinen dünnen Kleidern, seiner Betkunst" (T 19); "damals vor der Kirche" (T 17).

16 "Nachm. Baden. Gerudert mit Kafka u. dessen Cousine. —Todesahnungen. —In demselben Moment der Selbstmörder, wir sehn ihn herausgezogen auf den Brettern, zitternd, glotzen [sic], schwitzende Wachleute, Zuseher in Boten [sic], auf der Brücke."

17 "die giftige Welt wird mir in den Mund fließen wie das Wasser in den Ertrinkenden" (T 20).

18 "Wie ein Faulpelz auf dem Quai stehst Du dort und ich liege da wie ertrunken" (BeK 119).

19 "so wie man plötzlich an seinem Leib ein Geschwür bemerkt" (T 20).

20 "15. November, zehn Uhr. Ich werde mich nicht müde werden lassen. Ich werde in meine Novelle hineinspringen und wenn es mir das Gesicht zerschneiden sollte" (T 26).

21 "fünfmal so viel als ich überhaupt je geschrieben habe" (T 29).

22 "nun schon fast ein Jahr dauernden Zustand" (T 27).

23 "Ich werde das Tagebuch nicht mehr verlassen. Hier muß ich mich festhalten, denn nur hier kann ich es" (T 28).

24 "Zeno sagte auf eine dringliche Frage hin, ob denn nichts ruhe: Ja, der fliegende Pfeil ruht" (T 29).

25 "Wenn die Franzosen ihrem Wesen nach Deutsche wären, wie würden sie dann erst von den Deutschen bewundert sein" (T 29).

26 "Daß ich soviel weggelegt und weggestrichen habe, ja fast alles, was ich in diesem Jahr überhaupt geschrieben habe, das hindert mich jedenfalls auch sehr am Schreiben" (T 29).

27 The passage beginning "Finally, we may conclude . . . " was translated by the editor.

28 The critical edition of the *Tagebücher und Reisetagebücher* has meanwhile appeared. See Franz Kafka, *Tagebücher. Kritische Ausgabe*, eds. Hans Gerd Koch, Michael Müller, and Malcolm Pasley (Frankfurt, 1990).

'Eine gewaltige Erschütterung des Tradierten': Walter Benjamin's Political Recuperation of Franz Kafka*

Michael Jennings
Princeton University

In the English-language world, Franz Kafka has long been enshrined in the pantheon of high modernism. In courses, where he is regularly compared to Joyce, Eliot, and Pound, and in study after study of canonical modernism, Kafka figures as principle German-language exemplar of a modernist literature defined by its extreme autonomy and its extreme aestheticism.[1] Indeed, the current debate on central categories of twentieth-century literary history—modernism versus avantgarde and popular culture, modernism versus postmodernism—has as yet hardly touched Kafka.[2] Walter Benjamin's groundbreaking work on Kafka is a notable exception here. Benjamin's late thinking on Kafka reveals aspects of Kafka's work which call radically into question the place usually accorded Kafka in the histories of twentieth-century literature.

Benjamin's great essay "Franz Kafka" of 1934 is frequently adduced in support of arguments for Kafka's essential modernism. This essay, though, stands as something of an anomaly in the corpus of Benjamin's late work. With a few notable exceptions, every major essay Benjamin wrote after 1928 was related in a direct manner to the massive project of constructing an *Urgeschichte*—a primordial or true history—of modernity and drawing from that *Urgeschichte* its political consequences.[3] This project took shape under the sign of the *Passagen-Werk* (Arcades project), his study of mid-nineteenth century France and the arcades which he took to be its consummate symbol.[4] "Franz Kafka," however, bears the

mark of the focus on the arcades only in its form; Benjamin's construction of the essay provides us with an early approximation of
the dialectical strategies that will shape Benjamin's writing of the
Passagen-Werk itself.[5] The essay's thematic concerns, on the other
hand, are dictated by close reading of a broad spectrum of Kafka's
texts and thus address directly none of the concerns which dominate the essays in the orbit of the *Passagen-Werk*:   capitalism,
commodity fetishism, the disappearance of the aura.

Benjamin's engagement with Kafka hardly came to an end with
the writing of the 1934 essay, however.   After 1935, Benjamin
attempted intermittently to integrate a reading of Kafka into his
late theory of modernity.   Adorno was the first to challenge Benjamin to extend his thinking on Kafka into the conceptual realms
of the *Passagen-Werk*; already in December 1934, Adorno pointed
to the "unfinished" quality of "Franz Kafka" precisely as it related
to the Arcades: "The relationship of Urgeschichte and Modernity
has not yet been properly conceptualized and the success of a
Kafka interpretation is dependent on that."[6]

It was not until 1938 that Benjamin produced further material on
Kafka.   In 1938 and 1939 he attempted, with Gershom Scholem as
intermediary, to interest Salman Schocken in a book-length study
of Kafka.   In a letter to Scholem of June 1938, Benjamin articulated his new thinking on Kafka; the letter, intended as an exposé
of Benjamin's ideas that could be shown to Schocken, has all the
polish and epigrammatic force of a Benjaminian essay.   That letter
has to date been read as an *extension* of the ideas in the 1934 essay
and thus viewed in isolation from Benjamin's other work in the late
1930's.[7]   Yet Benjamin offers in this letter a reading of Kafka
which marks a radical break with that contained in the earlier
essay, a reading which not only makes explicit the connections
between Kafka and Benjamin's late work, but which might serve as
the starting point for a rethinking of Kafka's place in twentieth-
century literary history.

Benjamin begins his consideration of Kafka thus: "Kafka's work
is an ellipsis whose foci, which lie at a great distance from one
another, are determined by mystical experience (which is above all

the experience of tradition) and by the experience of the modern person in the metropolis."8 To take the latter point first: Benjamin asserts that Kafka depicts in his works a particular kind of modern experience, that determined by life in the capitalist metropolis. He attempts to get at the exact character of that experience by adducing a contemporary essay on modern physics, Eddington's "Weltbild der Physik":

> I stand on the threshold of the door, about to enter my room. That is a complicated undertaking. First I must struggle against the atmosphere . . . I must furthermore attempt to land on a board that is flying around the sun at 30 kilometers a second; only a fraction of a second's delay, and the board is already miles away. . . And the board has no solid substance. To step on it is to step on a swarm of flies. Won't I fall through? No, for if I dare and step on it, one of the flies meets me and gives me a shove upwards. . . (761).9

The intended analogy is clear: the modern world has a substance like that depicted in Kafka's short prose text "The Trees" (Bäume), a temporality like that in "A Common Confusion" (Eine alltägliche Verwirrung), and a causality akin to Odradek's. Benjamin's essay accords unusual emphasis, though, to the social and economic determinants of this experience. Benjamin reads Kafka's figurations of experience as a series of shock-like occurrences whose principles, origins, and effects remain opaque. In fact, the human agent in Kafka's world remains wholly unaware that experience is thus constituted. Benjamin insists, in other words, that humans are at once inalterably shaped by the character of their experience and *denied* any awareness of its character as a series of shocks.

It is Kafka's particular genius to have found a form that can reveal the true character of modern historical experience. And that form was accessible to him only because of his awareness of mysticism.

> It is the really and in a precise sense madly wonderful thing (Tolle) about Kafka, that this newest world of experience was born to him precisely through mystical experience. . . . One must appeal to nothing less than the forces of this tradition if the individual . . . is to be confronted with that reality which projects itself theoretically in modern physics and practically in the technology of war. I mean to say that this reality is hardly experienceable any

longer for the individual, and that Kafka's often so cheerful world that is per-
meated with the angelic is the exact complement to his epoch (762).[10]

In the 1934 essay, Benjamin had argued for Kafka's particular gift
for "Studium," for a particular kind of attentiveness that made
present to him aspects of a forgotten "pre-world" (Vorwelt), a
sphere of pre-rational, inchoate myth whose laws nonetheless
determine the course of human existence. Now, in 1938, that same
mystical capability is shown to orient itself instead toward the
"Urgeschichte" of modernity, that underlying stratum of the true
character of the age concealed beneath the phantasmagorias of
commodity capitalism and further obscured by the fragmentary
character of modern experience.[11]

Benjamin's apodictic assertion of an intimate connection
between the fragmented, inassimilable experience of the individual
in the big city and the integral and integrative experience of the
mystic is notable first of all for its density and allusiveness. And the
formulaic character of Benjamin's utterance depends, in fact, upon
a series of coded references to a fully developed theory of experience "beneath" the essay. Benjamin's antithesis exactly parallels
the structure upon which he builds his interpretation of Charles
Baudelaire in the essay "Über einige Motive bei Baudelaire;" in its
crudest form, it is the distinction between *Erlebnis* and *Erfahrung*
(fragmented, shock-like, isolated experiences versus experience as
an integral, discursive continuum) articulated in that essay. The
1938 letter—and its late interpretation of Kafka—arose from a
parallel process of thinking about Kafka and thinking about
Baudelaire, who had by 1938 emerged as the protagonist of the
Passagen-Werk, and indeed of the drama of modernity itself.[12]

In the late draft of Benjamin's book on Baudelaire now in the
Bibliothèque Nationale,[13] Benjamin argues that Baudelaire's
"sensitive disposition"—the tendency toward the Swedenborgian
mysticism of the *correspondances*, toward the apperception of subterranean interconnections between things—granted to Baudelaire
the intermittent rumor of a now lost integrated and meaningful
experience. "The *correspondances* are the data of remembrance.—... What makes festive days great and significant is the

encounter with an earlier life."[14] Such days are exceptions, however, breaks in a pattern of shocks dealt the individual by life in the
capitalist metropolis. An adequate synthesis or understanding of
the character of that experience is denied the human resident in
the urban metropolis. Paradoxically enough, it is mystical remembrance of an integrated experience which casts into a harsh light
and so brings to consciousness the true condition of historical
experience in the mid-nineteenth century. For Benjamin, mysticism functions together with, as a sort of counterpoint to, the structures of modern alienation and precipitates itself in the stark con-
tours of Baudelaire's poetry. "Baudelaire in 'Spleen' and 'Vie
antérieure' holds in his hands the scattered fragments of genuine
historical experience."[15] It is in this sense that Baudelaire becomes
for Benjamin the representative poet of modernity.

In a wonderful aside in another letter, Benjamin shows just how
deeply his thinking on Kafka and modern experience has become
embedded in his thinking on the arcades and Baudelaire. He
claims for that special class of Kafkan figures, among whom the
helpers are most prominent, a function analogous to that of the
flâneur. Just as the flâneur wanders the Grands Boulevards,
allowing a series of disparate, shock-like experiences to be
inscribed on his body as he preserves them visually; so do the
helpers, in a state of intoxication akin to a mystical trance, wander
though the Kafkan universe. Such figures, in their difference and
apparent groundlessness, alone seem capable of bringing to consciousness the fragmented and alienating character of historical
conditions. It is not so much that they penetrate the facade of the
apparently integral social world, but rather that they reveal it
through their very brokenness.[16] Benjamin attributes to Kafka,
then, a socially transformative impulse, the impulse to allow masses
of human beings to transcend the brute, reactive character of their
experience of the world and to become aware of its character and
the conditions which produce it.[17]

The primary thrust of the parallel between the late Kafka essay
and the late work on Baudelaire is not, however, in any sense thematic; the analysis of experience is in both instances the precondi-

tion to a crucial discrimination of form. The depiction in the late letter on Kafka of the relations between a mystically-derived but finally irrecoverable wisdom and the shock-driven, wholly discontinuous character of modern experience clearly emerged out of Benjamin's long-term redefinition of the nature of the modern work of art. Benjamin in his late work distinguishes the symbolic or auratic work of art as an autonomous, integrated aesthetic object from the non-auratic or allegorical work of art which actively resists those qualities.[18] For Benjamin, Baudelaire's status as the hero of modern life derives in large part from his strategic deployment of spleen and its attendant poetic device, allegory, against the emerging structures of capitalism. Random, esoterically charged allegorical images, in their similarity to the denatured things of the world, reflect a history that itself has become increasingly analogous to the natural and capitalistic production of shattered, fetishized objects. For Benjamin, Baudelaire's use of allegory — his notion that "l'imagination décompose toute la création" — was an essential aspect of the rational project of demystification Habermas associates powerfully with modernism. Baudelaire's work has a "destructive, purifying character. This art is useful, in that it is destructive. Its destructive furor is directed not least toward the fetishized conception of art. It thereby serves 'pure' art in the sense of a purified art."[19] Allegory breaks down the fetishized appearance of the commodity, breaks through the mythic, phantasmagorical powers that distort and deflect our ability to apprehend the structure and character of present historical conditions. "Baudelaire's allegory shows the traces of the violence that was necessary to tear through the harmonic facade of the world that surrounded him."[20] This power was obtained at the cost, though, of an "abstinence from the enchantment of distance,"[21] at the cost of giving up the seductive glimmer of the auratic work of art.

It is important to note here that Benjamin's discrimination of auratic and non-auratic forms is neither progressive nor period-fixed. The typology in question here is not the description of a historical progression from one form to a later, more "advanced" form. Allegory, the non-auratic form Benjamin discusses most extensively, is typical of the Baroque and Baudelaire; he finds allegorical features in places as unlikely as Russian naturalism and Cocteau's dramas. The film, with its "optical unconscious," the photomontages of the Berlin Dadaists, with their attempt to retrain modern political perception, and of course Brecht's epic theater all perform an analogously revelatory function and must be classed as non-auratic forms. Similarly, the auratic, totalizing work of art occurs in the renaissance, in all forms of neoclassicism, and in the twentieth century in a high modern novelist such as Thomas Mann. Precisely because of this capacity to characterize varied works usually subsumed under one period style, the term aura emerges from Benjamin's discussion as a potentially powerful intervention in the current debates regarding high modernism and mass culture and modernism versus postmodernism.

Andreas Huyssen's designation of the boundary between modernism and mass culture as the "great divide" of course speaks directly to this problem. Yet Huyssen's attempts to discern breaks in the monolithic facade of the modernist project—his focus on "strategic moves tending to destabilize the high/low opposition from within"—loop back repeatedly to admissions of the "resilience" of this opposition.[22] The isolation of moments of opposition to totalizing, autonomous art has become especially pressing today, as attacks upon modernism's purportedly *inherent* tendency toward reaction and even fascism have begun to proliferate.

We cannot claim that Kafka's work wholly denies its auratic—and thus in a certain sense retrograde—status. One need think only of the trance-like state in which Kafka claims to have produced so apparently hermetic a text as "Das Urteil." "Nur so kann geschrieben werden," Kafka's evaluation of writing that story, points to a seamless, integral, and inspired model of artistic production. The Anglo-American reception of his work, the seemingly remainderless absorption of Kafka into that canon of high modernism, also clearly points to affinities between Kafkan form and Benjamin's definition of the auratic text. Yet the late essay covertly claims for Kafka a status as a paradigm of his class and time, and for Benjamin, that status is consistently related to the formal strategies at work in an oeuvre. My title—which comes from the essay on technologically reproducible art—is intended to mark out the entry into this problem: Kafka's work stands for Benjamin precisely at the crucial instant of a typological turn from auratic to non-auratic works. For Benjamin, Kafka's texts do not so much stand at a particular point on the continuum from symbolic to non-auratic art as *embody* the crucial antithesis itself.

The 1934 essay begins with the words "Es wird erzählt:" it is told or narrated. In the late essay on Nikolai Leskov, "The Storyteller," Benjamin argues for oral storytelling as the privileged form for the transmission of a community's wisdom—like the concept of Erfahrung, an integrated, epic, and socially productive force. Benjamin evokes that same sense in the late Kafka essay: "One has occasionally attempted to define wisdom as the epic side of truth. Wisdom is thereby characterized as the stuff of tradition; it is truth in its haggadic consistency" (763).[23] This wisdom, indeed truth itself, is, however, no longer available under the economic and social conditions which determine modernity; it is Kafka's particular greatness to have figured that loss. The mere awareness of what Benjamin elsewhere calls the human *Leidensgeschichte* of course hardly distinguishes Kafka from his contemporaries; instead, it is the discovery of a particular form which brings this loss to consciousness which constitutes his genius. For Benjamin, the form of Kafka's parables is, irrespective of content, the emancipatory element in his work.[24] "He surrendered truth in order to hold fast to the transmissibility, to the haggadic element" (763).[25] Kafka's works constitute a "sickening of tradition;" they mark the point at which the transmission of wisdom is hollowed out, becoming transmission *tout court*.[26] In this they are like allegorical works, which "know many riddles but no secret. The riddle is a fragment that makes a whole together with another fragment that fits together with it. One has addressed secrets since time immemorial in the image of the veil, which is the accomplice of distance. Distance appears veiled."[27] In their pretense to wholeness, organicism, and finally wisdom, the parables share, in other words, certain properties with auratic art. Yet they remain at the same time resolutely non-auratic, they distinguish themselves in their essential hollowness from works founded upon the symbol. Kafka's parables attain their simultaneous beauty and misery from the persistent sense that they had to be more than parables.

In this they reveal their social determination. Benjamin relates the hollow, brittle character of Baudelaire's art to societal processes: "in the nineteenth century the number of 'hollowed-out' things increased at a pace previously unknown, since technological progress constantly put new functional objects out of circulation."[28] Benjamin's emphasis here—and in particular the shift from his position in "Franz Kafka" with its privileging of depth and wisdom—shows, among other things, his ability to incorporate a Brechtian component in his thinking after about 1935. His earlier conversations with Brecht show him defending an auratic, secret core to Kafka's work against Brecht's insistence on Kafka's demystifying potential.[29] Now, in 1938, we find a Brechtian emphasis where we might least expect it, in reference to a cognitive and linguistic world that is anything but crude (*plump*). Kafka's texts, like mechanically reproduced forms and like commodities, include a moment of resistance to characterization by such terms as uniqueness and authenticity. "In the instant at which authenticity fails as an evaluation of the work of art, the entire social function of art is transformed. In place of its grounding in ritual, a grounding in another form of praxis emerges: namely its grounding in politics."[30] In its resistance to a rhetoric of totalization, indeed in its resistance to the transmission which occurs in narrative, Kafka's works make problematic their assimilation into a tradition of domination.[31] Benjamin's late reading shows high modernist form, and especially its pretension to wholeness and signifying potential, as it breaks down toward the popular and the avantgarde, in short toward the social and the political.

Of all the artists treated by Benjamin, Baudelaire and Kafka must occupy a unique position. All others stand on one side or another of the great divide between allegory and symbol; only Kafka and Baudelaire show the aura *in the process of its decay*.

Kafka's parables are at once auratic and allegorical; they distinguish themselves by their unique ability to *rehearse the processes* which hollowed them out. The antitheses in Kafka's work between mysticism and shock, between aura and its destruction constitute its greatness. Rethinking Kafka in this manner means rethinking his relationship to the historical avant-garde and especially his incorporation into his texts of what Peter Bürger has called the praxis of life.

Benjamin's essay sheds new light not only on the progressive tendency of Kafka's formal strategies; those same texts that stand on the fault lines between popular and modernist forms also precondition the character, and especially the diversity, of their reception: "As the use value dies away from things, these alienated objects are hollowed out and attract to themselves meanings in the form of ciphers."[32] The promise of wisdom and the frustration of that desire in the black hole of Kafka interpretation emerge in Benjamin's reading as the result, then, of a reciprocal process involving technological progress and cognitive regression. Interpretation in its diversity attempts to fill the void haunted by the penumbra of departed wisdom; Kafka criticism, with its seemingly endless willingness to carry on the chain of mutually replaceable signifieds and sigifiers, assures the ongoing emancipatory force of Kafka's work, as such substitutions are always only inadequate replacements for wisdom. In the letter to Scholem, the revelatory and even transformative potentials in Kafka emerge only when Kafka's texts are brushed against the grain.

> In every true work of art, there is a point at which anyone who puts himself into it will feel it blowing toward him like the cool wind of the coming dawn. It becomes apparent that art, which has often been considered resistant in any connection to progress, can give the latter its true determination. Progress lodges, not in the continuity of the course of time, but rather in its moments of interference: where the truly new first makes itself felt with the sobriety of the dawn.[33]

Benjamin's understanding of Kafka's liminal position between auratic and non-auratic art enjoins the reader, then, not so much to invest new meaning in these ciphers, but to move beyond the com-

mentator's despair and to question the conditions that produced—
and produce—such art. We might paraphrase Benjamin's final
verdict on Baudelaire the poet in the following way: "It is nearly
worthless to want to draw the position of a Kafka into the network
of the most advanced positions in the struggle for human liberation. It appears from the first more propitious to trace his machi-
nations there, where he is doubtless at home: in the enemy camp.
. . . Kafka was a secret agent—an agent of the secret unhappiness
of his class with its own rule."[34]

Notes

* I am grateful to Eric Santner and Alain Toumayan for perceptive critiques of this essay.

1 Cf., for example, Martin Greenberg, *The Terror of Art: Kafka and Modern Literature* (New York, Basic Books, 1968).

2 On the question of the relations between modernism, avantgarde, and popular culture, see esp. Andreas Huyssen, *After the Great Divide: Modernism, Mass Culture, Postmodernism* (Bloomington: University of Indiana Press, 1986), pp. vii-xii and 3-15. Huyssen draws heavily on the work of Adorno, Benjamin, and especially upon Peter Bürger's *Theorie der Avant-garde* (Frankfurt/M: Suhrkamp Verlag, 1974).

3 The essays on Brecht, for example, have an only tenuous relationship to the larger project; a seemingly unrelated essay, however, such as "Karl Kraus," emerged directly from the thinking on nihilism and the theory of citation Benjamin developed in connection with his study of the Parisian arcades. On the concept of Urgeschichte, see my *Dialectical Images: Walter Benjamin's Theory of Literary Criticism* (Ithaca: Cornell University Press, 1987), pp. 78-79, 87-88, 207.

4 Benjamin began collecting material for his massive sociocultural history of mid-nineteenth century Paris in 1927; only his death at the Spanish border in 1940, in flight before the Nazi death machine, brought his work on the project to a standstill. The volume edited by Rolf Tiedemann in 1981 and titled *Das Passagen-Werk* consists of Benjamin's massive accumulation of citations from nineteenth-century sources, commentary on those sources, and a highly developed theoretical model which he hoped to apply to them. On the *Passagen-Werk*, see my *Dialectical Images*, pp. 15-41, 204-219; Susan Buck-Morss, "Benjamin's Passagen-Werk: Redeeming Mass Culture for the Revolution," *New German Critique* 29, 1981, pp. 211-40; and James Rolleston, "The Politics of Quotation: Walter Benjamin's Arcades Project," *PMLA* 104, no. 1 (1989), pp. 13-27.

5 In an unpublished essay, Roland Dollinger has demonstrated that the essay's form is determined by the principle of the dialectical image developed in conjunction with the Arcades Project.

6 "Das Verhältnis von Urgeschichte und Moderne ist noch nicht zum Begriff erhoben und das Gelingen einer Kafkainterpretation muß in letzter Instanz davon abhängen." Adorno to Benjamin, Dec. 17, 1934, cited in Benjamin, *Gesammelte Schriften*, ed. Rolf Tiedemann and Hermann Schweppenhäuser (Frankfurt am Main: Suhrkamp Verlag, 1972-85), II, p. 1175. All translations are my own unless otherwise noted.

7 Cf., e.g., Bernd Witte, "Feststellungen zu Walter Benjamin und Kafka," *Neue Rundschau* 84 (1973), pp. 480-94.

8 Kafkas Werk ist eine Ellipse, deren weit auseinanderliegende Brennpunkte von der mystischen Erfahrung (die vor allem die Erfahrung von der Tradition ist) einerseits, von der Erfahrung des modernen Großstadtmenschen andererseits, bestimmt sind. Walter Benjamin, *Briefe*, ed. Theodor Adorno and Gershom Scholem (Frankfurt am Main: Suhrkamp Verlag, 1966), p. 760. Hereafter cited in the text by page number.

9 Ich stehe auf der Türschwelle, im Begriffe, mein Zimmer zu betreten. Das ist ein kompliziertes Unternehmen. Erstens muß ich gegen die Atmosphäre ankämpfen. . . . Ferner muß ich auf einem Brett zu landen versuchen, das mit einer Geschwindigkeit von 30 Kilometer in der Sekunde um die Sonne fliegt; nur den Bruchteil einer Sekunde Verspätung, und das Brett ist bereits meilenweit entfernt. . . . Auch hat das Brett keine feste Substanz. Darauftreten heißt auf einen Fliegenschwarm treten. Werde ich nicht hindurchfallen? Nein, denn wenn ich es wage und darauf trete, so trifft mich eine der Fliegen und gibt mir einen Stoß nach oben; ich falle wieder und werde von einer anderen Fliege nach oben geworfen.

10 Es ist das eigentlich und im präzisen Sinne *Tolle* an Kafka, daß diese allerjüngste Erfahrungswelt ihm gerade durch die mystische Tradition zugetragen wurde. Das Kurze und Lange von der Sache ist, daß offenbar an nichts Geringeres als an die Kräfte dieser Tradition appelliert werden mußte, sollte ein Einzelner (der Franz Kafka hieß) mit *der* Wirklichkeit konfrontiert werden, die sich als die unsrige theoretisch z. B. in der modernen Physik, praktisch in der Kriegstechnik projiziert. Ich will sagen, daß diese Wirklichkeit für den *Einzelnen* kaum mehr erfahrbar, und daß Kafkas vielfach so heitere und von Engeln durchwirkte Welt das genaue Komplement seiner Epoch ist.

11 Walter Sokel has argued for the presence of a parallel, though not identical, dichotomy in Kafka's poetics, a tension between a "communal, collective, and universalist" project and an "inward and subjective" element with a "Gnostic spiritualist" dimension. Sokel, "Language and Truth in the Two Worlds of Franz Kafka," *German Quarterly* 52 (May 1979), p. 374.

12 The Kafka-Baudelaire connection remains wholly subterranean in the letter. Most obviously, Benjamin would have attempted to keep anything "dangerous" out of an initial approach to Schocken; Scholem would certainly

have considered categories of historical materialism, however idiosyncratic, dangerous in the extreme. More importantly, though, the simultaneous existence of surface discourse and master sub-discourse marks the letter as a canonical Benjamin essay.

13 My reading of the Kafka-Baudelaire connection is based not so much on Benjamin's two famous essays on Baudelaire as on the late draft for the book *Charles Baudelaire: A Lyric Poet in the Age of High Capitalism.* This draft, now in Paris at the Bibliotheque Nationale under the title "Notes et fiches pour *Charles Baudelaire: Ein Lyriker im Zeitalter des Hochkapitalismus*", was discovered in 1981; it will appear as an appendix to Volume VII of Benjamin's *Gesammelte Schriften.* Essentially a selection and ordering of portions of the *Passagen-Werk* (it includes fully developed section and chapter headings), the draft of the Baudelaire book lends us the most complete picture of Benjamin's astonishingly original reading of the poet.

14 Die correspondances sind die Data des Eingedenkens. Sie sind keine historischen, sondern Data der Vorgeschichte. Was die festlichen Tage groß und bedeutsam macht, ist die Begegnung mit einem früheren Leben. Walter Benjamin, *Illuminations*, ed. Hannah Arendt, trans. Harry Zohn, (New York: Schocken Books, 1969) p. 182; *Gesammelte Schriften*, I, p. 639.

15 Wenn Baudelaire im spleen und in der vie antérieure die auseinandergesprengten Bestandstücke echter historischer Erfahrung in Händen hält, . . . Benjamin, *Illuminations*, p. 185; *Gesammelte Schriften* I, p. 643.

16 Benjamin, *Briefe*, p. 807.

17 In a way absolutely characteristic of the structures of Benjamin's thought, this awareness is described as bound tightly to a pervasive nihilism. "The experience that corresponds to that of the private individual Kafka may well be obtainable by great masses of humans only on the occasion of the experience of their annihilation." Die Erfahrung, die der des Privatmanns Kafka entspricht, dürfte von großen Massen wohl erst gelegentlich dieser ihrer Abschaffung zu erwerben sein (762). The mystic light flares up only in the moment of destruction. For Kafka as for Baudelaire, mysticism is the horizon against which decline must be judged, against which the adequacy of the new is to be measured.

18 On symbol, allegory, and aura, see my *Dialectical Images*, pp. 166-78.

19 Sie besteht in dessen zerstörendem, purifikatorischen Charakter. Diese Kunst ist nützlich, indem sie zerstörend ist. Ihr zerstörender Ingrimm richtet sich nicht zum wenigsten gegen den fetischistischen Kunstbegreiff. Dadurch dient sie der 'reinen' Kunst im Sinne einer gereinigten. Benjamin, "Notes et fiches pour *Charles Baudelaire. Ein Lyriker im Zeitalter des Hochkapitalis-*

mus," unpaginated; also in *Das Passagen-Werk* J 49, 1 (*Gesammelte Schriften* V, p. 399).

20 Die Allegorie Baudelaires trägt Spuren der Gewalttätigkeit, welche von Nöten war, um die harmonische Fassade der ihn umgebenden Welt einzureißen. Benjamin, "Notes et fiches pour *Charles Baudelaire*," unpaginated; also in *Das Passagen-Werk*, J 55a, 3 (*Gesammelte Schriften* V, p. 414).

21 Der Verzicht auf den Zauber der Ferne. Benjamin, "Notes et fiches pour *Charles Baudelaire*," unpaginated; also in *Das Passagen-Werk*, J 56a, 12 (*Gesammelte Schriften* V, p. 417).

22 Huyssen, p. vii.

23 Man hat die Weisheit gelegentlich als die epische Seite der Wahrheit definieren wollen. Damit ist die Weisheit als ein Traditionsgut gekennzeichnet; sie ist die Wahrheit in ihrer haggadischen Konsistenz.

24 Heinz Politzer's approach to Kafka is of course also informed by an emphasis on parabolic form and by the conviction that such forms communicate no wisdom, but only paradox—what we might now call aporia. Politzer, *Franz Kafka: Parable and Paradox* (Ithaca: Cornell University Press, 1962).

25 Er gab der Wahrheit preis, um an der Tradierbarkeit, an dem haggadischen Element festzuhalten.

26 Two recent discussions of the problem of truth in Kafka deserve mention here. Stanley Corngold has argued—largely on the basis of a reading of Kafka's aphorisms—for the existence of a "system of affirmations" ("truth," "the splendor of life") in Kafka's texts. Manfred Frank and Gerhard Kurz insist on the absolute unavailability of truth, of the absolute otherness of knowledge in Kafka's works. Benjamin's concentration on Kafka's parabolic *form* produces an argument for the production of a kind of negative knowledge, the consciousness of the absence of truth. Frank and Kurz, *Ordo Inversus: Geist und Zeichen* (Heidelberg: Carl Winter Universitätsverlag, 1977), pp. 75-92; Corngold, *Franz Kafka: The Necessity of Form* (Ithaca: Cornell University Press, 1988), pp. 123-136.

27 Die Allegorie kennt viele Rätsel aber kein Geheimnis. Das Rätsel ist ein Bruchstück, welches mit einem andern Bruchstück, das zu ihm paßt, ein Ganzes macht. Das Geheimnis sprach man seit jeher im Bilde des Schleiers an, der ein alter Komplize der Ferne ist. Die Ferne erscheint verschleiert. Benjamin, "Notes et fiches pour *Charles Baudelaire*," unpaginated; also in *Das Passagen-Werk*, J 77a, 8 (*Gesammelte Schriften* V, p. 461).

28 . . . daß im neunzehnten Jahrhundert die Zahl der 'ausgehöhlten' Dinge in vorher ungekanntem Maß und Tempo zunimmt, da der technische Fortschritt immer neue Gebrauchsgegenstände außer Kurs setzt. Benjamin,

"Notes et fiches pour *Charles Baudelaire*," unpaginated; also in *Das Passagen-Werk*, N 5, 2 (*Gesammelte Schriften* V, p. 582); in English as "Theoretics of Knowledge; Theory of Progress," trans. Leigh Hafrey and Richard Sieburth, *The Philosophical Forum* 15, nos. 1-2 (1983-1984), p. 12; translation slightly amended.

29   See Benjamin, "Conversations with Brecht" in Fredric Jameson, ed., *Aesthetics and Politics* (London: New Left Books, 1977), pp. 88-91.

30   In dem Augenblick aber, da der Maßstab der Echtheit an der Kunstproduktion versagt, hat sich auch die gesamte soziale Funktion der Kunst umgewälzt. An die Stelle ihrer Fundierung aufs Ritual tritt ihre Fundierung auf eine andere Praxis: nämlich ihre Fundierung auf Politik. Benjamin, *Illuminations*, p. 224; *Gesammelte Schriften*, I, p. 482.

31   The draft of the Baudelaire book suggests that the following series of terms are related in an essential way: totality — aura — narrative — domination.

32   Indem an Dingen ihr Gebrauchswert abstirbt, werden die entfremdeten ausgehöhlt und ziehen als Chiffern Bedeutungen herbei. Benjamin, "Notes et fiches pour *Charles Baudelaire*," unpaginated; also in *Das Passagen-Werk*, N 5, 2 (*Gesammelte Schriften* V, p. 582); in English as "Theoretics of Knowledge; Theory of Progress," trans. Leigh Hafrey and Richard Sieburth, *The Philosophical Forum* 15, nos. 1-2 (1983-1984), p. 12. Stanley Corngold has counted, for example, more than two hundred published commentaries on "Das Urteil." Corngold, *Franz Kafka: The Necessity of Form*, p. 24.

33   In jedem wahren Kunstwerk gibt es die Stelle, an der es den, der sich dareinversetzt, kühl wie der Wind einer kommenden Frühe anweht. Daraus ergibt sich, daß die Kunst, die man oft als refraktär gegen jede Beziehung zum Fortschritt ansah, dessen echter Bestimmung dienen kann. Fortschritt ist nicht in der Kontinuität des Zeitverlaufs sondern in seinen Interferenzen zu Hause: dort wo ein wahrhaft Neues zum ersten Mal mit der Nüchternheit der Frühe sich fühlbar macht. Benjamin, "Notes et fiches pour *Charles Baudelaire*," unpaginated; also in *Das Passagen-Werk*, N 9a, 7 (*Gesammelte Schriften* V, p. 593); in English as "Theoretics of Knowledge; Theory of Progress," trans. Leigh Hafrey and Richard Sieburth, *The Philosophical Forum* 15, nos. 1-2 (1983-1984), p. 22.

34   Es hat wenig Wert, die Position eines Baudelaire in das Netz der vorgeschobensten im Befreiungskampfe der Menschheit einbeziehen zu wollen. Es erscheint von vornherein aussichtsreicher, seinen Machenschaften dort nachzugehen, wo er ohne Zweifel zu Hause ist: im gegnerischen Lager. . . . Baudelaire war ein Geheimagent — ein Agent der geheimen Unzufriedenheit seiner Klasse mit ihrer eigenen Herrschaft. Benjamin, *Gesammelte Schriften*, I, p. 1161.

Silence Audible:
Mauthner, Hofmannsthal, Wittgenstein, and the Vindication of Language

Michael Morton
Duke University

I

For Vico, as is well known, the movement of history took the form of a great spiral. Regularly recurring cycles of cultural advance and decline, growth and decay, yield at the same time a certain linear progression, in the sense that at any point in the overall pattern a given historical period or moment recapitulates essential features of stages occupying the same relative position in earlier cycles, but, as it were, at a "higher" level. That does not mean, of course — or need not at any rate — that the later stage, simply by virtue of coming after earlier ones, automatically embodies a greater degree of perfection on some absolute scale of value. The point is primarily a conceptual rather than a normative one. It is that the later stage has as a crucial part of its foundation something that its earlier counterparts obviously could not have had, namely those earlier stages themselves. Thus within a framework of broad parallels in forms of thought and action, the specific character of a given later period will be determined in large part by the particular ways in which it assimilates, reactivates, and thereby also transforms the characteristic outlooks, interests, and tendencies of developmental stages corresponding to it at points falling further back up the line in the overall sweep of historical time.

Speculative philosophy of history of this sort has, of course, to put it mildly, slipped somewhat in prestige in the twentieth century, with the decline becoming steeper as one approaches the present day. Despite the efforts of thinkers such as Spengler, Croce, or Toynbee to keep the tradition alive (or perhaps, at least in part, as a consequence of those very efforts), the prevailing mood today is rather one of pervasive suspicion of all so-called "grand narratives."[1] And yet this suspicion (whatever may be said for or against it in its own right) does not render Vico's insight altogether valueless. Employed as a historical heuristic, it can aid us in recognizing parallels of the type that he believed he could discern everywhere, as direct manifestations of fundamental laws of history, where they actually do present themselves — as it seems to me they clearly do from time to time. One especially important instance of such a parallel, though one whose implications for literary criticism in particular are still for the most part too little appreciated, appears in the relationship between the massive change in the philosophical climate of the West that takes place in the eighteenth and early nineteenth centuries, and the almost equally profound shift in intellectual direction that occurs a hundred years later, at the turn of the nineteenth to the twentieth century.

Historians often speak of two major "turns" in Western philosophical thought since the eighteenth century, one of them "epistemological," the other "linguistic." Each of these involves a fundamental reordering of the ways in which philosophers frame their questions and the methods by which they seek to resolve them. The first has generally been regarded as the work chiefly of Kant, though the recognition is growing today of the extent to which others among Kant's contemporaries, notably Herder, contributed decisively to bringing it about as well.[2] The effect of the "epistemological turn," as formulated, for example, in the *Critique of Pure Reason*, is to reinterpret basic questions of the nature and forms of Being, that is, the traditionally primary questions of philosophy per se, as issues to be resolved through, in Robert Paul Wolff's words, "an analysis of the limits and preconditions of knowing."[3] The "linguistic turn," which is accomplished definitively in the years around 1900 (though its roots extend back into the eighteenth century, with Herder being in this case the pivotal figure[4]), stands in relation to the "epistemological turn" as that watershed in thought stood to the sort of philosophizing that it succeeded. Where Kant and others reanalyzed questions of Being as questions of knowledge, modern linguistic philosophers reanalyze questions of knowledge as questions of language. Each of these transformations occurs, moreover, in two stages: first, the very possibility of reliably grounded knowledge or communication is called into question by a skeptical assault on its foundations; the crisis thus brought about leads in turn, however, to a critical response, in which the nature of thought itself is reexamined and the validity of its operations reestablished in new terms. In the eighteenth century, the principal figures associated with these two stages are, respectively, Hume and, as noted, Kant. Analogous positions are occupied at the *Jahrhundertwende* by Mauthner and Wittgenstein. Both these "turns," finally, have associated with them, and in each case with both their stages, correlative developments in the realm of literature.

In the mid-1700s, British empiricism, though as a philosophical movement barely a century and a half old, reaches a kind of culmination (if scarcely the one envisaged by its founders) in the all-consuming phenomenalist skepticism of Hume. The arguments of the *Treatise of Human Nature*, as well as the more popularly intended works that follow it, are designed to show that, our ordinary beliefs to the contrary notwithstanding, we possess genuine knowledge neither of the external world nor even of our own identities. What we take to be a firmly grounded natural order, governed by the law of cause and effect, is reduced in Hume's analysis to a series of radically discrete (and thus, in principle, wholly unpredictable) events, which are reflected in the correspondingly discontinuous succession of sense impressions to which they give rise in us. In the same way, the unity of consciousness, and with it our intuitive belief in a stable and enduring Self, is dissolved into a play of individual impressions and ideas, bound together by no underlying principle of unification. In his *Life and Opinions of Tristram Shandy*, developing the (itself still relatively young) form of the novel in the direction of a kind of anti-autobiography, Laurence

Sterne provides a comic reflex of the philosophical assault on the Self.[5]   At about this same time in Germany the twin themes of skepticism regarding the possibility of attaining certain knowledge of the external world and the imperiled identity of the individual also begin to assume increasing prominence in literary works. One example from among many that could be cited of the former tendency is the opening monologue of Goethe's *Faust*, while the latter is virtually a signature theme of the *Sturm und Drang* generally, being treated (if not always exactly with Sterne's humor) in numerous works, from a novel such as *Die Leiden des jungen Werther* to dramas such as *Die Zwillinge* or *Julius von Tarent*.

In both their literary production and their theoretical and critical writings, however, the *Stürmer und Dränger* also take the crucial step of introducing the notion that the world is itself ultimately *constituted* by the very forms of mental activity through which we apprehend it.   In the various ways in which they develop that pivotal idea, Goethe, Herder, Lenz, and others thus actually anticipate by several years Kant's accomplishing of the "epistemological turn" in the more conventional form of a philosophical treatise. Kant establishes both the validity of our knowledge of reality and the substantial, continuous existence of the Self by means of an argument showing that the world of experience is at once a creation of consciousness and yet also—indeed, precisely for that reason—objectively real. This philosophical development, in turn, has a literary counterpart, or rather several literary counterparts, in its own right. To my mind, among the most "Kantian" of these are a number of works for which the traditional designation "poetic realism" still seems to me an apt enough characterization, albeit in a modified and, with respect to historical periodization, significantly expanded sense of the term. Beginning already in the 1790s, and continuing throughout the nineteenth and well into the twentieth century, writers as otherwise diverse as Tieck, E.T.A. Hoffmann, Eichendorff, Storm, Kafka, and many others develop and perfect a form of narrative in which the *entirety* of the world of the text, the *whole* of the fictive reality that at once defines and is defined by it, becomes a kind of meta-reality. Rather than being given in advance, independently of a human subject, as the scene of action, conflict, and the like, this "world" is embodied quintessentially in the effort on the part of the subject to create and sustain a "reality" at all—including, not incidentally, its *own* existence as well. That effort, moreover, is thematized not merely, or even primarily, in the overt content of the work. The truly distinctive quality of these texts lies rather in their ability to exemplify in their own narrative structures the very project of "world-creation," with its never entirely certain outcome, that they are at the same time concerned to represent—insofar literally self-creating (rather than self-consuming) artifacts.[6]

At the *Jahrhundertwende*, a two-stage development in almost all respects exactly analogous to the one just described occurs again. The one principal difference from a century earlier is that by this time the locus of concern has shifted decisively to *language*. Stirrings of the same sort that in the 1700s led ultimately to the "epistemological turn" are felt anew. Whereas in the eighteenth century, however (notable exceptions such as Herder and Humboldt notwithstanding), inquiries into the foundations of knowledge were still being pursued in terms of "mental representations" and the various "faculties" of mind thought to produce them, by the turn of the nineteenth to the twentieth century essentially the same issues are increasingly being formulated as questions regarding the status of *knowledge claims*. Instead of trying to deal with knowledge by way of a vaguely conceived (not to say wholly mysterious) internal topology of cognition, the predominant tendency is now to think of knowledge as embodied above all in *propositions* or other *linguistically* interpreted entities. And hence forms of language, rather than, for example, as earlier, "ideas," gradually become the primary objects of investigation.[7] Within this new context there occurs again a crisis of skepticism, followed by a critical revolution and reconstitution of thought. Corresponding to Hume and Kant in the realm of philosophy proper are, as noted earlier, in particular Mauthner and Wittgenstein. And just as the *Goethezeit* produced literary counterparts of both aspects of the "epistemological turn," so the *Jahrhundertwende* generates poetic expressions of both the so-called "crisis of language" and its over-coming. The names of a number of writers come to mind at once here, of course, especially among those active in Vienna—but perhaps none more so than that of Hugo von Hofmannsthal. Among Hofmannsthal's works, one in particular, the much discussed, analyzed, and argued over "Brief des Lord Chandos,"[8] written shortly after the turn of the century, has, indeed, acquired for many a kind of archetypal status in relation to the issues at stake here.

II

Both Hofmannsthal's acquaintance with Mauthner's philosophy of language and the actual (if somewhat limited) contact between the two men are well documented. Among the books in his personal library, Hofmannsthal numbered the first and third volumes of Mauthner's main work, *Beiträge zu einer Kritik der Sprache*; and the underlinings in the text indicate that he read at least the first of these, entitled *Sprache und Psychologie*, with some care.[9] In addition, there has been preserved what appears to be virtually the entire correspondence between the two. This is, to be sure, not extensive—a total of twelve letters (seven from Mauthner, five from Hofmannsthal), written between 1892 and 1907. The correspondence falls into four groups, separated by intervals of from one to ten years. Of these groups, the most interesting and significant is the second, an exchange of three letters in October and November 1902, occasioned by the publication of the "Chandos-Brief" on the 18th and 19th of October in the Berlin periodical *Der Tag* (BHM, 22).[10] In that same month—indeed, if Joachim Kühn is right,[11] the next day, October 20—Mauthner writes to Hofmannsthal in what is clearly a somewhat animated state:

> I have just read your "Letter." I saw in it the first poetic echo of my "Critique of Language." Confident that my perception was correct, I felt a profound joy of a sort not afforded me by even the most heartfelt praise of

my book. I saw fulfilled what had been my greatest dream: to have an effect
on the best among my contemporaries. (*BHM*, 33)[12]

Mauthner evidently believes both that he has suggested to
Hofmannsthal for the first time the idea of a skeptical critique of
language and that in so doing he has also succeeded in convincing
him of the validity of such a critique.

That opinion, or the first part of it at any rate, is shared by Kühn
(pp. 21-29), though in doing so, of course, he is obliged to overlook
the central position of precisely this same theme in Hofmannsthal's
own work from the very beginning of his career, well before even
the earliest of Mauthner's thoughts on language had appeared in
print.[13] Walter Eschenbacher offers what seems a decidedly more
balanced view of the matter. In particular, his study of Mauthner is
tempered throughout by a recognition of the fundamental point
that Mauthner's works do not in themselves constitute an epochal
event, revolutionizing intellectual and artistic life.[14] Neither his
actual ability as a philosopher nor the degree of originality represented by his writings is sufficient to gain for Mauthner a position
of influence on the literature of the *Jahrhundertwende* comparable
to that exercised, for example, by Nietzsche, Schopenhauer, or
Mach (p. 133). What he offers is rather a particularly extreme, and
thus, if for no other reason than that, also widely noticed, expression of a direction of thought already being reflected in one way or
another in much of the philosophy and literature of the period.
And this is in fact also how he tends for the most part to be viewed
by his contemporaries. He assumes, in other words, as Eschenbacher puts it, "a kind of herald's role in relation to the
phenomenon of linguistic crisis" (p. 130); he is by no means its
originator or prime mover (no matter what he may have thought).
That state of affairs is reflected in Hofmannsthal's reply to him of
November 3, in which Hofmannsthal undertakes, as he says, to
explain "the actual relationship to each other of the matters that
you touch on in your letter" (*BHM*, 33).[15] Hofmannsthal acknowledges having read with pleasure the first volume of Mauthner's
Beiträge and adds, "My own thoughts proceeded very early along
similar lines . . . " He mentions several of his works that in various

ways reflect a questioning of the ability of language to capture and convey meaning. And he concludes, "There is, in the end, present here both agreement between us and certainly a reinforcement of these thoughts through your book" (*BHM*, 33-34).

Putting aside for the moment the issue of intellectual priority, however, and pursuing the more interesting question of the significance of the *substance* of Mauthner's views for the literature of the *Jahrhundertwende* (and thereafter), we at once encounter a fundamental paradox. For the very thing that arouses the interest of poets and others in his thought—namely his uncompromising expression of *Sprachskepsis*—also sets definite limits to the extent to which that thought is likely to be reflected at the concrete level of literary production. Mauthner's critique issues, by his own admission, in a radical negation of all language, and there are (understandably) few writers prepared to follow him that far. At the same time, however, the wholesale challenge to the ability of language either to embody knowledge or to serve as a reliable vehicle of communication is not something one is able simply to ignore. The issue of *Sprachkritik* and the questions raised by it have simply acquired too much intellectual momentum by this time for that to be, as a practical matter, at all a possible alternative.

One consequence of this is that consciousness of a "crisis of language" becomes itself at once a condition of and an impetus to literary activity. The artistic and intellectual validity of the writer's work is increasingly felt to depend on the incorporation in it of a self-reflexive questioning of the terms of its own existence. In this way, writers at the *Jahrhundertwende* begin to develop, in place of the outright rejection of language that is Mauthner's last word, a more differentiated, and correspondingly more sophisticated, response to the challenge of linguistic skepticism. The initial loss (or at least wavering) of confidence in the capacity of language to function as either an organon or a medium of truth, the assumption—much in vogue now as then, of course—that there exists an inevitable gap between meaning and linguistic form, in sum, the first, necessarily negative, moment in the "linguistic turn," elicits an effort to reground language in a way that both acknowledges the force of the critique and yet at the same time avoids its nihilistic implications. As was the case in the eighteenth century, so once again skepticism, having been pushed to the limit and beyond, undergoes a kind of dialectical reversal. And that in turn leads once more, by means of a thorough reanalysis and reinterpretation of the object of the skeptical assault, to the reinstatement of that object in a new form and on new foundations.

The considerable extent to which this transition to the second stage of the "linguistic turn" occurs in the medium of *literature* — an extent, if anything, even greater than in the case of the "epistemological turn" — points, in addition, to a second consideration severely limiting the degree of influence Mauthner would ever have been able to exert on the writers of the period. The ferment at this time around the effort to create a new sort of literary language affords a singular opportunity for a sufficiently bold and imaginative theoretician or critic (the sort of opportunity seized, for example, with brilliant success by Friedrich Schlegel a century earlier). It is at just this point, however, that Mauthner's own deep-seated literary conservatism — specifically, his apparent inability to appreciate the significance of the formal innovations in literature taking place all around him — precludes his assuming such a role himself. His sense of what literature ought to be seems to have been fixed relatively early in his career, at the time of his association with the Naturalist movement in Berlin.[16] In his view (strangely enough perhaps), it is the poetics of Naturalism that represents the literary realization of his philosophy of language. And thus it is not surprising to find him reserving some of his harshest criticism for a poet such as Stefan George, whose self-consciously esoteric aestheticism and hyper-elitist cultural messianism represent in all respects the antithesis of Naturalism. In the second volume of his *Wörterbuch der Philosophie* of 1911, Mauthner asserts, with George and others in mind, "The word-artists . . . , who have nothing to say but who nevertheless, as a kind of automatic reflex, wish to appear to be creating something new, have become [mere] virtuosos of linguistic form."[17]

Some of Mauthner's contemporaries were puzzled (to say the least) by what seemed to them his unaccountable obliviousness to the manifest affinities between his critique of language and the work of modernist poets. His friend and admirer Gustav Landauer speaks of Mauthner's thoroughly "uncomprehending assessments" of contemporary literature. In his failure to recognize the extent to which that literature is "intertwined precisely with his own most extreme skepticism," says Landauer, Mauthner shows himself "unequal to his own thought."[18] In his *Skepsis und Mystik* of 1903, which even bears the subtitle *Versuche im Anschluß an Mauthners Sprachkritik*, Landauer makes the point at greater length, displaying as he does so a clear sense for the distinctive quality of much of modernist literature generally:

> To be sure, Mauthner says on several occasions that Naturalism is for him a gratifying corroboration of his critique of language. For my part, I will not pursue the question further, inasmuch as I see in Naturalism no artistic significance but, at most, a degree of social relevance . . .

> On the other hand, I find—perhaps to Mauthner's horror—deeper connections between his critique of language and the poets Stefan George, Hugo von Hofmannsthal, Richard Dehmel, and Alfred Mombert. . . . [I]f in the case of Schiller the realization that the world of sensibility cannot be expressed in language was only a flash of insight with little influence on his work, now, however, poets give us in the same way not only the rhythms of their lives and feelings but also images of the external world—that is, precisely *as the unsayable. This reciprocal resonancing of unsayables (Ineinanderschwingen der Unsagbarkeiten) . . . : that is what I find in the works of those poets I have mentioned, and it is in this way alone, it seems to me, that a path is to be found from the critique of language back to linguistic art.*[19]

For Landauer, "the practical value of the critique of language" (*ibid.*, p. 107) for literature lies in the stimulus it provides to a rejuvenation of literary art, precisely (if paradoxically) through its relentless exposure of our naively held notions of the nature of language and what it can accomplish as illusions (just as we saw earlier Hume had done, with ultimately similar effect, in the case of our conventional notions of natural phenomena and the Self).

In sum: The current of radical linguistic skepticism epitomized (if not originated) by Mauthner's work leads increasingly to the adoption of a stance of critical reflection on language as itself a condition of language use. In the sphere of literature, this tendency manifests itself in the development of ever more elaborately self-implicative and multiply ironic forms of textual construction.[20] Although not an aspect of his thought that Mauthner either emphasized or (apparently) even recognized, it can nonetheless (as the example of Landauer demonstrates) be discerned there at least by implication. And it is here, if anywhere, that the constructive aspect of his contribution to intellectual history ultimately lies. It is, in particular, the most important point of contact between his efforts in philosophy and the creative forces at work in the literature of the *Jahrhundertwende*. The primary need at this time, one felt by virtually all the leading writers of the period, is for what Eschenbacher terms a "reestablishment of viable forms of thought and speech" (p. 111) *after*—that is, in full cognizance of—the critique of language (p. 106).[21] At one point in his *Beiträge*, Mauthner himself suggests at least a glimmer of awareness of this latent dimension of his philosophy. Echoing Goethe's famous exhortation "Stirb und werde!," from *Selige Sehnsucht*, he asserts, "Language, too, must be able to die, if it wishes to live again."[22]

III

Landauer's notion of an *Ineinanderschwingen der Unsagbarkeiten* in the work of modernist poets expresses with admirable succinctness much of what is most characteristic of this new, "post-critical" literature. How that notion can function as the governing principle of an entire text is illustrated in exemplary fashion by a work mentioned earlier, Hofmannsthal's "Brief des Lord Chandos." It is, indeed, at least conceivable that the "Chandos-Brief" served Landauer as the direct inspiration for his formulation.[23] At a key juncture in the text (about which there will be more to say below) Chandos employs the phrase "Zusammensetzung von Nichtigkeiten" (p. 17)—more or less literally, "composite of bits of nothingness." And it turns out, as we shall see, that that concept is not merely thematically central to the essay, but that it also provides the key to resolving the formal paradox that lies at the heart of it — namely, that, on its own terms, it should not be able to exist at all.

To anticipate a bit, the "Chandos-Brief" *displays* rather than recounts — in the terms of Wittgenstein's *Tractatus Logico-Philosophicus* (to which we shall turn presently), it "shows" rather than "says" — exactly why a crisis of language should befall a certain sort of poet. In so doing, it also *exemplifies* (again, rather than attempting to describe discursively) how the poet can confront squarely the experience of such a crisis and yet not be reduced completely to silence by it. The text thus faces in two directions at once, a consideration that I think goes a long way toward explaining the literally pivotal position it has come to occupy in the canon of major twentieth-century works. In its thematization of the inadequacy of language, the affinity to Mauthner is clear (something that, as we have seen, Hofmannsthal freely acknowledged). In the means that the text employs to deal with the crisis, however, Hofmannsthal looks ahead to Wittgenstein. He thereby combines in a single, at once poetic and philosophical, work *both* aspects of the "linguistic turn" — both the moment of extreme skepticism and the transcendental revolution in thought and expression called forth in response to the skeptical challenge.

Mauthner is one of relatively few philosophers mentioned by name in the *Tractatus*, though not in a way likely to have given him much pleasure from the recognition. Wittgenstein writes, "All philosophy is 'critique of language.' (To be sure, not in Mauthner's sense.)" (4.0031). The distinction to which Wittgenstein alludes here is between what can be called an "external" and an "internal" approach to language, or, in other words, between a reductive analysis in the manner of Hume and a transcendental deduction of the sort carried out by Kant.[24] Like Mach in his own day and, for example, Derrida in ours, Mauthner bases his enterprise on principles whose sources lie outside of, and, more important, which are themselves *logically subsequent to*, what is nominally his primary object of investigation. He approaches the study of language and of the concepts embodied in it from the standpoint of what he takes to be their psychological origin and historical development. Wittgenstein, on the other hand, focuses his attention from the outset on language itself. Adapting Russell's distinction between the "real" and "apparent" form of a proposition (to which he alludes in the same section in which he distinguishes his conception of "critique of language" from Mauthner's), he develops an analysis of the way propositions actually function, individually and in combination with one another. He thereby *exhibits* linguistic structure as a logical scaffolding in which forms of description of every sort — *including any that might be employed in an attempted skeptical assault on language* — are already located, and which thus functions as the basis at once of signification and of the world of possible experience (see, for example, 4.022-4.023 and 6.124).

In one of the key propositions of the *Tractatus*, Wittgenstein says, "We make for ourselves pictures of facts" (2.1). These *Bilder*, however, are very different from the *metaphorical* descriptions of reality that, in Mauthner's view, are the most language can provide us with. For Mauthner, linguistic "images" are not simply more or less unreliable indicators of how things stand in the world; they are inherently incapable of conveying such information. There is in the first place the merely contingent nature of the human sensory apparatus. What Mauthner terms our *Zufallssinne* are, in the nature of the case, able to perceive only a small portion of the ontological spectrum.[25] In addition, we have to reckon with the inevitable distortions of memory, which, even if it were not fallible, would still be unavoidably selective, retaining only a part of even those sense impressions that we do register. Both these considerations taken together guarantee for Mauthner that our representations of the world are not merely *unlikely* to be accurate; it is rather in principle *impossible* that they should be.

Wittgenstein's "pictures," on the other hand, are not metaphors but *models*, necessarily isomorphic with the reality they represent, precisely because they are *constitutive* of that reality in the first place.[26] With the determination *a priori* of both the possible forms of the proposition and a procedure for analyzing more complex propositions into simpler ones, an exhaustive account of the phenomenal order is given.[27] Logic makes possible the existence of an intelligible world (which is to say, everything of which it can make sense to say anything whatever) by making intelligible discourse itself possible (see, for example, 5.526, 6.124, 6.3211, and 6.341-6.343).[28] Both Wittgenstein's procedure and the end he achieves are, as suggested earlier, analogous to Kant's transcendental deduction of the categories in the *Critique of Pure Reason*. The heart of the Kantian critical philosophy is the demonstration that such "pure concepts" as causality, and the "synthetic judgments *a priori*" in which they figure, although neither derived nor derivable *from* experience, are nonetheless objectively valid *for* experience by virtue of constituting the basic forms of *all possible* experience in the first place (cf. *Tractatus* 6.341-6.361). Like Kant in the sphere of epistemology, Wittgenstein is able by means of a similarly conceived "mapping from within" to display at once the structure and the limits of language.[29] He thus simultaneously grounds the scope and validity of the sayable and in so doing plants markers enabling us to recognize the realm of nonsense lying beyond it (see 4.113-4.115, also 6.53).[30]

But what of the formulation of this distinction itself? Can such a statement, on its own terms, be given at all? The problem is analogous to one that arises in connection with the notion of a universal set — a set, that is, that would contain absolutely everything, including itself. As Russell noticed, permitting sets to be members of themselves (as, for example, Frege had done) leads to paradox. For we can raise the question: given the set of all sets that are *not* members of themselves, is *it* a member of itself? Obviously, by the terms of the definition, if it is, it isn't, and if it isn't, it is. Gödel's incompleteness proof and Heisenberg's uncertainty principle also establish, in the realms of mathematics and physics, respectively, that the problem is in fact a permanent one. No system can include in itself a wholly adequate self-validation. And that entails with respect to the *Tractatus* in particular, as Wittgenstein recognizes, that the logical form of the linguistic model cannot represent itself.

What makes the existence of facts possible as elements in an ordered network of describable phenomena cannot itself be represented as a fact. The overall relationship between logic and the world is not itself susceptible to logical demonstration. That relationship remains, like other considerations lying beyond the realm of the strictly factual, in a sense ultimately ineffable. In the terms of what is arguably Wittgenstein's most important distinction, it is *shown* but not *said*:

> Propositions can represent the whole of reality, but they cannot represent that which they must have in common with reality in order to be able to represent it — logical form.
>
> In order to be able to represent logical form, we would have to be able to position ourselves, with a proposition, outside of logic, that is, outside of the world. (4.12; cf. 3.32-3.333 for a slightly different argument establishing essentially the same conclusion)
>
> Propositions cannot represent logical form; it is reflected in them. That which is reflected in language, language cannot represent.
>
> That which expresses *itself* in language, *we* cannot express by means of language.
>
> Propositions *show* the logical form of reality.
> They manifest it. (4.121)
>
> What *can* be shown, *cannot* be said. (4.1212)

The rest, however, is not silence, or not yet at any rate. Indeed, if some way cannot be found to elucidate the relationship between logic and reality, the entire exposition of the *Tractatus* is brought to a halt before it can begin. There thus arises the need (as it has repeatedly in the history of philosophy) for a form of *indirect communication*.[31] If it is the case that the most fundamental truths are not directly communicable in language, it does not follow that there is not a need — in Wittgenstein's view, indeed, an obligation — to seek some other means by which those truths can be conveyed. The key to doing so is to use language in such a way that it actively *affects* the one addressed. The relationship between language and the world must be spoken of (in a sense) figuratively, or rhetorically, that is, in a way calculated not so much to compel the reader's assent to the conclusion (as, for example, at the end of a chain of deductive reasoning), nor even to persuade him or her of its probable correctness (as when setting forth a hypothesis and the evidence that appears to support it), but rather to *move* the reader simply to "see" the ultimate equivalence of the two. Wittgenstein wrote of the *Tractatus*, "The work is strictly philosophical and literary at the same time . . . "[32] And thus his language moves, with perfect lucidity throughout, in the realm of what is by its own assertion nonetheless unsayable. In so doing, it achieves the kind of sustained tension between sense and nonsense appropriate to being positioned, as it were, at the edge of the world, at once inside and (almost) outside of logic. Much as in the case of two other seminal thinkers on language, Herder and Nietzsche, Wittgenstein bases his work finally on what I would like to call a *gestural* use of language.[33] The text so constructed exploits the resources of discursive utterance in order to transcend, precisely in the *image* of transcendence thereby achieved, the limits of standard discourse.

In the frequently cited penultimate section of the *Tractatus*, Wittgenstein writes:

> My propositions elucidate in this way: he who understands me recognizes them in the end as nonsensical, when he has by means of them—on them—climbed up over and beyond them. (He must, so to speak, throw away the ladder after he has climbed all the way up on it.)
>
> He must overcome these propositions; then he will see the world correctly. (6.54)[34]

Mauthner also employs the image of the ladder in speaking of his critique and its relationship to the reader. His way of doing so is telling in the extreme. It reflects with graphic precision the difference in both tenor and substance separating his approach to language from Wittgenstein's. Even the location of the passage is symptomatic, coming as it does on the first page of his major work, rather than, as with the corresponding passage in the *Tractatus*, on the last. There Mauthner declares:

> I must destroy language within me, in front of me, and behind me step for step if I want to ascend in the critique of language . . . ; I must shatter each rung of the ladder by stepping upon it. He who wishes to follow me must reconstitute the rungs in order to shatter them once again.[35]

Both Mauthner and Wittgenstein recognize a dimension of the "mystical," encompassing both the foundations of reality and the meaning of human existence. This dimension lies beyond language, and therefore nothing pertaining to it can be a proper object of deliberation or *a fortiori* admit of rational grounding.[36] Mauthner, however, reaches that point as the final stage of what we have seen to be an externally based, reductive analysis, the consequence of which is to annul the possibility of language altogether. The end is for him the silence of skeptical resignation—ideally, as he says, "the quietly despairing suicide of thought or language."[37] For Wittgenstein, on the other hand, having proceeded not *toward* language from a point outside it, but rather *through and by means of* language, the end is also silence of a sort, but silence comprehended in a dialectical relationship to the sayable. In the Preface to the *Tractatus*, he asserts that the entire sense of the work can be summed up in the two principles, "Whatever can be said at all can be said clearly; and on that of which it is not possible to speak, we must remain silent" (cf. 4.116 and 7). And in a famous letter to Ludwig Ficker he provides, in effect, a gloss of that centrally important passage:

> I once meant to include in the preface a sentence which is not in fact there now, but which I will write out for you here, because it will perhaps be a key to the work for you. What I meant to write, then, was this: My work consists of two parts: the one presented here plus all that I have *not* written. And *it is precisely this second part that is the important one*. My book draws limits to the sphere of the ethical[38] from the inside as it were, and I am convinced that this is the ONLY rigorous way of drawing those limits.

> In short, I believe that . . . I have managed in my book to put everything firmly into place by being silent about it.[39]

The same dialectic of speech and silence that is Wittgenstein's goal in philosophy receives, as suggested earlier, perhaps its best, and in

any case almost certainly best-known, poetic expression in
Hofmannsthal's "Brief des Lord Chandos."

IV

Hofmannsthal's task in the "Chandos-Brief," like Wittgenstein's in
the *Tractatus*, is to show *by means of* language what (as he recognizes) cannot properly be expressed *in* language. The problem is,
indeed, if anything still more apparent in Hofmannsthal's case than
in Wittgenstein's. As the literature on the "Chandos-Brief" regularly notes, there is something paradoxical at the very least in the
fact of a letter whose fictive author claims to have lost the ability to
use language, but who does so in a text of surpassing eloquence.
The path toward a resolution of that paradox leads by way of a consideration of a question that has received a good deal less attention
in the literature, namely, why does Chandos experience a
Sprachkrise at all? What is it about Chandos in particular, or, more
generally, about the mode of existence that he represents, that
brings him to the pass that he seeks in some way to describe in his
letter?[40]

The answer to that question emerges implicitly in the first of the
letter's three principal sections, in which Chandos describes both
his completed poetic works and those that he had planned but now
finds himself unable to carry out.[41] What Chandos in effect
recounts here—he is, of course, himself unaware of the full implications of what he is saying; if he were not, that is, if he could actually recognize for what it is the causal chain that his description in
fact lays out for the reader, he would *eo ipso* not be experiencing
the crisis at all, or at any rate not the one that he describes in the
letter as having befallen him—is a progression by incremental
stages toward the ultimately impossible situation of the self-conscious mystic. This is a problem by no means peculiar to Chandos
(or his creator). Rather it is one of the hallmarks of the *Jahrhundertwende* generally. Wolfdietrich Rasch speaks of the desire felt
by many at this time, animated by a "feeling of all-encompassing
unity," to render "bewußtseinsfähig"—that is, to realize as a

possible object of consciousness—"the oneness of the individual human being with . . . [the] underlying connectedness (*Zusammenhang*) of all things."[42] That attempt, however, as Rasch also notes, is encumbered by a latent contradiction. For it requires that the individual be, in effect, in two places at once. The person seeking this state must be simultaneously object and subject, both one with the totality of existence and yet also aware that precisely that is his or her condition, absorbed into a mystical, all-encompassing unity of Being and yet at the same time sufficiently distinct from that Oneness to permit conscious articulation of that very fact.

Bewußtseinsfähig entails *sprachfähig*—what can be conceived can also be spoken. That is true for everyone, of course, but its force is felt perhaps most acutely by the poet. As the contradiction inherent in Chandos's implicit project intensifies to the breaking point, he thus experiences the crisis as a rift at once in his sense of his own identity—"I hardly know if I am even the same person any longer . . . " (p. 7), he writes near the beginning of the letter—and in the fabric of language. In one of the most frequently cited passages in the entire text, he maintains, "My situation is, in short, this: I have completely lost the ability to think or to speak coherently (*zusammenhängend*) about anything whatever" (p. 12). Language for Chandos has lost what he had once felt to be its quasi-magical power to assert the true links between phenomena and so to disclose their deeper meaning. Where once it was able to mediate, unify, and reveal, language now seems to him only to distort, even to debase, what it tries to express. Rather than establishing and embodying essential connections, language now testifies only to the gulf between it (and *a fortiori* the person attempting to use it) and reality. As the crisis unfolds, it manifests itself, accordingly, as a progressive disintegration of phenomena. "Everything," says Chandos, "dissolved for me into pieces, and those pieces in turn into still smaller pieces; it was no longer possible to grasp and hold anything together by means of a concept" (p. 14).

Also frequently cited is Chandos's evocation of his "post-crisis" state of being. Although he now leads, as he says, "a life of almost incredible vacuity" (p. 19), that life is nonetheless "not entirely without its joyful and animating moments" (p. 15). These moments consist in occasional experiences of what has been called a kind of *Dingmystik*. At any time, without warning, says Chandos, "any phenomenon whatever of my everyday environment" (p. 15) can become the vehicle of an immediate and profoundly felt sense of the infinite oneness of Being and his own identity with it. To the extent that there is a key to the occurrence of these epiphanies, Chandos finds, it lies simply in maintaining a stance of passive openness toward them. They will arise, he says, "suddenly, at any moment, which I am utterly powerless to bring about" (p. 15). In this circumstance, language, whether thought of as a means of access to reality or as a vehicle for conveying truths gleaned from it, can only be a hindrance, and Chandos has accordingly resolved to renounce it.

It is easy to see here the two aspects of the "Chandos-Brief" that would have led Mauthner to regard it as a "poetic echo" of his own philosophy. There is, first, the collapse of a belief in the legitimacy of language and the consequent loss of ability to employ it, and secondly, the lapsing into a state of resigned silence, while at the same time remaining open to direct manifestations of the inherently inexpressible fullness of Being — an attitude for which Mauthner coined the expression *gottlose Mystik*.[43] There remains, however, a dimension of Hofmannsthal's text — in the end the most important one — that Mauthner appears not to have seen.

We noted earlier Mauthner's evident blind spot for *formal* modes of signification in literature. It is just this sort of thematic use of textual structure, however, that ultimately holds the key to the "Chandos-Brief." In a variation on the originally Romantic technique of a *produktiver Gebrauch des Negativen*, Hofmannsthal constructs his text in such a way that it is able to move beyond the crisis of language, not by denying the skeptical critique that gives rise to the crisis, but rather precisely by continuing in the direction initiated by that critique and following it out to its conclusion.

Again, considerations of space preclude showing in detail exactly how this is accomplished. Briefly, however, the crucial move is this. By exploiting the space between, on the one hand, Chandos's attempts to say what (as he at once recognizes) cannot properly be "said" at all, and, on the other, his immediate rejection of these (false) attempts, Hofmannsthal creates a sort of linguistic Gordian knot, in which the crisis of language effectively functions *as its own representation.* In a manner in some ways reminiscent of the medieval *via negativa,* the mode of discourse that was developed in order to be able to speak intelligibly of things recognized to be by nature inexpressible, Chandos is thus able to "show" what is necessary for the purposes of his letter.

It is in fundamentally this same way that he also manages to evoke a sense for his state of being following the crisis. Referring to his occasional "joyful and animating moments," he gives several examples of the sort of thing that can give rise in him to these experiences of the "presence of the infinite" (p. 17). Intent on emphasizing the utter disproportion between cause and effect in such cases, he characterizes one of these instances as, in a key formulation noted earlier, a "Zusammensetzung von Nichtigkeiten" (*ibid.*). Anything whatever, he continues, can affect him in this way. *"Even my own torpor, the dullness that otherwise lames my mind"* (p. 18, emphasis added) can do so. That is, precisely his *inability* to function any longer as he had before the crisis, precisely the *dissolution* of the world for him into a congeries of ever more minute pieces, can, as a "composite of bits of nothingness," assume for him an epiphanic, revelatory quality. And he continues, "When, however, this singular spell leaves me, in that moment I am at once unable to say anything about it" (*ibid.*). But at the moment in question Chandos obviously *is* able to say a good deal about "it." And from this it follows that the letter itself can only have been composed in the course of one of his "joyful and animating moments." Thus in the end he does accomplish what, with perfect consistency, he terms the "depiction of an inexplicable condition" (p. 21), and in so doing also implicitly provides the solution to the paradox of how on its own terms the letter can exist at all.

Through an indirect communication of the sort Wittgenstein will later employ in the *Tractatus*, that is, by weaving the dialectic of "saying" and "showing" into the fabric of the text itself, Hofmannsthal creates in the "Chandos-Brief" a linguistic structure that, like Wittgenstein's, is able to represent adequately the reality with which it is concerned by virtue of being itself *isomorphic* with that reality. For Wittgenstein, completing the "critical" phase of the "linguistic turn," the reality in question is the identity of logic and metaphysics, embodied in the basic forms of language and their constitution of the world of objective fact. Hofmannsthal, however, coming slightly earlier, has in some respects a significantly more difficult task. The direction of thought that will eventually issue in Wittgenstein's carrying out of the "linguistic turn" is, at the time of the "Chandos-Brief," still taking shape. Its first stage, that of the skeptical assault on language, has been largely accomplished; but its second, the reanalysis and reconstitution of linguistic foundations, is as yet barely (if at all) visible, even in outline. The reality coordinate with the "Chandos-Brief" is, in other words, precisely the phenomenon of *Sprachkrise* itself. Hofmannsthal's way of dealing with that reality in the fictive context of Chandos's letter does full justice to *both* aspects of the crisis—both the extreme, Mauthnerian skepticism that initiates it, but also the Wittgensteinian transcendental critique and reaffirmation of language that will be called forth in response. In what is far from the first instance of a poetic anticipation of a philosophical or scientific advance in the German or Austrian tradition, Hofmannsthal, through techniques of composition that point directly to Wittgenstein's principle of "mapping from within," treats the crisis of language in such a way that it *becomes itself articulate*. And thus, rather than having to be attacked from a standpoint external to it, it renders any such refutation superfluous in advance; for it has, in effect, already succeeded in overcoming itself.

Here in particular, of course, it becomes especially important to distinguish sharply between Hofmannsthal and Chandos. For while the final stage of Chandos's development is what Hofmannsthal terms the "decorum of silence"—the famous "Anstand des

Schweigens"[44]—the same fate obviously does not befall his creator. The "Chandos-Brief" does, however, mark a watershed in
Hofmannsthal's career, the most visible manifestation of which
being, of course, the change from lyric to dramatic forms as the
primary vehicles of literary production. The works that he goes on
to produce following this shift, however, continue to reflect essential elements of the "linguistic turn" as adumbrated in the
"Chandos-Brief." There is, again, a parallel here to the
"epistemological turn" and the consequences that followed upon it.
Kant's resecuring of the foundations of knowledge brought with it
not merely a radically new conception of what knowledge
is—indeed, of what a "fact" itself is. It also established an overall
context of thought in which a broadly "Kantian" critical reflection
on these very foundations would continue to function as an
indispensable prerequisite, not only of all subsequent philosophy,
but of virtually every other form of intellectual and artistic
endeavor as well. Analogous considerations apply both to
Hofmannsthal's "post-Chandos" works in particular and to a
significant portion of twentieth-century literature at large. From
opera (*Der Rosenkavalier*) to comedy (*Der Schwierige*)[45] to tragedy
(*Der Turm*), Hofmannsthal continues to explore and develop
possibilities inherent in the new foundation for literature
established with the "Chandos-Brief." This is a foundation in
which, on the one hand, a full awareness of the linguistic
constitution of reality and, on the other, a persistent questioning of
language's ability to do more than signal its own inadequacy stand
in uneasy tension with one another, as henceforth permanent
principles of discourse.

Notes

1 Lyotard, for example, has given influential voice to this suspicion (or, as he terms it, "incredulity"), albeit with, to my mind, questionable consistency at best. For if his global typology of *modern* vs. *postmodern* does not itself constitute a "grand narrative," one surely has to wonder what *would* count as such a thing. See *The Post-Modern Condition: A Report on Knowledge* (Minneapolis: U of Minnesota P, 1984).

2 I discuss this point at greater length in "Changing the Subject: Herder and the Reorientation of Philosophy," in *Herder Today*, ed. Kurt Mueller-Vollmer (Berlin: de Gruyter, 1990).

3 See *Kant's Theory of Mental Activity: A Commentary on the Transcendental Analytic of the Critique of Pure Reason* (Cambridge: Harvard UP, 1963; rpt. Gloucester, MA: Peter Smith, 1973), p. 320.

4 See my *Herder and the Poetics of Thought: Unity and Diversity in "On Diligence in Several Learned Languages"* (University Park and London: Pennsylvania State UP, 1989). Much of the argument of this study is devoted to presenting Herder as engaged in an effort to accomplish simultaneously *both* the "turns" in question here, the "epistemological" and the "linguistic."

5 The philosopher most often associated with *Tristram Shandy* is, of course, Locke, whose theory of "association of ideas" Sterne adapts for his narrative. The result of that adaptation with respect specifically to the person of the narrator, however, seems to me to accord rather more with the import of Hume's arguments than with those of Locke, for whom the integrity of the Self is not yet an issue.

6 In this connection, see the illuminating discussions of a number of nineteenth- and twentieth-century novels (beginning with *Die Wahlverwandschaften*) by Claudia Brodsky in *The Imposition of Form: Studies in Narrative Representation and Knowledge* (Princeton: Princeton UP, 1987).

7 The development I am sketching in outline here did not, of course, occur in reality in anything like so neat or uniform a fashion as I may appear to be suggesting. Husserl, for example (to mention but one particularly prominent case), with his belief in a fundamental level of non-linguistic ideation, somehow accessible through a sort of ultimate intuition, remained in effect a

holdout for what had by then become an all but entirely obsolete point of view.

8 "Ein Brief," *Gesammelte Werke in Einzelausgaben: Prosa II*, ed. Herbert Steiner (Frankfurt: Fischer, 1951), pp. 7-22. References to the "Chandos-Brief" will be given parenthetically in the text.

9 Martin Stern, ed., "Der Briefwechsel Hofmannsthal-Fritz Mauthner," *Hofmannsthal-Blätter*, 19-20 (1978), pp. 21 and 30. Cited hereafter in the text as *BHM*.

10 See also Rolf Tarot, *Hugo von Hofmannsthal: Daseinsformen und dichterische Struktur* (Tübingen: Niemeyer, 1970), p. 360.

11 Joachim Kühn, *Gescheiterte Sprachkritik: Fritz Mauthners Leben und Werk* (Berlin: de Gruyter, 1975), p. 27. Cited hereafter in the text.

12 Unless otherwise noted, all translations here are my own. In the case of Wittgenstein's *Tractatus*, I have generally relied on the outstanding Pears-McGuinness translation, but have also felt free to adopt my own wording where that seemed preferable.

13 Kühn sees in the "Chandos-Brief" a merely aesthetic exercise on Hofmannsthal's part (p. 24). "The linguistic collapse of Lord Chandos," he maintains, "has nothing to do with Hofmannsthal's own experience" (p. 27). That view, however, is as wide of the mark to one side as the once-prevalent tendency to read the text as a thinly-disguised bit of autobiography was to the other side. The best treatment of which I am aware of the relationship between the figure of Chandos and his creator Hofmannsthal is by Benjamin Bennett in his essay "Werther and Chandos," *MLN*, 91 (1976), pp. 552-58.

14 Walter Eschenbacher, *Fritz Mauthner und die deutsche Literatur um 1900: Eine Untersuchung zur Sprachkrise der Jahrhundertwende* (Frankfurt: Peter Lang; Bern: Herbert Lang, 1977), p. 131. Cited hereafter in the text.

15 This letter was not available to Kühn at the time of his study (*Gescheiterte Sprachkritik*, p. 27), which may in part explain the conclusion he reaches regarding the extent of Mauthner's importance for Hofmannsthal.

16 Mauthner was in fact one of the co-founders, in 1889, of the *Freie Bühne*. With his departure from Berlin in 1905, moving first to Freiburg im Breisgau, and later settling at Meersburg on Lake Constance, he effectively cut himself off from (among other things) the continuing developments in the literature of his time; nor does he seem to have felt any inclination to take any steps that might have relieved that isolation.

17 Cited in Kühn, p. 61.

18 Cited in Kühn, p. 60.

19 Cited in Eschenbacher, pp. 106-07; emphasis added.

20 It is surely not entirely coincidental that the principal forerunner of this mode
of writing, namely Romantic irony, should have been developed at precisely
the same time as the other of the two philosophical "turns" with which we are
concerned here.

21 As Allan Janik and Stephen Toulmin show, versions of precisely this same
problem appear in one field of intellectual and artistic activity after another at
the turn of the century, and, again, nowhere more so than in Vienna. See
Wittgenstein's Vienna (New York: Simon and Schuster, 1973), pp. 30-31,
165-66, passim.

22 Cited in Eschenbacher, p. 111.

23 *Skepsis und Mystik*, in which, as noted, the phrase in question appears, was
published in the year following the "Chandos-Brief." That Landauer, of
course, knew Hofmannsthal's text goes so nearly without saying as to render
documentation almost superfluous; but see, for example, Eschenbacher, p.
106.

24 For a fuller treatment of this and other points discussed in the present section
of the essay, see Janik and Toulmin, especially chapters five and six.
Although occasionally, if quite mistakenly, dismissed as mere eclectic summa-
rization, Janik's and Toulmin's study remains among the most lucid,
informed, and insightful commentaries available anywhere on the philosophical structure of the *Tractatus*.

The distinction between "external" and "internal" approaches is introduced
relatively early in the *Tractatus* (2.01231), and along with the distinction
between "saying" and "showing," to which it is closely related, it remains one
of the keys to the entire exposition of the work. It receives further development, variously more or less explicitly or implicitly, throughout the text, in
particular in sections 4.122-4.1252 and 5.2-5.233. Much of what might be
thought of as a kind of deep structure of the *Tractatus* comes to light in the
network of references and allusions (again, both explicit and implicit) that
takes shape as one moves back and forth among the sections of the work
having to do with this distinction alone. One sees, for example, how 4.122
develops implications of 4.121, while at the same time anticipating 4.125; and
how those two sections together (4.122 and 4.125) lead in turn to the key
6.54; also how the entire constellation 4.122-4.1252 is linked to the group 5.2-
5.232, which yields 5.233, which, again, merges into 6.54. It is a mark both of
Wittgenstein's care in composing the *Tractatus* and of the extent to which, as
a result, techniques of indirect communication (see below) pervade the work
that this same experience of finding oneself directed back and forth in the

argument, discovering ever new combinations and permutations of elements, can be repeated *mutatis mutandis* starting almost anywhere in the text.

25 See Gershon Weiler, "Fritz Mauthner," *The Encyclopedia of Philosophy*, ed. Paul Edwards (New York: Macmillan and The Free Press; London: Collier Macmillan, 1967), V, p. 221; Linda Ben-Zvi, "Samuel Beckett, Fritz Mauthner, and the Limits of Language," *PMLA*, 95 (1980), pp. 190 and 199; Janik and Toulmin, pp. 125-26.

26 In a somewhat different connection, Arthur Danto considers the question of whether or not language is fundamentally metaphorical and shows why, on conceptual grounds, it not only does not *happen to be*, but indeed *cannot be*. See *Nietzsche as Philosopher* (New York: Macmillan; London: Collier Macmillan, 1965), pp. 38-47.

27 It is a fundamental mistake, by the way, to regard the *Tractatus* as having been repudiated lock, stock, and barrel by the *Philosophical Investigations*. Nevertheless the "Two Wittgensteins"-dogma, which sees him as essentially two distinct philosophical personae, one "earlier," the other (the good one) "later," remains among the most pervasive misconceptions (as well as, increasingly, hoariest clichés) of contemporary critical theory. What actually induced Wittgenstein to return to active philosophizing after 1929 is better viewed as a recognition of the *limits* of the *Tractatus*-analysis, not a rejection of that analysis altogether. Apart from the logical atomist strain of the *Tractatus*, which certainly is abandoned in the so-called "later" period, but which had also always been both the weakest and most dispensable element of the earlier work, largely incidental to its central and most important line of argument, Wittgenstein, so far as I know, nowhere recants his belief in the fundamental validity of that analysis *within its proper sphere of competence*. His chief mistake, as he sees it, had been to assume (more or less unreflectively) that the particular use of language dealt with in the *Tractatus* — in essence, the discourse of natural science — was co-extensive with language as such. What he came to recognize, however (as he indicates in the Preface to the *Investigations*, largely under the impetus of criticisms of that earlier view by his colleagues Frank Ramsey and the economist Piero Sraffa), was that there are in fact a host of things that we do with language *besides* "picturing facts to ourselves," and for which a *Tractatus*-like analysis of logical form is, accordingly, unlikely to be of much use. On this entire issue, see Anthony Kenny, *Wittgenstein* (Cambridge: Harvard UP, 1973), in particular the final chapter, "The Continuity of Wittgenstein's Philosophy."

28 This conclusion, as suggested earlier, cuts the ground out from under linguistic skepticism, whether of the Mauthnerian sort or in any of its more current versions. For *any* coherent utterance, by the very fact of *being* coherent, must of necessity already be located within a context of intelligibility of the sort that Wittgenstein delineates. Arguments for adopting a skeptical attitude toward language — on the grounds, for example, that there is always, in the nature of

the case, an ultimately unbridgeable gap between meaning and linguistic form—are thus implicitly committed to the very thing they purport to undermine, *precisely to the extent that they can be understood at all.* There is no Archimedean point outside of language (see, in particular, *Tractatus* 3.42) from which a skeptical assault on it could be mounted (or if there were, it would, by hypothesis, be one about which nothing could be said and from which nothing could issue). Linguistic skepticism faces the dilemma of being either intelligible, and so self-refuting, or unintelligible, and so unable even to get off the ground (see 6.51; also, on the issue of solipsism and realism, 5.6-5.64, as well as Wittgenstein's *Notebooks, 1914-1916* [New York: Harper and Row, 1969], p. 85).

29 See the Preface to the *Tractatus*; also Janik and Toulmin, pp. 146, 168.

30 In the second edition of his *Fragmente über die neuere deutsche Literatur* of 1768, Herder provides a striking anticipation of this twofold move with his programmatic sketch for what he calls a "negative philosophy." See *Sämtliche Werke,* ed. Bernhard Suphan (Berlin: Weidmannsche Buchhandlung, 1877-1913), II, p. 17.

31 See Janik and Toulmin, pp. 159-61 and 196-200, on the affinities in this regard between Wittgenstein and both Kierkegaard and Karl Kraus.

32 Cited in Janik and Toulmin, p. 192.

33 For a discussion of the relationship between "discursive" and "gestural" modes of exposition in one text by Herder in particular, see *Herder and the Poetics of Thought.*

34 Cf. the similar dialectic of affirmation and negation in Zarathustra's dismissal of his disciples. Nietzsche, *Werke,* ed. Karl Schlechta, 2nd ed. (Munich: Hanser, 1960), II, pp. 339-40.

35 Cited in Ben-Zvi, p. 187.

36 Cf. "Wittgenstein's Lecture on Ethics," ed. Friedrich Waismann, *Philosophical Review,* 74 (1965), pp. 12-13.

37 Cited in Janik and Toulmin, p. 131.

38 What Wittgenstein calls (here and elsewhere) "the sphere of the ethical" includes as well aesthetics (*Tractatus* 6.421; cf. "Lecture on Ethics" [p. 4]) and logic (6.13). It is equivalent in his terminology to the dimension of "the mystical" (6.41-6.42, 6.432-6.522).

39 Cited in Janik and Toulmin, p. 192.

40 Limitations of space make it necessary to confine the discussion of the "Chandos-Brief" here to an overview of only the most salient points. I treat a number of these issues at greater length in my "Chandos and His Plans," *Deutsche Vierteljahrsschrift*, 62 (1988), pp. 514-39. The most recent extended discussion of the text of which I am aware, and one that will have to be consulted by anyone wishing to do work on it in the future, is Andreas Härter's monograph *Der Anstand des Schweigens: Bedingungen des Redens in Hofmannsthals "Brief"* (Bonn: Bouvier Verlag, 1989).

41 The second and third sections of the letter deal, respectively, with the nature of the crisis itself and with the mode of existence that Chandos has been led to adopt as a result of it.

42 "Aspekte der deutschen Literatur um 1900," in *Zur deutschen Literatur seit der Jahrhundertwende* (Stuttgart: Metzler, 1967), pp. 13 and 48.

43 See Ben-Zvi, p. 197; Weiler, *Mauthner's Critique of Language* (Cambridge: Cambridge UP, 1970), p. 294; William M. Johnston, *The Austrian Mind: An Intellectual and Social History, 1848-1938* (Berkeley: U of California P, 1972), p. 198.

44 See "Ad me ipsum," *Gesammelte Werke in Einzelausgaben: Aufzeichnungen*, p. 215.

45 On *Der Schwierige*, see in particular Richard Brinkmann, "Hofmannsthal und die Sprache," *Deutsche Vierteljahrsschrift*, 35 (1961), pp. 90-92.

PART III

FROM MODERNITY TO POSTMODERNITY

Normative Gender Discourse: Laplanche vs. Freud's Critics

Sylvia Schmitz-Burgard
Princeton University

> Was ist also Wahrheit? Ein bewegliches Heer von Metaphern, Metonymien, Anthropomorphismen, kurz eine Summe von menschlichen Relationen, die, poetisch und rhetorisch gesteigert, übertragen, geschmückt wurden, und die nach langem Gebrauch einem Volke fest, kanonisch und verbindlich dünken: die Wahrheiten sind Illusionen, von denen man vergessen hat, daß sie welche sind . . . .
>
> Friedrich Nietzsche[1]

Societal norms of gender still inform psychoanalytic discourse. While Freud had recourse to biological findings and economic metaphors in explaining and substantiating his psychoanalytic concepts of sexuality, he also reaffirmed the prevailing contemporary notions of femininity and masculinity. The absence or presence of the male secondary sexual organ structures the identity of wo*man in the writings of the founding father of psychoanalysis. In "Drei Abhandlungen zur Sexualtheorie" Freud acknowledges the equality of wo*man by defining the biological norm as bisexuality or as he calls it, anatomical hermaphroditism:

> In seltenen Fällen sind nebeneinander beiderlei Geschlechtsapparate ausgebildet (wahrer Hermaphroditismus); zu allermeist findet man beiderseitige *Verkümmerung.*

> *Ein gewisser Grad von anatomischem Hermaphroditismus gehört nämlich der Norm an*; bei keinem normal gebildeten männlichen oder weiblichen Individuum werden die Spuren vom Apparat des anderen Geschlechts vermißt, die entweder als rudimentäre Organe fortbestehen oder selbst zur Übernahme anderer Funktionen umgebildet worden sind. (my emphases)[2]

Gender differentiation emerges after the concession of a biological standard of sameness; according to Freud, wo*man exists by virtue of the atrophy of primary, secondary and tertiary sexual organs.[3] The possession or lack of the penis and its signification determine in Freudian psychoanalysis the identity of wo*man.

Psychoanalytic discourse since 1968 has either ignored Freud's idea of difference based on sameness, or has countered the synecdochical preference of one organ over the body by focusing on the body, by subrogating the attached organ with the (w)hole, and by supplanting the interest in desire with the exploration of *jouissance*.[4] The attribution of gender to the unconscious results, for example, in texts addressing the phallic unconscious, such as Nicolas Abraham's essay "The Shell and the Kernel."[5] The feminist psychoanalyst Luce Irigaray connects (menstrual) blood with the unconscious, but does not speak of a feminine unconscious; like Nietzsche, in "The Eternal Irony of the Community" she writes of truth as of something that comes about through forgetting:

> Woman is the guardian of the blood. But as both she and it have had to use their substance to nourish the universal consciousness of self, it is in the form of *bloodless shadows* — of unconscious fantasies — that they maintain an underground subsistence. And self-certainty — in masculinity, in community, in government — owes the truth of its word and of the oath that binds men together to that substance common to all, repressed, unconscious and dumb, washed in the waters of oblivion.[6]

This study will focus on language and forms of communication as informers of wo*man's conscience — the predecessor of the Super-Ego, the antagonist of the Unconscious. The atrophy of biological bisexuality still goes hand in hand with a normative gender-alignment of wo*man, and the prevalence of a discourse caused by and in turn causing what Freud calls cultural atrophy is not questioned. I will examine the problems and implications of such a discourse against the background of Freud's sexual theory and Nietzsche's views on language. The investigation of Post-Freudian writing on gender will proceed by contrasting Laplanche's assimilation of Freud to the more critical reception of Freud by Abraham, Irigaray and Cixous.

In addition to intellectual concepts Freud needed empirical (confessional) material on human sexuality. He refused, however, to take all of his patients seriously. The use of language by wo*man led Freud to give preference to the study of man's sexuality over the study of woman's sexuality. He considered only the man's statements on his couch truthful and therefore reliable, and implicitly deemed only the man receptive to his help, since truth and trust would yield the insight necessary to make man's life bearable. Although Freud names the reasons for his gender-specific studies, he only states, but does not further investigate, the cause of woman's supposedly questionable relation to truth. He therefore perpetrates gender-prejudices in his psychoanalytic theory and praxis by taking the undistorted accessibility of man's love life for granted:

> Die Bedeutung des Moments der Sexualüberschätzung läßt sich am ehesten beim Mann studieren, dessen Liebesleben allein der Forschung zugänglich geworden ist, während das des Weibes zum Teil infolge der *Kulturverkümmerung*, zum anderen Teil durch die konventionelle Verschwiegenheit und Unaufrichtigkeit der Frau in ein noch undurchdringliches Dunkel gehüllt ist. (my emphasis)[7]

Conventions of culture and language assure man the central position in Freud's studies, ideas and conclusions. Freud sees *Kulturverkümmerung* as the cause of the inaccessibility of the love life of woman. He does not, however, then go on to question his own discursive argumentation regarding the cause of this atrophy of culture, or even to recognize that his preference for man over woman is a consequence of this atrophy. The unreflected shift from the notion of organ-atrophy to that of cultural atrophy in a patriarchal society becomes an act of deformation that furthers wo*man's psychological problems instead of counteracting them. Freud prefers to study man without considering the possibility that the undeformed might be the deformer; he equates the seemingly undeformed with truth, endowing man with the exclusive power of self-knowledge and of providing the norms for the investigation of sexuality. In addition to the *Kulturverkümmerung*, Freud sees the conventionally silent or lying expression of woman as an obstacle for his sexuality studies. He is neither interested in analyzing a deformed culture and its effects on its representatives—a culture he even acknowledges as existing simultaneously with the one he intends to study—nor in probing the peculiar effect of convention on wo*man's use of language or of his own perception of such a convention on his work and the language he creates.[8] Because of his assessment of woman's stance towards sexuality in language, he deems it inevitable to accuse, mistrust and finally ignore woman. Hu*man* sexuality is defined, elucidated, by one gender alone; since the love life of the other is inaccessible by its own fault; it is irrelevant, if not (therefore) non-existent. Freud derives psychoanalytic truth from conventional discourse of/on gender.

In Nietzsche's text, "Über Wahrheit und Lüge im außermoralischen Sinn," language serves human beings as a survival device. Nietzsche does not discuss gender in his study of language, but he does examine the function of conventions as the basis for our ability to distinguish between truth and lie. For Nietzsche only in art does the instability of language prevail as the freedom from conventions. Except in the case of "fresh" metaphors in art,[9] speakers fail to recall, after prolonged use of metaphors, that all of language consists of rhetorical figures—not truth, but arbitrary assumptions of *truth*. The conventional use of language creates the illusion of truth and the illusory distinctions between truth and lie. We can see this illusory functioning of language in Freud's conventional, normative discourse on gender—a discourse that reflects his own race and gender. The conventionality-character of truth, which Nietzsche discerned, induces Freud to compose a gender-truth of/for an exuberant (man's) culture, which for lack of recollection, co-exists with a mutilated culture, and by virtue of its innumerable, interconnected, intra-supportive conventions, closes out wo*man's expression of/about gender.

Freud and Nietzsche both discuss tradition as the basis of conventions and as the informer of our conscience—the locus of knowing and differentiating good and bad (truth and lie as well as masculinity and femininity). Both their investigations address the influence of conventions on conscience as a discriminating and censoring device which serves an already existing order. Whereas Freud merely describes the shaping of the conscience he posits as a precursor of his new concept of the Super-Ego,[10] Nietzsche goes on to advise the reader to undermine power structures by questioning their norms as to their mere conventionality:

> *Inhalt des Gewissens.* — Der Inhalt unseres Gewissens ist alles, was in den Jahren der Kindheit, von uns ohne Grund regelmäßig *gefordert* wurde, durch Personen, die wir verehrten oder fürchteten. Vom Gewissen aus wird also jenes Gefühl des Müssens erregt ("dieses muß ich tun, dieses lassen"), welches nicht fragt: *warum* muß ich? — In allen Fällen, wo eine Frage mit "weil" und "warum" getan wird, handelt der Mensch *ohne* Gewissen, deshalb aber noch nicht wider dasselbe. — Der Glaube an Autoritäten ist die Quelle des Gewissens: es ist also nicht die Stimme Gottes in der Brust des Menschen, sondern die Stimme einiger Menschen im Menschen.[11]

In order to break free from gender determination and limitation by authoritarian forces, wo*man has to explore the use of language as creating and transmitting gender conventions. Language crises, however, interfere with the formulating of questions aloud, s*he searches desperately for acceptable words — words which will not be met by indifference, words which will not be dismissed as lies — to describe wo*man's unacceptable situation. Wo*man's silence is due to conventional indifference towards the statements or questions s*he voices; the power structures that oppress, determine and exclude wo*man forbid subversive questions, and in order to silence wo*man, they either ignore anything s*he says or they disparage conspicuous statements as lies — just as s*he had apprehended. The accusatory and mistrusting attitude towards wo*man speaking, let alone questioning conventions, obstructs the undermining of normative gender discourse and the initiation of gender dialogue. Language, as a means of survival, cannot be contained within the questioner of conventions, yet to be understood s*he gropes for a language expressing the inexpressible: that there is no wo*man with-in language's conventional use. Trying to create oneself in a language that offers no space for one's creation frustrates and silences. Rather than to speak only to be called a liar, wo*man prefers to remain mute for Freudian psychoanalysis.

For wo*man, gender and truth are informative conventions of a prevailing and deformative [i.e., atrophy-producing] power, which can be questioned by anyone on the grounds of its normative conventionality.   Metaphor and metonymy—human relations, as Nietzsche connotes[12] the rhetorical figures of similarity and contiguity[13]—are used, with a vested interest in gaining or retaining power, to create an illusory truth about gender. By questioning the informative conventions of a deformative power one frees oneself of the normative gender discourse of the past for the gender dialogue of the immediate future. The destabilizing use of language stabilizes gender dialogue. The discourse of logic, reason, and teleology disdains dialogue as that which uses associative language. As we have seen in Freud's method of sexual theorizing, discourse acquaints itself preferably with the known, while disregarding its inherent contradictions. Communicating about problems, caused by normative conventions, fails with-in conventional language, since wo*man may only ask questions for which conventional answers are available.

Wo*man resorts to art as a haven from conventional language. Yet even as an artist s*he is scorned as unreadable[14] by readers looking for the familiarity of stale metaphors. Wo*man writes unreadable language, because, following the Lacanian model, s*he is the other of the self-identical subject and therefore can only have restricted access to art, since she is limited by being the domain of the Other[15]. "Fresh" metaphors are acceptable within reason, but wo*man opens up the abyss of a new style. S*he rejects *mirror writing* [*Spiegelschrift*], as Helene Cixous calls it[16]; this non-visually oriented writing will remain *uncanny* to those readers looking for stale metaphors, since they make no attempt to decipher the metaphors and metonymies of wo*man's style. Frustration builds between writer and reader, speaker and listener. While art finally offers to wo*man the possibility of expressing the inexpressible, s*he then encounters linguistic rejection other than indifference, especially when s*he plays with grammar.   The politics of writing as a wo*man—that is, to open the gender dialogue, to subvert existing discourse—terminates frequently in frustration on both sides. Speaking in tongues might provoke (verbal) violence, s*he, who will not listen, must feel. In other words, anyone who attempts to create a language might provoke violence, because s*he attacks conventional language and thus frustrates the reader or listener, who profits from the conventions and makes no attempt to enter the questioning language, no attempt to leave the realm of conventionality. Wo*man's expression might seem unreadable or unreasonable, and yet it is still a desperate attempt to break the silence, to encroach on indifference.

Unable to contain wo*man's language any longer, any wo*man may burst out into *nonsense*. Luce Irigaray's woman articulates a *song*, instead of remaining silent. A *song* whose expression evades recognition:

> Words begin to fail her. She senses something *remains to be said* that resists all speech, that can at best be stammered out. All the words are weak, worn out, unfit to translate anything sensibly. For it is no longer a matter of longing for some determinable attribute, some mode of essence, some face of presence. What is expected is neither a *this* nor a *that*, not a *here* any more than a *there*. No being, no places are designated. So the best plan is to abstain from all discourse, to keep quiet, or else utter only a sound so inarticulate that it barely forms a *song*.[17]

The mystic's expression, as a historical example of nonsensical wo*man, is insensible; the content makes no sense, yet the form reminds one of a known form of art, of a somehow recognizable but foreign form of communication. At the beginning of *"La Mystérique"* Irigaray discerns man's eagerness to understand this language as a vested interest to partake through language of the mystic's relation to god. The mystic worships without/outside the institutionalized connection between human beings and god. To reject this unsanctioned communication as a lie would question god as a wonder-doer; to treat the mystic's claim with indifference might result in the abandoning of the institution by too many followers/imitators of the mystic's liberating form of communication. Thus some representatives of institutional authority temporarily disregard the known and superficially adapt to the mystic's expression. After having discovered all they need to know in order to preserve the institutional authority that sustains them, they use their access to the other's [Other] language against it—they cast out the mystic as an eccentric. And after having slipped back into their clerical authoritarian habit, they stress the known order and admonish everyone to stay on the known, institutionalized path of communication with divinity. Irigaray's discussion of the mystic's communication and the cleric's participation helps to decipher the difference between discourse and dialogue. Wo*man's form of communication cannot become a dialogue in the face of authority that prohibits any participation in wo*man's expression. Woman gains a short-lived audience because of the threatening content—a mystical love affair with god/god-son—in an *uncanny* form of communication. Wo*man's expression has occasionally provoked an interest which seems only too easily satisfied: once the known in wo*man's expression is discerned, the wo*man's text is aligned according to commonplace categories.

Freud did not attempt to communicate with wo*man, but resorted to the known—to the normative gender discourse as a framework for the analysis of psychological problems. The equation of passivity and lack with woman and of activity and sufficiency with man (in other words, non-existence and existence, respectively), lead into a dead end approach of psychoanalysis. No cure could be conceived of as long as the disease—phallogocentric discourse—was not diagnosed by Freud and his disciples. Language (some languages more than others, due to grammatical gender alignment) is always a manifestation of prevailing power structures and is at the same time a testimony to the attempt to change the language that survives the overthrown power structure. Hegelian lord-servant dialectics inform language in the aftermath of violence. A creative deciphering of language may reveal previous changes of power structures in what one might call the sedimentation of languages. In the recently acquired superior position, the victorious group strives to stabilize its position by abolition, exclusion or reversal of the predecessor's *truth*. And yet long before the decisive confrontation to overcome an authority, the subversion and the questioning of conventions, as wo*man practices it now, begins. It builds up until wo*man's expression becomes too loud, too persistent to be ignored. Or until so many voices join into the *song* to surpass self-assuredly the accusation of lie and falsehood leveled by the dominating group against the subordinated one in order to discredit its protest.

To survive as wo*man by questioning conventions includes the investigation of "penis-envy" and its symbolic signification as well. Why does the girl immediately accept and envy the penis,[18] realize its signification and even try to fabricate an *Ersatz*?[19] Freud, anticipating such questions, launched a preclusive attack against anyone advocating gender equality:

> Man zögert es auszusprechen, kann sich aber doch der Idee nicht erwehren, daß das Niveau des sittlich Normalen für das Weib ein anderes wird. Das Über-Ich wird niemals so unerbittlich, so unpersönlich, so unabhängig von seinen affektiven Ursprüngen, wie wir es vom Manne fordern. Charakterzüge, die die Kritik seit jeher dem Weibe vorenthalten hat, daß es weniger Rechtsgefühl zeigt als der Mann, weniger Neigung zur Unterwerfung unter die großen Notwendigkeiten des Lebens, sich öfter in seinen Entscheidungen von zärtlichen und feindseligen Gefühlen leiten läßt, fänden in der oben abgeleiteten Modifikation der Über-Ichbildung eine ausreichende Begründung.[20]

Freud elaborates on the traditional gender-alignments of justice, submission to the great necessities of life, and emotionality, while at the same time dismissing the objections of feminists by referring once again to the bisexual basis of all human beings.[21] So why then do the two genders differ in their sense of justice, necessity and emotionality?[22] Justice is born out of agreement on laws, necessity results from adoption of public standards either in accordance with or despite personal inclinations, and emotion becomes the inferior counterpart of reason. Acceptance of these underlying connotations of justice, necessity and reason would reveal a desire to identify with those who laid down the laws, those who defined the standards and those who accorded reason superiority over emotion. Disagreement with and disregard of these connotations would aim at the redefinition of those norms, because they posit some human beings as more equal than others. The atrophy of primary, secondary and tertiary sexual organs of the bisexual body demarcates the societal norms of gender just as the *forgotten* poetic and rhetorical alteration and canonization of metaphor, metonymy and anthropomorphism demarcate the societal norms of *truth*; both norms, in turn, are cause and consequence of the cultural atrophy. Abnormalities inform the arbitrary norms on which power structures base themselves.

Anxiety about and repression of the arbitrariness of normative gender and *truth* discourse structure our thinking in language. Wo*man's play with language is a desperate game against oppression, suppression and finally repression. However, a playful use of language is always in danger of remaining soliloquy, or of being uncritically identified with the imitated, adopted or assumed language. Beyond such misunderstandings on the side of the reader or listener, the writer or speaker puts her*himself constantly in jeopardy of slipping into reversion, of losing the playfulness, of forgetting the illusory character of what s*he might put forth as *truth*. In the face of these dangers silence sounds safe. Proverbially golden, silence is valued higher than communication. Is silence then a privilege, or is it a refusal to participate in a certain discourse, or is it a sign of pressure exerted socioeconomically, politically and ultimately psychologically in order to keep one not only from protesting against, from undermining prevailing power structures, but also from questioning them as such in language? Wo*man might remain silent about normative gender discourse, because she does not know better or because s*he believes criticism futile or even dangerous. And then again, wo*man might attempt to translate the inarticulate expressions mistaken for muteness, classified as wordless genre, or labeled nonsense into a language that considers a reader or listener grounded in pervailing language. While playing with the given language in order to translate, wo*man has made little or no sense to man — except as a mystic, an eccentric, a madwoman, a liar, a feminist. S*he still is considered to speak in tongues. S*he remains a curiosity unless she speaks the prevailing power's tongue, in which case man then always knows better than to pay attention to what he has inscribed as his ot*her.*

Wo*man, however, has to play with language, has to question prevailing discourses in order to survive. The analysis of normative gender discourse harbors in its language critique the danger of foul play—the danger of doing someone injustice by misinterpreting sound and silence, by mistaking associative language for normative discourse, or by misconstruing playful language renewal as fossilizing language preservation and thus feeding the anxiety informed by the old power structures. How can we resolve this dilemma? Harold Bloom interprets all misinterpretations as expressions of anxiety in language. Thus writing about normative gender discourse in psychoanalysis involves misreading, or misprision, as Bloom calls it.[23]

Freud's establishment of normative gender discourse has caused his critics to attribute gender to the unconscious, to question the effect of the penis-envy on the unconscious, or to re-elaborate his ideas. Nicolas Abraham speaks of "the Phallus of one's own Unconscious,"[24] while Luce Irigaray's questioning of psychoanalytic discourse centers more generally on the gender divisions; for example, she writes about the feminine:

> Psychoanalytic discourse on female sexuality as the discourse of truth: namely, that *the feminine occurs only within the models and laws devised by male subjects.*

Irigaray goes on to reveal the following gender/power structures of psychoanalytic discourse as a gender-specific discourse of truth:

> Mastery clearly acknowledges itself, except that no one notices it. Enjoying a woman, psychoanalyzing a woman, amounts then, for a man, to reappropriating for himself the unconscious he has lent her.[25]

For Irigaray, the notion of truth as masculine mastery sustains itself by discriminating against its own creation—the feminine; in short, it is the psychoanalytic rewriting of the story of creation. Just as Eve cannot exist independently in the paradise of man, so Luce cannot exist in the psychoanalysis of man (and she was, indeed, expelled from the Freudian School and from her teaching position at Vincennes).

In *Life and Death in Psychoanalysis*, Jean Laplanche re-elaborated Freud's ideas in order to outline them historically, in order to explain, clarify and stabilize the emergence of psychoanalytic terms and concepts. However, his point of departure fosters rigidity precisely where a destabilizing of the norms is needed in order to call forth the other and its outlawed language that one can glimpse in the breaks, ruptures and contradictions of Freud's writing. Laplanche's discipleship bears witness to the generational power struggle between the contemporary French psychoanalyst and the founding father of psychoanalytic ideas and vocabulary in that it is set up as a decipherable program subordinating or better subjugating specific writings of Freud to his own reading. Laplanche claims to represent the universal desire to redeem a lack in Freud's writings:

> But once the interaction of Freud's text and the terms it uses with the dialectic of what it describes is posited, we are obliged, as readers, in order better to *control* and detect the slippage in operation, to *force* the text in the direction of a certain terminological stability . . . . (my emphases)[26]

Laplanche seeks to explicate Freud's late "discovery" of the death drive, and to illustrate Freud's structuring of masochism and sadism, in order to offer the reader psychoanalytic *truth* by clearing away ambiguity and arbitrariness beyond Freud's attribution of truth to man regarding his own sexuality. But in his quest for language-stability as a prerequisite of *truth* in psychoanalysis, Laplanche does not assume the same critical approach to the gender discussions; rather, he simply adopts Freud's questionable discourse. He reads over the slippage from anatomical hermaphroditism to monosexuality and remains unperturbed by Freud's transition from biological and economic metaphors to gender conventions. He does not consider *this* slippage worth detection. (Not that I would advocate the application of *force* and *control*, but a discussion of shifting rhetoric and its assumptions, contradictions and consequences would seem appropriate in a book

with the title *Life and Death in Psychoanalysis*.) Laplanche feels
justified to claim he uncovers psychoanalytic truth without ever
considering the life-threatening quality of Freud's language for
wo*man. In search of *truth* in psychoanalysis, Laplanche strives for
control of/over Freud's texts by means of force. Laplanche's
vocabulary of domination reveals his assumption of authority
through verbal violence; his reading will produce a *truth* even
where he admittedly has trouble laying hold of one.

Instead of probing the incongruities of Freud's language,
Laplanche eradicates the ambiguities by glossing them over, by
claiming that Freud's own repression hindered a congruous delineation of the concepts Eros and Thanatos. Laplanche, however,
does not psychoanalytically preface his own desire or need for a
stabilized terminology which he considers a warrant of psychoanalytic *truth* discourse. In relying on Freud's biological and economic
metaphors as norms in his attempt to reach unambiguous psychoanalytic conclusions, he also adopts Freud's normative gender discourse. The unquestioned integration of Freud's conventions in
his criticism of Freud places Laplanche in a curious bind, since this
maneuver on the one hand frees him from rethinking those concepts, but on the other hand imprisons him in 19th-century conventions. Laplanche does not consider his own discourse — the
collage of his own and Freud's writing — a collage that itself might
constitute a form of repression; he writes *with* Freud:

> In this sense, the father is present from the beginning, even if the mother is a
> widow: he is present because the mother herself has a father and desires a
> penis; and also, as we know, because the mother has libidinal designs on her
> own child and, *beyond* him, on the penis she desires. These truths — which
> are verified daily in the psychoanalysis of women, but which are all too easily
> forgotten, when the children of these same women are in question —
> Kleinian theory, through its fantasmatic detour, has recalled to our atten-
> tion.[27]

The *truths* are: woman always desires the penis of a father, as well
as (judging from the use of the pronoun "him") that of the child.
The same woman becomes all women. Finally, Laplanche discred-
its the thoughts of a woman psychoanalyst with the adjective

"fantasmatic," except in his appropriation of her support of Freud's concept of penis-envy. This verification of the Freudian *truths* renders psychoanalysis a tautological enterprise. The known repeats itself, nothing new comes about with-in wo*man, with-in communication. Whatever does not verify the *truth* is dismissed as a lie. Given his authoritative knowledge of the Freudian model (as not only he has defined it), Laplanche could not consider the destabilization of/in language by/of the analyzed wo*man. Therefore he does not want to detect any slippage regarding gender.

Freud, whom Harold Bloom cites in *The Anxiety of Influence* as a strong poet, becomes for Laplanche, in accordance with his understanding of gender-normed psychoanalysis, the psychoanalytic/writing father. Bloom's summary in "Interchapter: A Manifesto for Antithetical Criticism" enriches the present discussion of Laplanche's contention with Freud. Laplanche's arrogation of Freud's ideas concurs with the three stages of *misprision*, which Bloom delineates and defines as follows: "For *clinamen* and *tessera* strive to correct or complete the dead, and the *kenosis* and *daemonization* work to repress memory of the dead, but *askesis* is the contest proper, the match-to-the-death with the dead."[28] The question about the effects of Freud's writings takes on a new aspect: how then does the criticized language influence the expressed misinterpretation? In *Life and Death in Psychoanalysis* Laplanche, at the first stage, explicates Freud's notion of the death-drive and illustrates his notions of sadism and masochism, and at the second stage he exerts verbal power over Freud's texts in order to stabilize the terminology and, finally, in order to render his predecessor impotent/lifeless. At the end of the *Anxiety of Influence* Bloom writes of the *apophrades*-stage as the one in which the dead re-enter the challenging text of the contender, and here we are reminded of how the Freudian normative gender discourse re-enters Laplanche's writing.[29] In writing of Freud's repression Laplanche reveals his own repression and in turn attempts to repress Freud in order to free himself of his precursor. Lying is part of the *askesis*: "To revise the precursor is to lie, not against being, but against time and *askesis* is peculiarly a lie against the truth of time, the time in which the ephebe hoped to attain an antonomy tainted by time, ravaged by otherness."30   While Laplanche tries to surpass Freud, he never departs from Freud or his discourse.   Since he never attempts dialogue in writing, but rather insists on domination, Laplanche's reading of Freud discloses itself as a rivalry in normative discourse.   Lying by counting on prevailing conventions of language-use in order to counter them is for Nietzsche one form of using the human survival device.   Laplanche, in order to survive as a Freudian psychoanalyst attempting to surpass Freud, has to make this discourse come true. Language as a binary system of lie and truth turns out to be a riddle about the use and purpose of the illusion about gender.   Truth is a convention to be reinforced or to be revealed as a lie; lie is a violation of convention "that could" expose the convention as a convention.   Any convention is dated, yet not the fluctuation within the binary system: the influence of lie on truth, of truth on lie delivers normative discourse.

Freud himself had used ideas from biology to explain his concepts of psychoanalysis; he had employed economic metaphors to write on psychic life as human productivity in the red or black, yet he did not reflect on the monopolization of the market through his own preconceived ideas of gender and the resulting normative discourse. In this respect Laplanche, in attempting to move ahead of Freud, ends up in stride with Freud and thus one step behind his own time; he relegates himself to the first half of the 20th century, rather than moving into the second.   In section V of *Jenseits des Lustprinzips* Freud writes of the "magic rhythm" as a possible interrelation of the drives, and projects a linearity which doubles back on itself in order to put off the end ("die eine Triebgruppe stürmt vorwärts, um das Endziel zu erreichen, die andere schnellt an einer bestimmten Stelle dieses Weges zurück, um ihn nochmals zu machen und so die Dauer des Weges zu verlängern"31), just as Laplanche in *Life and Death in Psychoanalysis* puts off the collapse of normative gender discourse.

Nicolas Abraham addresses Freud's problem of finding a language of his own to express his psychoanalytic ideas, while at the same time resorting to biology and economics. He asks how Freud can remain accessible to the reader while communicating in tongues. Not only through capitalization, Abraham writes, but especially by way of de-signification, Freud makes new use of the given language ("Pleasure, Id, Ego, Economic, Dynamic are not metaphors, metonymies, synecdoches, catachreses; they are through the action of discourse, products of de-signification and constitute new figures, absent from the rhetorical treatises"[32]), while at the same time his psychoanalytic terminology—Pleasure, Id, Ego, Economic, Dynamic—is no longer employable for an explanation, except by translation—by *de-signification.* Thus Freud, by creating for the most part a language of his own, instead of drawing on conventions, evades the arrest Laplanche attempts. Freud capitalizes on language and supports his theories by disfiguring some of the linguistic conventions he employs. Freud's innovative disfiguration turns out to cut both ways: linguistically it breaks the ground for a new field of thought and inquiry—psychoanalysis—and yet at the same time it supports and re-inforces existing norms at the expense of the social, economic, and cultural outsiders on whose psyche society exerts the greatest pressure as the psyche of the Other and who therefore might seek psychoanalytic help in the first place.

Laplanche takes over from Freud not only the gender conventions, the disfigured linguistic conventions, but also the concept of the centrality of the Ego. The Ego, as the battle ground of the Unconscious and the Super-Ego, is reframed by Laplanche between the discussion of Eros in Chapters 1 and 2 and that of the death-drive in Chapters 5 and 6. In leading up to the death-drive, which he makes into the kernel of understanding Freud, Laplanche spins around this nodus a terminologically stabilizing cocoon, which he then tries to harden into a shell by passing it off as the truth of/for institutionalized psychoanalysis. Laplanche frames his ideas by announcing his goal in the introduction and by explaining the use of the terms metaphor and metonymy in his own vocabulary. For Laplanche metonymy and metaphor stand in the following relation to ego, self and other:

What might one mean in speaking of a metonymical derivation of the "ego"? That between the ego as individual (in the "non-technical" sense) and the ego as "agency" or element in a physical structure, there would be a relation of differentiation. The ego appears here as a specialized organ, a veritable prolongation of the individual, no doubt charged with specific functions but serving ultimately to localize something which had originally been present in the whole organism.[33]

After having defined the metonymical as differentiation presupposing identity and wholeness, Laplanche then explains, three pages further on, his understanding of the term "metaphorical" in psychoanalysis:

This time, the ego is not conceived of as the prolongation of the living individual, but as a *displacement* of it, and of its image, to *another* site, and consequently as a kind of intrapsychical reality, an intrapsychical precipitate in the image of the individual. Is it the image of the self?

The crucial point, however, which is already indicated by Freud and renders useless and even fallacious a distinction between an "ego" and a "self," is the observation that the genesis of the ego itself is marked by the indissolubly linked image of self and other.[34]

Laplanche conceives of the Ego on the one hand as metonymically expressing contiguity, standing for difference of Ego and other, and on the other hand metaphorically implying similarity, standing for sameness of Ego as self and other. The Ego, as the crossing point of the unconscious and the Super-Ego, of Eros and Thanatos, now expresses difference and sameness simultaneously. Laplanche's structuring of the Ego brings the specific problem of normative gender discourse back into play, since penis-envy bases itself on difference determined by the assumption of sameness, i. e., the male organ is the standard of "to have" or "to be" vs. to have not and therefore not to be. Linking continuity to contiguity and simultaneity to similarity introduces the element of time into psychoanalytic discourse, which seems to bring about what Jacques Derrida has named *differance*[35], by which he indicates a combination of differing and both spatial and temporal deferring. We might more accurately describe this introduction of time into psychoanalytic discourse as *simulance*, by which I would indicate non-difference and non-deferral with-in language. How can one use discourses, such as Freud's and Laplanche's, after trying to expose them, and after recognizing that metaphor and metonymy barely touch upon truth and gender structures, on phallic/vaginal/menstrual power and subversion thereof, on silence and dialogue? Yet to declare psychoanalytic normative discourse (on truth/gender) a *taboo subject* is an increasingly futile attempt to prevent the contamination of psychoanalysis through the questioning of its conventions undertaken by analysands, analysts and especially readers.

To accept language as a responsibility seems to weigh down the Nietzschean notion of playing with language, yet in order to play with language, wo*man has to recollect the illusiveness of language and the implications of communication forms such as *differance* or *simulance*. Considering differing and deferring vis-à-vis their counterparts might help in rephrasing the problem of an underlying standard of identity which is subject to time and an underlying standard of authenticity (*Wahr*scheinlichkeit/probability, *Wahr*haftigkeit/veracity and finally *Wahrheit*/truth) which is subject to the process of forgetting and recollecting. To use language, then, is a game that becomes serious over time and with the increase of the power of some users. Thus the problem with-in the present normative gender discourse is: when merely a reversal of/with-in normative gender discourse takes place (i. e. discriminating against the other gender) another segment of society gains power and perpetrates the discourse of domination. Discourse remains the goal-oriented logical use of language designed to feed into the prevailing truth or to substitute one *truth* with another *truth*, to win an argument, to convince a doubter and to give the answer to a question. Dialogue, however, implies a back and forth of formulations, of endless questions, in the course of which the ending of an argument becomes impossible. According to René Girard, Hegelian dialectics of thesis and antithesis never reach a synthesis because of an insatiable desire for conflict[36], but dialogue is a conflict without violence, precisely because of a *jouissance* in nourishing conversation and avoiding the assumption of authority, which would end the dialogue; having found the one answer ends the autonomy of an other, no one has any longer a say in the matter. *Jouissance* of verbal exchange would then stimulate dialogue without the goal of synthesis. The idea of agreeing to differ then takes on two meanings: to call it quits in order to collect more material to strengthen one's argument (to defer until the answer is found) or to disagree for the sake of the argument. Psychoanalysis can insist on *normal* discourse, by which Richard Rorty means "that which is conducted within an agreed upon set of conventions."[37] Freud's normative gender discourse is a convention that is not disregarded one way or the other. What would the disregard of this convention "Freud" entail for psychoanalysis as well as for sustaining dialogue? For Freudian gender-oriented/normed illnesses the cure could be sought not only in the analysand's time and language but just as well or even more so in the analyst's. Could hysteria be made bearable simply by re-considering the gender frame or would a new word be the cure and the end of this illness for wo*man?[38] Would, instead of the desire for the penis (Laplanche), the pleasure in mothermilk (Cixous quoting Rimbaud) be an attempt to sustain a conversation or would the associative communication of menstrual/hymenal blood at one time be or become w*hole instead of phallogocentric normal discourse? And who is sustaining the conversation — the one who communicates, disregarding the conventions, or the one who listens/deciphers? Communicating in tongues and silence seems to be a conversation at odds with itself. Dialogue becomes a convention. How far can we differ and defer when disregarding conventions and yet stay accessible, comprehensible enough? Masculinity — femininity, truth — lie, normality — abnormality all come about through the use of language in order to survive despite conventions or in order to sustain conventions. To argue for the argument's sake may be the disregard of conventions, but it is also frequently the disregard for what is being said. Sexual abuse, for example, becomes a fantasy of/for the Freudian analyst, leaving little room to consider what the conventions allow the wo*man to reveal. The accusation of sexual abuse is believed to be disregard of the societal conventions by the woman/girl/analysand but not by the father/abuser/analyst.   Violence, especially when being dismissed as mock-violence, attempts to achieve submission, to achieve subjugation of the accuser; injustice is added to injury, the abuse is verbally repeated and it terminates a gender dialogue for the sake of the normative gender discourse.

How can the sustained conversation prevent itself from becoming what is has disregarded—a convention? The "anxiety of influence," in the margin groups of society, generates its own form of communication on which it thrives—priding itself on its marginality. Or might this marginal communication itself already be caught up in a binary system of center and margin, of discourse and dialogue, which feed upon one another? Nothing can be said in our time without considering gender implications. Luce Irigaray and Helene Cixous write about/in a wo*man's style; they do not define it, but rather only display some of its features. Freudian psycho-analysis offers itself as a target of criticism in search of such a style, because of psychoanalysis' breaks, ruptures and contradictions, because of its delineation of power structures at the same time that it succumbs to them, and because of its discussion of truth and gender with-out wo*man. In *rewriting* Freudian psychoanalysis the trinity of oppression, suppression and repression can be dethroned by extending the investigation, by questioning socio-economical, political and familial oppression as well as the induced and prolif-erating suppression thereof to the realm of repression. Repression is the least accessible for us, since we do not comprehend the degree of its inaccesibility and because we cannot estimate the extent to which the barriers of race, class or gender have been implanted in us. In order to initiate dialogue in an attempt to encroach on these barriers, we have to attempt a form of communication that probes for conventionality regarding truth and gender present in our own thinking, experiencing and communicating in order to avoid the creation of new *truths*. Otherwise we, like Laplanche, repeat the known and fall back into the trap of Freudian gender/truth discourse.

Notes

1 Friedrich Nietzsche, "Über Wahrheit und Lüge im außermoralischen Sinn," *Werke*, ed. by Karl Schlechta, 6th ed. (Frankfurt a/M: Ullstein, 1969), III, p. 1022.

2 Sigmund Freud, "Drei Abhandlungen zur Sexualtheorie" in *Gesammelte Werke. Werke aus den Jahren 1904-1905*, ed. by Anna Freud, et al., 4th ed. (Frankfurt a/M: Fischer, 1968), V, p. 40.

3 Sigmund Freud, "Drei Abhandlungen zur Sexualtheorie. Die sexuellen Abirrungen.1) Abweichungen in Bezug auf das Sexualobjekt. A) Die Inversion," in *Gesammelte Werke. Werke aus den Jahren 1904-1905*, ed. by Anna Freud, et al., 4th ed. (Frankfurt a/M: Fischer, 1968), V, pp. 40-47.

4 For connotations of the French term *jouissance* see Jacques Lacan "The signification of the phallus" and "Subversion of the subject and dialectic of desire," in *Ecrits*, trans. by Alan Sheridan (New York: Norton, 1977), especially pp. 282 and 317 as well as p. X of the translator's notes, and Julia Kristeva "About Chinese Women," in *The Julia Kristeva Reader*, ed. by Toril Moi (New York: Columbia, 1986), pp. 146-154.

5 Cf. Nicolas Abrahams, "The Shell and the Kernel," in *Diacritics. The Tropology of Freud*, Vol. 9, No. 1 (Spring 1979), p. 20.

6 Luce Irigaray, "The Eternal Irony of Community," in *Speculum of the Other Woman*, trans. by Gillian C. Gill (Ithaca, N.Y.: Cornell University Press, 1985), p. 225 and cf. Friedrich Nietzsche, "Über Wahrheit und Lüge im außermoralischen Sinn," in *Werke*, ed. by Karl Schlechta (Frankfurt a/M: Ullstein, 1969), III, pp. 1017-1030.

7 Sigmund Freud, "Drei Abhandlungen zur Sexualtheorie," p. 50.

8 For a discussion of a merging of empirical data and psychoanalytic theory in terms of case and socio-political history see D. LaCapra, "History and Psychoanalysis," in *Critical Inquiry. The Trial(s) of Psychoanalysis*, ed. by Françoise Meltzer, Winter 1987, Vol. 13, No. 2, pp. 222-252.

9 Friedrich Nietzsche, "Über Wahrheit und Lüge im außermoralischen Sinn," p. 1027.

10 In his lecture "Die Zerlegung der psychischen Persönlichkeit" Freud speaks
    of the power structure underlying the differentiation of good and bad:

    Sie werden gewiß mehr als eine bloße Illustration erwarten, wenn ich Ihnen
    ankündige, daß wir über die Bildung des Über-Ichs, also über die Entstehung
    des Gewissens, mancherlei gelernt haben.

    Die Rolle, die späterhin das Über-Ich übernimmt, wird zuerst von einer
    äußeren Macht, von der elterlichen Autorität, gespielt. Der Elterneinfluß
    regiert das Kind durch Gewährung von Liebesbeweisen und durch Andro-
    hung von Strafen, die dem Kind Liebesverlust beweisen und an sich
    gefürchtet werden müssen.

    Sigmund Freud, "XXXI. Die Zerlegung der psychischen Persönlichkeit," in
    *Gesammelte Werke. Neue Folge der Vorlesungen zur Einführung in die Psy-
    choanalyse*, ed. by Anna Freud, et al., 4th ed. (Frankfurt a/M: Fischer, 1968),
    XIV, pp. 67-68.

11 Friedrich Nietzsche, "Menschliches, Allzumenschliches," in *Werke*, ed. by
    Karl Schlechta (Frankfurt a/M: Ullstein, 1972), I, p. 902.

12 Connotation is here used in a Barthesian understanding of the term. In sec-
    tions III and IV of *S/Z* Barthes argues first against and then for the use of the
    term "connotation" and then sums his discussion up as follows:

    Then, what is a connotation? Definitionally, it is a determination, a relation,
    an anaphora, a feature which has the power to relate itself to anterior, ulte-
    rior or exterior mentions, to other sites of the text (or of another text): we
    must in no way restrain this relating, which can be given various names
    (*function* or *index*, for example), except that we must not confuse connotation
    with association of ideas, the latter refers to the system of a subject; connota-
    tion is a correlation immanent in the text, in the texts; or again, one may say
    that it is an association made by the text-as-subject within its own system.

    In the remainder of section IV, Barthes continues to discuss connotation
    under specific headings such as: topically, analytically, topologically, semio-
    logically, dynamically, historically, functionally, structurally, and ideologically.

    Roland Barthes, *S/Z*, translated by Richard Miller (New York: Hill and
    Wang, 1974), p. 8.

13 Friedrich Nietzsche, "Über Wahrheit und Lüge im außermoralischen Sinn,"
    p. 1022.

14 Helene Cixous describes, in *Die Weiblichkeit in der Schrift*, some aspects of
    the judgement "unreadable":

[U]nd es stimmt, daß ein Text aus Weiblichkeit gerade Wege bahnt, die keine Rückkehr versprechen, und eine ganz und gar abenteuerliche Leseweise ermöglichen; eine Leseweise von der man nicht berichten kann, die man nicht beherrschen kann, eine Lektüre, die gerade bewirkt, daß man oft sagt, diese Texte seien "unleserlich", man könne sie nicht zusammenfassen, nicht mehr als man ein Leben, etwas Lebendiges zusammenfassen kann.

Helene Cixous, *Die Weiblichkeit in der Schrift*, trans. by Eva Dufner (Berlin: Merve, 1980), p. 80.

15 Luce Irigaray discusses this limitation in her essay "Cosi Fan Tutti":

The relation to the Other of/by/in/through . . . the Other is impossible: "The Other has no Other." Which may be understood as meaning: there is no meta-language, except insomuch as the Other *already stands for it*, suspending in its own ek-sistence [ek-sistence – Existence as conscious separation or differentiation from nature: the state of being opposite to that generally ascribed to the feminine.] the possibility of an other. For if there were some other – without that leap, necessarily ek-static, of the capital letter – the entire autoerotic, auto-positional, auto-reflexive economy . . . of the subject, or the "subject," would find itself disturbed, driven to distraction. The impossible "self-affection" of the Other by itself – of the other by herself? – would be the condition making it impossible for any subject to form his/her/its desires. The Other serves as matrix/womb for the subject's signifiers; such would be the cause of its desire; of the value, also, of the instruments it uses to restore the grip on what thus defines it.

Luce Irigaray, *This Sex Which Is Not One*, trans. by Catherine Porter (Ithaca: Cornell University Press, 1985), p. 101 and [p. 220].

16 Helene Cixous describes this type of writing as follows:

Sie [die Stimmhaftigkeit] entsteht in der Auseinandersetzung, im Kampf mit der Sprache: Schreiben heißt für eine Frau lebhaft schreiben, frei schreiben, heißt gegen das Schriftbild, die *Spiegelschrift* ankämpfen, bedeutet, alles tun, damit die Sprache Dir nicht zuvorkommt, nicht vor Dir schreibt, heißt, sich mit aller Kraft von der furchtbaren Manie der Klischees loszureißen. (my emphasis)

Helen Cixous, *Die Weiblichkeit in der Schrift*, p. 85.

17 Luce Irigaray, "*La Mystèrique*," in *Speculum of the Other Woman*, trans. by Gillian C. Gill (Ithaca: Cornell University Press, 1985), p. 193.

18 Sigmund Freud "Drei Abhandlungen zur Sexualtheorie. Die infantile Sexualität," p. 96.

19   In his second set of lectures Freud writes about women's invention of the braiding technique as an attempt to fashion an *Ersatz* for the missing genital.

Man meint, daß Frauen zu den Entdeckungen und Erfahrungen der Kulturgeschichte wenig Beiträge geleistet haben, aber vielleicht haben sie doch eine Technik erfunden, die des Flechtens und Webens. Wenn dem so ist, so wäre man versucht, das Unbewußte dieser Leistung zu erraten. Die Natur selbst hätte das Vorbild für diese Nachahmung gegeben, indem sie mit der Geschlechtsreife die Genitalbehaarung wachsen ließ, die das Genitale verhüllt.

Freud chooses the subjunctive to imply that he is conjecturing about woman's ability to invent as well as about her incentive to invent, yet the last sentence changes the mode of the whole passage back into the indicative when he undermines possible objections to his theory by saying: "Wenn Sie diesen Einfall als phantastisch zurückweisen und mir den Einfluß des Penismangels auf die Gestaltung der Weiblichkeit als eine fixe Idee anrechnen, bin ich natürlich wehrlos."

Sigmund Freud, "XXXIII. Vorlesung. Die Weiblichkeit," in *Gesammelte Werke. Neue Folge der Vorlesungen zur Einführung in die Psychoanalyse*, ed. by Anna Freud, et al., 4th ed. (Frankfurt a/M: Fischer, 1969), XV, p. 142.

20   Sigmund Freud, "Einige psychische Folgen des anatomischen Geschlechtsunterschiedes" in *Gesammelte Werke. Werke aus den Jahren 1925-1931*, ed. by Anna Freud, et al., 4th ed. (Frankfurt a/M: Fischer, 1968), XIV, pp. 29-30.

21   Freud rejects the feminists' demand for equal rights and esteem with the admittance that the majority of men fail to represent the male ideal, as if women therefore should be satisfied to fall short, like men, of an ideal that does not even take them into consideration:

Durch den Widerstand der Feministen, die uns eine völlige Gleichstellung und Gleichschätzung der Geschlechter aufdrängen wollen, wird man sich in solchen Urteilen nicht beirren lassen, wohl aber bereitwillig gestehen, daß auch die Mehrzahl der Männer weit hinter dem *männlichen Ideal* zurückbleibt, und daß alle menschlichen Individuen infolge ihrer *bisexuellen Anlage* und der gekreuzten Vererbung männliche und weibliche Charaktere in sich vereinigen, so daß die reine Männlichkeit und Weiblichkeit theoretische Konstruktionen bleiben mit ungesichertem Inhalt. (my emphases)

Sigmund Freud, "Einige psychische Folgen des anatomischen Geschlechtsunterschiedes," p. 30.

22   At the very end of the lecture "Die Weiblichkeit," Freud gives his explanations for woman's deficiency regarding justice, lack of social interest and their limited ability to sublimate their drives. He lectures:

Daß man dem Weib wenig Sinn für Gerechtigkeit zuerkennen muß, hängt wohl mit dem Überwiegen des Neids in ihrem Seelenleben zusammen, denn die Gerechtigkeitsforderung ist eine Verarbeitung des Neids, gibt die Bedingung an, unter der man ihn fahren lassen kann. Wir sagen auch von den Frauen aus, daß ihre sozialen Interessen schwächer und ihre Fähigkeit zur Triebsublimierung geringer sind als die der Männer. Das erstere leitet sich wohl vom dissozialen Charakter ab, der allen Sexualbeziehungen unzweifelhaft eignet. Liebende finden aneinander Genüge und noch der Familie widerstrebt die Aufnahme in umfassendere Verbände. Die Eignung zur Sublimierung ist den größten individuellen Schwankungen unterworfen.

Freud's argumentation reveals itself as a circular reasoning, since his operation basis to prove the inequality of the genders are conventional notions on the soul, the family and individual divergencies.

Sigmund Freud, "Die Weiblichkeit," in *Gesammelte Werke. Neue Vorlesungen zur Einführung in die Psychoanalyse*, ed. by Anna Freud, et al., 4th ed. (Frankfurt a/M: Fischer Verlag, 1969), XV, p. 144.

23 In "Interchapter: A Manifesto for Antithetical Criticism" Bloom summarizes his idea on distorting someone's writing in one's *writerly reading*, as Barthes calls it in *S/Z*, in order to forego the binary system of interpretation/misinterpretation:

Every poem is a misinterpreation of a parent poem. A poem is not an overcoming of anxiety, but it is that anxiety. Poets' misinterpretations or poems are more drastic than critics' misinterpretations or criticism, but this is only a difference in degree and not at all in kind. There are no interpretations but only misinterpretations, and so all criticism is prose poetry. Misinterpretation is an act of rebellion, which perpetuates an acknowledged language.

Harold Bloom, *The Anxiety of Influence. A Theory of Poetry* (London: Oxford University Press, 1975), p. 94. See also the discussion of Bloomian anxiety of influence by Sandra Gilbert and Susan Gubar in "Infection in the Sentence: The Woman Writer and the Anxiety of Authorship," in *The Madwoman in the Attic* (New Haven: Yale University Press, 1979), pp. 46-53.

24 Nicolas Abraham, "The Shell and the Kernel," p. 22.

25 Luce Irigaray, *This Sex Which Is Not One*, p. 86.

26 Jean Laplanche, *Life and Death in Psychoanalysis*, trans. by Jeffrey Mehlman (Baltimore: Johns Hopkins University Press, 1976), p. 87.

27 Jean Laplanche, *Life and Death in Psychoanalysis*, p. 46.

28 Harold Bloom, *The Anxiety of Influence*, p. 122.

29   Harold Bloom describes this last phase as the blurring of poetics:

The *apophrades*, the dismal or unlucky days upon which the dead return to inhabit their former houses, come to the strongest poets, but with the very strongest there is a grand and final revisionary movement that purifies even this last influx.

For all of them achieve a style that captures and oddly retains priority over their precursors, so that the tyranny of time almost is overturned, and one can believe, for startled moments, that they are being *imitated by their ancestors*.

Harold Bloom, *The Anxiety of Influence*, p. 141.

30   Harold Bloom, *The Anxiety of Influence*, p. 130.

31   Sigmund Freud, "Jenseits des Lustprinzips," in *Gesammelte Werke. Jenseits des Lustprinzips und andere Arbeiten aus den Jahren 1920-1924*, ed. by Anna Freud, et al., 4th ed. (Frankfurt a/M: Fischer, 1969), XIII, p. 43.

32   Nicolas Abraham, "The Shell and the Kernel," p. 20.

33   Jean Laplanche, *Life and Death in Psychoanalysis*, p. 51.

34   Jean Laplanche, *Life and Death in Psychoanalysis*, pp. 53-54.

35   Jacques Derrida, *Of Grammatology*, trans. by G. C. Spivak (Baltimore: The Johns Hopkins University Press, 1976), p. 66.

36   René Girard, *Deceit, Desire, and the Novel* (Baltimore: The Johns Hopkins Press, 1965), pp. 110-111.

37   Richard Rorty, *Philosophy and the Mirror of Nature* (Princeton, N.J.: Princeton University Press, 1979), p. 378.

38   For a feminist discussion of hysteria see *In Dora's Case. Freud—Hysteria—Feminism*, ed. Charles Bernheimer and Claire Kahane (New York: Columbia University Press, 1985), where in her introduction Claire Kahane points out a feminist move in the opposite direction:

Although Freud's assertion that hysteria afflicted both men and women was a liberating gesture in the nineteenth century, contemporary feminists are reclaiming hysteria as the dis-ease of women in patriarchal society.

Claire Kahane, "Introduction. Part Two," in *In Dora's Case*, p. 31.

The Discovery of Austrian Literature Under the Shadow of Nazism: Autobiography as a History of Reception of Literature

Walter H. Sokel
University of Virginia
Translated by Steven Taubeneck,
in collaboration with the author

In the following I shall attempt the sketch of an autobiographical narrative by way of a description of my earliest confrontations with Austrian literature. Along the way I shall reflect on the significance that individual works, authors, and aspects of Austrian literature acquired for me at the time of my earliest contacts with them. I shall "remember," that is, I shall interpret and reconstruct past experience from my present perspective. My attempt is to suggest a kind of "auto-history" of literary reception. I am not the one who experienced Austrian literature at that time. I am his interpreter.

The topic will be approached from two perspectives. First, I shall describe a specific history of the reception of Austrian literature in one example—myself—; secondly, I shall try to represent one important component, namely literature, of my late childhood, adolescence, and young adulthood.

To begin with, I should confess that, despite voracious reading as a child, "Austrian" literature meant nothing to me. At that time, there was only reading for me, fanatic, indiscriminate, tasteless reading—Sir Walter Scott, Courts-Mahler, Dickens, H. G. Wells, Zane Gray, Dostoevsky, Wilhelm Hauff, Gustav Freytag, Karl

May, Bernhard Kellermann, John Galsworthy, Jakob Wassermann, and many others. It was not these authors who had a real existence for me, it was their books which I hungrily, indiscriminately devoured. A fanatical reader, I was illiterate for many years in regard to literary history. I basically threw myself at every book I could lay my hands on, and I read past the name on the title page. My life seemed to pass on two levels: the level of actual occurrences and the level of my imagination. The latter consisted of stories, self-invented as well as read in books and then freely—very freely—retold to myself. The worlds in my head seemed to me much more vivid, interesting, and real than reality, since "reality" for me meant the absence of stories. Now, in the world of stories, there was little talk of "Austrian," "German," "English" or "Russian" literature. I deeply experienced Raskolnikov's guilt and punishment, but for a long time I did not know that he was the creation of a famous author whose name I should have noted. My ignorance was a symptom of disregard for that reality to which authors, and especially their reputations, belonged.

When, in Gymnasium, the importance and significance of interpersonal reality became substantially clearer, I was more careful to note and memorize the names of authors and their place in space and time. It had become important to appear to be an "educated" person.

The concept of an "Austrian" literature assumed concrete form for me in the eighth grade of the Gymnasium, the year of graduation. Austrian literature then was literature of the turn of the century. It pointed unequivocally ahead to the apocalyptic end of our world. This end was certain. A new beginning beyond it was terribly uncertain and, in regard to its quality, completely unimaginable. Austrian literature for me, at that time, was above all Hugo von Hofmannsthal, and most particularly his "Ballad of Outer Life" ("Ballade vom äusseren Leben"). "And children grow up with deep eyes/which know of nothing" spoke to me of my own recently ended childhood. I had just become eighteen, and it was the year 1935/36. The "outer life" in the title implied, it seemed to me, an inner life, which expressed itself, at the end of the poem, in the weighty ambiguity of the word "evening" ("Abend"). In the contrast between an articulated external life that lies at hand, but leaves us deeply dissatisfied, and a vaguely sensed inner life that might be heavy and rich with unuttered significance, I felt again that contrast between my everyday, familiar reality and the worlds of my fantasy in which a stronger and truer life was lived. The historical moment at which Hofmannsthal's ballad became meaningful to me temporalized or historicized this contrast. The contrast between outer and inner life became the tension between a present nearing its end and a dimly sensed, scarcely conceivable beginning on the other side of the expected end of Austria and the world as we knew it. Austrian literature, as I encountered it in Hofmannsthal's poetry, portrayed a twilight world that foretold the approaching night. It also implied, however, the possibility, the premonition of a far-off dawn which was unspoken and inconceivable.

It seems to me now that my Hofmannsthal reception then was an interpretation of my own situation in the Vienna of Chancellor Schuschnigg. Hofmannsthal and his circle were, after all, our compatriots in time as well as in space. As *their* lives moved toward the threatening century that was to bring the First World War and smash their world, we graduates of the year 1936 faced an even more terrifying Second World War and, with it, the likely end not only of Austria, but of all of Europe in the abyss of a Third Reich whose shadows had been cast over our lives for the last three years: and only beyond those shadows, very vaguely, hardly hoped-for, the suggestion of a new and better world.

My Hofmannsthal reception coincided with the influence that Oswald Spengler as well as Marxism had had on me for the past several months. As it then seemed to me, we were living in a period that resembled the end phase of the ancient world. What Christianity had been then, socialism was for us, now. Apocalypse and Second Coming were comparable to the imminent World War and the world revolution which it, we were almost sure, would bring about.

In 1936 the poet Marcell Pellich became, for our little group of literarily inclined graduates, a figure of great importance. Pellich (ower), born in Vienna in 1908, died from leukemia in Swiss exile in 1945. He had already published two volumes of poetry and was now working on a lengthy novel, *The Magnifying Glass* (*Das Vergrösserungsglas*), which he compared to Joyce's *Ulysses*. Through Pellich I became acquainted with several contemporary or recently deceased Austrian authors, known as yet only to small groups of initiates, including Georg Trakl, Hermann Broch, of whose novel *The Sleepwalkers* I read the third volume, Elias Canetti whose novel *Auto-da-Fé* (*Die Blendung*) ends with a book burning, and above all Franz Kafka whose *Trial* I began to read but—and this is difficult to believe—found too boring to finish.

In school and everywhere around us, however, a wholly different kind of Austrian writing was being propagated, the so-called "nativist writing" ("bodenständige Dichtung"), which was supposed to have nothing in common with what that noun of foreign and subversive provenance, "*Literatur*," signified. Scornfully I turned away from that "wholesome" and "constructive" kind of writing—with the arrogance of the avant-gardist steeped in decadence. My contempt, unfortunately, included authors of the Austrian tradition, like Ferdinand von Saar, whom I have since learned to respect. Our professor of Greek, a tyrant of the type portrayed by Heinrich Mann in *Professor Unrat*, stormed into class one day and thundered at me: "Sokel, you may turn up your nose at Ferdinand von Saar, but thereby you only reveal yourself as what you are—a puffed-up, ignorant, and snooty fool. You should be ashamed of yourself!" To this day I can not say how he learned of my unpatriotic arrogance, but I owe to it a negative class mark on my transcript and the grade of "C" in our last semester of Greek.

From today's perspective I should like to examine more closely my anti-Austrian snobbishness of that time. It was a reaction against the narrow-minded regionalism and provincialism of the semi-Fascist "Fatherland Front," which tried to create a "native canon" of ideologically approved authors who were praised as "truly Austrian." Every modern, urban, skeptical, and cosmopolitan tendency was deeply suspect. These Austrian super-patriots sentimentalized "the homeland." For my friends and me it was simply self-evident that such "Austrian literature" was worthless. We wanted to have nothing to do with a provincial, self-congratulatory Austria.

In those years, the very concept of "Austria" was highly problematic for me. From the age of fourteen, when I had read Heinrich Mann's *The Man of Straw* (*Der Untertan*), I considered myself a socialist. At fifteen I joined a socialist student group and for a time was active in the underground, albeit in a ludicrously ineffectual manner. Marxism became problematic for me only with the Stalinist "Show Trials" of Zinovev, Kamenev, Bukharin, and others. The process of my disentanglement was to extend over many years. As a socialist I was, of course, above all an internationalist, and categorically rejected any emphasis of national difference. Austrian literature was for me nothing other than world literature written in Austria in the German language. If this literature had to be classified at all, then only as literature of the German language. Hence I could not accept the idea of an "essential Austria," propagated by the "Fatherland Front," nor that of an essentially Austrian literature, and I rejected such ideas with all the sovereign contempt of a youthfully self-assured "expert." The attempt on the part of the Fatherland Party to fabricate a specifically Austrian tradition in art, literature, and intellectual life seemed totally artificial to me, and its much-touted authors, including classics like Grillparzer, were marked for me by the blemish of provincialism. Literature proclaimed as "Austrian" bore the stigma of kitsch, as defined in Milan Kundera's *The Unbearable Lightness of Being* as the representation of a world without excrement and death. The worshippers of Austria in the "Fatherland Front" seemed to be bent on representing an Austria of total kitsch.

My equation of Austrian culture with kitsch changed, however, when, at the age of eighteen, I became acquainted with Viennese decadence or modernism of the turn of the century. In this *other* Austria, it was the experience of the end, which mocks all kitsch, that found its voice. My attitude towards Austria and Austrian literature also changed shortly thereafter under the influence of my friend and mentor Marcell Pellich. He was an intellectual who was also an Austrian patriot, a circumstance which gave a new meaning to patriotism. He saw in Austria a continuation of the best traditions of German Romanticism, those elements in it which had been spared Prussian militarization and able to develop further in Austria. For him Rilke, Hofmannsthal, and above all, Trakl were the true descendants of Hölderlin, and it was in *The Sleepwalkers, The Trial,* and *The Auto-da-Fé* that the German Romantic novel received its strongest expression. He also saw in the work of Broch and Canetti certain parallels to and continuations of the experiments of James Joyce. Pellich himself was working on that "Joycean" novel, *The Magnifying Glass,* which has not yet been published. He spoke sometimes of the literary axes Dublin-Vienna and Dublin-Prague in which Austria occupied a position vis-à-vis Germany analogous to that which Ireland occupied in relation to England. What that meant was Catholicism coupled with a romantic attraction to the past, fascination with dreams and fairy tales, obsession with the phenomenon of language, and a profoundly ironic attitude — the attitude of peoples who, defeated in and through history, had been almost able to turn defeat into triumph by means of culture. For Marcell Pellich, then, Austria represented a special value in the world, one that was worth defending, not to speak of the obvious fact that an independent Austria offered us our only protection and our only hope against National Socialist Germany.

This contrasting of Austria and Prussian Germany was, of course, not original. It belonged to a topos of long standing, as it became clear to me much later when I read Hofmannsthal's *Der Schwierige* and Musil's *The Man Without Qualities.* I would like to list some of the attributes of Austria as they appeared in light of such a contrast. Austria represented the soul or the spirit, freely imaginative and open, in contrast to German system-building. Austria stood for a receptive, understanding, and accommodating nature in contrast to German hardness, exclusiveness, and readiness to judge and to condemn the other, if his or her opinions deviated from one's own. For Marcell, Austria embodied the lyrical and Germany the dramatic, with Hebbel in the role of the quintessential German who stood at the opposite pole from the Austrian. (In today's situation, Marcell would probably see in the present director of the Burgtheater the successor of Hebbel, a figure antithetical to Austrian culture.) Yet, Pellich was not at all anti-German. He loved German Romanticism, the German *Lied*, Stefan George, and the Rhineland where, in Boppard, he had spent a childhood summer which appeared to him like paradise lost. I believe he needed Germany, Prussian Germany, to bring into clear and strong relief that which he loved about Austria.

In the seventh class of the Gymnasium, I read Franz Werfel's *Barbara or Piety* (*Barbara oder die Frömmigkeit*). It was in the streetcar on the long daily rides from Neubau, where we lived, to Gymnasium II in Zirkusgasse, to which I had been transferred after the dissolution of our class in the Akademische Gymnasium. I mention this because during the long rides across the Ring, the Quay and the Praterstrasse, on which I experienced *Barbara*, Werfel's novel appeared to me in the same context as the great novels of world literature, *Anna Karenina, The Brothers Karamazov, Père Goriot,* and *Buddenbrooks*, all books that I read on those streetcar rides. *Barbara* seemed one of them, of their rank, and it had the same epic format as they. Like these other, more famous examples, *Barbara* became for me a panorama of the world, the Austrian variant of those portraits of society and the individual which the great novels are. What fascinated me about it and what I most vividly remember is the typology of the Cafe Central, those types of eccentric intellectuality, each of whom embodied an esoteric, outrageous, and unheard-of position. One of the most egregious examples was Gebhardt, the sexual anarchist who preached absolute liberation of the libido and, preoccupied with love of humanity, allowed his own child to die of neglect. I did not know at the time that Werfel, in the figure of Gebhardt, had portrayed Otto Gross, Freud's anarchist disciple, who had tried to transform psychoanalysis into a gospel of sexual and social liberation, and whom his father, the famous law school professor, had arrested and brought home in shackles before committing him to the insane asylum.

Outstanding in my memory was the Jew Engländer who hated England because it was the fount of modernity and who cursed the enlightenment to which he owed his own freedom from the ghetto and the salvation of his people from the flaming stakes of persecution. In Engländer I first encountered that discontent with modernity which since then has seemed to me to be an essential characteristic of Austria and her culture—a cultural pessimism which had become dominant in Austria as in Germany, and which I subsequently found again in Broch's *Sleepwalkers* as a bemoaning of the loss of the "central value" in modern civilization. This cultural nostalgia was closely linked to the apocalyptic feeling that had struck me in Hofmannsthal and his circle. I began to see the apocalyptic element as the perhaps essential symptom marking that part of Austrian literature that impressed me most. I found it in *The Sleepwalkers* as in *Auto-da-Fé*, in my friend Marcell Pellich's *Magnifying Glass*, as later in Musil's *Man Without Qualities* and Doderer's *Demons*. Austrian literature was a literature of the end.

The long-awaited end of our world came shortly thereafter, on March 11, 1938. In the meantime, however, Austria had become precious to me in and through its literature, and I brought this affection with me across the ocean into the American emigration where nostalgia deepened and intensified. I found America at first to be truly foreign. I was, in the most fundamental sense of the term, "alienated." Austria, remembered in its literature, was a submerged homeland, from which, however, I had always been excluded, and which now, in the impending Second World War, faced probable annihilation.

Prompted by nostalgia, I read a great many of Schnitzler's works, especially his narratives. They became a substitute for a return that could never occur. In Schnitzler's work I discovered the mythologies of my family, the gossipy stories in the circle of relatives and acquaintances, which, in my childhood, as an observing outsider, I had only half understood. I saw these myths raised to a new level of clarity and insight, borne on the whiff of a poeticizing memory. But the familiar details evoked by Schnitzler had now themselves become history, mythical and unreal. My father, all my aunts, my mother's cousins, and many other people in our family and circle of acquaintances disappeared forever from my life. I knew they would be killed. The statistics of horror, of which we heard at the end of the war, confirmed only what we had known long before in our nerves and our nightmares. In February 1942, I had a dream that announced the death of my father to me. Only much later I learned that, in the week in which I had dreamt of him, he had died of a heart attack on the eve preceding his scheduled deportation to the East. In my dream, he strangled the National Socialist bureaucrat who, quite politely, had delivered the deportation order. The official, who had been my father's former business partner, had pretended not to know him. I see the scene quite clearly before me. My father, clinging desperately to the neck of the elegant gentleman, who wears a small silver swastika in his lapel, begs for a sign of recognition as if his salvation depended on it, while the official, disgusted, tries in vain to shake him off. My father tightens his grip on the official's throat and chokes him to death, intending not to kill, but merely to force him to acknowledge their one-time partnership. I mention this convergence of murder in the dream with death in reality to emphasize the monstrously personal relevance that the world of Schnitzler and Stefan Zweig acquired through the circumstances in which I read of it.

It was in an attic room in New Brunswick, New Jersey, where, endowed with a generous stipend, I was studying history and philosophy at Rutgers University, that I felt myself in the company of Schnitzler's characters far more Viennese than I had ever felt in Vienna. In a dialectics of exile and home, the closeness of a past which no longer was was juxtaposed to the remoteness of a present that held no value for me. This dialectics was driven home to me as I read of Schnitzler's world in a New Jersey that had never heard of him. It was then that Austria and Austrian literature took on that kind of intensity which for me had always marked the world of the imagination in contrast to reality. Austria and its literature had become myth.

It was not, however, nostalgia that moved me to study German literature, but something quite different—my encounter with Kafka. As mentioned before, I had begun to read *The Trial* in Vienna, but put it aside as too boring to finish. During the war, shortly after receiving my Bachelor's degree, I waited one afternoon for a woman friend in front of the New York Public Library. She stood me up. Melancholy, deprived of a promising evening, I went into the Public Library and, recalling my unfinished reading of Kafka, borrowed another work by the Prague author— "The Metamorphosis." This time I was shaken, stirred, carried away more than I had ever been in a reading experience. From that time on, I read all the writings of the still little-known Kafka and decided to take up graduate study of German literature in order to occupy myself with him. Kafka, at that time, was still undiscovered by the discipline. In Hitler's Germany this was, of course, to be expected; however, it was also the case in America. Kafka simply did not count among the authors accepted and recognized in the field. When I mentioned to a professor in the German Department of Columbia University that I wanted to write my dissertation on a comparison of the fantastic in E.T.A. Hoffman and Kafka, he merely laughed scornfully, saying: "There is, of course, no possible comparison between them. Their difference in rank (he meant in favor of Hoffman) precludes it." This attitude failed to deter my resolve.

Comparing the impact of Kafka on me with that of Schnitzler shortly before, I see an essential difference. With Kafka, nostalgia was a negligible factor. To be sure, many of Kafka's narratives could have occurred in Vienna, yet the essential point was that they could have occurred anywhere or nowhere. With Kafka the realm of the dream, the night dream, emerged. In night dreams fantasy and reality converged, and their opposition was overcome. While reading Kafka, I felt that everything could be said—as he himself had observed while reading over "The Judgment"—, that the most intimate and unheard-of could find expression in

language. It was Kafka who first inspired my own literary activity.
Under his influence I wrote stories in his manner that were derived
from my dreams of the preceding nights. I called their collection
my "nightbook" to which I gave the title, "Out of the World's
Night" ("Aus der Weltnacht").

Simultaneously with my Kafka experience, I came under the
spell of Surrealism, especially Jean Cocteau's film, *The Blood of a
Poet*, which fascinated me and seemed related to Kafka. Both
liberated from the necessity of choosing between the mimesis of
physical reality and the projection of imaginary worlds. Each
author seemed to make the interpenetration of dream and reality
the true goal of his art. At the same time, I discovered Soergel's
volume, *Dichtung und Dichter der Zeit*: *Im Banne des
Expressionismus* (*Authors and Works of Our Time*: *Under the Spell
of Expressionism*). Kafka, Surrealism, Expressionism—under their
banner, literature became the utopia of life freeing itself from the
constraints of a narrow concept of reality. Therefore, I could not
understand why many found Kafka depressing and unnerving. For
me, his writing had exactly the opposite effect. His irony, his
humor, his playful challenge to the normal expectations of his
reader, and the confusion which he caused: all these were
invitations to and promises of freedom. Through Kafka it became
clear to me that reading is never passive, but creative. As in a relay
race, it leads to further writing, to productive opposition, to
variation and alternatives. The fact that a horrifying reality was
only now, in the Second World War, catching up with the visions of
Kafka, Surrealism, and Expressionism, that in Hitler's "Fortress
Europe" reality resembled an Expressionist's or Surrealist's savage
fantasy, deepened my impression that Kafka's writing represented
the true realism of our time.

A further decisive experience of Austrian literature was Robert
Musil's *The Man Without Qualities*, which Leo Cohn, also a
Viennese refugee and somewhat older fellow-student in the
German Department of Columbia University, had recommended
and lent to me. It was in the early summer of 1944. The Second
Front had just been opened in Normandy and the hope began to

dawn that Europe, perhaps even Vienna, might escape without
total destruction. The time of the *partial* apocalypse had begun.
To be sure, Hitler had already been written off, but the postwar
period was to leave open two possibilities: the planetary completion of apocalypse or its avoidance. In the meantime, however,
there emerged the immediately more urgent question: Would
Central Europe be left an utter wasteland where the recovery of all
that had made Central Europe valuable would no longer be
possible? It was in this situation that *The Man Without Qualities*
contributed to a decisive broadening and illuminating of my
existential horizon. Here I found what I had at the same time
begun to find only in Nietzsche: the coupling of cultural-historical
nostalgia with a radical critique of ideologies and an unmasking of
illusions.

Cultural nostalgia had come to correspond to and take the place
of the fantasy worlds of my earlier years. Like the latter, it was a
siding with the non-existent against the existing world. In
formulations of brilliant wit, Musil returned to nostalgia an
element of futurity, a utopian dimension. In Musil I found my own
situation formulated: that of the irony of a consciousness of not
belonging and a knowledge that one did, after all, belong. This
"after all" of Musil defined my own relation to "Kakanien," the
name he gave to Austria. It was a feeling of "in spite of everything,
my Kakanien." What enabled such a repossession was Musil, an
author who represented an Austrian world championship in most
advanced thinking.

There was in Musil something that went even further. Musil's
irony, it seemed to me, was not only spatial, but temporal. For the
reader of *The Man Without Qualities* knows what the characters in
the novel do not, namely that the jubilee planned for 1918 can
never occur. For the object of the planned celebration, the old
emperor, will no longer be alive then and Kakanien itself will cease
to exist. The real achievement of the planned celebration will,
unknown to the characters but known ironically to the reader, be
apocalypse. With the narrator of the novel, however, the reader
has survived apocalypse. What appears unthinkable to the

characters, Kakanien's end, has already happened for the reader and he has survived it. Life is more powerful than the conceivable. The novel was a tour guide into existence in the shadow of apocalypse, but the existence of the novel itself guaranteed the possibility of surviving apocalypses. Delightfully entertained by the narrator's and the protagonist's wit, the reader, despite the end of the Kakanian world fares quite well, at any rate during the considerable time span it takes to read Musil's book.

For me who read *The Man Without Qualities* in New York in the summer of the invasion of Europe, while waiting to be drafted, the irony of the novel's temporal structure was a sign of hope. Of course, the terrible end of the Hitler horror still lay ahead. Apocalypse neared with giant steps. It came as the possibility of an absolute destruction of German-speaking Central Europe, its complete demolition as envisaged by the Morgenthau Plan, which would leave the universe of my childhood and youth, Vienna, behind as an unrecognizable mountain of rubble. Indeed the heaviest bombing of Vienna took place at the very last minute of the war, in 1945. Its complete destruction was thus very much a possibility, perhaps even a probability. In my dreams of Vienna, of which I had many at that time, the city always appeared in pale evening twilight and approaching night. On awakening I had the uneasy feeling that perhaps I had seen Vienna for the last time, and that I would never find it again. At that time, the sovereign irony of temporal structure in Musil's novel gave me the hope that perhaps this time too, Austria would survive her end, that she would awaken from this, the worst temptation she had ever succumbed to, and that there would be a reunion between my homeland and myself. This reunion would occur under the auspices of an Austrian avant-garde set by Musil and Kafka.

Imagining the Sixties: Herbert Marcuse and His American Opponents

James Rolleston
Duke University

Herbert Marcuse was the member of the Frankfurt School who became most fully involved in the American academic and political scene. For a time his name was a household word. Yet this familiarity is deceptive, for reasons that have partly to do with publishing history. Theodor Adorno and Walter Benjamin wrote exclusively in German and the translation of their works has been a project of recent years. Their formidable difficulties seem to appeal strongly to the current theoretically sophisticated readership. By contrast Marcuse wrote primarily in English from the time of his 1941 book on Hegel, *Reason and Revolution*. Most of his works are readily available, and his writing is far more accessible than that of Adorno or Benjamin. However, the extreme unfamiliarity of critical theory in the USA of the 1940's and 1950's caused Marcuse to be viewed as ponderous and Germanic. And since his rise to prominence in the 1960's it has seemed that his life and work can somehow be closed out, given an individualist story-line, assigned to a specific chapter in intellectual history. Marcuse, so the outline runs, began as a student of Heidegger devoted to arcane philosophy; forced into exile by the Nazis he began to work with the other members of the Frankfurt School on the structural features common to fascism and liberal capitalism; staying on in America after the war, Marcuse achieved considerable depth of insight into the conformist society of the 1950's, with its therapeutic cooptation of Freudian categories.

Then came the breakthrough book, *One-Dimensional Man* (1964), a total and pessimistic indictment of contemporary capitalism, with its ever more specialized and focused manipulation of human needs, its success in establishing its own universe of relentless work, profit, waste and exploitation as the only possible one. The story reached its climax as the Great Refuser suddenly became the guru of the 1960's rebellion, seeing the so-called new sensibility as the necessary rupture in the administered society. With the collapse of the 1960's movements, the aged Marcuse retreated into the world of art, as evoked by the title of his last book, *The Aesthetic Dimension* (1978).

This entire Bildungsroman structure—beginnings, maturation, social impact, resignation and closure—bears no relation to what one learns from an actual study of Marcuse's writings. Two features of his work seem crucial. First, there is a striking steadiness in his conceptual structures, leading occasionally to repetitiveness in the later texts; the task of critical theory as he sees it, namely reimagining and reapplying the ideals of the Western tradition, reason and freedom, in the context of the everyday experience of what we now call the consumer society—this task is laid out with full clarity in the major essays of the 1930's, mostly translated in the 1968 collection *Negations*. Second, there is an elusive flexibility in Marcuse's terminology, a flexibility which never amounts to inconsistency but which also never permits the reader a sense of comfort or closure. Unlike Adorno, say, Marcuse is not committed to a modernist view of art as uncompromising negation. Some of his formulations are more radically confrontational than those of any other Frankfurt School thinker; yet he is never frozen in a confrontational posture. Like a boxer he dances round the ring; yet he is no individualist gadfly, since his quest is always for the possibility of solidarity, the signs of awakening from the capitalist nightmare. In all Marcuse's analyses of social conditions, the rhetoric in which the analysis is conducted is both crucial and overt; and it is with that rhetoric that this paper is concerned. I shall define Marcuse's theoretical language in terms neither of synthesis nor of ambiguity but of bi-valence, a term he himself used. He has an intellectual double vision, a way of seeing the world as functioning on two time scales at once. Why two rather than more? Marcuse's perspective is precisely not that of anthropological neutrality, which would permit multiplicity, but that of the historical subject under late capitalism, on whom temporal duality is imposed. Daily we are forced to correlate our sense of progress and technological change with our insistent awareness that such change is directed, not towards freedom and life-enhancement but, on the contrary, towards the abolition of the past and our confinement within the eternal present of commodities. We have to seek our personal fulfillment within this anti-history; Marcuse is no ascetic. But we cannot even define what fulfillment could mean without keeping faith with the history and dreams that are being relentlessly commodified. A double vision of the world is forced upon us: even as we direct both our desires and our critique at the existing social system, we must go in quest of that "outside" which the system would exclude, images of human possibility embedded everywhere in philosophical and literary texts.

Marcuse's theoretical premise, outlined in the early essays "Philosophy and Critical Theory" and "On Hedonism" (reprinted in *Negations*), is the conceptualization of bourgeois consciousness articulated from differing perspectives by Hegel and the young Marx. Western philosophy since Plato has gradually secured the alignment of reason with the value of human freedom. However, the very moment of success, the idealist moment of the late 18th century, coincides with the capitalist structuring of the public world according to a more restrictive version of reason, namely rationalized domination and control. The instinctive response of philosophy, as Marx already diagnosed, was to assign the sacred value of freedom, hitherto defined in terms of the interplay between individual and society, exclusively to individual subjectivity. The result was an unacknowledged split between private and public which, throughout the 19th century, manifested itself on the one hand as a neo-Puritan contempt for bodily pleasures, now seen as degrading to the free individual; and on the other hand as a constant effort to dignify the sordid realities of capitalism, to sanctify the public realm in which the free individual actually had to live. Hence the paradox that fuels all of Marcuse's thought: in order to overcome the split between private and public, to achieve genuine experiential continuity, one must first launch a sustained attack on the illusory continuities which bourgeois individualism has produced. As he put it in a characteristically radical statement of Hegel's position: "Knowledge begins when philosophy destroys the experience of daily life." (*Reason and Revolution*, 103)

This sentence suggests the unusual immediacy and functionality of Marcuse's epistemology. Whereas most traditional philosophy, including the Marxist tradition, endeavors to distill experience into abstraction, to overcome contingency and "false consciousness," Marcuse insists on the responsibility of "knowledge" to the present moment, no matter how antagonistic the truth it has to tell. For him, the individual is a supreme achievement, the master-concept of the Western tradition, now under radical threat from the rationalized public world from which it has so fatefully averted its gaze. Certainly the experience of Fascism played a crucial rule in the formation of this view: but Fascism's impact was not uniform, the other members of the Frankfurt School did not embrace this passionate program of individual liberation.

What the individual has to be liberated from above all is the delusion of its own autonomy, the false dream of bourgeois Bildung or self-cultivation. For to assert the validity of the individual, Marcuse argues, is to declare allegiance to the philosophical tradition which produced it. And that tradition mandates the goal of community, of public values from which the private cannot be divorced without impoverishment. One of Marcuse's time scales, then, is historical in the fullest sense. Reactivating the moment of Hegel himself, he situates the drama of the individual consciousness in a variety of historical perspectives. It is vital to view modernity as a single whole, beginning as it were in 1776, when the dialectic of individual freedom and individual alienation was initiated. But history has other starting-points: it begins in ancient Athens, with the conversations of Socrates which give irrevocable shape to Western images of public value; it begins in primeval times, with the clashing myths of violence and fertility which resonate still in our mental structures; and it begins after World War 2, with the dramatic consolidation of the power of international capitalism, dispelling all illusions that the defeat of Fascism might involve a qualitative change in the world. For Marcuse all these ancient and modern struggles are historically *actual*, they are stories culminating in the present, exerting force upon us, not a mere anthology of the past which we could somehow view from a neutral-autonomous perspective. If we open our consciousness to these multiple narratives, resisting capitalism's strategy of neutralizing them as exotic fashion source or packaged "cultural" commodity, Marcuse argues that "philosophy" can once again "destroy the experience of daily life." This epistemological rupture is simultaneously an act of structuring, of re-locating the many dimensions of the present within the stories and myths of the past which insist on being actualized once more.

The "knowledge" that will begin when the everyday is disrupted is thus the actuality, the incompleteness of the many human stories. But what is to be the instrument of rupture itself? There can be no successful quest for the "outside" that capitalism represses without a powerful analytic instrument focussed wholly on conditions as they are, on the "inside." In common with many of his Frankfurt School colleagues, Marcuse finds the Marxist concept of class struggle no longer adequate for this task.[1] His answer—which establishes his double vision—is to view both the alienation and the potential wholeness of the individual with what I shall call the Freudian optic, although Freud did not move to the foreground of his thought until the 1950's. The exploration of pleasure in "On Hedonism" (1937) establishes this perspective, which is fully articulated in *Eros and Civilization* (1955). In the Freudian optic history becomes the individual struggle for subjective identity on the one hand and the struggle of the human collectivity against necessity and privation on the other. Until the bourgeois era subjectivity has been legitimately constrained by the collective need to limit and control the scope of erotic binding. The achievement of the bourgeois era has been to emancipate whole groups of individuals from these constraints, to enable them to develop concepts of identity, dignity, privacy and free expression hitherto unknown. Technology has potentially freed the collectivity from the anxieties imposed by necessity. And yet the capitalist reduction of the public sphere, its fetishization of private "needs," has ironically frozen the emancipation of subjectivity at its inception. In the dialectic of Marcuse's Freudian optic, which is certainly a revision of Freud's own pessimistic determinism, the individual has imposed "surplus repression" on himself. In the politically emancipated class, virtue strangles pleasure; in the exploited classes, work is ceaselessly promoted as being an end in itself.

Whereas the Hegelian timescale situates the present moment in a multiplicity of ancient and modern stories, the Freudian moment is always the present itself, the possibility of the now. In this perspective history is a product of Desire, and desire persists, with all its power, in a state of repression imposed by the subject on itself without the objective necessity of collective need. Marcuse's interest in so-called polymorphous perversity derives from his conviction that libidinal power, even in the confinement of perversity imposed on it, tells us of what a qualitative change in human existence might mean. Obviously Marcuse's view can be misinterpreted from almost any viewpoint beside his own. It is precisely his valorization of individualism that allows him to assign so urgent a role to the disfigurement of repression, and to insist that the individual can make the supreme free choice, namely the negation of that repression. This negation of the negation, this rupture of the privatistic shell imposed by bourgeois consciousness, means of course a risk-taking move beyond all too familiar psychic limits. But it is a choice that's ours to make, a choice given us by the human struggle against necessity, a struggle now objectively won, at least in the First World; and this concept of qualitative change, of breaching everyday limits, enables Marcuse to retain in place the cumulative insights of critical theory, and to assign actual content, albeit content of the future, to the word socialism.

The consistency of Marcuse's vision stems from the establishment early on of two categories which he sees as operative in any diagnostic description of culture: Contradiction and Art. Each category derives its elasticity and viability from Marcuse's double vision. The principle of contradiction involves for him an act of totalization: consumer society is to be indicted for its radical betrayal of the early bourgeois vision of individual dignity. For Marcuse the situation is not redeemable by any dialectical quest for the possibility of infrastructural change. And yet his Adorno-like diagnosis of the administered society leads him neither to mandarin conservatism nor to pessimism. Or rather: he was, as he said, a "cheerful pessimist." For a switch of perspective from the Marxian narrative of determinism to the Freudian exploration of the actual bourgeois subject leads to an unexpected richness of historical possibility *within* the self-conscious individual: specifically, what ultimately grounds erotic desire is a desire for community, a drive towards the collective which is potentially subversive at each and every moment. Conversely, to reaffirm the Hegelian story of modern subjectivity and to refuse the privatistic self, the ego with its will to retreat, points *not* towards a self-indulgent instinctuality but towards Robert Jay Lifton's "Protean" consciousness, openness to the multiple pasts simultaneously at work within us. We live in a doubly blocked condition: the blockage of the capitalist moment, which must force all human stories into the single shape of the act of commodity exchange, endlessly repeated; and the blockage of the ego-structure dominated by surplus repression, which similarly shrinks all desire to the one desire for self-validation within a structure of self-perpetuating social controls. These determinisms can be broken by mutually reinforcing acts of refusal—once the determinisms are understood as indeed totalizing. Thus *Eros and Civilization* simultaneously deconstructs the social categories which keep the ego encased in a self-repressive shell; and grounds the Freudian eros in images of community drawn from myth, art and anthropology in every age and place. The one move, in Marcuse's view, makes no sense without the other: he is particularly harsh on the group he calls Freudian revisionists, notably Erich Fromm, who would liberate the ego into so-called psychic wholeness and health, understood privatistically.[2]

Does Marcuse view his double liberation as likely or imminent? To the contrary: the principle of contradiction means precisely that these positive visions are *only* accessible through unflinching documentation of the negative totality—a documentation undertaken in *One-Dimensional Man*. The problems posed for readers of his time by this double functioning of knowledge, as critique and as expanded experience, become particularly striking as Marcuse enters his moment of fame in the 1960's. Again and again, he is stylized either as a dangerous nihilist or as an indulgent father-figure to the new rebels. And indeed, in his 1969 *Essay on Liberation*, he does explore "The New Sensibility" as an apparent emergence of the erotic celebration of the now and drive towards community such as he had anticipated in *Eros and Civilization*. But indulgent Marcuse never is; at this point he switches most insistently to the Hegelian optic, refusing all ill-defined hopes and confronting the massive power of established society as it moves to suppress or coopt the counter-culture. At best, from this historical perspective, a liberated sensibility establishes itself momentarily in a spatial sense, as a zone within the metropolis where the actual physical environment is symbolically colonized and bright colors and straight language prevail. But this space corresponds dialectically to that other, far larger space, the exploited and devastated countries on the margins of international capitalism.

It is Marcuse's concern for space, literal as well as figurative space, dystopia as well as Utopia, that underpins his second dominant theme, namely Art. His last book recapitulates the importance of art, and it is sometimes forgotten that he began life as a Germanist, with a dissertation on the "Künstlerroman."[3] Although Marcuse's view of art is close to Adorno's—and his contrast between aesthetic authenticity and an "affirmative culture" obviously nourished Adorno's famous essay on the "culture industry"—his double view of the world renders his version of art's autonomy less abstract and uncompromising. Certainly art is the Hegelian negation of bad reality, the actual shape produced by the act of contradiction. But art is also the contradiction of ego limitations, an enigmatic image of what human living actually could be in the here and now. In this perspective too art is above all a form, a space, a constructed entity that refuses conventional use value, a production of eros that overflows the limits which the ego places on Desire.   Stylized by capitalist ideology as irrational/ spontaneous/subjective, art rigorously keeps faith with "reason" as it was understood before its seemingly inescapable subordination to the laws of domination and exchange. The values of reason which originally nourished the image of the individual — Western civilization's major achievement to date — have been driven into the confines of the art-work. Bourgeois society, by labelling art as "irrational," has unwittingly endowed it with its subversive power — the power, precisely, of the rational understood dialectically. Unlike Adorno, Marcuse does not confine art to the sphere of absolute negation; his view of the aesthetic is not weakened by the decline of modernism, since consumer society simply cannot coopt the ontological ground of art, which is reason itself. Marcuse's aesthetic is well adapted to post-modern guerrilla tactics: art occupies a specific space, emancipating that space from the irrationality of capitalist rationalization; once the ordinary human consciousness ventures into that space, it is touched with suspicion of existing life-structures. Whether or not that suspicion accumulates towards resistance depends on the historical moment, the effectiveness of the controls currently operating to confine human experience.

To clarify the point I cite a paragraph from *One-Dimensional Man*, a book that barely mentions art, devoted as it is to documenting the seemingly impregnable controls dominating the psychic space of the early 1960's:

"Like technology, art creates another universe of thought and practice against and within the existing one. But in contrast to the technical universe, the artistic universe is one of illusion, semblance, Schein. However, this semblance is resemblance to a reality which exists as the threat and promise of the established one. In various forms of mask and silence, the artistic universe is organized by the images of a life without fear — in mask and silence because art is without power to bring about this life, and even without

Imagining the Sixties

power to represent it adequately. Still, the powerless, illusory truth of art (which has never been more powerless and more illusory than today, when it has become an omnipresent ingredient of the administered society) testifies to the validity of its images. The more blatantly irrational the society becomes, the greater the rationality of the artistic universe." (238-39) By "universe" Marcuse means something explicitly spatial, as he pursues the dialectic provoked by the reality of the aesthetic. On the following page he invokes the Hegelian optic of mastery, the necessary control of Nature in the sense of controlling "poverty, disease and cancerous growth." Western civilization has achieved this—but within specific, localized, essentially "aesthetic" space, "liberating transformation in its gardens and parks and reservations. But outside these small, protected areas, it has treated Nature as it has treated man— as an instrument of destructive productivity." (240) The way in which parks "interrupt" our homogenized social space opens a perspective on the continuing historical struggles which the system conceals. It is precisely the quasi-aesthetic achievement of parks—and, a few years later, of counter-cultural communities— which enables Marcuse to grasp the full, Hegelian context of any functioning erotic space in today's world: "In the contemporary era, the conquest of scarcity is still confined to small areas of advanced industrial society. Their prosperity covers up the inferno inside and outside their borders; it also spreads a repressive productivity and 'false needs.'" (241)

Insofar as the word Utopia is to be taken literally—as "no place"—it defines a value indispensable to the principles of Contradiction and Art. For Marcuse's reasoning moves always from "no place" to "place." Utopia is essential to the dialectical understanding of the sheer irrationality structuring modern human lives: in the Hegelian optic it constitutes the Archimedean point, the perennially produced human image of the "whole" against which all self-justifying social systems are to be judged; in the Freudian optic it embodies the instinctual dream of unity nourishing all desire. In either guise, as locus of desire or as zone of contesting historical perspectives, Utopia is no-place demanding to become a realized "place." In other words, it has meaning only as provocation, as stimulus to action. And it is this logic of action which most clearly distinguishes Marcuse from others who sought to "imagine" the 1960's. I conclude by briefly sketching contrasts between Marcuse and three other social thinkers of the time, Erich Fromm, Norman O. Brown and Eliseo Vivas, contrasts rendered meaningful by the very extensive common premises in the cases of Fromm and Brown.

What they share is the basic neo-Marxist analysis of liberal capitalism as a stunting of human potential through specialization of tasks and what Marcuse calls surplus repression. In Fromm's long 1961 essay introducing Marx's *Economic and Philosophical Manuscripts* there are socially descriptive sentences which Marcuse could certainly have written.[4] Indeed Fromm expressly praises Marcuse's book on Hegel, *Reason and Revolution*. And yet the acrimonious breach between them of 1955-6, concerning neo-Freudian therapeutic goals, cannot have been forgotten. What is evident in Fromm, I think, is that drive for intellectual synthesis which looks in retrospect so very like the language of domination which it seeks to overturn. Fromm quotes extensively from Marx's text, dwelling in his own commentary on the concept of alienation. Although he never says so, indeed the Marxian context would prohibit it, he implies that this alienation is remediable, once recognized. Under capitalism, to be sure, alienated work is intensifying, but yet . . . without clear transition the move is made to proclaim Marx a "humanist." Indeed he is said to be fundamentally at one with contemporary theologians such as Tillich and Teilhard de Chardin. The argument is conducted wholly through the Hegelian optic, as I have defined it here. If the antithesis, namely the diagnosis of alienation, is pressed hard enough, it will, Fromm implies, flip over inevitably, through sheer intensity of consciousness, into the synthesis called humanism. No action is necessary, no outward qualitative social change, only thought and the desire to overcome antagonisms. It is remarkable to see a text expounding Marx move without irony to "transcend" class conflict.[5]

An appropriate contrasting Marcuse text would be the famous essay "Repressive Tolerance" (1965), since, as Martin Jay reminds us, Fromm himself was the first to point, in a 1935 essay, to the tradition of bourgeois tolerance as "a mask for moral laissez-faire . . . never extended to protect serious threats to the prevailing order." (Jay, 97) Given the neo-Marxist diagnosis shared by Fromm and Marcuse, the question of action becomes crucial. And the stakes are all the greater because of Marcuse's profound commitment to the historical achievement of individualism. He can neither endorse the revolutionary overthrow of the freedoms achieved in the early modern era, nor be content with simply describing the subversion of those freedoms by the administered society. The only answer is to switch from the Hegelian to the Freudian optic, to challenge the here and now with a rhetoric that forces the abstraction (tolerance) in front of the mirror of its actual functioning in contemporary society. Marcuse is very much aware of the corrupting power of language, the web of complacency which must be torn apart. The form of action at this moment can only be the simulated violence of linguistic rupture, as is suggested by Marcuse's definition of the intellectual's task: "to break the concreteness of oppression in order to open the mental space in which this society can be recognized as what it is and does." ("Repressive Tolerance," 81-82) Eruptive assault aims at a kind of beachhead, a "mental space"; nothing could be more unlike Erich Fromm's synthesizing consciousness in which all hard cognitive edges become blurred.

It is not my purpose here to re-stage the argument of the essay itself, the notorious "withdrawal of tolerance" from certain extremist movements of the Right. This was Marcuse's most celebrated breach of manners, quoted against him by every ignorant editorial writer. And the purpose of the breach was to enable "knowledge" to "begin," by "destroying the experience of daily life"; for that experience was continually shrivelling, its rhetoric of complacency becoming a denial of the original goals of Jeffersonian democracy. The current struggle in 1965 was of course the one for civil rights, involving the breaking of laws for reasons of conscience; Marcuse addresses these activists at the close of the essay: "If they use violence, they do not start a new chain of violence but try to break an established one." (117) To refute the charge of authoritarianism Marcuse states flatly that "censorship of art and literature is regressive under all circumstances" (89), and suggests that intolerance towards Hitler at the right time would have given us a chance of avoiding Auschwitz. (109) The multiplicity of connections he sets up, the refusal to provide polite historical qualifiers: all this is a specifically linguistic strategy, aimed at the very language which uses tolerance as a cushion against any and all authentic resistance. Tolerance, a treasured achievement of the Enlightenment, has become unrecognizable in its dialectical inversion, its deployment as a mask of power. In 1971, when General William Westmoreland, commanding general of US forces in Vietnam, was scheduled to speak at Yale, I discovered to my surprise that my German class disapproved of plans to protest and disrupt his speech. He should have the freedom to speak, the students argued. My counter-argument, to the effect that we already knew what he would say, that it would not concern Aristotle or Shakespeare, that his very appearance was already "language," the language of power—all this fell on deaf ears. I knew then that the "Sixties" were ending, that Marcuse had lost the struggle for a public language, as of course he knew he would, at least for a time.

Language and action began to interact in quite new ways in the 1960's, with the result that apparently closely related arguments could separate into different worlds when the writer chose a specific audience, a historical reference-point, even a charged phraseology. It is clear to us now that Fromm's choice of synthesizing blandness was as "political" in its way as Marcuse's provocative formulations. The Sixties became "imaginable" insofar as inherited political and social formulae suddenly proved powerless to contain events within their elaborate linguistic neutrality. Many new "languages" asserted their universality, notably Norman O. Brown's lyrical depth psychology in *Love's Body* (1966). Again, there is a common source with Marcuse, namely a Freudian interpretation of history and a revaluation of Eros and Thanatos. But whereas Marcuse works always with limits and acts of enclosure, epitomized in his principles of contradiction and art, Brown's whole project is to collapse distinctions, to generate a language of Dionysiac inclusiveness: Latin quotations, neo-Marxist politics and primeval mythologies jostle each other in a text that is unmistakably performative, a language of action. The trouble is that this "action" amounts to pure incantation, linguistic narcissism nourished by transcendental gestures: "The dance of life, the whole story of our wanderings; in a labyrinth of error, the labyrinth of this world" (40); "And with the doctrine of no-self goes the doctrine of non-action: action is proper only to an ignorant person, and doing nothing is, if rightly understood, the supreme action." (105) I have chosen quotations that illuminate the radical otherness of Brown from Marcuse; Marcuse's polite yet firm review of the book explicitly switches from the Freudian to the Hegelian optic, refusing the refusal of history, resisting all self-consuming ecstasy: "the political fight is the fight for the whole: not the mystical whole, but the very unmystical, antagonistic whole of our life and that of our children —the only life that is." (*Negations*, 243)

The furthest Marcuse goes in Brown's direction occurs in the section of *An Essay on Liberation* entitled "A Biological Foundation for Socialism?" Essentially this is a restatement of the bivalent thesis of *Eros and Civilization*, wherein the material achievement of the collective in overcoming "necessity" mandates a revaluation of the "present moment," a Freudian-erotic transformation of human instinctual self-understanding. Even as Marcuse allows himself to affirm the new spaces and languages of radicalism, particularly the events of May 1968 in Paris, he renews the Hegelian optic, insisting on the multiple levels of ethical consciousness, on the complexity of social organizations, on time that is not the Now: "The construction of such a society presupposes a type of man with a different sensitivity as well as consciousness: men who would speak a different language, have different gestures, follow different impulses: men who have developed an instinctual barrier against cruelty, brutality, ugliness. Such an instinctual transformation is conceivable as a factor of social change only if it enters the social division of labor, the production relations themselves." (21)

Marcuse's third American opponent is of a very different sort. The assault on him is frontal and from the right. One ironic aspect of Eliseo Vivas' book-length attack on Marcuse, *Contra Marcuse* (1971), is that the target sounds more like Norman O. Brown: "Why should he want to turn every man, woman and child into a polymorphous and narcissistic erotophiliac?" (Vivas, 135) So bizarre and vitriolic are some of Vivas' verbal assaults that the reader with any knowledge of Marcuse quickly becomes more interested in Vivas' own linguistic predicament. Clearly this is a man who, in the decade since Erich Fromm envisioned a new humanism, has been drastically deprived of the comfortable liberal language so readily available to Fromm. Vivas hates dialectic above all: it enables the dialectician to make bold connections from which the empiricist shrinks, while refusing to permit the empiricist to stand in his familiar and indispensable posture of "neutrality." And the dialectic, with its rhythm of *Aufhebung*, appears to destabilize the fixed historical perspective beloved of an academic like Vivas: "The uselessness of the past is a deeply hidden assumption of the revolutionist, seldom stated, never examined ironically, always present, nevertheless, in his chiliastic dreams. In this respect Marcuse is a typical revolutionist." (196) Vivas struggles to salvage commonsense "American" values; by psychic necessity he is blind to Marcuse's insistence on individual dignity as the basis of his entire critique of modern society. Most surprising and revealing are the moments when Vivas' language betrays him. Suddenly the vigorous defender of the status quo speaks with a pessimism far more intense than Marcuse's most relentless indictment of one-dimensional culture: "it is because (morality) is not observed that the world we live in, the world man has always lived in, is and has always been a stinking chaos." (188) The intensity of the phrase is not accidental; we learn that Vivas is a pessimistic Freudian who sees social life as a "temporary truce. Schopenhauer said that human beings are gregarious porcupines. He should have said that we are not only gregarious but bristling porcupines. We need to get near one another but when we do we manage inevitably to hurt one another." (204)

We would now call Vivas' stance "essentialist" (that is, he regards the prevailing characteristics of society as reflecting "essentially" fixed, unchanging structures); but it is a rhetorically beleaguered essentialism, a double optic of his own whereby contradictory views are simultaneously asserted: on the one hand modern society is perfectly O.K. with its tolerance and its abstract truth and it is nihilistic of Marcuse to trash it; on the other hand modern society simply keeps animalistic humans under control and Marcuse is a fool to imagine some higher agenda to be feasible. The hysterical tone of his book adds another dimension to Fredric Jameson's remarks on the closure of the 1960's: "the intellectuals associated with the establishment itself . . . begin to recover from the fright and defensive posture which was theirs during the decade now ending, and again find their voices in a series of attacks on 60s culture and 60s politics which . . . are not even yet at an end." (Jameson, 204-5) What Vivas' text suggests — and the polemics of such current sages as William Bennett and Allen Bloom have a comparable effect — is that the 60's have fractured the conservative discourse irreparably.   There is seemingly no return to the "humanistic" assumptions on which Erich Fromm could rely.

Marcuse's 1974 lecture on "Marxism and feminism" is peculiarly relevant to the project of evaluating the 60's dialectically. As ever, he deploys a double optic, simultaneously an engagement with the present and a marshalling of historical counter-narratives; and is able to make a historical point which feminists themselves are reluctant to stress: because of marginalization of women under patriarchy, and especially under high capitalism, a storehouse of subjective values has been accumulated by women, *not* because of biological difference but through historical pressure. The public-private split meant that a whole group of qualities, valued in any definition of the individual, were specifically assigned to the "spiritualized" domestic zone. It is easy to mock the enforced delicacy and prudery of 19th century womanhood. But by a simple dialectical shift of perspective, these values can be re-stated as grace, warmth, restraint, in other words precisely the values essential to a qualitative change in civilized existence. Marcuse can thus view the liberation of women, which was and is on the immediate social agenda, as a first step towards human liberation, without resorting to any biological a priori. Indeed, that first step has already been taken. The identifiable social achievement of the 1960's, surviving the rhetorical and political failures, has been to open the way for feminism to enunciate, as a practical agenda, what Marcuse calls "the legendary idea of *androgynism.*" This single word both ruptures the patriarchal present and reactivates cultural material from the past, in the interest of transcending our self-perpetuating obsessions with otherness and our need to dominate that otherness. To that possibility Marcuse continues to give the name of socialism, now "feminist socialism." And his fundamentally bivalent rhetoric is confirmed when, at the very moment of endorsing the feminist vision, he renews his allegiance to the conflictual story of the individual as such. The Refusal of the capitalist-patriarchal present is counterpointed by a "refusal" of all escapist visions of an end to conflict. Utopia is a conceptually essential no-place. But human beings always live in place: " . . . no degree of androgynous fusion could ever abolish the natural differences between male and female as individuals. All joy, and all sorrow are rooted in this difference, in this relation to the other, of whom you want to become part, and who you want to become part of yourself, and who never can and never will become such a part of yourself. Feminist socialism would thus continue to be riddled with conflicts arising from this condition, the ineradicable conflict of needs and values, but the androgynous character of society might gradually diminish the violence and humiliation in the resolution of these conflicts." ("Marxism and feminism," 287)

In any overall assessment of Marcuse's project we must bear in mind that the principle of contradiction never involved the negation of either individualism or technology, but always their emancipation from the grim constraints of a repressive society. Conversely his endorsement of 1960's activism, even in some of its extreme forms, was never a deluded surrender of the critical faculties. Precisely the immediate impact of certain radical events impelled Marcuse to contextualize them in every way possible: to confront soberly the certainty of the radicals' defeat while strengthening the links of their projects to the diverse Utopian and aesthetic glimpses of a whole human society which pervade cultural traditions. This is not relativism but a sustained attempt to maintain the inner linkage between immediate social possibilities, the realm of action, and the best that has been dreamed and acted out in the past, the dialectic of the whole. In an age when international capitalism is exploiting its most successful tool of repression to date, collective amnesia, it is hard to see how we can do without Herbert Marcuse's double vision.

Notes

1 "The First International was the last attempt to realize the solidarity of the species by grounding it in that social class in which the subjective and objective interest, the particular and the universal, coincided . . . The narrowing of the consumption gap has rendered possible the mental and instinctual coordination of the laboring classes: the majority of organized labor shares the stabilizing, counterrevolutionary needs of the middle classes . . . " *An Essay on Liberation*, pp. 14-15.

2 "Fromm revives all the time-honored values of idealistic ethics as if nobody had ever demonstrated their conformist and repressive features. He speaks of the productive realization of the personality, of care, responsibility, and respect for one's fellow men, of productive love and happiness—as if man could actually practice all this and still remain sane and full of 'well-being' in a society which Fromm himself describes as one of total alienation, dominated by the commodity relations of the 'market.'" *Eros and Civilization*, pp. 258-59.

3 The dissertation is summarized by Barry Katz, pp. 40-53.

4 For example: "I shall try to demonstrate that . . . the very aim of Marx is to liberate man from the pressure of economic needs, so that he can be fully human; that Marx is primarily concerned with the emancipation of man as an individual, the overcoming of alienation, the restoration of his capacity to relate himself fully to man and to nature." To be sure, Fromm's rhetoric never overlaps with Marcuse's for more than a few sentences. His very next assertion is "that Marx's philosophy constitutes a spiritual existentialism in secular language . . . " *Marx's Concept of Man*, pp. 4-5.

5 Thus: "It is hardly possible to talk about Marx's attitude toward religion without mentioning the connection between his philosophy of history, and of socialism, with the Messianic hope of the Old Testament prophets and the spiritual roots of humanism in Greek and Roman thinking . . . The process of history is the process by which man develops his specifically human qualities, his powers of love and understanding; and once he has achieved full humanity he can return to the lost unity between himself and the world." *Marx's Concept of Man*, pp. 64-65.

Works Cited

Adorno, Theodor W. *Aesthetic Theory*. New York: Methuen, 1986.

Brown, Norman O. *Love's Body*. New York: Vintage, 1966.

Fromm, Erich. *Marx's Concept of Man*. New York: Ungar, 1961, 1966.

Jameson, Fredric. "Periodizing the 60s." *The 60s Without Apology*. Eds. Sohnya Sayres, Anders Stephanson, Stanley Aronowitz, Fredric Jameson. Minneapolis: U of Minnesota P, 1984. 178-209.

Jay, Martin. *The Dialectical Imagination*. Boston, Toronto: Little Brown. 1973.

Katz, Barry. *Herbert Marcuse and the Art of Liberation*. London: Verso, 1982.

Lifton, Robert Jay. "Protean Man." *History of Human Survival*. New York: Random House, 1970. 311-331.

Marcuse, Herbert. *Negations: Essays in Critical Theory*. Boston: Beacon, 1968. Includes "The Affirmative Character of Culture" (1937), "Philosophy and Critical Theory" (1937), "On Hedonism" (1938) and "Love Mystified: A Critique of Norman O. Brown" (1967), together with other essays.

——————————. *Reason and Revolution: Hegel and the Rise of Social Theory.* New York: Oxford UP, 1941. Boston: Beacon, 1960.

——————————. *Eros and Civilization: A Philosophical Inquiry into Freud.* Boston: Beacon, 1955, 1966.

——————————. *One-Dimensional Man: Studies in the Ideology of Advanced Industrial Society.* Boston: Beacon, 1964.

——————————. "Repressive Tolerance." *A Critique of Pure Tolerance.* By Robert Paul Wolff, Barrington Moore, Jr., Herbert Marcuse. Boston: Beacon, 1965. 81-117.

——————————. *An Essay on Liberation.* Boston: Beacon, 1969.

——————————. "Marxism and feminism." *Women's Studies* 2 (1974): 279-288.

——————————. *The Aesthetic Dimension: Toward a Critique of Marxist Aesthetics.* Boston: Beacon, 1978.

Vivas, Eliseo. *Contra Marcuse.* New Rochelle, N.Y.: Arlington House, 1971.

Music and Fluidity in Bachmann's "Undine geht"

Karen R. Achberger
St. Olaf College

Virtually nothing has been written about the musical under-pinnings of Ingeborg Bachmann's story, "Undine geht." This is particularly surprising given the musicality of both author and subject. Ingeborg Bachmann is a writer whose literary works are in large part about music. A woman of letters, she "composed" with words and played with the idea of music, as few writers have, in her verbal "compositions."[1] In addition, the tale of the water nymph Undine has been a frequent subject for operas and ballets.[2] The musicality, by comparison, of a subject like Tristan by a writer like Thomas Mann has not at all escaped the attention of literary schol-ars, whose discussion of the work has focused above all on this very aspect.[3]

Beyond the musical histories of both Undine and Bachmann, one further musical connection is Bachmann's friendship and collaboration with the German composer, Hans Werner Henze, whose ballet, "Undine," premiered less than three years before the publication of her own story in 1961.[4] It is probably no coincidence that they each completed an "Undine" a short time after the years which they spent together in Italy (from 1953-57). Bachmann attended the premiere of Henze's ballet in October of 1958 in London, dressed so dazzlingly that she appeared, in Henze's words, "wie die Meerjungfrau persönlich."[5]

Since we can safely assume that Bachmann associated the Undine tale with music, her own narrative around the material needs to be viewed in the context of both its intrinsic musicality and its frequent musical treatment. For this reason, I would like to discuss Bachmann's story, "Undine geht," in light of both Henze's ballet, and other musical treatments of the tale, as well as Bachmann's own development and concerns as a writer.

There is strong evidence in both Bachmann's life and work of an intense relationship to music. As a child, she wanted to be a musician, began composing at the early age and admitted to having what she called "ein besonderes Verhältnis zur Musik" as a result.[6] In her interviews, she spoke of ". . . Musik, zu der ich eine vielleicht noch intensivere Beziehung als zur Literatur habe"[7] and told of writing her first poems because she needed texts for her music.[8] She lived for some time with the composer, Henze, who wrote the music for her radio play, *Die Zikaden* (1955), and for whom she wrote a ballet scenario (1953)[9] and two opera librettos (1958 and 1964).[10] She wrote essays on music, the singer Maria Callas, the interrelationship of music and literature, and Weber's *Freischütz*.[11] In her interviews, she refers to her novel *Malina* as an "Ouvertüre,"[12] terms her writing "Komposition,"[13] and points out that she attempted to write the final section of the novel "wie eine Partitur"*[14]* for two voices in unison and opposition, complete with Italian markings, such as *rubato, dolcissimo,* and *senza pedale.* Bachmann even includes musical notation in the novel: Near the beginning and near the end, she cites a passage from Arnold Schönberg's song cycle opus 21, "Pierrot lunaire." By framing the novel in a motif from Schönberg's work, enclosing it in a musical parentheses, as it were, Bachmann is signaling the central importance both of music and of the composer Schönberg for an understanding of this work. References also to Richard Wagner and Gustav Mahler are recurrent in Bachmann's oeuvre, as are references especially to compositions of the Second Viennese School around Schönberg. In her penultimate poem, "Enigma" (1968), which she dedicates to Henze, Bachmann quotes both the children's chorus from Mahler's Second Symphony ("Du sollst ja nicht weinen, sagt eine Musik") and the Peter Altenberg-Lieder of Alban Berg ("Nichts mehr wird kommen").[15]

At the heart of all of Bachmann's writing is her concern, informed by the study of Ludwig Wittgenstein's philosophical writings, with the limits of language and the borderline between the sayable and the ineffable. She believed in poetic language as a means to transcend these limits and thus to expand human possibilities by providing a glimpse of the impossible. Much of her work can be seen as an attempt to reach beyond linguistic limits and to allow what Wittgenstein termed "das Mystische" to manifest itself through poetic language. In music she saw the most powerful metaphor for this creation, which may explain such things as her consistent reference to her own writing as "Komposition,"[16] her portrayal of one of her writer figures in the process of creating a literary work with the Mozartian title, "Exultate jubilate," and her response in April of 1971 to an interviewer's comment about her novel's apparent lack of social relevance with the statement: "Ich schreibe keine Programmusik."[17]

The story of the water nymph who gains a soul through union with a mortal probably dates from the 14th century Stauffenberger saga, which was recorded in the mid-16th century by Paracelsus and rediscovered by the Romantics in the early 19th century. After the publication of de la Motte-Fouqué's story, "Undine," in 1811, there followed a series of Undine operas by E. T. A. Hoffmann (1816), Girschner (1837), and Lortzing (1845), as well as dramas by Hauptmann (1896) and Giraudoux (1939), a fairy tale by Hans Christian Anderson (1837), and ballets by Gyrowetz, Schmidt (1836), Perrot (1844) and, in this century, Hans Werner Henze (1958).[18]

Henze's story does not differ significantly from that of the earlier male writers and composers. In all instances, a man vacillates between two women: a human, like himself, and a sea creature, whose "otherness" simultaneously attracts and frightens him. The story of Undine thus appears as the story of male ambivalence vis-a-vis woman. Man's initial attraction to the water nymph is quickly followed by fear and revulsion as soon as he notices her difference from himself, especially her supernatural power over the sea. He chooses to marry the less powerful woman, a human like himself, while at the same time still unable to free himself from a fatal fascination with the sea creature. Their final kiss results in his death.

Until Bachmann, the story has always been told from the male perspective, where the female sea creature is clearly the "other." For Henze, it is the ethereal quality of Margot Fonteyn's dance, and her ability to suggest weightlessness and only a shadow of a body which separates her from the humans. It is just this magical appearance of bodilessness which Bachmann also mentions in reference to Fonteyn: " . . . diesen Körper, der doch beim Tanzen kaum vorhanden ist, die schwebt doch Zentimeter über dem Erdboden."[19] Henze questions in his diary of the ballet to what extent Undine does physically exist at all and is not merely a dream image, a hallucination, a figment of the male imagination which has brought her forth from the deep.[20] Told from the male point of view, the soulless sea creature Undine wants most of all to become human and have a soul, that is, to become like the man.

Told from the perspective of the woman, however, Bachmann's story gives voice to that part which is usually confined to silence. As soon as the water creature is allowed to speak for herself, the desire to become human—in this case, to have a soul—is not at all what seems to motivate her. Critically distant from the world of humans, whom she addresses throughout the monologue as "Ihr Ungeheuer,"[21] she has no desire to become like them. She has no desire to share in their lives without integrity: "Verräter! Wenn euch nichts mehr half, dann half die Schmähung (. . .) Vor euren großen großen Instanzen wart ihr so tapfer, mich zu bereuen und all das zu befestigen, was in euch unsicher geworden war." (259-60) She has no desire to share in their exploitation of women: "Die ihr die Frauen zu euren Geliebten und Frauen macht, Eintagsfrauen, Wochenendfrauen, Lebenslangfrauen und euch zu ihren Männern machen laßt. (. . .) Ihr mit euren Musen und Tragtieren und euren gelehrten verständigen Gefährtinnen, die ihr zum Reden zulaßt" (255-6). She therefore leaves their world and returns to the sea, but in so doing longs for reunion with her human lover. Thus the male ambivalence of the earlier story is now a female one. One can view Undine as that part of themselves which humans have repressed in their will to master and to name: she stands for the instinctual, the incomprehensible part which has been sacrificed to the will for rational control over nature. And Bachmann consistently associates this vulnerable, indeterminable part, this water world beyond words, with music. Undine's world is portrayed in images of fluidity and sound, she is the call of the wild, "den Muschelton, die Windfanfare" (255), she is "gurgelndes Gelächter"(256), she is the "Ruf von weither, die geisterhafte Musik" (255), the siren who seduces "durch einen Schmerzton, den Klang, die Lockung" (256).

Henze, together with his British choreographer, Frederick Ashton, took care to "southernize" the saga, replacing the dark Germanic setting with radiant southern Italy. Names were changed accordingly, and Henze's music is also said to have "gone south," taking on a natural flow which is characteristically Italian and "uninhibited." The knight Huldbrand becomes the fisherman Palemon; his fiancee Bertalda becomes the fisher maiden Beatrice; and Undine's rather picaresque uncle Kühleborn becomes the demonic Lord of the Water, Tirrenio. The demons of the haunted Germanic wood become a whole company of Mediterranean tritons and water nymphs.

In contrast, Bachmann eliminates all the specificity and uniqueness of the encounter, which now takes on a timeless, placeless, absolute quality. The water creature — and all that she suggests — is united with a human whose lack of individual specificity is already signalled by his name: He is the generic *Hans*. Like the *Jan* before him, who survives Jennifer in the radio play, "Der gute Gott von

Manhattan" (1958), and the *Ivan* after him, who survives the
nameless female narrator of the novel, *Malina* (1971), he is not at
all the unique lover she would like him to be, but just an average
guy who never loses touch with reality. Bachmann lets Undine tell
us about him, in his various incarnations:

> Ich habe einen Mann gekannt, der hieß Hans, und er war anders als alle
> anderen. Noch einen kannte ich, der war auch anders als alle anderen. Dann
> einen, der war ganz anders als alle anderen und er hieß Hans, ich liebte ihn.
> In der Lichtung traf ich ihn, und wir gingen so fort, ohne Richtung, im
> Donauland war es, er fuhr mit mir Riesenrad, im Schwarzwald war es, unter
> Platanen auf den großen Boulevards, er trank mit mir Pernod. Ich liebte
> ihn.[22]

The repetition which is introduced here suggests a timeless,
recurrent condition. Each encounter is like the preceding one and
has its parallel in the short, repeated phrases which are variations
on the Hans theme. Here, as throughout the entire first-person
narrative, the language is simple, repetitive, and hypotactical, each
sentence consisting of many short, independent clauses, which flow
along easily and are often connected by the coordinating conjunc-
tions "und" or "denn." Undine's language, like her world, is fluid
and instinctual, a language whose semiotic motility, to use Julia
Kristeva's distinction,[23] seems to disrupt the strict symbolic order
of German syntax.

It is also the language of Bachmann's utopian "Ein Tag wird
kommen," which serves as a counterpoint to the everyday reality in
the novel, *Malina*:

> Ein Tag wird kommen, an dem die Menschen schwarzgoldene Augen haben,
> sie werden die Schönheit sehen, sie werden vom Schmutz befreit sein und
> von jeder Last, sie werden sich in die Lüfte heben, sie werden unter die
> Wasser gehen, sie werden ihre Schwielen und ihre Nöte vergessen.[24]

What Bachmann has created out of the "Undine" material is not
so much a story any longer; like most of her narratives, it has virtually no plot. It is rather the opposition of images from two separate
worlds. One can read the story as the sketching out of Bachmann's
ideas about those two opposing realms: On the one side, the world

of humans, of firm ground, social order, law, authority, and language, the world of light and reason; on the other, the world of water creatures, of fluidity and impermanence, of vitality and unbound nature, of feeling and sensuality, the world of "grenzenlose Wortlosigkeit,"[25] the world of the ineffable, indefinable, uncontainable, the world of sound and of sirens.

It is this very opposition which Bachmann has also given shape to in the "Doppelgänger" of her novel *Malina*.[26] By splitting the protagonist into the rational, logical, male and the sensual, nameless, female, Bachmann is again playing with this tension. In both works, the male half is shown to be superior and to survive the female, which is left to retreat from the world: Undine into the water and the novel's narrator into a crack in the wall. In both cases, the persona associated with music is destroyed by the one associated with language. The primacy of *logos* over *melos* is clearly portrayed in the novel's closing scene, where the writer, Malina, survives the narrator and destroys her glasses and her phonograph records. Her musical vision has yielded in the end to his logical "superiority." This theme is first sounded at the end of the novel's "overture," where the narrator recalls a moment in which the shouts of a heated discussion from the next room drown out and shred ("zerfetzen") the music of Offenbach's "Tales of Hoffmann," which the narrator is trying to hear over the words.[27] That the smashing of records and the shredding of music in these two scenes framing the novel is by no means a peaceful superiority, but rather the destructive violence which the word exerts over music is suggested at the close of the earlier work as well, when Undine refers to Hans' speaking about himself as "Beinahe wahr. Beinahe mörderisch wahr,"[28] thereby sounding the "murder" theme with which Bachmann closes the novel ten years later.[29]

If Undine represents art and if Bachmann is then on the side with those called Hans, as she has indicated in an interview,[30] then the central opposition here is one of language (and the writer struggling with language) and art. And the epitome of art for Bachmann, the art *par excellence*, which she continually sought to emulate in her own verbal "compositions," was, of course, music. For Henze, too, Undine represents an artistic ideal: "Das Meermädchen besitzt statt eines Menschenherzens nur Charme, Grazie, vielleicht unnennbare Eigenschaften, wie Musik, schwebend und alterslos."[31] Henze sees Palemon's desire for Undine as a futile longing for transcendence through art: "Wenn Palemon in Undine verliebt ist, ist er gleichsam in die Kunst verliebt und die Vereinigung mit einem Traumbild oder Kunstwerk (diese nur im Wahnsinn oder im Tod erreichbare höchste Verbindung), das begehrte Vergessen wird Palemon nicht gewährt, die ersehnte Umwandlung stellt sich nicht ein, immer wieder stößt ihn seine menschliche Unzulänglichkeit zurück unter die Menschen." Unable to forget her and prevented by his human shortcomings from undergoing the transformation necessary to join her, Palemon finds deliverance in a final moment which transports him to that perfection of love in death, that "Liebestod" which he has been seeking all along: "Bis zum letzten Herzschlag dem oft nur ungenauen, fast unkenntlichen Bild verfallen, wird ihm ein Tod zuteil, dem er inkonsequent entgegengegangen ist und dessen erlösende Schönheit er sich nur durch seinen Schmerz, nicht durch Glauben, verdient hat."[32]

Bachmann's narrative, by contrast, ends without resolution. While the "Liebestod" theme is not entirely absent in Bachmann's works — and one can view the deaths of both Jennifer (in *Der gute Gott von Manhattan*) and the female narrator (in *Malina*) as such[33] —, Undine retreats from the world of humans, not as a "death" or an act of transcendence, but as an assertion of her difference. She returns to her element and remains separate by nature from the world of humans.

For Bachmann, music's most salient quality is its freedom from words. It lies beyond the will to name, beyond the rationality which is founded on mastery and dominance. Only when we are at a loss for words, when words fail and we can think of nothing more to say, can the two worlds (language and art/music) meet in a moment of truth. In addressing Hans, Undine describes this utopian meeting as the powerful overflowing of the sea onto the earth:

> Wenn dir nichts mehr einfiel zu deinem Leben, dann hast du ganz wahr geredet, aber auch nur dann. Dann sind alle Wasser über die Ufer getreten, die Flüsse haben sich erhoben, die Seerosen sind gleich hundertweis erblüht und ertrunken, und das Meer war ein machtvoller Seufzer, es schlug, schlug, und rannte und rollte gegen die Erde an, daß seine Lefzen trieften von weißem Schaum.[34]

This scene offers one metaphor for that utopian moment of truth which Bachmann had described a year earlier in her closing "Frankfurt Lecture" (1960) on the subject, "Literatur als Utopie." It is only in transcending the customary limits of our "wretched language"—what she terms "die schlechte Sprache"[35]—that we can glimpse a new language, one imaginative enough for us to speak the truth about ourselves. The act of writing poetry is an attempt to come to such a language. The transcendence of the limits of our language, which Bachmann believes we can experience in poetic language and in music, finds its parallel here in Undine's vision of the spontaneous flooding of the waters over the solid structures of the human world. Hans' moment of speechlessness opens the floodgate, and the powerful utopian thrust of Undine's element, "a mighty sigh," beats against the earth with foaming lips.

We have in this one vision a composite of images of the utopian which are recurrent in Bachmann's work: the elemental, unbound, fluid, musical, all of which function in the tale, and in her entire oeuvre, to suggest that which is "other" to the rational world of language, order, law, authority.[36] And therein lies for Bachmann the utopian function of music.

Notes

1 Cf. I. B., *Wir müssen wahre Sätze finden. Gespräche und Interviews* (Munich: Piper, 1983), 96, 114, 126. Cf. also Suzanne Greuner, *Schmerzton. Musik in der Schreibweise von Ingeborg Bachmann und Anne Duden*, Literatur im historischen Prozeß, N. F. 24, (Berlin: Argument-Verlag, 1990).

2 Cf. Françoise Ferlan, *Le thème d'Ondine dans la littérature et l'opéra allemands au XIXième siècle*, Bern: Peter Lang, 1987.

3 Cf., for example, Frank W. Young, *Montage and Motif in Thomas Mann's "Tristan,"* (Bonn: Bouvier, 1975).

4 "Undine geht" appeared as the seventh and final story in her first prose collection, *Das dreißigste Jahr* (Munich: Piper, 1961).

5 "Wenn die Sprache versagt," *Profil*, 26 (23 June 1986), 50-51.

6 I. B., *Gespräche und Interviews* (Munich: Piper, 1983), 124.

7 Cf. her interview of 5 May 1971, ibid., 107.

8 Cf. her interview of 23 March 1971, ibid., 83.

9 "Ein Monolog des Fürsten Myschkin zu der Ballettpantomime 'Der Idiot,' " after Dostojevsky, I. B., *Werke*, 4 vols. (Munich: Piper, 1978), I, 62-79.

10 "Der Prinz von Homburg," after Kleist, and "Der junge Lord," after Hauff, I. B., *Werke* I, 331-368, 375-432. The operas were premiered in 1960 and 1965 respectively. For a summary of the Bachmann-Henze collaboration, see Elizabeth Schrattenholzer, "I.B. und Hans Werner Henze: Sprache und Musik in gemeinsamer Sprache," *Jahrbuch der Grillparzer-Gesellschaft*, 3.Folge, 17. Band (1991).

11 Cf. I. B., *Werke* I, 437-442; IV, 45-62, 342-3.

12 I. B., *Gespräche und Interviews*, 95.

13 Ibid., 95-6, 114, 126.

14 Ibid., 75.

15   I. B., *Werke* I, 171.

16   I. B., *Gespräche und Interviews*, 95-6, 114, 126.

17   Ibid., 99.

18   Cf. Elizabeth Frenzel, *Stoffe der Weltliteratur* (Stuttgart: Kröner, 1970), 757-9. Cf. also Ferlan, op. cit. and H. W. Henze, *Undine. Tagebuch eines Balletts* (Munich: Piper, 1959), 36; and Ria Endres, "Die Paradoxie des Sprechens," *Kein objektives Urteil-nur ein lebendiges. Texte zum Werk von I.B.*, eds. Christine Koschel, Inge von Weitenbaum (Munich: Piper, 1989), 448-62; also Wolfgang Gerstenlauer, "Undines Wiederkehr. Fouqué-Giraudoux-I.B," *Die Neueren Sprachen* 10 (Oct. 1970), 514-27.

19   I. B., *Gespräche und Interviews*, 115.

20   Cf. Henze, *Tagebuch eines Balletts*, 17, 20-21, 54-55.

21   Cf. I. B., *Werke* II, 253-263. Page numbers in parentheses following subsequent quotes from the text of "Undine geht" refer to this edition. Undine also addresses humans as "Ihr Monstren" (253), "Verräter!" (259), and "Ihr Betrüger und Betrogene" (256).

22   Ibid., 258.

23   Cf. Julia Kristeva, *Polylogue*, (Paris: Seuil, 1977).

24   I. B., *Werke* III, 121.

25   Rilke describes Trakl's poetry as consisting of enclosures around "grenzenlose Wortlosigkeit."

26   In reference to the persona of her novel, Bachmann herself consistently used the term "Doppelgänger" or "Doppelfigur." Cf. I. B., *Gespräche und Interviews*, 87, 89, 101, 88, 104, 108.

27   Cf. I. B., *Werke* III, 26-27.

28   I. B., *Werke* II, 262. Hans Höller connects this with what Julia Kristeva terms the "killing of substance" in the structures of the sociosymbolic order. Cf. Hans Höller, *Ingeborg Bachmann. Das Werk*, (Frankfurt: Athenäum, 1987), 139.

29   *Malina* ends with the statement, "Es war Mord." Cf. I. B., *Werke* III, 337.

30   Cf. Bachmann's statement in Nov. of 1964: "Die Undine ist keine Frau, auch kein Lebewesen, sondern, um es mit Büchner zu sagen, 'Die Kunst, ach, die Kunst.' Und der Autor, in dem Fall ich, ist auf der anderen Seite zu suchen,

also unter denen, die Hans genannt werden." I. B., *Gespräche und Interviews*, 46.

31   Henze, *Tagebuch*, 21. Here Bachmann refutes the suggestion that her first-person narrative could somehow be interpreted as autobiographical, a misjudgment given support by such things as Henze's association of the two (cf. note 5), her friends in Vienna terming her a "Wasserwesen" (cf. Andreas Hapkemeyer, *Ingeborg Bachmann. Entwicklungslinien in Werk und Leben*, [Vienna: Verlag der österr. Akademie der Wissenschaften, 1990], 111), and her birthday, like Henze's, falling under the water sign Cancer.

32   Ibid., 21.

33   Beth Bjorklund refers to Jennifer's death as "a modern love-death" in her article, "Ingeborg Bachmann," in *Major Figures of Modern Austrian Literature*, ed. by Donald G. Daviau, (Riverside: Ariadne, 1988), 63. In light of the extensive references to Wagner's "Tristan" and parallels between Isolde and the female narrator in the novel *Malina*, her death can also be viewed as a "Liebestod" of sorts.

34   I. B., *Werke* II, 259.

35   I. B., *Werke* IV, 268.

36   The consistent association of water images with the utopian and the feminine in Bachmann's work has been noted by, among others, Höller, op. cit., 139, and Kurt Bartsch, *Ingeborg Bachmann*, Sammlung Metzler 242, (Stuttgart: Metzler, 1988), 126.

The Staging of Memory: Rewriting the Past in Contemporary German Cinema

Anton Kaes
University of California, Berkeley

I

Let me begin by briefly delineating the larger framework of my inquiry with three quotations from 1945, 1977, and 1986. In the last days of the Second World War, on April 17, 1945, Joseph Goebbels spoke of the historical UFA film "Kolberg," a multi-million Reichsmark epic made by Veit Harlan in 1944/45, in the following prophetic terms: "Gentlemen, in a hundred years a great color film will show the terrible days which we experience now. Don't you want to play a role in that film? Hold out so that the spectators in a hundred years don't yell and hiss when you appear on screen."[1] Goebbels's perverse command, which in effect asked the Germans to play their part well in the staging of their own destruction, to be, as it were, worthy actors in their own historical film, can only be understood as the outgrowth of a politics that was based on spectacle in general and the aestheticization of war in particular. The question that follows from Goebbels's — how to distinguish the experience of history from its representation — has haunted historical fictions dealing with the Third Reich to this day. Is it possible to use, as Joachim C. Fest has done in his film "Hitler — a Career" in 1977, documentary footage from the Nazi period itself, or are these images hopelessly tarnished, as Wim Wenders believes in his polemic against Fest's Hitler film?

"I do not believe," Wenders wrote in 1977, "that any other people have experienced as great a loss of confidence in their own images, their own stories and myths, as ours. We, the directors of the New Cinema, have felt this loss most acutely in our work. The lack, the absence of an indigenous tradition has made us parentless. (. . .) Never before and in no other country have images and language been handled as unscrupulously as here, never before and in no other place have they been so debased as vehicles for lies." (18) What Wenders does not mention, however, is the unquestionable suggestive power which is associated with these images, a universally acknowledged attraction that over the last forty years has cast its spell over dozens of historical films in Europe and the United States alike.[2]

Only recently, in a February 1986 review of Claude Lanzmann's film "Shoah," — a film which reveals the horrors of the Nazi period in interviews and recollections of KZ survivors and administrators — the endless fascination with the images of Fascism, their morbid appeal to the irrational and subliminal, was again recognized as a prime source for cinematic spectacles of history:

> Some images never seem to lose their appeal. Take, for an apparently inexhaustible example, Nazi Germany. The Third Reich is only partly the embodiment of evil; on a subterranean level it represents an unholy mixture of order and audacity, life lived as spectacle, an alternative universe as exotic as found in any space opera. Who is truly immune to the Nazis' machinelike pageants of obedience, with their organized stupidity and exciting sense of Modern Times? Or the torchlight rallies orchestrated for the camera — Hitler's face etched in flames, emblem of the megalomania anyone might experience in their dreams?[3]

The question remains: How can one deal today with the images and collective myths that kept a country mesmerized for twelve years? How can one represent and come to terms with the German Nazi past and its aftermath without falling prey, once again, to the lure of its images? These are the questions to which numerous German history films over the last decade sought an answer, culminating in the period between 1978 and 1984. Such films as Hans Jürgen Syberberg's "Hitler — a Film from Germany," Rainer Werner Fassbinder's "Lili Marleen" and his so-called "BRD trilogy" (with "The Marriage of Maria Braun," "Lola," and "Veronika Voss"), Helma Sanders-Brahms's "Germany — Pale Mother," the collective film "Germany in Autumn" and Kluge's "The Patriot," Schlöndorff's "Tin Drum," Margaretha von Trotta's "Marianne and Juliane," Lilienthal's "David," and above all Edgar Reitz's 16-hour film chronicle "Heimat,"—all these films (despite the considerable differences in narrative strategies and visual styles) conjure up images of the Third Reich and the immediate postwar years. As if in response to Wenders' remarks of 1977, these films do not shy away from evoking images and narratives of recent German history or from exploring various strategies of reintegrating these images and myths again into popular memory.

Studying these fictional representations of German history in the New German Cinema, one is struck not only with the great diversity of pictorial techniques with which the past is represented, but also with the shift in political emphasis that occurred after the mid-seventies. German films dealing with the Third Reich are no longer accusatory or openly didactic but more ambivalent, more interested in the subjective and personal dimension of German history. Dealing with the period of the Hitler regime in the late '70s and early '80s, German films not only had to address the question of the past but also acknowledge the lingering traces of that past in the present. Marked by the stigma of the recent German past, the German history film has the specific burden of confronting questions of historical continuity and discontinuity, of national self-representation and self-image, and of collective memory and identity. The discourse surrounding the events of Bitburg in 1985 on the occasion of the 40th year of liberation from Fascism demonstrated, in an uncanny way, the unrelenting presence of the past.[4] It is, I believe, no coincidence that German history has become the secret center of the New German Cinema.

Although the moral and political heritage of the Third Reich has occasionally been thematized in the New German Cinema before (particularly in the early films of Straub/Huillet and Alexander Kluge), the urgent desire for a true historical understanding of Germany's repressed past was not felt until the fall of 1977 when Germany experienced for a few months its most severe political crisis since its inception. The events of Fall '77, the kidnapping and murder of German industrialist and former Nazi party official Hanns Martin Schleyer, the Mogadischu hijacking of a Lufthansa jet by German terrorists, and the mysterious deaths of Andreas Baader, Gudrun Ensslin and Jan Carl Raspe in a maximum security state prison as well as the severe counter-measures of the government (such as the news black-out and the officially condoned witchhunt of leftist sympathizers) — all these events resonated with memories of the psychological terrorism of the Hitler regime — memories which suddenly ruptured, as Alexander Kluge pointed out, the collective amnesia.[5] German filmmakers considered it their mission in the Fall of 1977 to look for the roots of this crisis in the German past. The compilation film "Germany in Autumn," collectively made by a group of nine filmmakers under the coordination of Alexander Kluge, spawned a whole series of history films: Fassbinder's "The Marriage of Maria Braun," Kluge's "The Patriot," and Reitz' "Heimat" are already foreshadowed in brief episodes in "Germany in Autumn."

Another jolt to the collective memory of Germans was the showing of the American TV series "Holocaust" on German television in January 1979. Imported from Hollywood as historical fiction film, "Holocaust" not only triggered an unprecedented flurry of emotional reactions and probings into a past which had been taboo for so long, it also came to stand as document for the supposed failure of German filmmakers to grasp images and stories from recent German history in a way that engages the emotions of the audience.[6] Two years before "Holocaust," another film dealing with the Third Reich had captured the imagination of Germans, Joachim Fest's above-mentioned controversial and revisionist documentary film "Hitler — a Career," in which the history of Nazi Germany was simply mirrored in the charismatic career of their Führer. It seems that all historical films of the New German cinema between 1977 and 1984 are part of, and answers to, a discursive context determined not only by historical events but also by these two films, Fest's "Hitler" and the American television series "Holocaust." Syberberg's six-hour "Hitler — A Film from Germany," for instance, was made in response to Fest's Hitler film, and

Edgar Reitz's sixteen-hour TV-chronicle "Heimat" is a programmatic counterproduction to the American "Holocaust." History itself appears as a vast textual field in which recurring images and stories are being used and re-used, expanded, exchanged and reinterpreted again and again; historical fiction itself becomes an intertextual enterprise in which the relations between historical and fictional narratives are constantly changing.

II

What are the narrative models used to construct historical fiction in film? Like the historical novel, the historical film is based on the interplay between two narratives: a fictional narrative, on the one hand, freely invented, the result of the imagination of the author, and a historical narrative, on the other, bound by the factual existence of historical persons and events. Every historical film must anchor its fictional story in some verifiable past with references to historically true incidents and circumstances; thus it validates its fiction as "true" and "real." By having a referent that is grounded in a known historical event or period, historical fiction tends to appear both "truer" and more realistic than a pure fiction film. We are all familiar with certain images of the Hitler regime and the war which have over the years become conventionalized as valid representations of that period; in fact, these images, precisely because they look like old photographs and newsreels, persuade the audience to accept the film as a historical film. The recognition effect of "that's the way it was" in a historical film appeals above all to the visual memory of the spectator and is less a product of the historical narrative than that of the careful attention to the image: the history film must *look* historical. Film by virtue of its multi-channelled textuality can present the past with a higher degree of referentiality and authenticity than is possible in any other medium.

Classical historical films such as Griffith's "The Birth of a Nation," for example, deploy a dual narrative focus: one is the domain of historical events, while the other deals with familial or private affairs. All classical history films explore the tension between the public and the personal, the division and disjunction between family relations and larger political structures. Historical film is thus the locus where *Geschichte* and *Geschichten*, history and stories intersect, where historical fact and present fiction blend into one another. If this interlocking correlation between history and fiction is constitutive of the genre of history film, then one can differentiate various ways in which the factuality of history is encoded in narrative fiction. I am thinking of three major paradigms of narrative construction in historical fiction.

In the first paradigm, the narrative deals with historical events and personnages in an authentically reconstructed setting. Past events are translated into a story by emphasizing certain of them while suppressing others, and by such literary techniques as characterization, motific repetition, various points of view, in short, by what Hayden White has called "narrative emplotment."[7] History displays itself as fiction which unfolds by itself because the source of enunciation is erased and the constructive work necessary in the representation of the past is hidden. Following the film theorist Christian Metz one might say that by effacing the point of origin, history disguises itself as a story from nowhere, told by nobody — it is simply there as a story of already completed events which propose to tell everything.[8] History is encoded in the story as a closed discourse with a finality and an end. History in this paradigm is absorbed by fiction.

The second paradigm retains the illusion of an autonomous historical fiction but brackets it by a discursive framework which actually shows history as a production of discourse in the present. The historical fiction is presented in a way that calls attention at least occasionally to the fact that we are watching a construct of history from a certain point in time and a certain perspective. Thus the reconstructed past stands in some tension with the process of reconstruction. The positivistic idea that "the Past" can simply be reproduced is shown as a convention in the realistic depiction of the past. History is presented in this paradigm as a fictional construct from the perspective of the present.

The third paradigm is dominated by a self-reflexive discourse on the very act of reconstructing and reconstituting the past from a heterogeneous mass of historical fragments. The source of enunciation is itself foregrounded and thematized; the reconstructive, creative process of reconstituting the past in the present becomes the object of the historical fiction. This anti-historicist conception of history is based on the workings of a selective and often capricious and playful memory; it thereby criticizes classical-dominant modes of historical representation. History is here conceptualized as constituted in and by knowledge which draws heavily on archaeological work to excavate historical signs: events, names, documents, characters, stories, images—a large body of references which overwhelms any linear narrative. History comes to exist as a product of fragmentary traces and contradictory indices of the past. In this paradigm the gap between historical documents and their use in the fictional narrative is clearly accentuated.

Although this typology of German history films is by no means complete or exhaustive, it does provide, I think, a useful framework for discussing German history films in analytical terms because it highlights the tension, central to historical fiction, between history and narrative, between verifiable historical events and their narrative encoding. It is within the framework of narrative construction that questions of historical representation can best be broached.

III

I would like now to examine three recent films of the New German Cinema that narrativize German history in ways that follow the paradigms mentioned above. Edgar Reitz's "Heimat," Helma Sanders-Brahms's "Germany—Pale Mother," and Alexander Kluge's "The Patriot" present German history and, at the same time, reflect upon the question of historical representation. For the sake of comparison, I will concentrate on the first few minutes of film time in each of the three films.

Edgar Reitz's "Heimat" is a nearly sixteen-hour chronicle of over sixty years of family life in the fictitious German village of Schabbach in the Rhineland, beginning in 1919 and ending in 1982. It was screened as a film in two parts in European film festivals and all major German cities in Summer 1984 and then released as an eleven-part TV series in September and October of that year; it was also shown in the United States in 1985 and was recently playing on subscription cable television. It is probably the most widely known—over 20 million viewers saw it on German TV—and also critically acclaimed history film of the New German Cinema.

"Heimat" tells, or more precisely, re-tells German political history of the 20th Century in terms of its impact on private lives in a rural village, far removed from the public events that we associate with political history. The emphasis is on the history of daily life, on *Alltagsgeschichte* with its constricted political horizon. According to Reitz, the attention to detail in the reconstruction of the various historical periods from 1981 to the present distinguishes his film from previous history films, including the American Holocaust film which, says Reitz, showed no sensibility for "German images."[9] The original title of "Heimat," "Made in Germany," a polemical title directed against the Holocaust film which presented German history "made in Hollywood," is still visible in the first image of the film, engraved in a milestone.

The film starts out, after the title sequence, by establishing the link between the private story, which the film will present, and the larger political events which, as it were, Paul has left behind. The story begins, in other words, after Paul has been released from the firm grip of History. By providing the exact date, May 19th, on which the film's protagonist Paul Simon returns from the War, the film constitutes itself as a chronicle which will be concerned—this is clearly connoted—with the truthful and accurate recording of events as they unfold. This play with exactitude in the case of a fictive character is part of the documentary illusion which the film—as historical film—wishes to establish from the beginning. The superimposed title shows an anonymous chronicler as narrator who seems to be responsible for selecting, ordering and dating of events.

The camera has been stationed just outside of the village as if it had been waiting for Paul's return. As soon as he appears on the horizon it approaches him in a fast tracking shot. The camera acts in the rest of the scene as an alert recorder of village life as Paul perceives it—although nothing seems to have changed, he sees, the emphatic camera movements seem to suggest this, the village with new eyes after his long absence. The camera introduces the two women, Apollonia and Maria, and lingers on them, anticipating their importance for the development of Paul's story. By pursuing history in terms of personal stories, Reitz seeks to restore a sense of continuity in the discontinuous and fragmented history of Germany. "We Germans," he said in an interview, "have had a hard time with our stories. Even now, 40 years after the war (. . .), we are still afraid that our little personal stories could recall our Nazi past and remind us of our mass participation in the Third Reich." (23) It is no coincidence that Reitz lets his film begin in 1918 and end 35 years after the Hitler regime. He thus historicizes Nazism and integrates it into the lived experiences of simple German folk who appear more as victims than agents of History.

The realistic narrative, which re-presents history as a complex web of interrelated family stories, offers the spectator a large identificatory potential. We follow most of the characters through much of their life and experience with them historical events as fate that cannot be explained or prevented. Our identification with the characters is facilitated by the faithful reconstruction of the locale. History in this film is encoded with a strong sense of time (through three generations) and place (through dialect and almost excessive attention to detail in the mise-en-scène). The film dissolves German history into many fictional private stories with the Hunsrück region as a strong geographical referent which, in the last analysis, transcends history.

My second example, "Germany—Pale Mother," ("Deutschland—bleiche Mutter") was written and directed by Helma Sanders-Brahms; it was released in 1980 and subjected to fierce criticism in Germany. The film begins abruptly with the written text of a poem by Bertolt Brecht whose central metaphor is that of the mother and her sons: the poem thus pictorializes the Nazi terror as a family conflict tearing the very fabric of social order: not only have the brothers killed the best among themselves, they also humiliate the mother. It suggests an image of Germany which causes not only fear and mockery but also pity. The poetic narrator distances himself from Germany (he speaks of his own shame), while at the same time preserving an undying attachment to it as if it were his mother who, having been victimized by her own sons, tries to cover up the crime committed against her. Despite the intense pain a possibility of reconciliation and a sense of solidarity with the victim is suggested. It is an attitude that also informs the film: crimes have been committed in the name of Germany, but the mother cannot be blamed.

The poem, whose first line is also the title of the film, serves not only as a prologue to the story, it also leads the implied spectator to an allegorical reading according to which the mother is equated with the mythic Germania whose sons have betrayed and befouled her. The fact that the poem is not part of the diegesis and is read by a person outside the historical world which is set up by the film, suggests a complex relationship not only between the past and a present which comments on the past but also between the visible space of the screen and the acoustical space of the film. The lyrical text spoken by a voice off screen establishes from the outset the independence of sound from the image, which is characteristic for this film. Because the screen only shows the printed poem, no images, we are forced to listen to the sound track. The voice displays what is inaccessible to the image, what exceeds the visible; at the same time, by emanating from outside the field of vision, it connotes some disturbing oracle-like quality, at least until we are given the necessary information on the screen, namely that it was Brecht who wrote this poem with uncanny foresight in 1933 and that his daughter recited it. That it is Brecht's daughter who reads the account of the past, alludes to one of the central concerns which the film itself explores: the problematic, tense relationship between generations, and, more specifically, between daughter and father, daughter and mother.

The first image, the reflection of a gigantic red swastica flag in the middle of a lake, localizes the historical period in which the story takes place; it provides, literally speaking, the foundation on which the ensuing love story is built. As in Edgar Reitz's "Heimat," the private narrative is linked right from the outset to the public political narrative with which we are already familiar. The image of the Nazi flag serves as marker of historical time and space; even if we don't know its symbolic value from own experience, we recognize it because it has become a conventionalized sign, a kind of visual shorthand, for the period after 1933. While a rowing boat enters from the left and cuts through the image of the flag, a female voice from off-screen says: "I can remember nothing about the time before my birth. I cannot be blamed for events before my birth. I didn't exist then. I began when my father first saw my mother." The voice, detached from a represented body, thus identifies itself as the voice of the daughter who comments on the image from the perspective of the present, acknowledging thereby the temporal split between the narrated past and the moment of speaking. The voice-over that recurs throughout the film addresses the audience without mediation, interpreting the images and expressing what cannot be visualized: her memories, her inner thoughts, her own later value judgements. In an autobiographical monolog, directed at the spectator, she introduces both her father—he is the one who is not a Nazi, as she is quick to point out—and her mother who is shown from the start as victim of men. At our first glimpse of her we see her accosted and commented on as sexual object by the two men in the boat and harassed by four men in Nazi uniforms who let their huge dog loose on her. The first scene then alludes to several stories which are developed in the film: the story of a woman victimized in a world populated by men, the unprovoked aggression toward her as woman, her quiet defense and expression of melancholy—the heavily symbolic foreshadowing of much unhappiness to come—and the domination of the private realm by politics, alluded to by the obtrusive display of the swastika.

"Germany—Pale Mother" tells the story of the filmmaker's mother from 1939 to 1955 from the perspective of the daughter who herself is the mother of the child who plays the daughter in the film. Autobiographical, fictional, and historical elements blend into each other here; political history is filtered through the semi-fictional private autobiography of the filmmaker as a young girl. If autobiography is, as Paul de Man maintains, "a discourse of self-restoration," (925) then the old dichotomies of past and present, public and private, have to be challenged and realigned. Even the concept of history needs to be reconsidered, as Judith Mayne recently argued: "The task of rendering ourselves visible has, for feminist historians, entailed a process of re-reading the very notion of history: not as a series of Grand Events in the public domain, but as a constant interaction of the realms of private and public life. For women have always participated in public life, although most frequently through the mediation of domestic life. 'The personal is political' has by now become a truism for feminists. Yet we are only beginning to realize the extent to which the so-called 'personal' areas of existence are shaped and shape in their turn the nature of social relations." (122)

Women's experiences of German history, particularly of the Hitler regime and the war, are for Sanders-Brahms the point of reference for portraying the past. She attempts to write history not from the perspective of those who won or lost the war but from the perspective of those who suffered from Fascism. Women appear as victims of men's wars. She believes that women have their own history, and possibly a different history than men have. Her feminist perspective challenges the very notion of history as the collective memory of the past. Whose experiences constitute collective memory and history? Sanders-Brahms records many life experiences which are gender-specific and typically absent from the male version of history: the meaning attached to childbirth, the fear of rape, the physical reaction of women to violation, the relationship between mother and daughter. She opens up to the public what historically has been defined as private and personal and she portrays the true experience of many German women who discovered their own strength during the war and then suffered the devaluation of those strengths and their achievements when the men returned after the war. Historical fiction as autobiography assimilates real historical time and space in a highly subjective way; the radical subjectivization of history, dramatized mainly through the confessional and often defensive voice-over, stands in stark contrast to the more objective chronicle style of "Heimat". Although Sanders-Brahms still translates history into a continuous fictional story, she freely acknowledges her contemporary feminist point of reference from which images of history are being interpreted and judged. The very act of reconstituting history in film is foregrounded by her deliberately subjective voice-over; she comments on and criticizes the past from her present perspective.

If we compare now the beginning of Alexander Kluge's film "The Patriot" ("Die Patriotin") with the two previous beginning scenes, then we will see that the rift between representation and its referent has widened. The very practice of representing the past in a self-contained story becomes problematic; historical representation for Kluge is a matter of production, an archaeological process in and for the present; history is no longer conceived in terms of a sequential series of events (as it still was for Reitz and for Sanders-Brahms), but of a disparate number of unique contacts between past and present which have to be constituted and constructed by the historian. Kluge's misgivings about progress in history has led him to reject also the narrative mode of history-writing which believed in the idea of historical continuity and linear development. He follows Walter Benjamin's "constructivist principle," according to which the historian "grasps the constellation which his own era has formed with a definite earlier one." (263) In contrast to the chronological and additive method of traditional historiography which establishes a "causal nexus between various moments of history," Benjamin's and Kluge's critical historiography is based on the principle of montage. History is presented as something that needs to be dissolved and put together again in a different way. The gaps and breaks between the shots as well as the heterogeneity of forms are intended to demonstrate time and again the impossibility of a narrative totality and closure in history. By accentuating the process of historical representation, Kluge distances the spectator and opens up space for inspection and reflection. The first five minutes of this film are fairly characteristic for Kluge's technique and concept of history and historical representation.

At first sight the mosaic of disparate verbal and visual quotations resembles the Surrealist technique of *écriture automatique* with its principal category of chance. Kluge's radical departure from the narrative emplotment characteristic of traditional historiography has led him to a nomadic approach which ranges freely over 2000 years of German history. By suspending the time-space continuum he also suspends causality; the spectator is forced to be active in combining the various fragments and thereby co-produce, rather than simply consume, the meaning of the film.

Kluge's theory of history owes much to postmodern aesthetics which repudiates the principles of organic wholeness, teleology, and even intelligibility for the sake of the fragmentary and the dispersed. The filmmaker's activity is seen by Kluge as that of the bricoleur engaged in collecting, arranging, and reordering the scraps of history: literary, filmic, and musical quotations, fragmentary observations, paintings, photographs and newsreels, fairy tales and science-fiction fantasies, free associations and flashes of remembrance. They are designed to illuminate each other by way of correlation and juxtaposition. Kluge privileges anonymous visual and textual quotations; origins are deliberately left obscure. Torn from their original context and placed in constantly new constellations, these quotations preserve the past in a fragmented form; at the same time they act as disruptive elements: through them the past breaks into the apparent immutability of the present and challenges its illusion of permanence. It is this dual function of preserving the past and challenging the present which to me characterizes Kluge's concept of filmic historiography as well.

Kluge wants to recharge the past with the energy which comes from the sudden convergence of past and present in the consciousness of the observer. His project is predicated on the compelling claim which the past inevitably has on the present: "It is an error," the narrator says in the film, "to believe that the dead are simply dead. They are full of protest and energy." Kluge's focus is neither on the past nor exclusively on the present but on the constantly shifting dialectical constellation between past and present. As a consequence the interpretation of history becomes a process of continually remapping and rewriting the past in the eyes of the present. The film as it constitutes itself as a historical film creates multiple, simultaneous and contradictory temporalities.

"The Patriot" is made up of several representational modes. There is, first of all, a fragmented fictional narrative whose central character is introduced in the first shot of the film: Gabi Teichert, a history teacher in the state of Hessen, where there were plans in 1979 to abolish history altogether as a subject in schools. She is the patriot of the title, concerned as a German patriot with all who died for the fatherland. She is shown shouldering a spade with which she wants to dig for the roots of German history—again a metaphor taken literally and visualized. The fictionality of Gabi Teichert is later called into question when she visits the Party convention of the Social Democrats which took place in fall 1979 and involves known figures like Herbert Wehner in the dialogue about ways to change the raw material of history.

The second mode of historical representation, interspliced with the first, is based on documentary evidence. Kluge's interest does not lie in the fictional reconstruction of history but in the preservation of historical documents: in the first five minutes alone we see archival film footage, newsreels from Stalingrad with haunting images of emaciated German prisoners of war, pictures of open graves, reproductions of romantic paintings by Caspar David Friedrich, a photograph of the Brandenburg Gate of 1870 festively lit for the victory celebration after Sedan, comic strip pictures of war battles, and some unlocalizable "found footage" of the moon rotating around the earth. Intercut are also documentary-style shots of ruins in Swabia in the midst of meadows with cherry trees in full blossom, signifying the tensions between cyclical, ever-present nature and history which leaves its traces on the land. The drastic shifts of perspective and dislocations of space and time, dramatized further by intertitles, mark the materiality of the film and emphasize its montage construction.

The montage of fictional and documentary footage is accompanied by a complex soundtrack which by itself is a montage of voice-over and musical quotations. Significantly the film begins with the music which Hanns Eisler composed for Alain Resnais' classical 1955 film about Auschwitz, "Nuit et brouillard" ("Night and Fog"), which is about memory and forgetting, about the horrors of history, exemplified by grainy documentary footage from the concentration camp, and the obliviousness of nature, illustrated by the peaceful landscape surrounding Auschwitz now, shot in color. Where does memory lie if not in the documents of the past? How are people made to remember without the historical evidence preserved in films like "Night and Fog" and "The Patriot?" The musical quotation from "Night and Fog" which Kluge uses in "The Patriot" resonates with questions of remembrance and the presence of the historical past.

The poem by Christian Morgenstern, "The Knee," read by Kluge off-screen, would seem to be a nonsense text that actively encourages us to forget the real world and enter a fictional counter-world where poetic freedom reigns supreme and knees fight for their right to speak. Kluge associates the knee as the surviving fragmentary part of a German soldier who died in Stalingrad; he has the part speak for the whole person who lies buried in Stalingrad. The introduction of a speaking knee displaces the narrator: not only the survivors speak, the defeated and dead are also given a voice.

In contrast to traditional historical films which attempt to reconstitute the past "the way it really was," Kluge does not situate us within the world of the past. On the contrary, the past is perceived as "other," as foreign, as something that must be recovered, not in its totality, but as trace, as part of a whole. The task of a historian is closely tied to that of an archaeologist, and it is no surprise that Gabi Teichert is an amateur archaeologist looking for traces which the past yields up to the present in the form of conflicting documentary material.

Kluge's intertextual approach to history may have the effect of ultimately dehistoricizing the past: by dislocating historical images and text fragments from their habitual relations and by recombining them in the present, he injects into historiography such a degree of playful arbitrariness that undeniably forceful dependencies and contingencies (for instance, in the economic sphere) remain simply excluded. At the same time, the film, perpetually aware of its own process of enunciation and bent on deconstructing all cinematic conventions, tends to disorient and overtax the spectator who is used to traditional modes of historical exposition and reconstruction as well as to narrative closure. As a discourse on the very possibility of historical representation, Kluge's film calls into question not only our habitual knowledge of history but also our willingness to decipher images that are mere fragments — unfamiliar and opaque — of a whole that is irrevocably lost. In contrast to Reitz and Sanders-Brahms, Kluge no longer believes in reconstituting the past as historical fiction. His aesthetics of dispersion not only differs greatly from Reitz's and Sanders-Brahms's construction (and deconstruction) of family histories against the background of German history, it also shows a way to break with the conventions of narrative history altogether.

Despite their radical stylistic differences all three films attempt to rewrite recent German history from the perspective of the present. In "Heimat" an attempt is made to integrate the political and moral anomaly of the Third Reich into a narrative that deliberately does not begin with 1933 but with 1918; by showing fifteen years before as well as the three decades after the Hitler regime, Reitz historicizes and thereby normalizes German Fascism. To the extent that he narrativizes political history in a chronological fashion and embeds it in the private stories of his characters, he tends to trivialize the political dynamics of Fascist politics. Sanders-Brahms premises her film on the victimization of women by the "male" politics of Nazi men. Her narrative construct of Germany's crucial period which is centered around the conflict between genders and generations, again deflects from the political and ideological force of Hitler. To translate questions of politics of war into gender-specific issues carries with it the obvious danger of shutting political history out and refracting it in private histories/stories. Kluge's concept of history and his post-modernist, dispersed aesthetics free him from the shackles of narrative, linear history writing. Still his all-encompassing, intertextual approach to history deemphasizes historical causes and effects, explainable conditions and dispositions and developments. Breaking the narrative hold over history and ranging freely over 2000 years of German history, he prods the imagination of the spectator to adopt a critical, often ironically detached attitude vis-à-vis history. In his film "The Patriot" the Nazi period is hardly ever mentioned or shown; it is there only by implication and occasional allusion.

If it is true what Foucault has said about the power of film to "re-program popular memory" (22), then it might prove interesting to follow closely the future of the German history film because the various visual and narrative appropriations of the past will say much about the memory of the present.

Notes

1 Cited in Courtade/Cadars 7 (my translation). The quotation (in a different translation) also serves Saul Friedländer as an apt motto to his evocative essay on representations of Nazism in literature and film of the 1970's.

2 For a discussion of images of fascism in contemporary European film, see Baudrillard, Fischli, Friedländer, and Insdorf.

3 Jim Hoberman 62. His review "Shoah Business" was written in response to the critique of the film by Pauline Kael.

4 For an intertextual account of the filmic dramaturgy of the Bitburg ceremony, see Rentschler's article.

5 I discuss Kluge's views on the "German Autumn" in my essay on Kluge, 133.

6 The factual evidence seems to speak against that accusation; see films cited in Knilli/Zielinski; Zielinski, 84.

7 For a theoretical discussion of "narrative emplotment," see White, 92ff.; cf. also Danto, Koselleck, Koselleck/Stempel, Quant/Süßmuth.

8 For Metz, who takes his terms "histoire" and "discours" from the linguist Emile Benveniste, *histoire* is disguised *discours*; according to Metz *histoire* hides its own means of production, its marks of énonciation. See Bordwell 21-26 for a discussion and critique of this distinction.

9 Reitz, Interview, 23. See also Hansen and Geisler for a critical examination of the more troubling political assumptions of "Heimat."

Works Cited

Baudrillard, Jean. "L'histoire: un scénario rétro." *Ça* (1977): 16-29.

Benjamin, Walter. *Illuminations*. Ed. Hannah Arendt. Trans. H. Zohn. New York: Schocken Books, 1969.

Bordwell, David. *Narration in the Fiction Film*. Madison: The University of Wisconsin Press, 1985.

Courtade, Francis, and Pierre Cadars. *Geschichte des Films im Dritten Reich*. Trans. Florian Hopf. Munich: Wilhelm Heyne Verlag, 1977.

Danto, Arthur. *Analytical Philosophy of History*. Cambridge: Cambridge University Press, 1968.

deMan, Paul. "Autobiography as De-Facement." *Modern Language Notes* 94 (December 1979): 919-930.

Fischli, Bruno. "Rekonstruktion, Retro-Scenario, Trauerarbeit, Aufarbeitung—oder was? Neue Filme über den deutschen Faschismus." *Jahrbuch Film* 79/80. Ed. H. G. Pflaum. München: Carl Hanser Verlag, 1979: 63-75.

Foucault, Michel. Interview. *Edinburgh Magazine* 2 (1977): 20-25.

Friedländer, Saul. *Reflections of Nazism. An Essay on Kitsch and Death*. New York: Harper & Row, 1984.

Geisler, Michael E. "'Heimat' and the German Left." *New German Critique* 36 (Fall 1985): 25-66.

Hansen, Miriam. "Dossier on Heimat." *New German Critique* 36 (Fall 1985): 3-24.

Hoberman, Jim. "Shoah Business." *Village Voice* (28 January 1986), p. 62.

Insdorf, Annette. *Indelible Shadows. Film and the Holocaust.* New York: Random House, 1983.

Kael, Pauline. "The Current Cinema." *New Yorker* (30 December 1985): 67-72.

Kaes, Anton. "Über den nomadischen Umgang mit der Geschichte. Aspekte zu Alexander Kluges Film 'Die Patriotin.'" *Text+Kritik* 85 (January 1985): 132-144.

Kluge, Alexander. *Die Patriotin.* Frankfurt am Main: Zweitausendeins, 1979.

Knilli, Friedrich, and Siegfried Zielinski. Eds. *Holocaust zur Unterhaltung. Anatomie eines internationalen Bestsellers.* Berlin: Elefanten Press, 1982.

Koselleck, Reinhart and Wolf-Dieter Stempel. Eds. *Geschichte — Ereignis und Erzählung.* (Poetik and Hermeneutik V) München: Wilhelm Fink Verlag, 1973.

Lanzmann, Claude. *Shoah. An Oral History of the Holocaust.* New York: Pantheon Books, 1985.

Mayne, Judith. "Visibility and Feminist Film Criticism." *Film Reader* 5 (1982): 120-124.

Metz, Christian. "Story/Discourse: Notes on Two Kinds of Voyeurism." *Movies and Methods*. Vol. II. Ed. Bill Nichols. Berkeley: University of California Press, 1985, 543-549.

Quant, Siegfried, and Hans Süssmuth. Eds. *Historisches Erzählen. Formen und Funktionen*. Göttingen: Vandenhoeck & Ruprecht, 1982.

Reitz, Edgar. *Liebe zum Kino. Utopien und Gedanken zum Autorenfilm 1962-1983*. Köln: Verlag KÖLN 78, 1984.

——————. "Interview." *tip-Magazin* 16 (1984): 23-25.

Rentschler, Eric. "The Use and Abuse of Memory: New German Film and the Discourse of Bitburg." *New German Critique* 36 (Fall 1985): 67-90.

Ryan, Judith. *The Uncompleted Past. Postwar German Novels and the Third Reich*. Detroit: Wayne State University Press, 1983.

Sanders-Brahms, Helma. *Deutschland, bleiche Mutter. Film-Erzählung*. Reinbek: Rowohlt, 1980.

Wenders, Wim. "That's Entertainment: Hitler, Eine Polemik gegen J. C. Fests Film 'Hitler—eine Karriere.' " *Die Zeit* (8 May 1977).

White, Hayden. "The Historical Text as Literary Artifact," in *Tropics of Discourse. Essays in Cultural Criticism*. Baltimore and London: The Johns Hopkins University Press, 1978, 81-100.

Zielinski, Siegfried. "History as Entertainment and Provocation: The TV Series 'Holocaust.' " *New German Critique* 19 (Winter 1980): 81-96.

Bloom, Nietzsche, and the Critique of Postmodernism

Steven Taubeneck
University of Washington

> Philosophy has made no progress? If somebody scratches
> where it itches, does that count as progress? If *not*, does that
> mean it wasn't an authentic scratch, or not an authentic itch?
> And couldn't this reaction to the irritation go on for a long time
> before a remedy for itching is found?[1]

The concept of postmodernism is one of the most irritating problems in recent philosophical writing, but also one of the most widely discussed. Perhaps the roots of the problem lie in the paradoxical nature of the term itself. For if the "modern" concerns that which is most contemporary, how could there be a collection of "post-contemporary" phenomena? Or again, from another perspective, it could be said that postmodernism is the rejection of any totalized conception of truth. But on what grounds could the truth of that statement be shown? The notions of a "post-contemporary" place in history or a "groundless ground" for truth are only two of the many troubling issues that arise. Yet despite such difficulties it is certain that much current writing deals with the problem of postmodernism. Indeed, in the following I shall argue that Alan Bloom's main concern is not with things German, as it may at first seem. Rather, Bloom's sharpest attack is directed against the widespread effects of postmodernism, and in this critique his writing can be related to the arguments of many other contemporary critics, from Lyotard to Habermas to Rorty.

Much of Bloom's polemic in *The Closing of the American Mind* is directed against Nietzsche, Heidegger, Freud, and Weber.[2] For example, the middle section of the book is dominated by a chapter entitled "The German Connection," in which Bloom mounts a strong attack against "German thinkers" in general:

> In short, after the war, while America was sending out its blue jeans to unite the young of all nations, . . . it was importing a clothing of German fabrication for its souls, which clashed with all that. . . . Our intellectual skyline has been altered by German thinkers even more radically than has our physical skyline by German architects. (C, 152)

It is instructive to note Bloom's polemical style at this point. In this passage, as elsewhere, "America" for Bloom is the land of the young, the naive, people who are eternally innocent, unsuspecting, but too quickly seeking mere self-satisfaction and a merely comfortable or pleasant existence. "America" is the land of blue jeans, whereas the "clothing of German fabrication" is made of fundamentally sterner stuff.

Germany, by antithetical contrast, is the land of dangerous but exhilarating thinkers like Nietzsche. Undoubtedly Bloom's most polemical statements are directed against Nietzsche, whom he sees as one of the great prophets of contemporary life and a fitting example of the sinister potential everywhere visible today. What astounds Bloom is the extraordinary breadth of Nietzsche's impact:

> In politics, in entertainment, in religion, everywhere, we find the language connected with Nietzsche's value revolution, a language necessitated by a new perspective on the things of most concern to us. Words such as "charisma," "life-style," "commitment," "identity" . . . all of which can easily be traced to Nietzsche, are now practically American slang, although they, and the things to which they refer, would have been incomprehensible to our fathers, not to speak of our Founding Fathers. (C, 146-147)

Bloom does not reject Nietzsche out of hand, but seems to admire him in a contradictory way that wavers between love and hate. For Bloom, Nietzsche is one of the greatest thinkers in Western history. Similarly, Bloom seems in awe of German intellectual history as one of the greatest traditions in the West. What bothers him about both Nietzsche and the German tradition is the recent Nazi past. The Nazi period for Bloom is inextricably bound up with German cultural and intellectual history, and Americans have been too quick to forget it. This is the hidden danger of Nietzsche and the "German connection," namely, that Americans have been too quick to swallow the "value relativism" suggested by Nietzsche and others, while forgetting the horrors of Nazism built into their tradition.

Bloom clarifies the point in his argument with an explicit disclaimer of anti-German paranoia:

> My insistence on the Germanness of all this is intended not as a know-nothing response to foreign influence, the search for a German intellectual under every bed, but to heighten awareness of where we must look if we are to understand what we are saying and thinking, for we are in danger of forgetting. (C, 152)

I am inclined to accept the disclaimer, though Bloom's often bizarre formulations could lead one to suspect him at first of extreme national chauvinism. What is bothering him most, I believe, is not the specific "Germanness" of recent American cultural history, but the refusal to take "the German connection" seriously. In fact it would seem that his greatest anger is directed against an imagined, Miami Vice-style production of German thought: "We are like the millionaire in *The Ghost (Geist) Goes West* who brings a castle from brooding Scotland to sunny Florida and adds canals and gondolas for 'local color' " (C, 153). It is the Disneylandification of German thought which bothers him most, the unwillingness to remember the dangers of such a tradition, in short, that very phenomenon of radical cultural pluralism and late capitalist insouciance which has come to be known as "postmodernism."

Both with his appraisal of Nietzsche, and with the analysis of the postmodernization of Nietzsche, Bloom joins company with some of the most influential theorists in the recent Ameroeuropean context. From Bloom to Jürgen Habermas, Jean-Francois Lyotard, and Richard Rorty, many critics internationally have reasserted the importance of Nietzsche for contemporary thought. Of course each of these writers has evaluated Nietzsche differently, but they are nevertheless in agreement on the point that Nietzsche's thought has become central. A brief discussion of Bloom's position in relation to Habermas, Lyotard, and Rorty should clarify some of the context of the debate on Nietzsche and postmodernism today.

In striking agreement with the basic outlines of Bloom's argument is the speech given in 1980 by Jürgen Habermas, entitled "Modernity—An Incomplete Project."[3] Habermas rejects postmodernism outright and instead attempts to rescue modernism from its would-be usurpers. For Habermas, then, postmodernism is essentially anti-modernism. He sees in postmodernism above all the attempt to sacrifice "the tradition of modernity in order to make room for a new historicism" (M, 3), an "anarchistic intention of blowing up the continuum of history," and a "rebelling against all that is normative" (M, 5). Habermas attacks specifically the "aesthetic modernity" of Baudelaire, the "French Nietzsche," Dadaists, and the Surrealists in the "Cafe Voltaire" (M, 5). Such recent writers as Georges Bataille, Michel Foucault, or Jacques Derrida are for Habermas simply continuations of the tradition of "aesthetic modernity" from the nineteenth century (M, 14).

The biggest problem with these writers, as Habermas sees it, is that they have perverted the basic presuppositions of modernism as they were first formulated by Kant and the Enlightenment philosophers of the late eighteenth century. Whereas Bloom argues for a return to the Greeks, and especially Plato and Socrates as the normative models, Habermas argues that Kant, among others, distinguished three autonomous spheres of reason that were nevertheless integrated into a unified and coherent field. These three spheres were science, morality, and art, and they each had an internal logic of their own: cognitive-instrumental, moral-practical, and aesthetic-expressive (M, 9). The three spheres and their distinct logics were separate but joined into a unitary multiplicity that was essentially optimistic about the potential of human reason. Habermas thus goes to great length, in the 1980 speech and in many later writings, to revitalize the original and still incomplete project of modernism as it was founded in its most optimistic form by the Enlightenment. Like Bloom, Habermas wants a rejuvenation of the claims of reason to establish a coherent value system more clearly. Both want to reform society and contemporary education along the lines of more reasonable principles and values.

Quite in contrast to Bloom and Habermas is the work of the French theorist Jean-Francois Lyotard. His *The Postmodern Condition: A Report on Knowledge* of 1979 is among the texts most concerned with the concept of postmodernism.[4] As the title suggests, this text is offered as a commentary on a contemporary historical situation, namely, "the condition of knowledge in the most highly developed societies." Lyotard summarizes the events of recent decades under the headings of poststructuralism, deconstruction, and the critique of metaphysics. In the process, he defines some of the terms that have influenced the discussion of the contemporary world ever since.

Lyotard's most prominent usage involves the term "postmodern" itself, which he articulates right at the outset: "Our working hypothesis is that the status of knowledge is altered as societies enter what is known as the postindustrial age and cultures enter what is known as the postmodern age." For Lyotard, then, it is primarily the transformations in the "status of knowledge" that indicate the fundamental changes in the contemporary world. Knowledge has been "mercantilized" (PC, 26), translated into computer language and quantities of information to be bought and sold (PC, 23). The old idea of personal development or "Bildung," involving the belief in the formation of the mind and the personality, has been replaced, according to Lyotard, by a sense of knowledge as a commodity to be produced, distributed, and consumed (PC, 24). Knowledge has become one of the major instruments in the worldwide competition for power (PC, 26).

With the reduction of knowledge to mere information, infinitely transferable through an economy of exchange and susceptible to hoarding by various competing interest groups, the old dream of establishing a timeless foundation for knowledge has been exhausted. Undoubtedly, Lyotard's most famous remark on this point is that postmodernism involves incredulity towards "metanarratives" (PC, 33; 109-112). Metanarratives are those "big-picture stories" in which knowledge is given a foundation and all parts of human activity find an ultimate meaning. According to Lyotard, philosophy has been dominated by different metanarratives at different times. There were initially the great narratives of Platonism, in classical philosophy, or Christianity, in medieval philosophy. Philosophy reached its modern period when these metanarratives were no longer mythical or religious, but became rational, scientific, and asserted the authority of reason. Now, Lyotard suggests, philosophy has grown suspicious of any generalized system or authority, and as a result the great foundational metanarratives have lost their power. Of course, the "incredulity towards metanarratives" is seen by Bloom and Habermas as one of the greatest problems of contemporary intellectual life, and it is one of the tendencies they would most like to overcome.

By contrast, Lyotard's attitude towards the impotence of metanarratives is basically positive, for he wants to hasten the downfall of all claims to a general truth. He writes explicitly against every form of totalization, for he sees in totalizing narratives the danger of a totalitarian world view. Hence his own position is not meant to be just another metanarrative, as he explicitly denies any truth value for his own account and considers it to be of hypothetical character at best (PC, 31). What he wants to endorse instead of the grand metanarrative is the multiplicity of individual language games, following Wittgenstein (PC, 56), which have primarily an "agonistic" character (PC, 41), and which have no ultimate legitimacy outside of the negotiations between players in a language community (PC, 40). Lyotard's position is one that Bloom and Habermas would clearly want to reject. Bloom decries the loss of values and of belief in reason's power in a little allegory he tells of Odysseus's journey: "Values are not discovered by reason, and it is fruitless to seek them, to find the truth or the good life. The quest begun by Odysseus and continued over three millennia has come to an end with the observation that there is nothing to seek" (C, 143).

There is in the American context another analysis of postmodernism, by Richard Rorty, who seeks to maintain that insouciant attitude so infuriating to Bloom while combining the disparate narrative of Habermas and Lyotard.[5] Rorty thinks, for example, that

Habermas is making a desperate effort to reaffirm the position of rational enlightenment and progress, and that his position is not very useful:

> To accuse postmodernism of relativism is to try to put metanarratives in the postmodern's mouth. One will do this if one identifies "holding a philosophical position" with having a metanarrative available. If we insist on such a definition of "philosophy," then post-modernism is post-philosophical. But it would be better to change the definition. (PBL, 389)

Rorty evidently chooses not to challenge Habermas on the grounds of a more reasonable argument. He avoids the contest with Habermas over the issue of rationality and considers simply the view of greatest utility. This ironic skepticism on Rorty's part is quite in contrast to Habermas's (and Bloom's) missionary insistence on the dangers or perversions of postmodernism. Rorty's position, then, would seem to be that the use of irony is more characteristic and effective in a postmodern situation than the direct, outspoken, and passionate statements made by Habermas and Bloom.

Rorty, in other words, would put Habermas and Bloom into the modern camp and attributes to himself a postmodern position. His postmodernism, however, goes beyond mere ironic skepticism and supports practical attitudes in the art of living, such as curiosity or an "intellectual analogue of civic virtue—tolerance, irony, and a willingness to let spheres of culture flourish without worrying too much about their 'common ground' " (HL, 38). He thinks that Habermas "is scratching where it does not itch" (HL, 34), and that his story of modern philosophy is "both too pessimistic and too German" (HL, 38-39).

Rorty's story in part combines the two narratives of Habermas and Lyotard. This story would not expose the power of "ideology," as would Habermas, but it would, in contrast to Lyotard, suggest how some other people might acquire power and "use it for other purposes" (HL, 41-42). Rorty also suggests creating "a new canon," based on an awareness of "new social and religious and institutional possibilities," instead of producing a "new dialectical twist in metaphysics and epistemology" (HL, 42). In conclusion he sounds a nearly optimistic note: "Those who want beautiful social harmonies want a postmodernist form of social life, in which society as a whole asserts itself without bothering to ground itself" (HL, 43).

If we consider Bloom in light of these various examples from recent philosophical writing there are a few points that can be made. Clearly, the debate around postmodernism has emerged as an international dispute in which writers from many different traditions take part. Moreover, there seems to be a general consensus that postmodernism emphasizes fragmentation over totality, indirect over direct discourse, irony over solemnity, heterogeneity over unity, and uncertainty over certainty. And yet, despite the widespread consensus over the shape of postmodernism, there is very little agreement on the evaluation of this constellation. Bloom and Habermas may see it as catastrophic, Lyotard may see it as positive, and Rorty may see it as mildly amusing. My point is that, far from trying to resolve the debate over postmodernism, we might keep in mind both the general agreement that it represents a problem, and the general irritation over how the problem should be treated. In this way, the persistent scratching identified by Wittgenstein as philosophy might continue to be productive.[6]

Notes

1 Ludwig Wittgenstein, *Vermischte Bemerkungen* (Frankfurt/M: Suhrkamp, 1977), pp. 165-166.

2 Alan Bloom, *The Closing of the American Mind* (New York: Simon & Schuster, Inc., 1987). Further references given in the text as (C).

3 Jürgen Habermas, "Modernity—An Incomplete Project," trans. Seyla Ben-Habib, in *The Anti-Aesthetic. Essays on Postmodern Culture*, ed. Hal Foster (Port Townsend: Bay Press, 1983), pp. 3-15. References given as "M" in the text. For a further discussion of this topic see *Habermas and Modernity*, ed. Richard J. Bernstein (Cambridge, MIT Press, 1986).

4 Jean-Francois Lyotard, *The Postmodern Condition: A Report on Knowledge*. Trans. Geoff Bennington and Brian Massumi. Foreword by Fredric Jameson (Minneapolis: University of Minnesota Press, 1979). Further references are given in the text as (PC).

5 Richard Rorty, "Postmodernist Bourgeois Liberalism," *The Journal of Philosophy* 80 (1983), pp. 580-594, and "Habermas and Lyotard on Postmodernity," *Praxis International* 4 (1984), pp. 32-44. References will be given as either (PBL) or (HL) in the text.

6 For more on Bloom and Rorty in the specific context of Nietzsche criticism, see my "Afterword," in Ernst Behler, *Confrontations. Derrida/Heidegger/Nietzsche*, trans. Steven Taubeneck (Stanford: Stanford University Press, 1991).

Past Intention and Present Meaning: Reflections on the Limits of Accommodation

E. D. Hirsch, Jr.
University of Virginia

Since Walter Sokel is one of my favorite people, I hope you will indulge me if on this occasion I return to one of my favorite subjects. Because I have often stressed the importance of authors' intent, I could not blame anyone for supposing that I value authors above readers. But on the contrary I believe that living readers should take precedence over dead authors, and I am sympathetic to what is called "the readers' liberation front" (as distinct from the professors' liberation front). Thomas Jefferson firmly held the principle that we the living must resist binding ourselves to the conceptions of the dead. He recommended revising the U. S. Constitution every 20 years, and he framed legislation to abolish property entail. Entail was the practice of narrowly prescribing in one's last will and testament exactly how one's property shall be passed down through all future generations. Modern criticism, applying Jefferson's spirit to the literary sphere, has abolished intellectual entail. Dead authors may not restrict their meanings forever to some original historical moment, nor narrowly control how their texts shall be passed down in perpetuity among future readers.

But simply to assert the rights of living readers over dead authors is not to say anything specifically useful for literary culture or academic learning. Having abolished the principle of literary entail, shall we also abolish the principle of inheritance itself? Shall we place no limits upon our liberation from the dead hand of the past?

That is a significant question for literary culture and for writing in general. It is also a vexed question in the law.

The law is where I wish to begin, because our experience of the Bork Hearings in 1987 has made it all too clear that one has to distinguish between sophisticated and unsophisticated intentionalists. People like Robert Bork and Ed Meese give intentionalism a bad name. All the good guys who favor civil rights and tolerance and vote Democratic are anti-intentionalists, and this moral embarrassment must be piled upon other well-known intellectual embarrassments of original intent. But it turns out that the embarrassments of totally abandoning intent are even more troubling.

In law, for instance, the total abandonment of intent would result in there being no hindrance to making the law an instrument of judges' politics rather than of litigants' justice. Litigants *must* believe that judges try to be objective interpreters. Otherwise, they lose faith in law, and in the essential principle of our society—"a government of laws not of men." Can we avoid both embarrassments? Can we preserve a necessary faith in law yet still not fall into simplistic notions of original intent? In the literary sphere we ask the equivalent question: how can we preserve a necessary faith in reason and scholarship, and at the same time avoid the literary equivalent of Bork-Meesism? That is the problem I want to address.

Writing was invented to overcome the restriction of speech to one time and place. But, as Plato, ruefully observed in *The Phaedrus*, writing abandons living conversation and suffers from the artificial yoking of two historical worlds. Obsoleteness is inherent in the very nature of writing. That disadvantage is of course trivial compared to the advantages of writing. The fixing of speech in written form makes its meaning permanently available, and enables human experience to be cumulative to a degree that oral societies could not hope to match. By enabling the present to build upon the knowledge of the past, writing has been the chief agent of intellectual and technical progress.

This momentous, cumulative function of writing has required the myth of a *communication* between the past and the present. Mankind advanced in knowledge because what writing said in the past is communicated to the present. But the model of communication is, as Plato observed, problematical. In oral communication speaker and audience inhabit the same moment, but in writing they occupy different moments, making the model of communication an analogy or metaphor rather than a reality. From the start and forever after, communication through writing has required imaginative adjustments. Chief among these is the adjustment required for datedness, which I take as a general term for the unacceptability of a past meaning in a present context.

Literate cultures have developed in their religious and legal institutions techniques for overcoming the datedness of past writing. These may be called, generally, techniques of "accommodation." In oral societies, as Goody and Watt have explained, the accommodation of past traditions to present circumstances was accomplished not by interpretive strategies but by directly changing the words that carried the traditions. Such a mode of direct adjustment of past to present is not acceptable to literate cultures. *Scripta manent.* Writing stays. Since we cannot adjust the words we must adjust our interpretations of the words.

In literate cultures that endure a long time, writing almost always uncovers conflicts between the beliefs of past authors and those of present readers. This problem of datedness was the intellectual focus of the Bork hearings. The datedness of past writing gradually introduces into literate cultures a spirit of skepticism towards authority and tradition, which, in the secular sphere, encourages the rise of science. But in spheres where authority and tradition must be preserved, that is in religion and law, literate societies have developed interpretive techniques designed to overcome datedness by accommodating past texts to present readers.

In religion, such accommodation is based in a distinction between the literal and the spiritual senses of scripture. When God revealed His truth to historical persons He accommodated His meaning to their historical understandings in the form of a literal meaning. Later times must re-accommodate that literal meaning to uncover the hidden spiritual sense. When we interpret a holy text we go beyond its original, literal sense to grasp the trans-historical principle it represents. We must re-accommodate God's eternal meaning to our own understandings in our own time and place. On this conception of divine texts, the problem of datednesss does not and cannot arise in a fatal form, as St. Augustine argued so brilliantly and at such length in the *Confessions*.

But what of non-religious texts? A divine text permits indefinitely many acts of historical accommodation without fear of anachronism. But with merely human texts, datedness is a permanent danger. How, for instance, do we accommodate our present interpretations of the Constitution to the fact that its framers accepted racial segregation? We cannot assume that this literal belief hid a more acceptable spiritual meaning. That is why we have reserved the right to amend the Constitution, and did amend it to address the question of race. With secular texts, we cannot always rely on the human author's authority. Perhaps, therefore, we must conclude that the communicative, author-based model of interpretation is inadequate for accommodating literary and legal texts. Perhaps we will have to repudiate the communicative model in the secular sphere. We would accept the authority of the divine author but not that of the human one. We would preserve the communicative model in religion, but abandon it in all other spheres of textual interpretation. We would solve the problem of datedness by abolishing its very existence in the secular sphere.

Some recent literary theorists have encouraged us to make that move. But that way of abolishing the datedness of human authors also abolishes their authority, and vests the authority for textual meaning in ourselves. Justice Douglas made the point well when he said to his colleagues on the nine-person Supreme Court. "With five votes, we can do anything." By the same token, a literary critic can do anything with just one vote.

Another way of stating Justice Douglas's declaration of freedom is to say that no limit is placed upon the principle of accommodation when we interpret merely human texts. We can accommodate a secular text to our beliefs and desires, without allowing any hindrance to be imposed by the beliefs and desires of the merely human author. By making a radical distinction between religious and secular interpretation, we find ourselves using a communicative model to understand all language *except* the language of law and literature. But the only intellectual justification for this inconsistency in our practice is that it avoids the problem of datedness. Thus, the solution to the problem suffers from the difficulty of all arbitrariness in the intellectual sphere. We are left with no way of being wrong. Under a non-communicative model of interpretation, one is, as Justice Douglas observed, automatically right. Might makes right.

Literary theorists who belong to the tribe of Justice Douglas counter this objection by saying that interpretive arbitrariness is not complete. It is limited in actual practice. But this move from logic to actual practice is unconvincing, because real interpreters are invariably infected by the communicative model of interpretation that is ubiquitous. Real interpreters would have to be inhumanly sophisticated and alert not to be infected by normal, everyday principles of verbal interpretation that are used everywhere else in their lives. Those very theorists who accept Justice Douglas's principle in literature forget it when they appear as litigants in court. Like everyone else, they wish their legal cases to be decided objectively on consistent principles rather than arbitrarily on the preferences of judges. For the sake of consistency, rationality, and for other theoretical and practical reasons, it is very desirable to save the communicative model of interpretation even in the sphere of literature, if we can do so and still overcome datedness.

Notice that the principle of accommodation is basically the same in the religious and the secular sphere. Whenever we accommodate a human text to the present, we are obliged to assume that it resembles the sacred text in that it has a spirit as well as a letter—a core meaning that can be transported from one historical era to another. This notion of a trans-historical meaning in literary texts seems a radical doctrine in our historicist era. Nonetheless, the very *idea* of accommodation, whether secular or sacred, logically implies a trans-historical core meaning that can be lifted from the past and applied to the present.

The distinction between letter and spirit is fundamental to all accommodation, and therefore to the interpretation of all past texts. If the literal sense of a past text could be directly applied to the present, there would be no datedness, and no accommodation would be needed. The spirit and the letter would be the same. The distinction between letter and spirit arises because the literal sense becomes outdated. We know why a trans-historical, spiritual sense exists in Holy Scripture, but can we justify finding a trans-historical spiritual sense in the secular texts of literature and law?

Not always. We know that some texts seem irretrievably dated. Let us look at an example of literary datedness: Chaucer's "Tale of Melibee." It is an allegorical tale that goes as follows: a rich young man named Melibee has a wife named Prudence and a daughter named Sophie (or Wisdom). One day Melibee abandons Prudence and Wisdom, and goes to sport in the fields of temporal delight. While he is thus occupied, three foes enter his house, beat his wife and wound his daughter in five places. Should Melibee take revenge? After long discussions, in which many learned authorities are quoted, Prudence persuades Melibee to forgive his foes, which he does to his great benefit.

On the first level of allegory, by attending to temporal delight, and by leaving behind prudence and wisdom, Melibee has allowed the three external causes of sin, the world, the flesh and the devil, to enter his house (that is, his soul) and commit an unjust act. The five wounds inflicted upon Wisdom and Prudence represent the five senses.

On a second or moral level, we are to understand that Prudence and Wisdom are wounded by the *internal* causes of sin, ignorance, lust and malice. The healing of the soul is symbolized by the healing of Wisdom, which is the paramount virtue of the soul.

Finally, on the third level, concerning things of salvation, Melibee's forgetfulness of God, like his forgetfulness of prudence and wisdom, has wounded his soul unto death. His wife tells him directly that his name being Melibee means that he has drunk so much of sweet temporal riches that he has forgotten Jesus Christ his Creator. His return to Prudence and Wisdom foreshadows his final redemption.

This story is partly interpreted for us in the text itself, mainly by Prudence, who gives numerous citations from authorities whom we don't accept anymore, and uses arguments we don't any longer believe. The literal story makes little sense in realistic terms, and has little application to life. Thus the spiritual sense of the poem is confined to a very explicitly articulated moral and theological system—one that is not widely accepted today. This suggests a preliminary hypothesis about literary datedness: that a work of literature becomes irretrievably dated when its *spiritual* sense is no longer accepted as valid. When the spiritual sense of literature becomes itself obsolete, all is lost.

This hypothesis about datedness explains why much of our older literature is remarkably resistant to datedness. Most of the *Canterbury Tales* are unlike "The Tale of Melibee." They decline to express narrowly explicit systems of allegory and philosophy. That is what Sir Philip Sidney meant when he said (somewhat playfully) that the poet never affirms. The poet comes to us with a tale, and lets *us* supply the analogies by which we apply the tale to our lives. When a story is explicitly allegorical it often contains elements that quickly become dated. As Sidney so brilliantly suggested, truth claims are the words that most easily tell lies. The historian and the scientist tell lies, Sidney says, because they try to tell particular truths with great exactitude. Their literal and spiritual senses are the same. When their literal-spiritual sense proves to be wrong, their story is superseded by later literal stories which try to tell those truths with ever more precision and detail.

Stories that last in literature, no matter how detailed they are in their concrete descriptions of life, are able to support many different conceptual systems, and apply to human experiences in many different periods. I don't suggest by this that literature is innocent of conceptual systems. Quite the contrary; the conceptual element alone gives literature breadth and duration of application. For unless an example implies a concept, that example cannot embrace further analogues beyond the one in the story. Rather, it is the vagueness of the conceptual systems in literature that enables it to remain true of human life. We can accommodate its broad concepts to our more explicit and current systems of belief, like Freudianism, or Marxism. The lack of conceptual specificity in literature helps it resist conceptual datedness, in the same way that, according to Nicholas Rescher, vague, stone-age physics resists datedness. It is last year's very specific physics that has become outmoded.

An inexplicit spiritual sense also enables law to resist datedness. It is well known that laws tend to become outmoded when they have painted with narrow rather than broad strokes. Justice Marshall famously observed that the framers of the U. S. Constitution deliberately wrote it broadly and vaguely to enable later readers to supply future accommodations. The statutes that are narrowest and most explicit are the first to become obsolete. So far then, we have found no compelling reason to make a radical distinction between the interpretation of secular and sacred texts. Literature has an underlying conceptual element that corresponds to the underlying conceptual element in law as well as to the underlying spiritual sense in scripture. We conclude from this that almost all textual interpretation is allegorical.

We are thus led to reject the doctrine of original intent as espoused by Bork and Meese, because they have not grasped the allegorical character of interpretation. They think of intent as constraining interpretation through literal meaning. But the intent of all writing directed to the future necessarily includes further intent to be accommodated, to be allegorized. For that is the only possible way the present text can communicate with the future reader. Indeed, I have argued elsewhere that all speech contains an allegorical dimension. All human speakers recognize the fallibility and correctibility of what they say. They intend the truth, even while knowing that the literal sense of their words may not hit the mark. Consequently, we always allegorize the speech of others when need be, and we expect them to return the favor.

A dated work like Chaucer's "Tale of Melibee" shows, however, that there are limits to secular accommodation. Sophisticated intentionalists have no difficulty in going beyond original intent to accommodate the spirit of a work, but they do recognize there may be a limit to accommodation in a given case. Is there a principle for determining this limit?

I once had an interesting debate with W. K. Wimsatt over the limits of accommodation. It concerned Blake's poem, "London," which ends with this stanza:

> But most thro' midnight streets I hear
> How the youthful Harlot's curse
> Blasts the new born Infant's tear,
> And blights with plagues the Marriage hearse.

Wimsatt had this to say about my description of Blake's original intent in using the phrase "marriage hearse."

> The following [example] may serve to define the issue. The materials are well known, but not the interpretive problem as I shall urge it. William Blake wrote in a sketchbook:
>
> > Remove away that blackening church
> > Remove away that marriage hearse
> > Remove away that man of blood
> > You'll quite remove the ancient curse.
>
> These lines remained in the sketchbook, where they deserved to remain. They are a raw expression of certain soreheaded antinomian attitudes which are beyond doubt a part of Blake's biography at the period when he was writing "London."
>
> Mr. E. D. Hirsch is well-informed about Blake and reliable, and I believe he gives us an accurate reading of a sort of intention [for the phrase "marriage hearse"] which Blake probably did entertain. "If there were no marriage, there would be no ungratified desires, and therefore no harlots."
>
> One thing, however, which perhaps he does not notice, or perhaps does not worry about is that these ideas are silly. (Why wouldn't there be *many* ungratified desires, as many at least as there were losers in stag combats, or wooers rejected, or pursuers eluded, or matings frustrated? and *many* harlots? and *many* whoremasters?) An admirer of Blake the poet might well be content to leave these ideas, if he could, on a back shelf in the doctrinaire part of Blake's mind. What if we actually do find them or manage to put them in the poem? Won't this make the poem silly? And, since evaluation

and interpretation are at the very least closely related, won't we be in danger of reading the poem as a pretty bad poem? And isn't this poem in fact supposed to be a masterpiece, "one of the best city poems every written"? Isn't it in fact a masterpiece?

Wimsatt has clearly laid out the puzzlements that arise when we are interpreting a text whose original intentions do not completely fit values and truths of current readers. The Blake poem is a particularly useful example of the problem, because the discussants have agreed upon the premises of the debate. Wimsatt accepts my view about what Blake originally intended, and I accept his view that Blake's ideas about marriage (which he shared with Godwin and other radicals of the early 19th century) are obsolete. Thus we agree about what Blake originally intended by "marriage hearse," and we agree about the datedness of his ideas. With those issues agreed upon, how shall we interpret the last line of his poem?

Wimsatt's answer is that we should not allow original intention to place *any* limits on our accommodation of the text. He reads the poem as being in *favor* of marriage. He says:

Blake's struggle with "London" was in part a struggle to make the last line of the last stanza viable. The tough fact was that the word "marriage" in the history of English usage and culture was not the name of an evil. . . . It was the name of a sacred institution and a first principle of stability for nearly every important value in a whole religiously and ethically oriented civilization and culture. . . . Let us imagine that some inquisitor of school curricula, reading Mr. Hirsch's gloss on "London," were to file a protest against corrupting the minds of schoolchildren by the required study of this depraved poem. . . . [An] answer that surely would not be long delayed would be to the effect that Blake's "London" in fact says no such thing.

And indeed Wimsatt sees to it that the poem says no such thing. He quotes with approval the comment of Joseph Wicksteed to the effect that the poem implies the "beauty of marriage." This direct inversion of Blake's intended meaning protects the poem from silliness and justifies it as a "masterpiece" that deserves to be taught in the schools.

But should a teacher-interpreter make Blake's poem say the very *opposite* of what the author intended? My own preference in this case would be to leave the local warts of datedness on a poem wherever they cannot honestly be removed. Even if the price of this approach were to exclude the poem from early grades. I'd be content for that price to be paid. *Amicus Blake, sed magis amica veritas.* Is there a rational demarcation-principle between an accommodation that is justifiable and one that is not? Whatever this principle might be, I would claim we have transgressed it when we understand Blake's "London" as being in *favor* of marriage.

When the Supreme Court overturned Plessy-Fergusson in the Brown Decision, all of their reasoning in nullifying the earlier decision would have been unnecessary on the Wimsatt or Douglas principle of accommodation. The Court could have simply announced that the spirit of Plessy-Fergusson was *against* segregation, regardless of what it said and intended. But courts in a democracy are reluctant to make quite such radical "accommodations," though one hears of Alice-in-Wonderland interpretations occurring under totalitarian legal systems. But in the U. S., judges are reluctant to go as far as some literary critics, because judges want to preserve respect for the law's objectivity, and for its governance by evidence and rational argument. (I would want to make the same point about literary scholarship, which should also be a democracy that depends on reason and evidence rather than authority.)

But can we generalize to find a universal demarcation-principle between justified and unjustified accommodations? In typical communicative situations, the demarcation-principle is of the following sort. We are broadly tolerant in our uses of language, but we reach a point at which we put our linguistic foot down. Typically, we will accommodate slight misstatements as meaning the truth. For instance, we would usually accept "cottage" as referring to a cabin. But we put our foot down at "mansion" as referring to a cabin. We would let "article" stand for "monograph," but not for "book"; "marriage hearse" for "repressive institution," but not for "sanctity of marriage." Thus, in the case of the Blake poem, if we wanted to carry out an acceptable accommodative interpretation, we would acknowledge Blake's mistaken views of the relations between marriage and prostitution, and emphasize the spiritual sense embracing all repressive institutions. We would not say Blake's poem means marriage is a good thing.

In the examples just mentioned, the implicit demarcation-principle that determined whether a text should sustain a particular accommodation was our conception of the breadth and character of the original intention. In literature, a very specific word may often stand for a very general range of applications. On the other hand, when the textual intention-convention is more specific, as often in the law, our tolerance of accommodation will be narrower, and the distance we allow between literal past sense and spiritual present reference will be proportionally smaller. Ultimately, then, the limits of accommodation are determined by the *breadth* of the actual historical intention that we infer.

That seems to me a basic principle of sophisticated intentionalism. It encourages us to accommodate our traditions to our changed beliefs, but also encourages us to reject those traditions whose very spirit runs against current beliefs. We are unwilling to preserve the empty husks of tradition at all costs, including the cost of saying that our texts mean the opposite of what they meant. We are willing to reject old literary works and bring in new ones, just as we do with our laws. At the same time, we recognize that we cannot completely remake our traditions every decade. In literary culture as in law, we need change *and* continuity but, above all, a reverence for truth.

Canonization and the Curriculum: George Orwell "In the Classroom"

John Rodden
University of Texas, Austin

How and when do books and authors become "canonized" in British and American schools and universities? Amid all the calls in literary studies during the last decade to "open up" the canon and the excellent research into the theoretical issues involved in canon-formation, this practical question has gone largely unexplored in the literary academy. And indeed, there is no simple or systematic way to answer it, for distinctive canons obtain for educational levels and nations. Quite apart from the high canon taught in upper-division university literature courses ("The Great Tradition"), a multiplicity of canons — pertaining to books, authors, genres, periods, national and regional literatures, institutional levels, and many other categories of literary repute — exists, formally or informally scaled according to aesthetic and other criteria (Tompkins; Rodden "Literary Studies").

Who can doubt that the widespread and lasting entry of an author's books into school and university curricula is of monumental importance to his or her reputation? If his work becomes required reading in school syllabuses, it reaches countless readers at an early age, receives support from the publishing industry, and tends to attract increasing critical attention. A case in point is the canonization of George Orwell, whose important place in school curricula discloses many of the institutional and historical factors conditioning the inclusion and exclusion of a writer's work in Anglo-American classrooms.

The variations in Orwell's reputation in the educational community are striking. Orwell's canonization was immediate, but it has also been eclectic. *Animal Farm* is a high-school staple. *1984* is also fairly widely taught in Anglo-American schools. His essays are likewise standard requirements in introductory university composition classes. Yet these writings are rarely encountered in more advanced courses. Nor, apart from the special attention accorded Orwell's *oeuvre* in 1984, are any of his other works usually taught in the academy. Nor are there any Orwell literary societies or publications (aside from an occasional xeroxed newsletter published by the Society for Orwell Studies, edited by Dennis Rohatyn of the University of San Diego). And yet, except possibly for Lawrence, it is likely that Orwell has exerted deeper influence on young Anglo-American writers than any other English writer of the last half-century. Nonetheless he made a first appearance in *The Norton Anthology of English Literature* (fourth edition, 1980) only after many other modern writers, some of whom he directly influenced (Kingsley Amis, Robert Conquest, Thom Gunn, Philip Larkin, Dylan Thomas).[1] Indeed, since a fable and a dystopia do not fit easily into standard fiction categories, the result is that Orwell the fiction writer is reduced to a "Thirties" writer—his work falling, most inconveniently for reading lists in college literature courses, between the end of the modernist movement and the return to more traditional, realistic fiction of the 1950s.

Thus, understanding the story of the canonization of "St. George" Orwell is not merely a matter of "dissecting" his "sacred place in the school curriculum," as one hostile critic of Orwell has asserted (Norris paperback cover blurb). For that place, however sacred, is also highly ramified; Orwell's educational status is a puzzling mix of elevations and exclusions, a matter of selective enshrinement.

Such discrepancies in academic reputation warrant emphasis, for they are by no means unique to Orwell. All writers are selectively read and esteemed, according to a plethora of variables. The eclectic canonization of Orwell's work is of special interest precisely because its sharp discontinuities illustrate so graphically the heterogeneous receptions of all writers.

This case study, then, approaches Orwell from the standpoint of readers' professional affiliations: i.e., readers as students and classroom teachers. We are concerned here with the institutional setting of the reading act: we look at how Orwell is being read in the academy, "in the classroom." Our attention is directed less toward the various scholarly interpretations of Orwell by academic "critic-readers" than toward his reputation among classroom "teacher-readers" and "student-readers." This emphasis will allow us, as we grapple with the dynamics of Orwell's reputation, not only to examine the historical reception of his work but also to address periodically the institutional context of its production, distribution and transmission in the schools and in educational publishing.

We will return to these conceptual issues as we relate the anomalies of Orwell's present-day educational institutionalization and their implications for canon- and reputation-formation to the development of his curricular reputation. This history has evolved on three distinct educational levels (junior and senior high school, and college) and in four phases since the early 1950s.[2]

I

Like most countries, neither the U. S. nor Britain has a national syllabus of required school texts. In the U. S., individual schools, or school districts, usually establish curricula. Only elementary school textbooks are chosen at the state level (and only in 22 states). The traditional British "set book" policy, however, in which readings are "set" for external examinations by regional Examination Boards in cooperation with their Local Education Authorities, introduces a greater measure of uniformity and consensus about appropriate school texts—though by no means a "national canon." Orwell's work—specifically *Animal Farm*—first entered English O[rdinary]-level (16-year-old) classes in the 1950s. Composed of examiners and teachers, Examination Boards for O-level (and sometimes for the AO [Alternative Ordinary] level) began prescribing *Animal Farm* every three or four years after 1958 (Davidson; Galvin; Davis; King; Lambert). (The fable is also often read in British classes before the O-level year, as early as the age of 13, whether or not it is later studied for the external examinations.) (Squire and Appplebee 96). *Animal Farm* appears to have entered American eighth- to tenth-grade classrooms at roughly the same time.

Why did *Animal Farm* join *Silas Marner* and *Great Expectations* as a standard fiction assignment in many Anglo-American class-rooms in the late 1950s? "It is such a useful teaching text for pupils of a wide range of ability," wrote one British educational official. "It is short, entertaining, makes a suitable impact, and is acceptable at a variety of levels" (Fain). Surely brevity, readability, perceived literary merit, and sufficiency to the assigned task and grade level have been significant considerations — as in the case of such main-stays as *Silas Marner* and *Great Expectations*. But politically wary teachers might justly cast a cold eye on talk about the "usefulness" and "suitable impact" of *Animal Farm*. Indeed many interacting and overlapping factors, impossible to weigh precisely — some quite routine and others historically specific and particular to *Animal Farm* — obviously contributed to its acceptance in the 1950s: its wide availability in cheap paperback editions, the turn by American high schools away from anthology selections and back toward "high quality" paperback books, the shift toward contemporary literature in American secondary schools, the new orientation of the National Council of Teachers of English (NCTE) toward a balance of socially relevant and artistically respected fiction in the late '50s, the convenient existence of the 1954 cartoon film, the effects of the Cold War on Anglo-American curricula, the easy use of *Animal Farm*. Indeed many interacting and overlapping factors, impossible to weigh precisely — some quite routine and others historically specific and particular to *Animal Farm* — as an anti-Communist and anti-revolutionary lesson — all these factors, plus Orwell's rising status among intellectuals and the TV public's growing familiarity with his work in the wake of the 1953 NBC and 1954 BBC television adaptations of *1984*, doubtless helped lay the groundwork for the fable's canonization (and for the adoption of *1984* as a school novel a few years later).[3]

Equally important is the related question of how *Animal Farm* was actually taught in the 1950s and '60s. It is clear that the Cold War affected some English school programs, especially in the U. S., but hard to determine its precise impact on Orwell's work (Caute 320; Neumann). Scattered evidence suggests that teachers, then and now, have veered between two pedagogical approaches. Some have presented *Animal Farm* as an entertaining story, tacking on the bromide that "Power corrupts" but downplaying the Russian parallels (as does the Halas-Bacheler film). Other teachers have taught it point-by-point as a horrifying "animallegory" of Soviet despotism. Study guides dating from the mid-1960s (e.g., Cliffs Notes and Monarch Notes) take the latter approach, usually offering chapter-by-chapter summaries of the correspondences between Russian history and the fable's characters and events. Among the guides' sample test questions are the following, each of which receives a two-paragraph "model" answer:

Whom do Snowball and Napoleon represent? (Ranald 95)

How may the character of Boxer be interpreted? (Ranald 98)

Assemble details which obviously refer to characteristic aspects of Russian society. The decorations given and the naming of battles are two. Find as many as you can (Thompson 50).

O-Level exam questions in England, though more sophisticated, have been similarly phrased and have leaned in the same political direction, as the three questions below from two 1964 exams illustrate:

Give an account of the building of the Windmill and its interruptions; show how far this affected the animals and what, in real life, it is meant to represent.

Describe the origins of the seven commandments, and give an account of the changes they underwent later. What was Orwell's satire directed against in this part of the book?

Write an essay defending *Animal Farm* against a reader who tells you that it is 'merely anti-Communist propaganda.' Illustrate your answer with detailed reference to the book (cited in Brown 48-9).

Questions like this last one instruct students to defend *Animal Farm* by way of subtly inculcating a standard of political taste; the very tone of the question disposes the examinee to imagine that any radical critic of Orwell is invariably a tiresome nuisance, a mere propagandist himself. (One easily forgets Orwell's oft-declared view that "all art is propaganda.") (Orwell 4.359). Such questions do indeed verge on "a manipulative form of 'thought-policing,'" in one radical's pharse, and their ideological thrust is transparent (Brown 243). Another leftist, D.A.N. Jones, a teacher of Nigerian children in the 1950s, has written that his Commonwealth text of *Animal Farm* stressed Orwell's anti-Communism and passed over his socialist convictions altogether. If so, it would come as little surprise. In his introduction to the 1956 Signet edition, which has sold millions of paperback copies, C. M. Wodehouse quotes Orwell's famous statement in "Why I Write": "Every line I have written since 1936 has been against totalitarianism . . . " —thus vaporizing half of Orwell's sentence ("and for democratic social-ism, as I understand it.") and his radicalism with it (Wodehouse xi). Such use of ellipses is, unfortunately, a frequent practice in the politics of reputation.

Jones has further claimed that *Animal Farm* was chosen as a set book for the colonies because it was "a clear-cut expression of the anti-Communist orthodoxy" (159). Such a claim is impossible to verify. The preface to the special Overseas edition of *Animal Farm* by Longman in 1960, however, treats the fable as a general satire on revolution and makes no mention of Russia, Marx, Stalin or Lenin (Brander v-xxii).

Still, the prevalence of questions like those above since the 1950s suggests the structural "fit" between the demand, whether overt or implicit, for anti-Communist propaganda and a "simple lesson" like *Animal Farm.* Just as *Homage to Catalonia* supposedly filled a social-psychological need within the liberal New York intelligentsia for a fellow radical to furnish an eyewitness, unapolo-getic, moral and political condemnation of Stalinist practices in the Spanish Civil War, *Animal Farm* filled, as probably no other con-temporary work could, a public need during the Cold War era to wipe out the Communist menace, especially in the schools, and thereby safeguard impressionable youth. Alan Brown has argued persuasively that the fable has typically been taught since the 1950s as a "simple equivalence" between Soviet history and the book's events, with students then eagerly mining the allegory for parallels. The correspondences then become the basis for rote-learning, with students "regurgitat[ing] the equations of Cold War wisdom" (Brown 247).[4] My own experience in teaching *Animal Farm*, along with the film adaptation, to tenth-grade students in the 1970s, partly confirms Brown's indictment: I found my own teaching tending towards these reductionist practices, despite my attempts at nuance. Sometimes students concluded (prodded by their study guides) that the fable's version of history constituted the whole story; a few student essays slid into anti-Soviet tirades. And yet such dangers are hard to avoid entirely if *Animal Farm* is actually taught as a satiric allegory. I discovered that much of the excitement of the re-reading experience for my students lay in their realizing that the book *was* an allegory with a serious subtext (of which many were unaware until class discussion). With 14- and 15-year-old students who have never even heard the names Lenin and Stalin, it may not be possible to present the intricacies of socialist theory and Soviet history. Once again, the plain style of Orwell's "only seemingly simple" fiction masks the intricate context (Crick "Readings"). Indeed it may be that this little book, so clear on the surface, should be saved for the eleventh and twelfth grades. I have found that college freshmen discuss well all the issues which *Animal Farm* raises — e.g., the Russian Revolution, Bolshevism, utopianism, the rewriting of history, the deterioration of political language, the media's "proletarianization" of the citizenry, the betrayal of the intellectuals, the allegory and fable as literary forms.

II

Although a 1955 secondary school survey showed that *1984* was one of thirty novels most commonly read by college-bound seniors, it was not widely taught in schools until the early 1960s (Friedman

423). Its entry into senior high school classrooms at this time marks a second stage and level of Orwell's canonization. (The timing should make clear that, although Cold War politics no doubt conditioned how Orwell's work was taught, it was not the prime determining factor in the selection of his books for classroom use.)

1984 occupies a different, and less secure, place than *Animal Farm* in school canons. Invariably, *1984* is read at more advanced grades; it belongs to what could be called the "senior high school canon," whereas *Animal Farm* would normally be classed in the "junior high school canon." In the U. S., *1984* is most frequently read in the twelfth grade, sometimes as a science fiction novel (Burton 46).   In England *1984* has sometimes been set for A[dvanced]-level (18-year-old) students, though (except during 1983-84) it has never been so popular an examination text as *Animal Farm*.

Numerous reasons account for *1984*'s being less commonly taught than *Animal Farm* in schools. In America, its greater length has probably deterred teachers from assigning it. Whereas teachers not bound to anthologies are frequently encouraged to innovate in their selection of poems, plays, and short fiction for syllabuses, curricular guides have often advised caution in the choice of full-length novels, since a month or more of class time may be required for a novel (Knapton and Evans 19-21). Parents and educators have also found the love scene between Winston and Julia objectionable; a few school boards have even banned *1984*. Controversy about its sexual content was probably a key factor in its delayed entry into American schoolrooms. Even during the McCarthy era, parental opposition to *1984* on moral grounds was evidently more powerful than anti-Communist support for it on political grounds. (In fact, one comprehensive retrospective survey in the 1970s found that *1984* "never failed to appear" on postwar lists of censored books.) ("Censorship" 65-6).

In England, where censorship in the schools in rarely a community issue, the examination structure largely explains why *1984* is less often set as an exam book than *Animal Farm*. *1984* does not easily fit examiners' expectations for texts at either O- or A-level.

Understandably, it is often regarded as too difficult to be an O-level set book. The A-level exam for which *1984* could be set in the "Practical Criticism" exam, where traditional critical standards (organic unity, character development, etc.) have often made it appear inappropriate, a "failed" novel possessing insufficient literary merit. As the following three A-level questions from 1972-73 illustrate, the judgment of *1984*'s "failure" is usually advanced indirectly. Students are invited to "agree," rather than contest, the authoritative statements (enshrined in quotation marks) of the anonymous examiners that *1984* is "diminished" as literature by its political purpose:

> "*1984* is unashamedly a book with a message." Do you consider that this diminishes its merits as a novel?

> "The political message is constantly getting in the way of the story, and this diminishes its interest and excitement." Do you agree with this view of *1984*?

> "Characterization in this novel is negligible. It is completely subordinated to the political message." Do you agree? (cited in Brown 55-6)

Needless to say, the very idea of "testing" readers about a book indicates how the conditions of the student-reader differ from those of most other readers. And this raises the large, elusive question of how the institutional reading experience of Orwell—as a classroom "assignment"—has conditioned his public reputation. But we should immediately distinguish between those books set for examinations and those suggested as "outside" reading. Studies show that students strongly prefer books they choose to read, and that they enjoy a book less once it becomes an examination subject (Protherough 131-32, 139). *1984* is possibly read more outside class than for class by students; reading surveys show that it is one of the few "classics" many students buy for leisure reading (Algra and Fillbrandt). This element of student choice probably has contributed to *1984*'s popularity among students. In a 1969 survey, university-bound British and American students ranked *1984* among their most "personally significant" books. British students also listed Orwell in fourth position as "the author who had greatest influence on them" (Squire and Applebee 110-11). A 1971 survey among A-level students found Orwell, after Lawrence, the most popular "serious" author (with Hardy third, and Shakespeare fourth) (Yarlott and Harpin 92). Orwell was also the only author with two books among students' top twenty "favorites," as judged by a 1975 survey of American teachers (Hipple 23).[5] Asked to suggest titles which should be added to the required English program, both British and American students also cited *1984* among their first choices. (One wonders whether such a curricular change would undercut *1984*'s appeal, particularly since most of the students' suggested additions were "forbidden fruit," in the survey editor's phrase — e.g., *Catcher in the Rye* and *Brave New World*.) (Squire and Applebee 110).

A great deal of reading is conducted, of course, within the school as a social institution, with numerous attendant advantages and constraints. Certainly many teacher-readers and critic-readers return to Orwell, not always eagerly, with a professional purpose (to teach, to write criticism). The student-reader, however, is in a slightly different situation. For a sizable number of students, even their first reading of Orwell's work is not self-initiated: they encounter *Animal Farm* and *1984* as "required reading." Possibly the majority of young readers would never otherwise read Orwell, and doubtless many of them profit from reading him under the guidance of teachers. Surely a large number, however, do not enjoy reading Orwell in class, and find the experience vulgar with purpose in that its end is examination performance. One 1979 British educational report found that reading had been "impoverished" in secondary schools by a concentration on exam requirements (Reported in Protherough 10). Another report showed that "Practical Criticism" is the exam most frequently failed at A-level (Mathieson 21). (One recalls the hostile attitude of the author of "Such, Such Were the Joys" toward exams.) The situation may be even worse in Britain than in the U. S., at least during the O- and A-level years, when the small number of set books are sometimes analyzed in excessive detail, critical terminology is drummed into students, and classes are turned into cram sessions —

all directed toward an artificial situation, in which the student has an hour, without the text, to deal with topics like "the merits of *1984* as a novel." Exams, of course, may be among the necessary evils of student life. But there is no need that student answers be mired in the overuse and misuse of critical terms—or that exam questions, as exemplified by those about *1984* mentioned above, impose categories on students' reading experiences, thereby constricting, rather than awakening, their responses to books.

III

While both British and American schools have each accorded Orwell's fiction a place of comparable significance and taught it similarly, the same cannot be said for Orwell's nonfiction. Only occasionally have English schools set Orwell's documentaries and selections of his essays as exam books (variously at O-level, AO-level, and A-level since the early 1960s, assigned approximately every other year by at least one examination board) (King; Lambert; Fain); and English teachers have taught his essays as much for their subject matter as style (See Bott). By contrast, in the U. S. Orwell's essays are standard reading, being taught as prose models in introductory college composition courses. Because most British universities do not have courses comparable to these American writing courses, British students do not normally encounter Orwell's essays in class at the post-secondary level.

Indeed, so widely used are Orwell's essays in American composition courses that it may be a more common experience for an American to read an Orwell essay in college than to read either *Animal Farm* or *1984* in high school. Most frequently anthologized are "Politics and the English Language" and "Shooting an Elephant," both of which began to enter composition readers in the early 1950s (On PEL, see O'Connor; Stone and Hoppes; on SAE, see Locke; Wise). After the 1956 publication of *The Orwell Reader*, composition anthologies also began to include some selections from *Down and Out in Paris and London*, *The Road to Wigan Pier*, and *1984*.[6] This development illustrates the interaction between publishing and canon-formation.   By making handily available "pre-packaged" excerpts from an author's *oeuvre*, a well-edited collected volume can facilitate the institutionalizing of new works and the growth of a reputation.[7]

Orwell's essays acquired the status of composition classics in the 1960s. Per the Matthew Effect, which postulates that the status system operates to award recognition disproportionately to those who already possess it, anthology editors aiming to avoid "overfamiliar" essays like "Politics and the English Language" and "Shooting an Elephant" often turned not to other essayists but to less familiar essays by Orwell himself (e.g., "Marrakech," "A Hanging," "Why I Write," "Such, Such Were the Joys," "Writers and Leviathan," "The Art of Donald McGill"), with even minor journalism ("The Moon Under Water") entering anthologies after the publication of Orwell's *Collected Essays, Journalism and Letters* of 1968 (See Shroder; Smart; Levin; Kennedy). Author of composition handbooks excerpted "exemplary passages" of Orwell's plain style, sermonized on prose style via "Politics and the English Language," and added luster to grammatical rules by name-dropping "Orwell."   Some composition handbooks of the 1960s and '70s quote Orwell more frequently than any other "authority" (Hodges and Whitten; Stone and Bell); in some composition readers of this period Orwell is represented by more selections than any other writer (Stone and Bell).[8]

Questions in instructors' manuals often serve as the basis of class discussion, suggesting even more clearly than in the case of the exam questions how images of an author radiate throughout an institutional audience — e.g., from editor to teacher to student. Biographical questions dominate some manuals' approaches to Orwell's essays, as in the following questions for "Marrakech" in the manual for William Smart's widely-used *Eight Modern Essayists*:

> Discuss the qualities you most admire in George Orwell.
> Based on "Shooting an Elephant" and "Marrakech," discuss V. S. Pritchett's statement that Orwell was "the conscience of his generation" (8).

Such questions place Orwell's personality center-stage, spot-lighting his "virtue" and "integrity." The study guides do likewise, uncritically identifying the writer's "pure" style with the man's "saintliness." "Orwell's style shows the simple, self-conscious qual-ity of his own personality," declares the Cliffs Notes for *Animal Farm*. The Monarch Notes for *Animal Farm* calls Orwell "a sort of modern-day saint" and asserts that Orwell and Eileen Blair had "an ideal relationship," since both of them were "saintly ascetics." The Cliffs Notes for *1984* likewise personalizes the prose craftsman, calling him a "lumberjack" who used words for an "ax" and a "magician" who wove a "spell" in language. It also asks the student to imagine, in inviting him to compare *1984* with the international political scene of the 1980s, that he *is* George Orwell. That these emphases on Orwell's character come within the context of discussions of *Animal Farm* and *1984* makes clear that his reputation as The Model Stylist and Defender of the King's English is not founded solely on the essays. The former image is partly based on the simple, economical style of *Animal Farm*; the latter image is significantly indebted to *1984*'s Newspeak and the Ministry of Truth (Hillegas 51; Ranald 22; see also Borman 44-5).

This double image of Orwell as prose laureate and guardian was officially institutionalized in the 1970s by the NCTE, which began making annual awards in Orwell's name. Following Orwell's "intention to expose inhumane propogandistic uses of language," the NCTE's Committee on Public Doublespeak presents the ironic tribute of the Doublespeak Award to a deserving public figure; and the NCTE also bestows the George Orwell Award for Distin-guished Contributed to Honesty and Clarity in Public Language. No other English or American writer has prompted the establish-ment of tributes to his legacy by an official national body like the NCTE; and certainly no other author bears positive and ironic awards in his name (*Cf.* Lutz).[9]

Orwell's distinctively plain style has obviously had much to do with the formation of these images and the canonization of his essays as composition models. And the ascension of his reputation as an essayist, in turn, is surely linked to the rise of the plain style in our postwar "information age." As late as the 1940s Cyril Connolly could still speak well of the latinate mandarin style of Gibbon and Carlyle, but by the 1960s the tradition of which Orwell has been regarded as the twentieth-century master—that "familiar" style represented by Dryden, Swift, Defoe and Hazlitt—informal, conversational, clean, fast-moving—had won the allegiance of most educators and intellectuals. Prose had come to imitate journalism, and journalism had become artistic and professional.

Yet Orwell's essays would probably never have been so widely adopted in introductory composition courses had it not specifically been for the changing conception of the college course during the 1950s. Until then, most freshman composition courses were literature survey courses, with selections from the classical literary canon serving as prose models. English departments saw their mission as the teaching of literature, not writing. "Error-Comp," which emphasized the ability to write "correct" English in the plain style according to certain modes (description, narration, exposition, argumentation) joined traditional "Lit-Comp" during the decade as the prevailing pedagogy (See Lloyd-Jones; Gould; Shugrue); the resultant combination of the two approaches and the fortuitous timing proved highly favorable to Orwell's work. Writing instructors discerned the pedagogical advantages of using Orwell's essays, which encourage good writing by both precept and example: "Politics and the English Language" and "Why I Write" discuss the "how" and "why" of writing; ""Shooting an Elephant" and "Marrakech" present themselves as the finished models. (Many composition anthologies of the '60s through '80s suggest student assignments such as "Evaluate 'Shooting an Elephant' according to Orwell's advice in 'Politics and the English Language.'") Also, Orwell wrote a sufficient number of varied, short essays that his work offered numerous excellent instances of the standard prose modes of Error-Comp: description ("Marrakech," "A Hanging"), narration ("Shooting an Elephant"), exposition ("The Art of Donald McGill," "England Your England"), and argumentation ("Why I Write").

It was perhaps inevitable that, after the NCTE's institution of the Doublespeak Award (1973) and George Orwell Award (1974), the pedagogical worth of Orwell's essays would be subject to reassessment in the late '70s and '80s. Revisionist judgment centered on "Politics and the English Language," on which one teacher archly bestowed "the golden essay award for 'most anthologized essay in college texts'" (Brouse 218). Teachers of the '50s and '60s had valued the essay for its discussion of economy and honesty in writing and its attention to the connection between good writing and good citizenship. Even as the Watergate Affair was providing fresh material for use in teaching the essay, however, liberals and radicals began disagreeing sharply about its merit — and about the wisdom of elevating Orwell's plain style as a writing model. Liberal-Left defenders praised the populism of the plain style and its fitness for a variety of tasks. Wrote Irving Howe: "And when my students ask, 'Whom shall I read in order to write better,' I answer, 'Orwell, the master of the plain style, that style which seems so easy to copy and is yet almost impossible to reach'" ("As the Bones" 34). Radicals saw such views as part of "the Orwell myth" and stressed getting beyond "the fifties relic" represented by Lionel Trilling's image of Orwell as the radiant "figure of the man who tells the truth" (McNelly 566; Trilling xi). Deriding Orwell's "fetishizing of the particular" and aversion to system, one teacher argued that the "liberal empiricism" of the plain style served to mask the interrelations between individualism and capitalist hegemony. The "immense academic prestige" of "Politics and the English Language" maintained the notion that the plain style was the only style, he added, urging that the plain style be taught *as* the plain style (i.e., with attention to its ideological implications) rather than as "good English" (Freedman 337-40).

Other teachers discussed the practical difficulties of teaching Orwell's essays in freshman composition. Cleo McNelly noted that "Politics and the English Language," though a fine essay, presumes far more than one should in speaking to beginning student writers, many of whom simply do not possess the level of cultural literacy and range of prose techniques necessary to benefit from the essay's advice; e.g., choose short words, avoid dead metaphors, and cut unnecessary words out. Many freshmen can't "follow" these and other "rules" of Orwell, argued McNelly, because they possess limited lexicons, can't distinguish between live and dead metaphors, and can't even meet minimum word limits. Orwell's famous sixth rule ("Break any of these rules sooner than say anything outright barbarous") doesn't help them because they often just can't recognize barbarisms. Most of her freshman, said McNelly, respond to this and other Orwell essays "with a neutral or negative stare." "Orwell's essays," she concluded, "are prime examples . . . of how *not* to teach composition" (McNelly 553; see also O'Shaughnessy).

Having taught several of Orwell's essays in freshman composition, I find myself in unfortunate agreement with McNelly's analysis, though my conclusions differ. To start off, the problem is not Orwell's essays but the poor writing skills of college students. Beginning student writers, especially those who do not read much and are from disadvantaged backgrounds, do find it difficult to model their work on Orwell's. They don't "hear" Orwell's "living voice." Asked to evaluate the prose of an editorial or public speech in light of Orwell's "Politics and the English Language," beginning students often ape the outraged, doubting tone of Orwell, but without his clarity and insight. Indeed Orwell's "rules" almost invite beginning writers to take a "detective" approach toward such an assignment, and to confuse the use of idioms with politically distorted language. Beginning students rarely possess the verbal and intellectual resources to engage in Orwell's skillful rhetorical analysis, so instead they reduce writing to rules and Orwell to a rules-monger. They seize on the "don'ts" and "nevers" of "Politics and the English Language." They mechanically "apply" Orwell's "rules"—but with little sense of appropriateness or audience, so that Orwell's caveats obstruct rather promote effective writing.

A different problem emerges when writing teachers take a non-rhetorical, "literary" approach toward Orwell's narrative essays. Writing instructors frequently teach an essay like "Shooting an Elephant" not as a prose model but as a short story—and engage chiefly in exegesis or biographical criticism rather than in rhetorical analysis. They conclude class sessions by giving students a comparative assignment in personal narrative, e.g., "Relate an incident in which you acted to 'solely avoid looking a fool.' Use concrete detail." Such courses no doubt heighten students' critical appreciation of Orwell's essays; but students' writing skills, especially in the area of their greatest weakness, analytical argument, remain undeveloped.[10] The fact is that introductory composition courses should place more emphasis on analysis and argument, for which essays like "Shooting an Elephant" are inappropriate models.[11]

Orwell's essays, then, are indeed examples of how not to teach composition—*to beginning students.* Model essays should be sufficiently accessible to allow readers to imitate the author's writing strategies and to identify with his or her writing situation; and more models of fine argument (and less devotion to the procrustean categories of Error-Comp) are needed. (Outstanding student essays would probably serve as better argumentation models.) Nevertheless, I have found several Orwell essays useful for advanced composition, where students usually do appreciate "Politics and the English Language" and are sufficiently skilled in prose argument to justify focusing on narration and description via Orwell's other essays. I have also discovered Orwell's essays fitting for introductory literature courses which include the short story. (Here again one notices the ironies in Orwell's canonical status; his firm place in freshman composition, where his work is not well-suited, and its exclusion from upper-class English literature courses, where he should, arguably, be better represented.)

Yet the issue of whether or not Orwell's essays are "appropriate" as prose models probably says more about American education than about Orwell's work per se. Moreover, we should remember that Orwell wrote for literate London audiences and never considered himself a "proletarian" writer, let alone a juvenile writer. "Politics and the English Language" originally appeared in *Horizon.* The essay assumed one could write, if badly, not that one needed to learn *how* to write. As editor of the London *Observer,* David Astor circulated the essay as a model to reporters in the late

'40s (Crick *George Orwell* 495). But that "Politics and the English Language" commends itself as a model fit for beginning student writers. Orwell freely admitted that the essay's advice was meant for himself as much as anyone else. His six "rules" were really based on his awareness of his own bad habits, which he constantly struggled to ward off. Indeed the essay should be read as a companion piece to "Why I Write" (written a few months later), showing an experienced writer with an irrepressible "joy of mere words" reminding himself and others to resist "purple passages" and write "less picturesquely and more exactly" (Orwell 1.9). Good prose is like window-washing: the writer as craftsman strives to wipe clean his smudges so that his clear pane or prose will let his meaning shine forth.

IV

An enormous upsurge of interest in Orwell's work occurred at all educational levels during the much-publicized "countdown to 1984" in the early 1980s. In England, Longman issued special school editions of *Animal Farm* and *1984* in 1984. *1984* was taught on all levels, with some schools even requesting that special O-level exams be devised at school expense. Orwell's essays were also set for A-level exams by many Boards in 1983-84.[12] The loudest discordant note was D. S. Savage's diatribe against Orwell in *The New Pelican Guide to English Literature*. It was the only hostile critique of a writer in the eight-volume series and most unusual in a "guide" book intended as a reference work (Savage).

Meanwhile, in the U. S., entire college courses were devoted to *1984* during the title year (Carpenter). Political theory, sociology, and history courses made increasing use of *Burmese Days, Keep the Aspidistra Flying,* and *Coming Up For Air*. Whereas in the 1970s British radicals were charging that *Animal Farm* was used in high schools as anti-Soviet propaganda, in the 1980s neoconservatives were protesting that *1984* was being taught as if it applied not just to totalitarian states but also (or primarily) to the Western democracies (Podhoretz). Lobbying efforts to proscribe *1984* by right-wing groups intensified, with the ironic result that *1984* was one of the most widely assigned *and* most severely criticized books in American schools in 1983-84. (In its 1983 list of Top Ten Classics, the Association of American Publishers ranked *1984* first [and *Animal Farm* third]; meanwhile the American Booksellers Association included *1984* on its 1983 list of books which libraries and bookstores had recently been pressured to remove from their shelves ("Politics"; Hechinger). Inevitably, civil libertarians like the editors of *Penthouse* used the occasion to warn against the coming spectre of a right-wing *1984*.) (Davis; see also Nellis).

With the passing of 1984, Orwell's fiction and nonfiction once again largely disappeared from upper-division college literature courses. The absence of Orwell's work from most courses in British literature is an interesting phenomenon. It is the result of an odd confluence of received truths: *Animal Farm* and *1984* are "high-school reading," the essay is not really "literature," and the "realistic" tradition of the modern British novel is inferior. How these three judgments have solidified and interacted, and how they have structured Orwell's academic reputation by level and genre, and have thereby operated to *exclude* as well as include Orwell as a "canonized author," merits attention here.

First of all, probably the rapid entry of *Animal Farm* into school curricula in the 1950s served to fix an image of Orwell as a "school" author. For academic reputation derives chiefly from the opinions of those "on high," not below, and it is typical for a reputation to radiate "outward" and "downward." The reverse, given the dynamics of reputation-formation, is less common. Moreover, just as critics' "first impressions" of an author continue to weigh heavily in subsequent evaluations of him, how an author makes his institutional "debut" — into the schools, media, or any other sphere of repute — often buoys or burdens him for years to come. For better or worse, revaluation usually lags behind reality. This tendency has operated both to win Orwell an enduring place in the schools and to frustrate his entry into university syllabuses. As one Examination Board official explained, once an author gets "set" in Britain, he tends to stay set. "Schools have only limited funds available for buying textbooks, and there is considerable pressure, therefore, on us to set texts that schools already possess" (Lambert). The same is true in American high schools. Economic considerations may out-weigh literary and pedagogical ones. (Which is another reason why *Silas Marner* and *Great Expectations* become school fixtures.)[13] When a high school has purchased 600 copies of a book, it will not only use them year after year, but often assign them, round robin, to several different grades throughout the years, thus maximizing their economic value through continuous use. (Hence the practical payoff of investing in an author "acceptable at a variety of levels.")

Such practices keep authors out as well as in. *Animal Farm* and *1984* are still taught in schools in the 1980s, sometimes for the rea-sons cited above. But I also suspect that *Animal Farm*'s institu-tionalization at the secondary school level in the 1950s—when the values of Matthew Arnold, T. S. Eliot, and the New Critics were dominant in Anglo-American academic criticism—added legitimacy to the dismissal of Orwell by some academic critics as a "lightweight" or "teenage" author. The entry of *1984* into British and American schools in the early 1960s probably reinforced this impression, as did the adoption of Orwell's essays in freshman col-lege composition courses.

In none of these cases did Orwell's work enter college literature courses. The essays were not treated as literature. No widely-used English literature anthologies of the '50s and '60s included Orwell's essays, though pieces by Chesterton, Maugham, Max Beerbohm, W. H. Hudson, H. M. Tomilinson, Lawrence, Woolf, David Cecil, C. P. Snow and others appeared. Not until the 1973 edition of the massive two-volume *Oxford Anthology of English Literature* did an anthology include a short excerpt (from "England Your England") of Orwell's prose. And here we should, strictly speaking, qualify our characterization of Orwell's essays as "canonical." Technically, they have been canonical as "prose models" but not as "essays." However widely they are anthologized and presented in freshman composition as "prose models," they are rarely taught as "essays" and do not really belong to any formal essay canon. English literature curricula—not anthologies—define periods and genres, and thereby establish formal, exclusivist, stable, professionally-recognized canons. English curricula feature period courses in poetry, fiction and drama—and even in "minor" genres like lyric, epic, romance, and so on—but not in the essay. Considered an amorphous genre, "a catch-all term for nonfictional prose of limited length," the essay is treated as a sundry, grabbag category, in to which is thrown "subliterary" prose like editorials, humorous sketches, and occasional journalism—anything that doesn't belong elsewhere (Scholes and Klaus).

The exclusion of *Animal Farm, 1984*, and the essays from the "high" canon further illumines the dynamics of reputation-formation in the academy. It first demonstrates that levels of canonization can and do conflict. In particular, entry into a "lower" canon often constrains, rather than facilitates, admittance into "higher" canons—usually according to some variant of the notion that an accessible, "popular" author cannot be "serious" too. "Generic hierarchy" plays a determining role in the making of reputation (Fowler). Where an author gets "placed" in the generic class-system—as "novelist" versus "literary journalist" or "essayist"—is crucial to the development of his or her reputation. Some genres get exiled from or discriminated against in the high canon. So even distinguished achievement in a genre of mediocre or vague literary status (the essay, the fable, the utopia) may doom a writer to exclusion from the high canon.

Furthermore, just as curricula establish formal canons, educators establish curricula. That is, literary academics—though admittedly influenced greatly by literary-political intellectuals, publishers, and others—ultimately "make" the university canon. Literary-political intellectuals do not. They may shape cultural opinion through their journals and books, "leading the way" for institutional acceptance, but they do not directly establish curricula. And so the fact that leading Anglo-American intellectuals of the liberal-Left (Trilling, Howe, Alfred Kazin, V. S. Pritchett, George Woodcock) and Right (John Wain, Norman Podhoretz) unite in their admiration for Orwell does not guarantee his entry into university literature classrooms. Intellectuals are often "reputation-makers" and even "figure-makers," but they are not necessarily "canon-makers." (Nor do historians or other academics exert great influence on the *literary* canon.) All this helps explain the apparent paradox of Orwell's eclectic educational canonization, especially his "relative absence from the literary scene," in Cleo McNelly's words. McNelly suggests that Orwell was too radical in the 1950s and '60s to be brought "above stairs" into college literature classrooms (McNelly 566, 554). But this seems doubtful. (Non-experimental writers of Orwell's generation, like Waugh, fared little better; Auden's early work was widely taught.) The crucial fact is that postwar literary academics, beholden to Arnoldian and modernist principles, approached Orwell according to formalist criteria — and judged his work "simplistic," with the meaning of books like *Animal Farm* just "there," lamentably "on the surface," and requiring no labor of exegesis. They therefore relegated Orwell to the schools as an admirably "accessible" author, but not "a major writer." (The verdict has persisted. Orwell was not an eligible choice for the "major author" category of my English Ph.D. examinations in the 1980s.) I suspect that Orwell's relatively lower standing with English professors than with politically-minded intellectuals has much to do with the differing identities of the two groups. Literary academics as a group have not expressed intense personal or professional admiration for Orwell. On the other hand, although Howe, Kazin and Woodcock has each taught for years in the academy, each has also seen himself as an intellectual rather than an English professor, and has seen Orwell in turn as a model writer and man.

This difference bears on the third reason for Orwell's exclusion from the high canon, namely the devaluation of the "realistic" or social-political novel of the twentieth century. In effect, Henry James "won" the so-called great debate against H. G. Wells on the purpose of the novel during the war years, and The Great Tradition of the modern British novel has been shaped accordingly. Orwell's absence from the high canon is partly explained by his fiction's lying outside the Jamesian-Eliotic-Leavisite tradition, which has retrospectively restructured not only authors but also periods into "major" and "minor" in terms favorable to itself. Its influence has been especially marked upon the reputations of authors and works of the late nineteenth and twentieth centuries; its version of "The Tradition" has largely won acceptance as "modern English literary history." Orwell is not alone among its prominent victims. (For instance, period courses in British literature often skip from the Victorians to modernists, giving cursory or no attention to the years of the Decadents, Edwardians and Georgians, since these do not constitute "major" periods.) In this respect Orwell's exclusion from The Great Tradition of the British novel takes on much larger implications than his own case. It points to the existence of a severely restricted canon ignoring another "great tradition," one which Orwell himself identified in his review of Leavis's enormously influential *The Great Tradition*. Orwell pointed to the realistic or rhetorical tradition, traceable to Defoe, Fielding, Smollett, and Dickens, which continues, albeit with little curricular acknowledgment, on through Butler, Gissing, Wells Bennett, Galsworthy, Orwell and Amis. "But surely a book on the English novel," Orwell concluded his review, titled "Exclusive Club," "ought at least to mention Smollett, Surtees, Samuel Butler, Mark Rutherford and George Gissing?" (3).

Silence, of course, is a major instrument in the politics of reputation. For reputations in the rarified "high" canon live or die on the oxygen of classes, criticism and new editions. This essay has not set itself the task of arguing the upward or downward revaluation of Orwell's reputation,[14] but we may note here that the banishment of an entire line of historically (and artistically) significant writers — a line of writers who, moreover, obviously derive more directly than Joyce and Woolf from the original "great tradition" of the British eighteenth-century novel — has reflected and reinforced Orwell's own exile.[15]

"Nature didn't intend him to be a novelist," Mrs. Leavis pronounced in her otherwise flattering 1940 essay-review of Orwell. One doubts that the appearance of *Animal Farm* and *1984* in the next decade would have broadened her categories or changed her mind. Yet she could hardly have pondered the consequences for the Leavisite Great Tradition when she concluded:

> Perhaps the best thing for him and the best thing for us would be to export him to interpret English Literature. . . . Everyone would benefit. . . . (189-90)

How inclusive she meant her "us" and "everyone" to be is hard to say. But not the least of the beneficiaries, one imagines, would be The Model Stylist and Defender of the King's English himself — and his "only seemingly simple" last works of fiction, *Animal Farm* and *1984.*

Notes

1. On Orwell's influence on these and other Movement writers of the 1950s, see Rodden "The Rope."

2. I based this historical reconstruction on teachers' discussions of curricula in British and American education journals, on personal correspondence with British and American education officials, on American study guides of *Animal Farm* and *1984*, on the contents of anthologies and composition textbooks, on personal conversations with instructors who have taught Orwell, and on my own experience as a college and high school teacher of English and composition.

3. On the turn by American schools toward paperbacks, contemporary literature, and "quality" fiction, see Applebee 129, 170, 189, 204.

4. Communists also betrayed a knee-jerk "Cold War wisdom" when it came to Orwell's work. See Thomas's humorous story of Chinese students asking to drop his course when "Orwell" appeared on the syllabus. (Notably, the class was not reading *Animal Farm* or *1984*, but rather "Marrakech," "The Sporting Spirit," and excerpts from *The Road to Wigan Pier*.) For a discussion of O-level exams and *Animal Farm*'s use, see Jackson.

5. Of course, students' reading preferences are surely influenced — indirectly, directly, or negatively — by teachers' preferences. A 1979 survey also showed *Animal Farm* among teachers' favorite books to teach. See Stephen and Susan Judy.

6. For instance, after the publication of *The Orwell Reader*, edited by Richard Rovere, excerpts from *The Road to Wigan Pier* identical to those in Rovere's collection appeared in Beal and Korg; and Rovere's excerpts from *1984* also later appeared in Kallsen and McCoy.

7. The interaction between literary reputation, canon-formation, and the sociology of occupations is well-illustrated by how the rise of the New York intellectuals to national prominence in the 1950s led to Orwell's increased representation in composition readers. As the New Yorkers became more influential in the New York publishing world, they edited more anthologies and readers — and, understandably, excerpted themselves and their favorite writers, one of whom was Orwell. See Howe "1984"; Fielder; Kazin; and Coser.

8. In my survey of sixty prose anthologies from the 1950s through 1980s, Orwell's essays were among the most frequent selections. See, for example, the widely-used readers by Muscatine and Griffith and by Stafford and Candelaria, both of which contain more essays by Orwell than any other author.

9. Lutz also edits the *Quarterly Journal of Doublespeak*, which devotes itself to Orwell's concerns about language abuse in public discourse.
   Well-known Doublespeak awardees have included Yasir Arafat (1975), the nuclear power industry (1979), Ronald Reagan (1983), and the U. S. State Department (1984). George Orwell Award winners have included Ted Koppel (1984) and Noam Chomsky (1988).

10. This is partly so because most introductory composition courses, at least in universities, are taught by graduate students, who aspire to teach literature — and so turn basic writing classes into "literary" courses. For a still-relevant critique of the problem, see Kitzhaber.

11. Another of the difficulties is the anthologies themselves, which feature selections more appropriate to literary analysis than practice in expository writing. See Kersoes.

12. Examination boards differ widely in their judgments about suitable set books. One board reported that *1984* was being set at O-level for the first time in 1985; another board set *1984* for the fourth time in a dozen years in 1984. See Davidson; Galvin; Davis; King; Lambert.

13. In Hipple's 1975 survey of high school reading, *Silas Marner* and *Great Expectations* were the two most frequently anthologized novels and among the most frequently taught (p. 33).

14. For an explicit attempt at an upward revaluation, see Lee. For downward revaluations, see Savage and Patal, respectively.

15. Interestingly, even when political-sociological writers like Conrad, Forster and Lawrence are admitted to the modern British novel canon, it is usually on tacit condition that they can be accommodated to the Arnoldian tradition. Instead of discussing these writers' treatments of imperialism or class conflict, that is, their work is characteristically approached exclusively by way of the formal and epistemological issues which it raises.

Works Cited

Letters to the author from:

Davis, A. R., Oxford and Cambridge Schools Examination Board, 13 May 1983.

Davidson, K., Schools Examinations Department, University of London, 23 May 1983.

Fain, M. T., Associated Board for the General Certificate of Education, Hampshire, 7 July 1983.

Galvin, K. M., Joint Matriculation Board, Manchester, 12 May 1983.

King, H. F., Oxford and Cambridge Schools Examination Board, 10 June 1983.

Lambert, G. M. University of Cambridge Local Examinations Syndicate, 13 June 1983.

"Censorship in the English Classroom: A Review of Research." *Journal of Research and Development in Education.* 12 (Spring 1976): 65-6.

"Politics Dominates Classics' Top Ten List." *The College Store Journal.* January 1984.

Algra, Cecilia and James Fillbrandt. "Book Selection Patterns Among High School Students." *Journal of Reading.* 14 (December 1970): 157-62.

Applebee, Arthur N. *Tradition and Reform in the Teaching of English: A History*. Urbana: NCTE, 1974.

Beal, Richard and Jacob Korg, eds. *Thought in Prose*. New York: Holt, Rinehart, & Winston, 1958.

Borman, Gilbert. *Cliffs Notes to Orwell's 1984*. Lincoln, 1967.

Bott, George. Introduction to Orwell's *Selected Writings*. London: Secker & Warburg, 1951.

Brander, Laurence, "George Orwell, His Life and Writings." In *Orwell's Animal Farm*. London: Longman, 1960.

Brown, Alan. "Examining Orwell: Political and Literary Values in Education." In *Inside the Myth*, ed. Christopher Norris, 31-43.

Brouse, Albert. "A Negative Response." *College Composition and Communication*. 25 (1974): 218.

Burton, Dwight. *Literary Study in the High Schools*. New York: Oxford, 1964.

Carpenter, Luther. "1984 on Staten Island." In *1984 Revisited: Totalitarianism in Our Century*, ed. Irving Howe. New York: 1984, 72-88.

Caute, David. *The Fellow Travellers: A Postscript to the Enlightenment*. London: Faber, 1973.

Coser, Lewis, ed. *Sociology Through Literature*. New York: Oxford, 1963.

Crick, Bernard. *George Orwell: A Life*. London: Secker, 1981.

Crick, Bernard. "Readings and Misreadings." *Times Educational Supplement*, 3 June 1983.

Davis, L. J. "Onward Christian Soldiers." *Penthouse*, March 1982.

Fiedler, Leslie, ed. *The Art of the Essay*. New York: Harper & Row, 1958.

Fowler, Alistair. *Kinds of Literature*. Cambridge: Harvard UP, 1982.

Freedman, Carl. "Writing, Ideology, and Politics: Orwell's 'Politics and the English Language' and English Composition." *College English*. April 1981: 337-40.

Friedman, Albert B. "The Literary Experience of High School Seniors and College Freshmen." *The English Journal*. 44 (1955): 420-26.

Gould, Christopher. "Freshman Composition As A Survey Course." *Journal of Education*. 34 (1981): 308-18.

Hechlinger, Fred. "Censorship of Books on Upswing in U. S., Report Shows." *Lexington Herald* (Ky.), 2 November 1981.

Hillegas, C. K. *Cliffs Notes to Orwell's Animal Farm*. Lincoln, 1967.

Hipple, Theodore. "The Novels Adolescents Are Reading." *Research Bulletin of the Florida Educational Research Council*. 10 (Fall 1975).

Hodges, John C. and Mary E. Whitten. *Harbrace College Handbook*. New York: Harcourt, 1972.

Howe, Irving. "As the Bones Know." *Harper's*. January 1969: 30-4.

Jackson, Lionel. "Getting Involved With the Text." *Times Educational Supplement*, 21 August 1970.

Jones, D. A. N. "Arguments Against Orwell." In *The World of George Orwell*, ed. Miriam Gross. London: 1971.

Judy, Stephen and Susan. "English teachers' literary favorites: the results of a survey." *The English Journal*. 45 (February 1979): 36.

Kallsen, J. J. and D. E. McKoy, eds. *Rhetoric and Reading*. New York: Random House, 1963.

Kazin, Alfred, ed. *The Open Form*. New York: Houghton Mifflin, 1960.

Kennedy, X. J. and Dorothy, eds. *The Bedford Reader*. New York, 1985.

Kersoes, Joseph. "Anthologies of Prose Models and the Teaching of Composition." Ph.D. Dissertation. Stanford University, 1983.

Kitzhaber, Alfred. *Themes, Theories and Therapy: The Teaching of Writing in College*. New York, 1963.

Knapton, James and Bertrand Evans. *Teaching a Literature-Centered English Program*. New York: Knopf, 1967.

Leavis, F. R. *The Great Tradition*. London, 1948.

Leavis, Q. D. "The Literary Life Respectable." *Scrutiny*. 16 (October 1940): 324-8.

Lee, Robert A. *Orwell's Fiction*. South Bend: U. of Notre Dame, 1969.

Levin, Gerald, ed. *Prose Models*. New York, 1975.

Lloyd-Jones, Richard. "The Study and Teaching of Writing." *PMLA*. 99 (1984): 980-81.

Locke, L. G. *Readings for a Liberal Education*. New York: 1952.

Lutz, William. "Scenerio: Setting Parameters for a Task Force to Implement Language Enhancement." *Social Education*. 13 (March 1984): 177-79.

McNelly, Cleo. "On Not Teaching Orwell." *College English*. February 1977: 554-68.

Mathieson, Margaret. *Teaching Practical Criticism: an introduction*. London: Milton Keynes, 1985.

Muscatine, Charles and Marlene Griffith. *Borzoi College Reader*. New York, 1968.

Nellis, Barbara. "The Dirty Thirty." *Playboy*. January 1984, 262.

Neumann, William. "Historians in an Age of Acquiescence." *Dissent* 4 (Winter 1957): 10-20.

Norris, Christopher, ed. *Inside the Myth*. London: Lawrence and Wishart, 1984.

O'Connor, William van. *Modern Prose: Form and Style*. New York: Knopf, 1954.

Orwell, George. "Exclusive Club." *Observer* (London), 6 February 1949, 3.

Orwell, George. *1984 — Text, Sources, Criticism*, ed. Irving Howe. New York: Harcourt, 1963.

Orwell, George. *The Orwell Reader*. Ed. Richard Rovere. New York: Harcourt, 1956.

Orwell, George. *The Collected Essays, Journalism, and Letters of George Orwell*, ed. Sonia Orwell and Ian Angus, 4 Volumes. New York: Harcourt, 1968.

O'Shaughnessy, Mina. *Error and Expectation: A Handbook for Teachers of Basic Writing*. New York, 1977.

Patai, Daphne. *The Orwell Myth*. Amherst: U. of Massachusetts P., 1984.

Podhoretz, Norman. "1984 Is Here: Where Is Big Brother?" *Reader's Digest*, January 1984, 37-41.

Protherough, Robert. *Developing Response to Fiction*. London: Milton Keynes, 1983.

Ranald, Ralph. *Monarch Notes to George Orwell's Animal Farm*. New York: Monarch Notes, 1965.

Rodden, John. "'The Rope That Connects Me Always With You': John Wain and the Movement Writers' Image of George Orwell." *Albion* 27 (Summer 1988): 46-60.

Rodden, John. "Literary Studies and the Repression of Reputation." *Philosophy and Literature* (forthcoming).

Savage, D. S. "The Fatalism of George Orwell." In *The New Pelican Guide to English Literature* vol. 8, *The present*, ed. Boris Ford. Harmondsworth, 1983.

Scholes, Robert and Carl Klaus. *Elements of the Essay*. New York, 1969.

Shroder, Caroline, ed. *Reading for Rhetoric*. New York: Macmillan, 1967.

Shugrue, Michael. *English in a Decade of Change*. New York: Holt, Rinehart & Winston, 1968.

Smart, William, ed. *Eight Modern Essayists*. New York, 1967.

Squire, James and Roger K. Applebee. *Teaching English in the United Kingdom: A Comparative Study*. Urbana: NCTE, 1969.

Stafford, William and Frederick Candelaria. *The Voices of Prose*. New York, 1966.

Stone, Wilfrid and Robert Hoppes. *Form in Thought and Prose*. New York: Oxford, 1954.

Stone, Wilfrid and J. G. Bell. *Prose Style: A Handbook for Writers*. New York, 1977.

Thomas, Donald. "The Red Line in a Literary Setting." *Times Educational Supplement*. 10 February 1967, 437

Thompson, Frank, *Cliffs Notes to Orwell's Animal Farm*. Lincoln: Cliffs Notes, 1967.

Trilling, Lionel. Introduction to George Orwell's *Homage to Catalonia*. New York: Harcourt, 1952.

Wise, J. Hooper. *The Meaning of Meaning*. New York: 1953.

Wodehouse, C. M. Introduction to *Animal Farm*. New York: Signet, 1954.

Yarlott, G. and W. S. Harpin. "1000 Responses to English Literature (2)." *Educational Research*. 13 (February 1971): 90-6.

Last Words
A Convention in Life, Literature
and Biography

Karl S. Guthke
Harvard University

> More are men's ends mark'd than their lives before.
> *Richard II*, II:1

1

"The unexamined life is not worth living," we've all been told and been left to gather that the examined life is (worth living). Such examination, such self-examination takes one form when we are young; it takes another form when we are middle-aged and yet a different one when we are old. And, to go one step further, it is only at the very end of life, Walter Benjamin has said in a famous essay on narration, that human life gains communicable "tradierbare Form," that is: that it reaches that stage which allows its essence to be articulated and transmitted. Or, as Hofmannsthal more than hinted in *Tor und Tod*, it is only the approach of death that may teach us "to see life clearly and in its entirety": "das Leben sehen . . . wach und ganz."

For this final (and most significant) self-articulation, there is a technical term: it is "the last word," of course; and "last words" is in fact a bona fide subject category in the classification system of the Library of Congress. But that's not the only reason why the subject is fascinating

Take Oscar Wilde, for example.

When Oscar Wilde lay dying in the Hôtel d'Alsace in Paris, his last words were: "I am dying, as I have lived, beyond my means."

How fitting. When the nurse attending Henrik Ibsen at his last illness whispered to bystanders that he seemed a little better, Ibsen retorted "on the contrary," and died. What could be more in character. Franz Kafka's last coherent remark was to his doctor: "Either you kill me or you will be a murderer." What could be more typical of the master and victim of paradox. Goethe muttered something about "more light" before he fell silent in his armchair, and it has been thought for generations that the epitome of the Enlightenment couldn't have chosen a more appropriate exit line. "But the peasants," said Tolstoy as the end was approaching in the Astapovo railroad station, "how do peasants die?" One might have guessed it. Diderot's final gem is reported to have been: "The first step toward philosophy is incredulity." Consistent until the end. King Umberto II of Italy expired on March 18th, 1983, in Geneva with just one word on his lips, according to *Newsweek*, of March 28, 1983: "Italia" (p. 60), while kings of Sweden tend to murmur "Sweden" when the curtain falls, according to usually well-informed Swedish sources. Brendan Behan, much like someone in a play of his, used his final breath to thank the nun who was wiping his feverish forehead: "Thank you, Sister! May all your sons be bishops." The last words heard from Cecil Rhodes, at the height of his imperial achievement, were: "So little done, so much to do." Suitable for framing. Heinrich Heine, predictably, checked out with a witticism: "Dieu me pardonnera, c'est son métier." Frederick William I of Prussia, father of a flute-playing son, on his death-bed listened to the hymn "Naked I came into the world, naked I shall go," and died claiming a royal exception to the clerical rule: "No, not quite naked, I shall have my uniform on." What else could the soldier king have said? Edith Sitwell's last words were in reply to being asked how she felt: "I am dying, but otherwise quite well." How Edith could Dame Edith be. Gainsborough's last thought, as the final darkness closed in on him, was of the one who mattered: "We are all going to heaven, and Van Dyck is of the company." Who else? First things last.[1] And finally, let me add that I read in some magazine that Conrad Hilton, in reply to the question whether he had one last message to the world, intoned: "Leave the shower curtain on the *inside* of the tub," and passed away.

I had better stop this random roll-call of quality ghosts before you murmur "Overkill" and lapse into a coma yourselves. If one is anything but clever one can go on like this forever. For the last words of hundreds and maybe thousands of people, mostly famous, are known and anthologized, quoted and misquoted until they become bon mots known by everyone including the dying, who have an unblushing way of quoting each other without attribution which would never be forgiven in closer-to-life scholarship. For example, at least six persons, when asked on their death-beds to renounce the devil, are reported to have replied: "This is no time to make enemies," according to Gyles Brandreth, *The Last Word* (New York, 1979), p. 6.

It seems safe to conclude from all this that particular importance is attached to last words in our civilization. Indeed, they have been treasured since time immemorial in communities which have little in common otherwise. As a result, they have survived and, in some instances, become proverbial.

> Dying words have a better than usual chance to survive. There are reasons, reasons rooted very deep in human nature, why men pay particular attention to them and preserve them. They answer an expectation. The interest, because so natural, is older than anyone can say. It is and has been for uncounted centuries the daily stuff of legends and biographies and histories and ballads, has pointed many a moral and adorned many a tale. Peoples far distant in time, place and customs have joined in the feeling that the utterance which is never to be followed by any other is by that very fact significant. Sometimes we remember nothing else, nothing of Nathan Hale or Captain Lawrence except their last words. Those who have never read Goethe in prose or verse can still tell you that he said on his death bed, "More light!"[2]

The process in which such a dying word becomes common property is observed with a keen eye by Carlos Fuentes in his novel *The Old Gringo* (New York, 1985): "Try always to get yourself killed—that was the last thing General Frutos García said before he died in 1964 in his home in Mexico City, and his words became famous among the anecdotes told by the men who had fought in the Revolution" (p. 92). To most readers, incidentally, this is probably one of the many cases where death is more memorable than the life preceding it or indeed the only reminder that there was such a life.

Last words, then, seem to have a status all of their own in life and literature in the Western world, to go no further afield for the time being, although there appears to be a similar convention in Japan, for example. This status is highlighted perhaps by the way we use the phrases like "kein Sterbenswort" or "the last word" (as in "the last word on" make-up, or life insurance), or by the way the idea of last words tends to provide inspiration for a special brand of joke (professors die, the *Edinburgh University Library Guide* no. 42 on *Dissertation and Report Writing* [1986] reminds us, whispering "Verify your references"; the condemned man in the Electric Chair regrets that he cannot offer his seat to a lady, etc.). It is true, of course, that the belief that the words of the dying have magical powers is a feature limited to "primitive" societies;[3] but *our* society still more or less expects significant persons to die with significant words. In the past the expectation was even stronger. Puritan "conduct books" of the 16th, 17th and 18th centuries for example were quite clear about the duty of the dying to depart from this world with words designed to leave an impression on the survivors,[4] and throughout the 19th century, if novels and biographies are any guides at all, the formal death-bed scene, complete with last words, was part and parcel of virtually everybody's life experience.[5] "In those days," one reads in Willa Cather's *Death Comes for the Archbishop* (New York, 1927), "even in European countries, death had a solemn social importance. It was not regarded as a moment when certain bodily organs ceased to function, but as a dramatic climax, a moment when the soul made its entrance into the next world, passing in full consciousness through a lowly door to an unimaginable scene. [. . .] The 'Last Words' of great men, Napoleon, Lord Byron, were still printed in gift books, and the dying murmurs of every common man and woman were listened for and treasured by their neighbours and kinsfolk. These sayings, no matter how unimportant, were given oracular significance and pondered by those who must one day go the same road" (pp. 172-173). Even in the twentieth century, this convention has not lost its power over our minds: the Mexican revolutionary Pancho Villa, assassinated on his ranch in Chihuahua in 1923, died imploring bystanders: "Don't let it end like this. Tell them I said something." Whether literally authentic or not, this remark makes a point. And how thrilling it can be to see this point, in a flash of revelation as it were, is illustrated, not entirely tongue-in-cheek, by William Saroyan in his essay "Last Words of the Great":

> When I was 10 or 11 years old I found an old almanac in the barn of the rented house at 2226 San Benito Avenue in Fresno, half gone, but I studied every page that was still in place. And all I remember is the feature entitled Last Words of the Great. I was so impressed by what people had said at death that I felt absolutely exhilarated by the promise that someday I would die, and say my last words. (*The Nation*, September 24, 1973, p. 282).

Last words—it is a curious experience to explore this little known, yet close-by territory whose natives we all are, though we may lack the love of dilettantism that gets us far into the interior. Everybody knows at least a few quotable last words as one can easily find out if one cares to make a capital bore of oneself by asking anybody one meets at a conference or cocktail party. Julius Caesar's proverbial "Et tu, Brute" may come up for instance, or the words that David Hume did *not* speak, or Queen Elizabeth's "All my possessions for one moment of time" (and she may have had as many dresses as Imelda Marcos had shoes). Finality commands attention: last words, unlike all others, cannot be taken back. Therefore, it seems, they are worth listening to and worth preserving, worth citing in the media even if the intended reader cannot be expected to know anything about the speaker, about Hapsburg Emperor Francis I e.g., whose dying words ("Don't change a thing," 1835) are believed to be an instructive warning with a view to the possible decline of the American "Empire" in a *Newsweek* article of February 22, 1988 (p. 63). At the very least, last words have a sort of curiosity value, which proves irresistible even to *The New Yorker* and *The New York Times*: both found it intriguingly newsworthy that French president Doumer "spent the last

conscious moments of his life wondering how an automobile got
into the charity book sale at the Maison Rothschild, where his
assassination occurred."[6]

Such attention paid to last words, whether they are highly
revealing or bizarrely haphazard, is simply a well-established convention in our society — no wonder *The Lazy Man's Guide to Death
and Dying* by E. J. Gold (Nevada City, Cal., 1983) recommends not
to say anything at all when the final opportunity presents itself (p.
2). This attention (which has its concrete antecedents in the literature and historiography of Antiquity as well as in the Old Testament)[7] is so ingrained that if a news magazine dedicates only half a
dozen lines or so to the death of a celebrity, or, for that matter, to
the bicentennial of the death of a celebrity, Samuel Johnson e.g.,
the last words will often be included. Front page or, at any rate,
lengthier and more than routine obituaries in the daily press would,
of course, be incomplete without the piquant detail of the dying
utterance, even in the (arguably less than world-shaking) case of
crooner Rudy Vallee — and no matter how trivial the words themselves, whoever the deceased (*The Washington Post*, July 5, 1986, p.
B 6). In a minor but telling way, last words of the newsworthy even
cast their mythical spell over the 1988 Democratic primary
campaign when the much publicized bloodstains on Jesse Jackson's
shirt suggested, in the words of New York mayor Koch, that
Jackson was "the last man to speak with" Martin Luther King — a
fact or claim deemed somehow significant (*The Christian Science
Monitor*, April 20, 1988, p. 32). But one did not need to be famous
to have one's last words recorded in the media, even in the late
1980s. On March 16, 1988 *The Boston Globe* reported that a New
Hampshire villager revealed on his deathbed the murderer of his
daughter-in-law's first husband — it was his own son, which elevated
the last word to the cue for what is known as poignant family drama
(p. 19); similarly *Newsweek* noted that when a 78-year-old Bible
teacher was stabbed with a 12-inch butcher knife by a teenager in
Gary, Indiana, she "recited the Lord's Prayer as she died"
(September 21, 1987, p. 37).

But to return from the obscure to the more prominent: When a panel of noted men of letters, W. H. Auden, Aldous Huxley and others, were interviewed on the BBC Brains Trust program in the 1950s, David Daiches, who was one of the participants, tells me, the question designed to get to the heart of the matter was what their last words would be if this were the occasion for them. Equally telling is the fact that a documentary film on Picasso will not fail to startle us in its concluding seconds with the revelation that the painter's last words were: "Painting remains to be invented."(In Paul McCartney's song "Picasso's Last Words" we hear about a different set of last words, based on the *Time* obituary of April 23, 1973, p. 93). In films, ranging from *Jules et Jim* to *Broadcast News*, there is a veritable cult of last words—which is beautifully parodied in Robert Bresson's *Le Biable probablement* where the protagonist pointedly has himself shot dead in mid-sentence, which in turn expressly thematizes the last word—the absence of it; and there is at least one film on the theme of the search for the meaning of a last word, *Citizen Kane*, no less, which not only encapsulates its message in the last word, but beyond that, has made the last word, "Rosebud," into a sort of shorthand symbol, among cognoscenti, of the unforgettable joys of youth, or rather, of what it is that makes life worth living.

Just how much last words have become a part of our everyday cultural heritage and our popular mythologies may also be gathered from the curious fact that "What were Mexican revolutionary Pancho Villa's dying words?" appears as the question of the day for October 17, 1987 in the popular *Workman Page-A-Day* "365 Trivia Calendar." There is, as Clifton Fadiman discovered in the early 1950s, "a worldwide fraternity of collectors of Last Words," for which he thought there was more to be said than for philatelists.[8] The London *Times Literary Supplement* hosted a competition designed to test readers' knowledge of last words of the famous (July 17, 1981, p. 814), while other publications may have a "contest" for the most appropriate "totally imaginary last words of famous real people, living or dead, in 25 words or less" (*The National Review*, June 14, 1985, p. 50; among the winners:

Descartes, "I think I'm dead, therefore. . ."). In England, during the years of the blitz, *The New Statesman* tried to cheer up its readers by running a similar competition which, however, included hypothetical last words of animals,[9] in the animal-loving British tradition of Robert Burns and others, one would like to think. *The New York Times* played a similar highbrow game, limited to imaginary last words of musicians, on October 11, 1987 (p. 27; Richard Wagner: "Ah, what lovely embossed wallpaper . . . is it paid for?"). In Germany, Hans Blumenberg, turned pop-philosopher at the height of his fame, has recently put the all-important matter of how certain philosophers died or might have died on the map by focussing on the genre of "imaginäre Anekdoten":

> Ich würde gern wissen, was man im nächsten Jahrtausend über den Tod und die 'letzten Worte' Heideggers und seiner Anhänger berichten wird, und hielte einen Wettbewerb für unbedenklich, der Vorschläge an die Tradition weiterzureichen hätte. Ich nähme es gern aus privater Indiskretion, habe es aber nicht. Dann hieße es: Was kann einer, den die Existentialanalytik ebenso getroffen hatte wie die Frage nach dem 'Wesen des Grundes', zum Schluß noch gesagt haben? Im günstigsten Fall von Evidenz: Was muß er gesagt haben? Etwa: *Kein Grund mehr zur Sorge.* (*Die Sorge geht über den Fluß*, Frankfurt 1987, p. 222).

To continue this necessarily haphazard tour d'horizon of the many manifestations of our attention to last words in the *Kulturgeschichte des Alltags*: there is a large number of anthologies in the manner of Herbert Nette's *"Hier kann ich doch nicht bleiben": Eine Sammlung letzter Worte* (Munich, 1983) and at least one "dictionary"[10] of last words, some of them kept handy in university library reference collections, somewhere between *Who was Who* and the *Encyclopedia Brittannica*; and several commonly used dictionaries of quotations contain sections entitled "Last Words."[11] Some people must want to check such facts regularly; indeed, reference librarians will confirm this (*Library Review*, XXIV, 1974, p. 255). Sacha Guitry even assembled a collection of last words on a long-playing record entitled "Leur dernier quart d'heure" (Pathe Marconi, n.d.). But it remained for Julian Barnes to bring the phenomenon truly into the late 20th Century: in his novel *Staring at the Sun* (London, 1986) the protagonist uses his computer to "call up the last words of the famous"—which allows the author to indulge in a fascinatingly whimsical reverie about the charm and pitfalls of the institution of paying attention to "last words" (pp. 152-153). Also, "Last Words" is guaranteed to be an attention-getting book title, whether for a collection of sermons or of newspaper articles, a novel, a comedy, an interview, or a bunch of stories or the autobiography of a dancer - just as *Last Days* is always an eye-catching title, whether it is the last days of Hitler or Bonhoeffer, Pompeii or United Pakistan or Mankind.

In Italy, according to an anonymous essay on "Last Words" in *Every Saturday*, "the sayings of the departed on their death-beds are sometimes written on scrolls, and hung in their parish church" (September 8, 1866, p. 276). And why did ordinary people go to see public executions? The 1985 Michelin guide to London instructs the tourist: "From the Tower or Newgate the condemned were drawn through the streets on hurdles to be hanged (and sometimes drawn and quartered too) before the great crowds who gathered to hear the last words . . ." (p. 99). Last words were indeed an important part of public executions for centuries. But this does not meant that the present-day sightseer has to miss out entirely on these specialized thrills. In Elizabethan England, and later, hundreds of broadsides and pamphlets, chapbooks and even ballads were printed and reprinted which reported the dying speeches (usually, but not always, carefully prepared and conforming to a *pattern* which allowed for little spontaneity or originality) made by traitors and highwaymen, pirates and murderers, royalty and dissenting ministers literally under the gallows or in front of the executioner's block.[12] There are, furthermore, entire collections of dying speeches and testimonies of Scottish Covenanters, of state prisoners of various kinds, freethinkers, saints, martyrs, infidels, children, American Indians, etc.[13] (By no means did one have to be a criminal to qualify for a broadside or chapbook preserving one's last words for posterity.) Sometimes, to be sure, there were public disputes about what was *really* said in the "last speech" as in the case of the traitor Thomas

Wentworth[14] (1641) and, with luck, one may chance upon a book like *The Tragical History of Jetzer [. . .] with an Epistle, wherein are some Soft and Gentle Reflections upon the Lying Dying-Speeches of the Jesuites lately Executed at Tyburn* (London 1679). Finally, if proof were needed of the immense popularity of the gruesome charm of the genre of "The Last Speech of . . ." writing, one might mention two broadside parodies which are representative of several others of this type: *The Last Speech and Dying Words of the Bank of Ireland Which was executed at College Green on Saturday the 9th inst.* (1721) and *The Last Speech, Confession, and Dying Words, of a Queen Ann's Guinea, Who was tried, and condemned, on a Late Act of Parliament, for being too Light; and executed by the Unmerciful Hands of a Butcher in Salisbury Market* (1774?). Later still, in France, the dying remarks of some victims of the Revolution, their words said on the way to the guillotine, became common knowledge, indeed part of the national folklore or the collective conscious: Marie Antoinette's "Pardonnez-moi, monsieur" for example, as she stepped on the executioner's foot. Similarly, the last words of heretics, patriots and soldiers dying on the battlefield have become part of our popular mythologies, our popular culture. Even in the second half of the 20th century, it is not uncommon to ask criminals on their way to the Electric Chair or to the gallows for their last words — and to write books about what they have to say under titles such as *Death Row Chaplain* and *By the Neck.*[15]

Biographies frequently start out with the death of their subject, and even when they do not, they often seem to have been written all along with at least one eye on the end or, more specifically, on the dying word which is somehow felt to give a summary of the life and to throw into relief its real significance. Lytton Strachey, "frank" even about himself, admitted that he had conceived (and written, as it were) his life of Queen Victoria from the death-bed scene,[16] and the book does in fact read much like a prologue to its deservedly famous last page — which indeed validates this biography as a superb example of what Strachey called, in the preface to *Eminent Victorians*, "the most delicate and humane of all the branches of the art of writing." Samuel Johnson must have had something remotely similar in mind when he quipped to Boswell that Gilbert Burnet's biography of the notorious Earl of Rochester, which makes great play of the death-bed repentance and conversion of the ingenious sinner, was "a good *Death*: there is not much *Life*."[17] (In Lytton Strachey's case, by the way, this biographical cult of death and last words was strangely ironic as he died with the remark: "If this is dying, I don't think much of it.") Harvard University's "institution" of honoring professors with a "Memorial Minute" even finesses the biographical convention by reporting the deceased's "last joke," though not in all cases, fortunately for those of us who might someday want to compete (*Harvard University Gazette*, April 22, 1988, p. 6).

One may go one step further and suspect that biographers are not the only ones who are convinced of the "telling" nature of someone's final words. Sometimes even their subjects share this view and cooperate by making the last moment count, writing their obituary on the death-bed as it were or at least trying to, as did Queen Elisabeth of Rumania: "'You are supposed—to say—beautiful things—and you can't,' the old woman rasped out with her last conscious breath before she fell into a coma and died."[18] The problem of the American writer Charles Wertenbaker was the opposite: "I'm running out of last words," his wife reports him to have said after various suicide attempts had failed.[19] Others succeed rather better. One of them is Henry Huntington, who staged his own farewell to life quite adroitly, according to a story that, I am told, goes back to one of those present, A.S.W. Rosenbach, a dealer in rare books and manuscripts who sold Huntington many of the treasures now in the Huntington Library. The other one present was Sir Joseph Duveen, the art dealer who had sold Huntington many works of art. Huntington, Rosenbach reported to Arthur A. Houghton, Jr., lay with his arms outstretched on either side. He looked at Rosenbach, then at Duveen. "Do you know what I feel like?" he asked Rosenbach. "What, Mr. Huntington?" "Christ between the two thieves," said Huntington and died.[20]

Some, in other words, try hard to die with a memorable last word, attempting to make up perhaps for a life they consider less memorable than what is yet to come, verbally, while time has not quite run out yet. One might want to think of this as a secular variation on the sinner's deathbed recantation (which, for all its seriousness, was a popular genre well into the 18th century): ending a less than beautiful life with a beautiful line that will survive.[21]

Of course, there are no guarantees, and the very opposite may happen: a dying word may "take back" whatever was beautiful about the life which it concludes. This, rather exceptional view is taken by B. Traven: "Das letzte Wort eines Sterbenden," he writes in *Der Ziegelbrenner* under his earlier pseudonym Ret Marut:

> Macht kein Wesens davon und haltet es nicht etwa heilig. Denn das letzte Wort ist nicht mehr sein eigenes Wort; es ist zur Hälfte schon das Hauchen aus einem anderen Zustand, der nichts mit Euch und Eurem Leben zu schaffen hat. Das letzte Wort eines Sterbenden hat noch nie jemand verstanden. Und noch nie jemand gehört. Aber dennoch hat es schon mehr Unheil angerichtet als die Worte Lebender. Und hütet Euch bei Menschen, die Ihr schätzt und hochachtet, ihr letztes Wort zu vernehmen! Es kann ihre ganze Lebensweisheit mit einer Silbe umwerfen und Ihr steht hülflos da. Das letzte Wort eines Sterbenden ist noch weniger wichtig als das eines Mannes, der sinnlos betrunken ist. (II: 3, 1918, p. 51)

Mark Twain may have had something like this in mind when he expressed the hope that "our great men" should cease to come up with those supposedly weighty but really "flat" statements in their last words and suggested that, instead, the survivors should concentrate on the next-to-last words of the great and not so great which might be more "satisfactory."[22] Mark Twain's iconoclastic reaction — just like his parody in *A Tramp Abroad*, where last words are prepared with great care before a duel[23] — of course only succeeds in pointing to the undeniable and unchangeable fact that in our civilization it is the last word and not the next-to-last word that carries weight, that is surrounded by the aura of the significant, that is treated with awe and reverence — the way a "Last Will and Testament" is *not*, necessarily, even if it does account for the best bed, as Shakespeare's does not. It is a curious fact that this is recognized even in the law courts of some countries or possibly "of all nations" if Chambers' *Encyclopedia* is correctly informed,[24] and *The Oxford Companion to Law* suggests it might be.[25] In Anglo-Saxon countries at any rate the so-called "dying declaration" enjoys a special evidential status, vastly superior to *in vino veritas*. Such a dying declaration is defined as "a verbal or written statement made by a dying person, which although not made on oath or in the presence of the accused, is admissible in evidence on an indictment for murder or manslaughter of that person, provided the person making it had a belief, without hope of recovery, that he was about to die shortly." Thus the succinct definition of the *Oxford Companion*. The American last word on this is the textbook *McCormick on Evidence*, which in its third edition (1984) devotes seven very large pages to this particular exception to the exclusion of hearsay, pages which also instruct the reader just how he can tell whether the "declarant" was conscious of impending death and how to assess the precise "weight" of his declaration (chapter 28).

Literature, not unexpectedly, has made the widest use possible of this highbrow folklore that surrounds us everywhere, this convention of our culture that attaches such great significance to the last words of a dying person. Many 17th century German poems e.g. as Ferdinand van Ingen has shown, are really versifications of the late medieval Christian instructions on how to die "well," i.e. of the many and popular *Artes moriendi* according to which the words spoken at the very last moment counted infinitely more than all others since they determined the destination of the soul about to depart: Heaven or Hell.[26] Similarly, 16th century Everyman plays thrived on this tradition.[27] Elizabethan drama, too, developed certain conventions of the magnificent dying speech; these, however, reflect not only the teaching of the *Artes moriendi* concerning the supreme horror of dying suddenly, unprepared, and the blessing of dying reconciled with one's Maker, but also the Renaissance desire to achieve immortal fame, last but not least at the moment of death, and needless to say through last words.[28] And the convention continued. Without deathbed speeches revealing a noble heart and everything else, genres as different as the Victorian novel and Sentimentalist middle-class tragedy in the manner of

George Lillo and G. E. Lessing would be as incomplete as the
Marlboro Man with empty hands and lips. But in other and more
recent literary genres, too, it seems that one cannot die without
saying something memorable. And these memorable literary exit
lines even develop their own generic leitmotifs — like "Wir sehen
uns wieder!" which in 18th century Germany became something
like a cipher of the belief in a secularized Heaven, as Eudo Mason
has shown.[29]

As for literary *techniques* and *devices* employing last words, they
are too numerous to even hint at here. They range from the
famous last words of Ibsen's *Ghosts* ("The sun, the sun" — where
the sun is, of course, symbolical) to the falsification of last words
for maximum political impact in Orwell's *Animal Farm*, from
Robert Burns's parody of the convention in his poem "The Death
and Dying Words of Poor Mailie, the Author's only Pet Yowe," to
Eugène Ionesco's spoof of the same convention in *The Chairs* or
Joe Orton's witticisms in *Loot*, from Captain Hook's premature
dying speech in *Peter Pan*, "lest when dying there may be no time
for it," to the carnival hit that was probably the longest-lived in the
annals of carnival, Teutonic style: "Schnaps, das war sein letztes
Wort,/Dann trugen ihn die Englein fort." Finally, when in Patrick
White's novel *The Twyborne Affair* (1979), Monsieur Vatatzes
expires saying to Madame Vatatzes: "I have had from you, dear
boy, the only happiness I've ever known" (p. 126), we know that we
are not being fooled — that we are indeed in Patrick White country.
There seem to be styles of dying and of corresponding last words in
literature, and at least one attempt was made to identify one
regional style on the basis of what is said just before nothing can be
said any more; it is entitled "Wie man in der norddeutschen Literatur stirbt" — which sounds as though it were a branch of "how to"
writing.[30]

2

One may wonder: What exactly is it that underlies all these
manifold manifestations of the convention of taking last words
seriously in our culture?[31]

There seems to be, first of all, some idea that the essence or the truth of a life—the "real" person—emerges in death and only in death. It is the idea that one dies as one lived (more so, perhaps) or as one "really" lived, whether one is, or is belatedly revealed to be, a saint or a sinner, a wit or a bore. It is the idea that a life should be rounded out, its pattern completed, perfect in its consistency, revealing that life's true identity as its unchangeable substance. It is no doubt this that accounts not only for the fact that according to the best of our information, martyrs invariably depart from this life with the name of their maker or his son on their lips and that patriots of all nations predictably turn their thoughts to the fatherland in their last moments on earth (having left little room for imaginative variation ever since Johann Zischka passed on in 1424 with the ultimate in patriotic last words: "Make my skin into drumheads for the Bohemian cause"). The idea of completing and perfecting a life by dying as one lived also accounts for the fame of the most famous of last words: Christ's words on the cross (repeated verbatim innumerable times by the dying, including Charlemagne, Christopher Columbus, Lady Jane Grey, Tasso and Martin Luther, who would probably have agreed on little else) and Socrates' proverbial remark to Crito moments after drinking the hemlock: "I owe a rooster to Aesculapius," the god of medicine and healing who had just cured him of what Alexander Pope was to call "this long disease, my life." A memorably consistent death, articulated in a characteristic last word, provides the motto for a life, or so it is believed only too willingly. Octavio Paz, a representative of a particularly death-obsessed nation, puts this line of thought, which has dominated occidental awareness for centuries in one form or another, rather more somberly, yet magisterially in a ponderous passage of the essay "The Day of the Dead," in his volume *The Labyrinth of Solitude*: "Death defines life [. . .]. Each of us dies the death [. . .] he has made for himself." Which is followed by the maxim which is not entirely logical but nonetheless clear in its meaning: "Tell me how you die and I tell you who you are."[32] Paz must mean roughly what Walt Whitman said with a rather greater sense of realism: "Last words are not samples of the best, which involve vitality at its full, and balance, and perfect control and scope. But they are valuable beyond measure to confirm and endorse the varied train, facts, theories and faith of the whole preceding life."[33]

On the other hand, a life, if not perfect, could be perfected in its last moments, through its last words, by a complete reversal of what it had been. This was the conviction underlying the *Artes moriendi*, which endeavored to show the way to a manner of dying that would save the soul, by achieving sinlessness, no matter how sinful a life might have been; the genre of deathbed recantation, mentioned above, simply continued in this vein.

One way or the other, then, it was the curtain line that mattered, regardless of whether it epitomized the play or gave it a surprise ending considered happy by the clerical audience that "collaborated." (The theater metaphor is quite common in such writing as there is on this subject.)[34] And perhaps it is not an overstatement to add that the curtain line mattered more than the play itself—to the protagonist and/or the audience, at least in some cases that became well-known. After all, for a long time, until the advent of the nondescript death made possible through the professionalism of modern medicine (which normally deprives us of last words)[35] dying was a public or semi-public act or even art (as Ariès, to mention just the best known authority, has amply shown). As such, the art of dying sometimes outdid the art of living, or might be said to have been designed to do so: designed to make up for opportunities missed, possibilities unrealized. As Malcolm says about the dying words of the Earl of Cawdor: "Nothing in his life became him like the leaving it" (*Macbeth*, I, 4).

Indeed, through a memorable last word, a kind of secularized immortality could be achieved. This is the second idea underlying our convention of taking last words seriously. For centuries, dying, more often than not perhaps, tended to be the act of survival in Last Words, of survival in the signature of a life that could not be erased again or in the intellectual or spiritual equivalent of the death mask. For a death mask is taken precisely because it is not a mask in the conventional metaphoric sense of the word, but the opposite: the real face which does not, it may be thought, emerge until the moment of death (as Tolstoy e.g. describes the emergence of the real self, of the ultimate that is within the individual's reach, in "The Death of Ivan Ilich"). Just as the death mask *preserves* that real face, the last word is the *enduring* legacy—life transcending itself into artefact, time transcending itself into timelessness, life transcending death.

This urge to self-transcendence, to leaving a monument that defies time and death, is a distinguishing, if often rather pathetic human trait. It is the Faustian need to assure oneself "daß die Spur von meinen Erdentagen nicht in Äonen untergeht." Egyptian pharaohs, heroes of Icelandic sagas and modern mausoleum builders from Franco to Stalin would agree, as would, outside the Western world, Yukio Mishima, who early in the morning of November 25, 1970, the day he committed his well-planned and well-orchestrated seppuku, just before leaving the house for his final and finest hour, placed a note on his desk which said: "Human life is limited, but I would like to live forever."[36] Similarly, William Butler Yeats describes in *A Vision* how touched he was by the sight of a barefoot girl on the beach in Normandy, who was looking out at the sea and singing a song about civilizations that had flourished on this coast and disappeared without a trace. The refrain of each verse she sang was: "O Lord, let something remain!"[37] This desire is universal in time and in space. If one visits the new Museo Nacional de Antropología in Mexico City's Chapultepec Park e.g., one is struck by verses from the Cantos de Huexotzingo, originally composed in Nahuatl, sculpted monumentally into the wall of the courtyard:

> ¿ Sólo así he de irme?
> ¿ Como las flores que perecieron?
> ¿ Nada quedará en mi nombre?
> ¿ Nada de mi fama aquí en la tierra?
> ¡ Al menos flores, al menos cantos!

"At least songs" will remain, or, sometimes, last words as the only mementos of a life troubling itself about one of the very few things worth troubling about, its temporality. No wonder so many of us "make a special effort" in this respect, an effort to "leave our stamp" on the world. Indeed, one might say that last words as an "institution" in our society encapsulate the very concept of culture and its tradition; for as the dying person endeavors to summarize his life experience or "the lessons that life has taught him"[38] in a last word, he does so with a view to passing this knowledge and this self-image on: with a view to adding something to the collective conscious of his civilization and its future.

But what is behind the age-old fascination with last words is not only this: not only, firstly, the obsession with life as the properly completed entity or pattern, or as the properly completed work of art, and not only, secondly, the obsession with self-transcendence and a secular kind of immortality. There is also, thirdly, quite apart from any individual case, the matter of *the mystique of the final moment*, and this becomes increasingly interesting as we move away, in time or in (intellectual) space, from any sort of religious framework of life. Of course, even in an age of belief, the final moment had its importance in that it provided the experience of the threshold to a "life" of a different kind. "It was believed in at least the early Middle Ages," writes R. C. Finucane, "that as [saints] neared death they could see over the boundary separating the worlds. Their deaths were transitions to another, higher and therefore more powerful state. This state could be anticipated: they could foresee their own deaths and other secrets of the future. Their statements were especially valued because in a sense they came from beyond the grave. It was a privilege to be present at their deaths and only 'worthy' auditors should hear their last words. Conversely, it came to be expected that the dying holy man or woman would, even should, bequeath his special knowledge to intimates."[39] But exciting and worthy of attention as such revelations may have been well into the 19th century, they were revelations within the framework of Christian beliefs and therefore, strictly speaking, not entirely surprising. One had an idea of what heaven and hell were like; and what saints, at any rate, had to say on their deathbeds was, in a way, predictable as their numerous biographies confirm. Others confessed and regretted their sins and accepted absolution with equal routine. As many anthologies recording Christian deaths amply and rather tediously demonstrate, these believers, whether long-term saints or sinners reformed in the nick of time, always knew what to say at the last moment. This was not a moment for originality. In fact, it was almost de rigueur to quote the very last words spoken on the Cross ("into Thy hands I commend my spirit"). It is only after and/or outside the supportive framework of orthodox religion that the dying "do not know what to say" and that what they do say becomes rather more interesting and original and less predictable. Their words do not fit into any dogmatically established pattern, and, as a result, the final moment gains a different sort of importance: a non-standardized one, so to speak. The search, the life-long search maybe, for a completed life is brought to a different sort of conclusion in the last moment in which words are uttered. As such, this moment is often seen to have a mystique all of its own.

Let me talk briefly about this moment, as briefly as one should about what is by definition beyond the ken of knowledge. Dealing as I am with an aspect of intellectual history, I may perhaps leave aside what physicians might have to say about the moments preceding death. For them the not uncommon state of serenity or even euphoria at the dying moment and, more specifically, "la vision panoramique des mourants" that Henri Bergson was so interested in,[40] is primarily a correlative of the physiology of incipient decomposition. More uninhibited is the imagination of folklore. It provides us with the notion (or is it an old wives' tale?) that a drowning or a hanged person sees his entire life recapitulated before his mind's eye in his last moments. But this does not take us very far either, even though it may inspire arresting literary works such as Ambrose Bierce's story "An Occurrence at Owl Creek Bridge" or William Golding's novel *Pincher Martin*, and even though Theodore Däubler was led by this bit of folk wisdom to realize that the life-review of a man being hanged "kann nur Expressionismus sein!"[41] Surely, there are more comfortable ways to achieve and to excel in Expressionist style.

And as far as the only clinical account of the state of mind of a person about to drown which I have found is concerned, it records nothing but trivialities, signifying nothing or very little.[42] In any case I find it difficult on the basis of such evidence (essentially a string of impressions of teen-age dating, a recent Rose Bowl game, etc.) to see that the folk belief in the life-review of the drowning or the hanged person is essentially a metamorphosis of the concept of the Last Judgment and the afterlife as A. Alvarez claims in his famous study of suicide, *The Savage God*.[43]

Whatever the significance of the moment, it is less specific and less dogmatically circumscribed than that, and it does not take hanging or drowning to see that. There is in fact quite a respectable if informal tradition of attributing special meaning—a mystique—to the last moment and the words said in it. This is, of course primarily a tradition outside the specific sphere of influence of the Christian churches, which teach that one's behavior at the last moment may decide the ultimate destination of the soul that is at that point preparing to embark on its journey to parts unknown to most. For Samuel Johnson notwithstanding—"the act of dying is not of importance" and "it matters not how a man dies," Boswell quotes him as saying[44]—there has been a fair amount of speculation, albeit frequently aphoristic, on the importance of the last moment and the utterance it yields, on the part of those not specifically committed to religious orthodoxy, and even on the part of those who are *not* eager for those glimpses of the life of the soul after death which have become the *dernier cri* in our postrationalist time.[45] Goethe e.g. in *Maximen und Reflexionen* comments on a victim of the French Revolution (whose last words are reported to have been "O Liberty! How are you mocked!"):

> Madame Roland, auf dem Blutgerüste, verlangte Schreibzeug, um die ganz besonderen Gedanken aufzuschreiben, die ihr auf dem letzten Wege vorgeschwebt. Schade, daß man ihr's versagte; denn am Ende des Lebens gehen dem gefaßten Geiste Gedanken auf, bisher undenkbare; sie sind wie selige Dämonen, die sich auf den Gipfel der Vergangenheit glänzend niederlassen. (H.A., XII, p. 415)

And in *Moby Dick* one comes across the sentiment: "For whatever is truly wondrous and fearful in man, never yet was put into words or books. And the drawing near of Death, which alike levels all, alike impresses all with a last revelation, which only an author from the dead could adequately tell."[46]

The reason why the "moment" is of such great interest to the "uncommitted," if one may call them that, is that it is the moment of a bona fide *Grenzerfahrung* as Existentialists of Jaspersian persuasion would say. It is a moment where being and non-being merge, a moment of experiencing what is indeed beyond experience and yet may leave a record actualized in language which forces or teases the ineffable into the effable, producing the last word. What passes understanding, the ultimate knowledge (or is it knowledge of the ultimate?) is seen through a glass darkly. Or is it? Whatever the answer, the mystique of this unique moment originates in this question.[47]

When it comes to this moment even present-day psychiatrists will sound mystical and mysterious, revealing the analogy of their craft to the practice of a rather different and more ancient breed of initiates. Gone are the days of physiological "realism" when an authority of the stature of Herbert Spencer could blithely assure his readers that near and at the point of dying both the "thinking faculty" and the "feeling faculty" are "almost gone," so that on the deathbed "the sentient state is the farthest possible from that which accompanies vigorous life";[48] in other words (as other observers have noted as well), there could not possibly be anything "telling" or significant about what a person utters as he dies. Modern psychiatrists do not necessarily agree; they may, in principle, return to a realization of what Goethe intuited about last moments and last words.

True, there are those who will go no further than stating the observational donnée "that the dying patient, [. . .] in the face of death, remains more or less true to his basic personality" which is then defined as "an individual's total responsive attitude to his environment and his habitual behavior patterns regarding his physical and mental activities irrespective of the picture he presents to the outside world." This last qualification allows for surprises in the deathbed scene, for if the patient's behavior in his last moments differs from "his earlier behavior," Arnold A. Hutschnecker continues in his essay "Personality Factors in Dying Patients," it is the final behavior that counts. For "an individual in his basic unrestrained structure" is "revealed" precisely at the moment of "a breakdown of conscious controls."[49] And it goes without saying that the most incisive breakdown that reveals the true face is what is commonly described as the last moment—from which the last word issues. This is really not much more than a translation of Edward Young's line "A deathbed's a detector of the heart" (*Night Thoughts*, II, v. 639) into polysyllabic jargon, although the Rev. Edward Young may be closer to disquisitions on "holy dying" than the New York M.D. Another psychiatrist, Gerald J. Aronson, however, does indeed see a remote connection between late medieval *Ars moriendi* and latter-day psychiatric bedside experience when he says that "no man is different from the martyrs who died according to a code of ethics, with an inbuilt script still rolling out."[50] Aronson's documentation—the case of A. E. Housman frivolously commenting with his last gasp on what is politely called "a thoroughly naughty story," told to the dying don and connoisseur of pornography by his thoroughly understanding physician—may be less than well chosen, but the point is clear: a dying man, in his final moment, retains "his sense of individuality and identity" and this, to some, has become the secular analogue of the *anima Christiana*. Such psychiatric evaluations of the significance of the dying moment and the last word do, however, almost explain away the "mystique."

Other psychiatrists, however, though no less secular in their basic outlook, give greater credit to the mystique of the last moment. When K. R. Eissler, known to Germanists as the author of a psychoanalytical biography of Goethe, in *The Psychiatrist and the Dying Patient* (New York 1955), a book widely considered a pioneering work, claims that "the moment of death is still the most important and the most decisive in man's life," he has rather more in mind than "the idea—often expressed by philosophers and well

supported by the psychoanalytic conception of the personality—
that the whole preceding lifetime is reflected in the terminal phase
of a human being"; he has more in mind than the idea (which he, of
course, finds psychoanalytically "correct" as far as it goes) that "in
dying, man consummates his whole previous life" (pp. 51, 263).
Eissler goes beyond this; yet in doing so, he too, like Aronson,
takes his cue from the Christian conception of death as the one
moment when, through repentance, absolution and Holy Commu-
nion, the state of sinlessness may be achieved by the believer. But,
unlike Aronson, he retains the sense of *tremendum* and *fascinosum*
that give this moment its unique aura in dogmatic contexts. For as
he translates the dogmatic concept of sinlessness into its secular
equivalent, namely "the state of maximum individualization," he
preserves a sense of the transforming power, or the mystique, of
the final moment. What may be achieved at that point is not only a
summation of a life or a given individuality (which may also
"immortalize" it in a secular sense). On the contrary, *beyond* the
stage of individualization attained in life some "last few steps of
individualization [. . .] may be possible along the terminal pathway." These steps beyond the *status quo*, these last stages of psychic "growth," significantly, may or may not "facilitate the last
farewell to life." For there is at least the possibility that "the futility" of the entire past life may be realized in the process of terminal, maximum individualization. On the other hand, even this perceived futility may be turned into what Eissler calls "a triumph of
individualization," adding that "the final processes of structuriza-
tion during the terminal pathway may provide the past life with a
meaning which it would never have acquired without them" (p. 55).
This formulation of the mystique of the last moment and, by implication, of the last word, is perhaps also to be understood as a
translation into psychiatric language of what Rilke in *Malte Laurids
Brigge* and the *Stundenbuch* had adumbrated poetically as the mystique of a "death of one's own" as opposed to the anonymous or, as
Rilke says, "factory-like" death of the modern Everyman who dies
in a Paris hospital ward designed for the masses. (As the century
progressed, there were, of course, other forms of mass death that

Rilke did not envision.) Eissler, like Rilke in his way, or Heidegger in his,[51] seems to articulate a secular form of salvation when he extols the individual and individuality-enhancing death: "The full awareness of each step that leads closer to death up to the last second which permits awareness and consciousness, would be the crowning triumph of an individually lived life. It would be taken as the only way man ought to die if individuality were really accepted as the only adequate form of living" (p. 57).

The all-importance of the dying moment, and the dying word, which the Catholic church has held axiomatic for centuries, reappears here in new language. But, of course, one cannot help noticing that, in a sense, secular psychiatry makes the mystique of the final moment even more mystical and mysterious, indeed more ineffable than it had been, and still is, in orthodox theology. Theology will speak of the certainties of heaven and hell, of the "fact" of the survival of the soul and meeting of its Maker (as does, for example, the Rev. Herbert Lockyer in his collection of *Last Words of Saints and Sinners*: "When the soul is face to face with eternal realities, true character is almost invariably manifest" and the believer may "bear witness [. . .] to the reality of Christ and the glorious assurance of heaven").[52] A modern psychiatrist, on the other hand, will speak of "possible stimulation of new structural processes through the terminal phase," which in his view is what raises the final moment and the final word far above the significance of a mere summing up or a consummation of previous life (Eissler, p. 263). But what does this, or what does "evolvement of new structures," or even "growth" mean to someone to whom "forgiveness of sins" no longer holds the meaning that was once self-evident? There is a curious emptiness of specific meaning about those "psychic processes of the terminal phase," and this void is not really filled by the negative definition, that is by the rejection of the common medical idea that it is "disturbed physiological functions" or the "disturbed biological apparatus" that account for whatever changes might be observable in the personality of the dying, and which might prompt last words (p. 263). Paradoxically, then, the ineffability of the significance of the last moment becomes even more ineffable if viewed within a secular horizon. Much the same is true of Jaspers, whose view has been summarized as follows: "Angesichts des Todes entspringt Existenz aus ihrer eigentlichen Tiefe zu ihrer wesentlichen Möglichkeit."[53] Again, what does this mean?

In comparison, the deathbed-scene in literature which habitually makes the ineffable effable—an exemplary literary rendering of existential "growth" may be found in the final chapter of "The Death of Ivan Ilich"—becomes all the more striking in its imaginative concreteness.

Not unexpectedly, poets will also come up with statements on the dilemma, on the commonly felt mystique of the last moment and the last word, which are rather more memorable than those of mental health professionals, and not only because poets do not normally have phrases like "the possible stimulation of new structural processes" in their active vocabulary. One could indeed have a field day going on a safari through the world's classics gunning down appropriate lines with minimal concern for the textual environment. I shall resist that temptation. I'll just mention that if one were game one could bag some birds of very different feathers which are not usually found in the same habitat. Shakespeare, of course, is hard to miss:

O, but they say the tongues of dying men
Enforce attention like deep harmony:
Where words are scarce, they are seldom spent in vain,
For they breathe truth that breathe their words in pain.
(*Richard II*, II, 1)

Typically, there is no suggestion here that the truth that emerges from the lips of a dying man might be illuminated by a ray of light from beyond. At the other extreme of the scale one might encounter a sentence from Willa Cather's *Death comes for the Archbishop*, describing the deathbed of Father Lucero: "Among the watchers there was always the hope that the dying man might reveal something of what he alone could see; that his countenance, if not his lips, would speak, and on his features would fall some

light or shadow from beyond."[54] Taken together, both quotations
capture well the arresting power that last words have over the
imagination of the survivors in our culture. And this is not entirely
a matter of the past. In Botho Strauß's much acclaimed *Paare,
Passanten*, published in 1981, one comes across the casual reference to the "allmächtige Kraft dessen, was ein Mann zuletzt gesagt
hat"; and the lifetime of the power of such a last word is described
here, with equal casualness, as nothing short of "ewig."[55] But
whether the truth of the dying pronouncement is seen as the reflex
of a *Grenzerfahrung* that involves the "totally other" in metaphysical terms (as in the passage from Willa Cather) or in what appear
to be purely human terms (as in the lines from *Richard II*)—there
is, in either case, a hint of an awareness that the moment and its
words are *sui generis*, distinct from any other ones. This paradox of
life articulating its own transcendence or, from the opposite point
of view, its own cessation (Albrecht von Haller, the physiologist, by
the way, is said to have expired diagnosing the cessation of his own
heartbeat) is expressed surpassingly well, I think, in Alice James's
remark in a letter to William James, dated July 30th, 1891: Death,
she says, is "the most supremely interesting moment in life, the
only one in fact, when living seems life."[56] One could ponder this
endlessly.

3

But let's not. Instead let's give vent to some pent-up common-
sensical reservations and objections that we have all been harbor-
ing throughout this time of unease that began when I began
speaking. If, as few would deny, the moment of dying is significant,
at least in principle, for our understanding of human nature, does it
follow that last words are of significance, be it as indicators of true
character or of the nature of the *Grenzerfahrung* from which they
supposedly derive? Last, but not least, last words themselves might
foster our doubts. True, Napoleon died with the name of his
beloved Josephine on his lips, and Josephine sank into a coma after
she pronounced the word Napoleon. But one of the greatest love

stories did not end with "Héloise" (Abélard's last word was a disappointing "I don't know"). Talulah Bankhead died saying bourbon, Chekhov died saying champagne — entirely insignificant it seems (even though Chekhov's coffin was shipped to its final resting place in a freight car labelled "fresh oysters"). Wordsworth said: "Is that Dora?"; Emily Dickinson's last remark was: "I must go in, the fog is rising"; Lord Chesterfield's last words referred to a visitor. "Give Dayrolles a chair" — writers, one feels, should be able to do better, should be able to die more memorably. Or take another disconcerting fact (as facts go in this line of inquiry; but more of that in a moment): George Washington, Immanuel Kant and André Gide not only died saying insignificant things, but they died with exactly the same last words, though their lives, personalities and claims to fame are arguably different (all three said: " 'tis well"). Rabelais and Beethoven and Emperor Augustus mumbled roughly the same statement about the farce of life being over; Harriet Beecher-Stowe and the Maréchal de Saxe said the same words as they lay dying, etc. etc.

About the last words of others there are and have been controversies. Everybody seems to have heard about Nelson's dubious exit line: Was it "Kiss me, Hardy" or "Kismet, Hardy"? I'll bypass the strange case of George V for fear of becoming obscene or guilty of *lèse majesté* in the pursuit of scholarship as it appears that "How stands the Empire?" were not the only recorded last words of the monarch. William Pitt is controversial in a less off-color manner: there are two main versions of his last words and both are saddled with internal problems of suspected textual corruption: "Oh, my country. How I leave [or was it love?] my country" and: "I think I could eat one of Bellamy's pork pies" or was it "veal pies"? *Many* of the famous apparently left more than one last word, leaving us wondering, in the absence of controversy, which was really last — and whether it was not followed by yet another one, deemed too insignificant or too revealing to be recorded or simply not heard by anyone. Goethe is one of them, so is Schiller. Oscar Wilde is another (he, at least, was dependably entertaining in the alternate, but again not literally "last" version as well: dying

in that dingy hotel room in Paris, he commented on the bad taste of
the wall-paper: "One or the other of us has to go." Did Diderot
have philosophy on his mind as he died, or an apricot? Heinrich
Heine can claim several last words, though not all witty, while the
world record is believed to be held by Rabelais, with a grand total
of five sets of last words, with Voltaire and Queen Victoria as the
runners-up—rather an odd couple when you visualize it. But let
me hasten to add that we may have our doubts even when there is
only *one* recorded version of the last word, as in "I have lived as a
philosopher and die as a Christian," supposedly the dying sentence
of Casanova, of all people. The reasons for all these problems are
obvious: whoever reports last words *as last words* (hence laden
with significance) may have a bad memory or a motive—to show
e.g. that Haller died a Christian death *or* the death of an empirical
scientist, with the name of his Savior on his lips or with his hand on
his pulse.

Authentic or apocryphal? That's the question that any master of
the raised eyebrow will pop the moment the matter of last words
comes up. What is behind this question or implied in it is the question of the significance or insignificance of the last word (indeed of
any last word) as a sort of testament or motto of a life. Of course,
one could, with a little effort, see some "telling" significance even
in the *prima facie* most insignificant last words, clearly not meant to
be a "message" or a "summation," e.g. Lord Chesterfield's offering
a visitor a chair: the man who was so concerned about manners
was "polite to the last," as one anthologist explains.[57] Much could
similarly be made of other last words which are not last by design,
but by chance: Marie Antoinette's "pardonnez-moi" to the
executioner, or Samuel Butler's "Have you the check-book,
Alfred?" And one might chuckle over the inappropriate appropriateness of Archduke Franz Ferdinand's muttering feebly: "It is
nothing" as he expired from the wound from that other gunshot
that was to be heard around the world. But even the trivial or
absurd last word that *resists* any efforts at interpretation (which
somehow are to show its telling appropriateness and symbolical
meaning) will find its connoisseurs who will be delighted by pre-

cisely its absurdity, pleading "human interest." And one can understand equally well the frame of mind of those who opt for meaningfulness and of those who opt for the opposite. A memorable life must have a memorable concluding line; an absurd last word, on the other hand, such as William Pitt's in version II, highlights the sorry fact of life that the sublime and the ludicrous are usually entangled with each other. We all know this, but while some would have it another way, some emphatically would not. Tragedy ends in sublime death, or does it end with the satyr play that follows? Writers of saints' lives ordinarily like to report last words of exemplary piety; modern biographers might be exhilarated by the find of a last word that lends itself to the debunking of a myth surrounding the great. While some make much of the Aufklärer's "Mehr Licht!," others hear the Frankfurt dialect in it ("man liegt. . ." — "so schlecht," perhaps). Both types of commentators, to be sure, do attach significance to the last word, one way or another. Whether profound or trivial, such last words are "telling" in that they affirm, and seal as it were, what this life was "really" all about or "really" amounted to — in *the observer's* view.

It seems, then, that this is a field of inquiry that allows anyone to play, to exercise his ingenuity, with only minimal demands being made on his sense of responsibility. Not only is the authenticity of last words questionable, but also, and even more so, their significance, if any.

To limit the damage, one should at this point introduce the *manner* and circumstances of death and the bearing that they may have, in a given case, on the last word and its alleged significance. To begin with, "last words" in the sense that the term is used here, should properly exclude what is frequently termed last words in a loose or metaphorical way:[58] suicide notes, documents such as the Antarctic explorer Captain Robert Scott's farewell message to his countrymen,[59] last diary entries and last letters such as *Letzte Briefe aus Stalingrad* (ed. Franz Schneider, Gütersloh, 1954), *Last Words: Letters and Statements of the Leaders Executed after the Rising at Easter 1916* (ed. Piaras F. MacLochlainn, Dublin, 1971), *Du hast mich heimgesucht bei Nacht: Abschiedsbriefe und Aufzeichnungen des Widerstandes 1933-1945*, collected by Helmut Gollwitzer and others (München, 1954), *Letzte Briefe zum Tode Verurteilter aus dem europäischen Widerstand* (eds. Piero Malvezzi and Giovanni Pirelli, Munich, 1962), and *La Dernière Lettre: Prisons et condamnés de la Révolution 1793-1794* by Olivier Blanc (Paris, 1984). Nor would one include reflections on life and death which are not the fruit of the extreme moment described earlier, even though this seems to be what Kierkegaard, for one, means by "the last word" in *Fear and Trembling*, where he says that many tragic heroes would all along have such a last word in themselves which would encapsulate the meaning of their life like an epitaph.[60]

Still, even if one excludes these varieties of "last words" entirely, there remains a whole range of circumstances of death which will make last words appear in a very questionable light. Last words, even if clearly "last," would arguably have to be considered and assessed differently if, on the one hand, they precede an unexpected or accidental death and therefore just happen to be the last (Abraham Lincoln being shot in his theater-box, e.g.) or if, on the other hand, they are the final death-bed utterance at the conclusion of a drawn-out process of dying which (to use Dr. Johnson's famous remark on the prospect of hanging) "concentrates [the] mind wonderfully."[61]

This is self-evident. Commonsense will have to be a guide here. But none the less, or perhaps precisely because of this, the question of authenticity of last words will keep dogging anyone in search of their possible significance. Authentic or not? Apocryphal or not? This question has all too often dominated the discussion of last words.[62] One collection of last words, Stevenson's, is prefaced by the well-meant warning that "the reputed last words of famous men are always open to suspicion"; but if this is "always" the case, Stevenson seems to draw the wrong conclusion when he continues by assuring his readers that the ones he has collected "are among the best known and best authenticated."[63] For quite apart from the suspicion that the best known may not be the best authenticated: Is "best authenticated" really good enough? To the purist turned cynic by experience the answer is most certainly no.

To him it is in the nature of things that last words are less likely to
be genuine, the less so the more proverbial they have become: history the inexact science once again.

In a spirited little "Study of Last Words" Nigel Dennis takes this
position, with all the wit and charm appropriate to the subject.[64]
He casts doubt on what D. J. Enright in the *Oxford Book of Death*
(1983) has called "the entire institution of Last Words," precisely
because so many of the reported last words of the great are so
appropriate or, as Dennis puts it, because they are "examples of
great men being expected to say what little men feel they should
say and thus being denied the right to speak for themselves" (p.
29). In other words, the recorded last words are inauthentic or
even deliberately falsified (as in Elisabeth Nietzsche's report on
her brother's last word being "Elisabeth"). Also, Dennis gleefully
points out the fact that for some great men more than one last
word has been transmitted to puzzled posterity. On the other
hand, where there is only *one* it is its metaphoric interpretation, so
welcome in some quarters, rather than its meaning in context that
has made it common knowledge, regardless of whether the
interpretation was called for or not. Goethe's "Mehr Licht" e.g.
had nothing to do with the Enlightenment, but everything with the
shutters at Goethe's window and even this remark, decoded as
harmless, was, Dennis claims, a last word deliberately induced by
bystanders who would have found the thought unbearable that the
grand old man died with something as banal as asking for the "little
paw" of his wife (who in fact had died many years earlier—so here
Dennis is being creative himself about the words of the dying man,
which in point of fact referred to his daughter-in-law). For such
reasons, Dennis at least sympathizes with the view that all last
words are "post-mortem counterfeits," pure invention by
interested parties (p. 30), and he goes on to suggest that since
modern death in the hospital bed under the influence of the
hypodermic needle does not lend itself to last words anyway, it
might be helpful to "postpone all last words until after
death"—which, in his opinion, is what in fact has happened. Such
a generally agreed-upon postponement "would have beneficial

results.   Genuine last words, often spoken in haste, could be replaced by falsifications more in keeping with the character and dignity of the deceased"; also such a practise would "supply biographers with a conclusion to their books" and finally "it would give each of us a chance to choose his official Last Wordster and so prevent the bickerings and differences that now attend upon the verbally intestate" (p. 30).   There is charity, in addition to wit, in this view, as Mr. Dennis warns that the effort involved in pronouncing last words should in any case be avoided, at least by "the common man," since it tends to raise the blood pressure which hastens the end and might in turn cut last words short so as to make the whole exercise self-defeating. . .

Such charm is difficult to argue with.   And I don't think that D. J. Enright, who does argue with it, in *The Oxford Book of Death*, comes up with the correct objection when he says that the last words *he* has collected at least are, "if not literally authentic, [. . .] authentically in character" (p. 314).   But he may lead us in the right direction, if *contre coeur*.   Authentic or not?   It seems to me that the correct answer is that it does not matter.

It does not matter because what aficionados of last words are *really* interested in, or should be, is not necessarily the empirical deathbed truth, but what we might call the legend, the *fable convenue* or the myth which may have a truth of a different kind.   Last words, more often than not, are not historical facts of documentary status but artefacts, and even when they are documented beyond the usual doubt, it is as artefacts that they survive: as the artefacts they have become through the collective imagination of those who have recorded them *as last words*, passed them on from generation to generation, and have thereby surrounded the possible empirical evidence with a far more appealing aura.   The question of authenticity vs. inauthenticity consequently becomes rather academic.   Is a myth authentic or inauthentic?   The question is relatively meaningless.   Myths are not transcriptions of historical, factual truth, but truths in their own right, truths which we live by, for better or for worse, and sometimes very much for worse.   And last words are somehow related to this category of artefacts that the human race leaves behind. Such myth-making begins at the deathbed. As a result, dying speeches and last words are, loosely speaking, a *literary* genre, not a class of historical documents the way last wills are, or death certificates.

4

As such, last words are a somewhat neglected genre. And yet one might say that, especially via the cult of last words in biographies and in the media which shape our popular mythologies, they invite a line of inquiry which might, in a minor and modest way, shed some light on an emerging lay anthropology or body of "truths" people lived by or thought or wished they had lived by. And one might suspect that these "truths" have changed over the centuries and that, as such changing guiding ideas, they might suggest something about the changing self-image of those who came before us, to avoid the term "the human condition." It is, for example, safe to say that in the Middle Ages (and wherever the Christian system of beliefs was and is unchallenged and unquestioned, since as historians we always have to allow for the "Gleichzeitigkeit des Ungleichzeitigen") one died in accordance with certain spiritual expectations and with corresponding last words. However, with increasing secularization, by the time of the Enlightenment (at the latest) one not infrequently died not knowing what to say or at any rate not repeating the standard Christian formula; one died, instead, with words that were unpredictable, original or conforming to a new, to an emerging convention (always assuming that the last words were not "chance" last words). That is, what last words reveal (beyond the image of the deceased, whoever he might be) may be something like the needs or intellectual profile of the time and the milieu: why is it *this* myth rather than *that* that is made at the deathbed at a given point in the history of a civilization? It may be arguable that there are styles, even fashions, of dying—with the corresponding styles and fashions of last words. What are these styles? And what is their history? To repeat: such questions become more interesting in and since the Enlightenment at the latest as dogmatic religious frameworks of intellectual life break down — and biography receives a new impetus. Beginning in the Enlightenment, then, or even the Renaissance, one might start looking for different, emerging trends in the kinds of last words reported and in the importance accorded to them. These would also be trends in the manner in which last words were made into literary artefacts, not only by biography but also by word of mouth as it were; for there is evidence of a significantly increased general or even popular attention at this time to what the great and the not so great had to say as they were about to die. For one thing, people started collecting last words after Montaigne confessed in his *Essais* that an anthology of dying words was one of his ambitions (I, 20; as for himself, Montaigne hoped to die while planting cabbages, of all vegetables). From the 17th century to the late 1980s, a steady and ever broadening stream of such collections of last words has continued unabated.[65] By the 18th century, as mentioned above, there are also those parodies of the genre of last words which attest to the vigor of the "institution" of last words. But whether a "history" of the "literary" genre of last words can be written, especially a history that contributes something to our knowledge of the intellectual life of the past and present that is not known from other sources, remains to be seen.

Notes

1 Throughout this essay, when no source is indicated, "last words" — what has come to be considered the dying words of the person in question — are cited from the numerous anthologies of last words which in themselves are part of the convention that is the subject of this essay. I have discussed these collections in my essay "Anthologies of Last Words," *Harvard Library Bulletin*, 1988. A good source for the purposes of this essay is cited in note 2. A considerably expanded version of this paper is part of my book *Letzte Worte*, Munich 1990.

2 Edward Le Comte, *Dictionary of Last Words*, New York 1955, p. vii. For similar statements concerning the age-old fascination with last words see, e.g. Rodger Kamenetz, "Last Words," *North American Review*, 269: 2 (1984), pp. 61-63; Thomas D. Bedell, "The Tongues of Dying Men," *The Reader's Digest*, 115, July 1979, pp. 122-125; anon. "Last Words," *Every Saturday*, II, Sept. 8, 1866, pp. 276-277; *Time*, Jan. 17, 1955, p. 53.

3 Åke Ohlmarks, *Sista Sucken*, Stockholm 1970, p. 93.

4 L. L. Schücking, *Die Familie im Puritanismus*, Leipzig u. Berlin 1929, p. 184.

5 For confirmation from a medical authority see *The Dying Patient*, ed. Orville G. Brim, Jr., New York 1970, p. XV.

6 *The New York Times*, May 22, 1988; quoted there from Janet Flanner's 1932 *New Yorker* piece, reprinted in her *Paris Was Yesterday* (New York 1972; new ed. 1988, p. 83).

7 Willibald Schmidt, *De ultimis morientium verbis*, Diss. Marburg 1914; cf. the last words of Jacob and Moses: *Genesis* 49; *Deuteronomy*, 23.

8 "Some Passing Remarks on Some Passing Remarks," in: Fadiman, *Party of One*, Cleveland 1955, p. 466 (first published in *Holiday* magazine in November, 1952); Fadiman's foreword to Barnaby Conrad, *Famous Last Words*, New York 1961, p. 7.

9 Fadiman, in Conrad, p. 14.

10 See notes 1 and 2 above.

11   E.g. Karl Petit, *Dictionnaire des citations du monde entier*, Verviers 1960, 3rd.
     ed. 1984, pp. 276-77; Burton E. Stevenson, *Home Book of Quotations*, New
     York 1937, pp. 413-417; E. Cobham Brewer; *Dictionary of Phrase and Fable*,
     first publ. 1870, London 1971, pp. 355-357.

12   Thomas Finkenstaedt, "Galgenliteratur.   Zur Auffassung des Todes im
     England des 16. und 17. Jahrhunderts," *Deutsche Vierteljahresschrift*,
     XXXIV (1960), pp. 527-553; Lincoln B. Faller, *Turned to Account*,
     Cambridge 1987.

13   See Note 1.

14   *A Collection of Scarce and Valuable Tracts* . . . , London ^{2}1810, IV, pp. 254-
     260.

15   Byron E. Eshelman, *Death Row Chaplain*, Englewood Cliffs, N. J. 1962, e.g.
     p. 26; August Mencken, *By the Neck*, New York 1942.

16   Michael Holroyd, *Lytton Strachey*, Harmondsworth 1971, pp. 808-9.

17   *Boswell's Life of Johnson*, ed. G. B. Hill, rev. L. F. Powell, Oxford 1934-1950,
     III, p. 192.

18   Hannah Pakula, *The Last Romantic. A Biography of Queen Marie of Rouma-
     nia*, London 1985, p. 182. Queen Elisabeth died on March 2, 1916.

19   Lael Tucker Wertenbaker, *Death of a Man*, New York 1957, p. 177.

20   Letter from Houghton to me.

21   Robert G. Walker, "Public Death in the Eighteenth Century," *Research
     Studies of the State College of Washington*, XLVIII (1980), pp. 11-24;
     "Rochester and the Issue of Deathbed Repentance in Restoration and
     Eighteenth-Century England," *South Atlantic Review*, XLVII (1982), pp. 21-
     37.

22   Mark Twain, *The Curious Republic of Gondour*, New York 1919, p. 135.

23   *The Writings of Mark Twain*, Definitive Edition, IX, New York 1923, pp. 51,
     60.

24   III, London and Edinburgh 1878, p. 722.

25   By David M. Walker, Oxford 1980, p. 386.

26   Ferdinandus Jacobus van Ingen, *Vanitas und Memento mori in der deutschen
     Barocklyrik*, Groningen 1966, pp. 120-130.

27 Walther Rehm, *Der Todesgedanke in der deutschen Dichtung vom Mittelalter bis zur Romantik*, Halle 1928, pp. 150-153.

28 Rudolf Böhm, *Wesen und Funktion der Sterberede im elisabethanischen Drama*, Hamburg 1964; Theodore Spencer, *Death and Elizabethan Tragedy*, Cambridge, Mass. 1936.

29 Eudo C. Mason, "'Wir sehen uns wieder!,'" *Literaturwissenschaftliches Jahrbuch*, n.s., V (1964), pp. 79-109.

30 By Johanna Gilhof, *Niedersachsen*, XIII (1907-8), pp. 359-61.

31 The evidence presented below is corroborated by the introductions to anthologies of last words (see note 1) as well as by remarks in a number of "popular" essays on the convention or institution of last words which, however, by and large, do not go beyond mere listings of last words considered interesting for one reason or another. Cf. anon., *Every Saturday* cited above; anon., "Last Words of the Poets," *Talks and Tales Magazine*, November 1899, pp. 30-32; Lance Morrow, "A Dying Art: The Classy Exit Line," *Time*, January 16, 1984, p. 76; E. V. Lucas, "Last Words," in E.V.L., *Luck of the Year*, New York 1923, pp. 180-184; Fadiman (see note 8); Charles D. Stewart, "The Art of Dying," in C.D.S., *Fellow Creatures*, Boston 1935, pp. 268-278; "Exit Lines," *Time*, January 17, 1955, p. 53; "Last Words," *Musical America*, December 15, 1954, p. 9; James Lindsay, "Last Words," *The Outlook*, April 14, 1928, pp. 470-471.

32 New York 1961, p. 54.

33 Cited from Le Comte, p. viii.

34 See, e.g., Thomas M. Kettle, "On Saying Good-Bye," in T.M.K., *The Day's Burden*, Dublin 1918, p. 105; Jay Weiss, "Last Words," *The Humanist*, XXXVI: 6 (1976), pp. 27-29; Lance Morrow (see note 31). For some other studies see note 31 above.

35 Cp. Kenneth A. Chandler, "Three Processes of Dying and their Behavioral Effects," *Journal of Consulting Psychology*, XXIX (1965), pp. 296-301; Lyn H. Lofland, *The Craft of Dying: The Modern Face of Death*, Beverly Hills and London 1979. This, as is well-known, is also the premise of Philippe Ariès. In the rare cases where a physician reports his patients' last words, nothing of significance seems to be said; see René Burnand, "L'Homme devant la mort," *Concours médical*, Oct. 1959, pp. 4113-4118. The hospice movement has of course changed the situation somewhat in recent years, as Elisabeth Kübler-Ross's interviews with the dying may suggest.

36 Robert Jay Lifton, *The Broken Connection: On Death and the Continuity of Life*, New York 1979, p. 277; cf. Marguérite Yourcenar, *Mishima: A Vision of the Void*, Henley-on-Thames 1986, p. 143.

37 New York 1966, p. 220. I owe this quotation to John S. Dunne, *Time and Myth*, Garden City, N. Y. 1973.

38 Heneage Ogilvie, *No Miracles Among Friends*, London 1959, p. 164.

39 "Sacred Corpse, Profane Carrion: Social Ideals and Death Rituals in the later Middle Ages," *Mirrors of Mortality*, ed. Joachim Whaley, London 1981, p. 51.

40 See Garrett Stewart, *Death Sentences: Styles of Dying in British Fiction*, Cambridge, Mass. 1984, p. 370, note 35. On physicians and last words see note 35 above. On the "review phenomenon" (also reported of falling mountain climbers) there are frequent comments, as distinguished from detailed accounts, in the psychological literature; see e.g. Zaleski (note 45 below), pp. 128-129; Hermann Nothnagel, *Das Sterben*, 2nd ed., Vienna 1908, pp. 40-41.

41 *Dichtungen und Schriften*, ed. Friedhelm Kemp, Munich 1956, p. 853.

42 Charles J. Thurmond, "Last Thoughts before Drowning," *Journal of Abnormal and Social Psychology*, XXXVIII (1943), Clinical Suppl., 165-184.

43 London 1971, pp. 234-5.

44 *Boswell's Life* (see note 17), II, pp. 106-7.

45 See e.g. William Fletcher Barrett, *Death-Bed Visions*, London 1926; Raymond A. Moody, Jr., *Life after Life*, Atlanta 1975; Carol Zaleski, *Otherworld Journeys*, Oxford 1987.

46 *Moby Dick*, New York 1952, p. 473.

47 Kenneth Burke, "Thanatopsis for Critics: A Brief Thesaurus of Deaths and Dying," *Essays in Criticism*, II (1952), pp. 369-75; Robert Detweiler, "The Moment Fiction," *Contemporary Literature*, XIII (1972), pp. 269-294.

48 "The Closing Hours," in Spencer's *Facts and Comments*, New York 1902, pp. 95-96.

49 *The Meaning of Death*, ed. Herman Feifel, New York 1959, p. 237.

50 "Treatment of the Dying Person," *The Meaning of Death*, p. 252.

51 *Sein und Zeit*, Tübingen 1957, p. 240.

52 Grand Rapids, Mich. 1969, p. 12.

53 Karl Lehmann, *Der Tod bei Heidegger und Jaspers*, Diss. Heidelberg 1938, p. 39. See also E. Kübler-Ross, ed. *Death: The Final Stage of Growth*, Englewood Cliffs, N. J. 1975.

54 New York 1927, p. 172. I owe this quotation to Frederick J. Hoffmann, "Mortality and Modern Literature," *The Meaning of Death* (see note 49), p. 154.

55 Munich 1981, p. 55. Karl Corino capitalized on this aura of the last word when he chose *Lauter letzte Worte* as the title for the collected poems of Dieter Leisegang, who took his life after a long illness (Frankfurt 1980).

56 Ruth B. Yeazell, ed. *The Death and Letters of Alice James*, Berkeley, Cal. 1981, p. 43; I owe this quotation to Garrett Stewart (see note 40), pp. 367-8.

57 Burton E. Stevenson (see note 11), p. 414. Paul J. Korshin points out in *TLS*, 29 Jan. 1982, p. 108, that this interpretation goes back to the first biography of Chesterfield which came out in 1777.

58 About such last words Lawrence L. Langer says, "nor do we know whether the condemned men were able to sustain [the sentiments expressed in written "last words"] when they stood alone before the final silence of extinction" (*The Age of Atrocity: Death in Modern Literature*, Boston 1978, p. 39).

59 *The World's Great Letters*, ed. N. Lincoln Schuster, New York 1940, pp. 458-60.

60 *Furcht und Zittern, Gesammelte Werke*, 2nd ed., III, Jena 1909, pp. 108-109.

61 *Boswell's Life* (see note 17), III, p. 167.

62 See esp. Le Comte (note 2 above), also Lindsay (note 31 above). Cp. note 1 above.

63 Stevenson (see note 11), p. 413.

64 "Arthur from the Barge: A Study of Last Words," *Encounter*, XCVIII (Nov. 1961), pp. 27-31.

65 See note 1 above.